A CRITICAL INTRODUCTION TO
MAO

Mao Zedong's political career spanned more than half a century. The ideas he championed transformed one of the largest nations on earth and inspired revolutionary movements across the world. Even today, Mao lives on in China, where he is regarded by many as a near-mythical figure, and in the West, where a burgeoning literature continues to debate his memory. In this book, leading scholars from different generations and around the world offer a critical evaluation of the life and legacy of China's most famous – some would say infamous – son. In the first part, chapters explore the historical and political context of Mao's emergence as a young man and revolutionary in the early twentieth century. Through this period it is possible to examine the nature of Mao's ideology in its purest form and to see why it was attractive to so many. This part also chronicles the main events of his life and individual aspects of that life: his key relationships with allies and foes, his followers, and his public persona; his philosophy; and his relationship with women. In Part II, chapters debate the positive and negative aspects of his legacy. In China, Mao has become a metaphor for the promises and betrayals of the twentieth century; in developing countries, he remains a beacon of revolutionary hope for some; and in the West, Mao continues to be the mirror of our hopes and fears. This book brings the scholarship on Mao up to date, and its alternative perspectives equip readers to assess for themselves the nature of this mercurial figure and his significance in modern Chinese history.

Timothy Cheek is Professor and Louis Cha Chair in Chinese Research at the Institute of Asian Research, University of British Columbia. His research, teaching, and translating focus on the recent history of China, especially the role of Chinese intellectuals in the twentieth century and the history of the Chinese Communist Party. He has written numerous papers and six books, including *Living with Reform: China Since 1989* (2006) and *Mao Zedong and China's Revolutions: A Brief History with Documents* (2002).

A CRITICAL INTRODUCTION TO
MAO

Edited by
Timothy Cheek
University of British Columbia, Vancouver

CAMBRIDGE
UNIVERSITY PRESS

CAMBRIDGE UNIVERSITY PRESS
Cambridge, New York, Melbourne, Madrid, Cape Town, Singapore,
São Paulo, Delhi, Dubai, Tokyo, Mexico City

Cambridge University Press
32 Avenue of the Americas, New York, NY 10013-2473, USA

www.cambridge.org
Information on this title: www.cambridge.org/9780521711548

© Cambridge University Press 2010

First published 2010

Printed in the United States of America

A catalog record for this publication is available from the British Library.

Library of Congress Cataloging in Publication data
A critical introduction to Mao / [edited by] Timothy Cheek.
    p. cm.
Includes bibliographical references and index.
ISBN 978-0-521-88462-4 (hardback) – ISBN 978-0-521-71154-8 (pbk.)
1. Mao, Zedong, 1893–1976. 2. China – Politics and government – 20th century.
I. Cheek, Timothy. II. Title.
DS778.M3C74 2010
951.05092–dc22   2010022109

ISBN 978-0-521-88462-4 Hardback
ISBN 978-0-521-71154-8 Paperback

Contents

List of Illustrations

About the Contributors

Geremie R. Barmé is Professor of History at The Australian National University, Canberra. His most recent book is *The Forbidden City* (2008). He codirected the documentary *Morning Sun* (Boston: Long Bow Group, 2003; www.morningsun. org) with Carma Hinton and Richard Gordon. He also edits the e-journal *China Heritage Quarterly* (www.chinaheritagequarterly.org).

Timothy Cheek is Professor and Louis Cha Chair in Chinese Research at the Institute of Asian Research at the University of British Columbia. His books include *Living with Reform: China Since 1989* (2006), *Mao Zedong and China's Revolutions* (2002), *Propaganda and Culture in Mao's China* (1997), and (with Roderick MacFarquhar and Eugene Wu) *The Secret Speeches of Chairman Mao* (1989).

Alexander C. Cook is Assistant Professor of History at the University of California, Berkeley. His contribution to this book was written with the support of the Stanford Humanities Fellows. He is completing a book on justice in the post-Mao transition, *The Cultural Revolution on Trial*.

Delia Davin is currently Acting Director of the National Institute of Chinese Studies at White Rose East Asia Centre of the Universities of Leeds and Sheffield. She lived in China for three years in the 1960s and 1970s. She is the author of *Womanwork: Women and the Party in Revolutionary China* (1978), *Internal Migration in Contemporary China* (1999), and *Mao Zedong* (Essential biographies, History Press, 1997 and 2009).

Joseph W. Esherick is Professor of History and Hsiu Professor of Chinese Studies at the University of California, San Diego, and author of *Reform and Revolution in China: The 1911 Revolution in Hunan and Hubei* (1976), *Origins of the Boxer Uprising* (1986), and *Ancestral Leaves: A Family Journey through Chinese History* (2010).

Charles W. Hayford teaches history at Northwestern University. His first book, *To the People: James Yen and Village China* (1990), investigated trans-Pacific liberalism. His current book project, *America's China: From the Opium War to Tiananmen*, traces the history of American images of China.

Hung-yok Ip is Associate Professor of East Asian History in the Department of History at Oregon State University. She is the author of *Intellectuals in Revolutionary China 1921–1959* (2005; paperback, 2009). In addition to examining

Chinese communism, she also studies Maoism, nonviolence, and modern Chinese Buddhism.

Jiang Yihua is Professor of History at Fudan University, Shanghai, China, where he has served as Dean of the School of Humanities and leader of several research groups on historical studies. His several books include studies on historiography and history of thought, including studies on Kang Youwei, Zhang Binlin, and Hu Shi. His scholarly edition of readings from Mao Zedong (1998) was copublished in Hong Kong and Taiwan.

Daniel Leese is Assistant Professor of Sinology at Ludwig-Maximilians University, Munich, Germany. In his Ph.D. dissertation, *Performative Politics and Petrified Image* (2006), he traced the evolution of the Cultural Revolutionary Mao cult. He is the editor of Brill's *Encyclopedia of China* (2009).

Roderick MacFarquhar is the Leroy B. Williams Professor of History and Political Science at Harvard University, where he has directed the Fairbank Center for East Asian Research and chaired the Government Department. He was the founding editor of the *China Quarterly* and is the author of the trilogy *The Origins of the Cultural Revolution* (1974, 1983, 1997) and, more recently, of *Mao's Last Revolution* with Michael Schoenhals (2006). In previous personae he was a print journalist, TV reporter, and member of Parliament in Britain.

Michael Schoenhals is Professor of Chinese in the Centre for Languages and Literature, Lund University, Sweden. His publications include *Saltationist Socialism: Mao Zedong and the Great Leap Forward 1958* (1987) and, together with Roderick MacFarquhar, *Mao's Last Revolution* (2006).

Frederick C. Teiwes is Emeritus Professor of Chinese Politics at the University of Sydney. His works include *Politics and Purges in China* (1979, 1993), *Politics at Mao's Court* (1990), and, with Warren Sun, *The Tragedy of Lin Biao* (1996), *China's Road to Disaster* (1999), and *The End of the Maoist Era* (2007). He wishes to thank the Australian Research Council for its generous support over many years.

Hans J. van de Ven is Professor of Modern Chinese History at Cambridge University. He has published *From Friend to Comrade: The Founding of the Chinese Communist Party* (1992) and *War and Nationalism in China* (2003). His current research interest is the history of globalization in China in the 1850–1950 period.

Brantly Womack is the Cumming Memorial Professor of Foreign Affairs at the University of Virginia. He is the author of *Foundations of Mao Zedong's Political Thought, 1917–1935* (1982), *Politics in China* (with James Townsend) (1986), *China and Vietnam: The Politics of Asymmetry* (2006), and *China Among Unequals: Asymmetric International Relationships in Asia* (forthcoming). Among his edited books are *Contemporary Chinese Politics in Historical Perspective* (1991) and *China's Rise in Historical Perspective* (2010).

Xiao Yanzhong is Associate Professor and Chair of the Department of Political Science, School of International Relations, People's University, Beijing, China. His research focuses on political thought and the history of the Chinese Communist Party. He is editor, with Shi Zhongquan, of the book series Guowai Mao Zedong yanjiu congshu (Foreign Studies of Mao Zedong), from the People's University Press.

Preface

This is a critical introduction to Mao Zedong, China's most famous (or infamous) leader of the twentieth century and still a force to contend with today. Mao warrants such a guide not only because he was such a significant historical figure – the recognized leader of China's Socialist Revolution and architect of the disastrous Cultural Revolution – but also because the ideas associated with him transformed a huge nation and still form the grounds of political argument in China today, as well as inspiring revolutionary movements across the world, from Naxalites in South Asia to the Shining Path in South America (and the gruesome example of Pol Pot in Cambodia in the 1970s). The controversies surrounding recent biographies of Mao in the West highlight the continuing significance of Mao even in the distinctly nonrevolutionary societies of "the West."

What this book offers is the benefit of the historian's perspective as addressed to the educated, nonspecialist reading public. How does one get beyond the partisan uses of Mao, whether by the current Chinese Communist Party (CCP) leadership in the People's Republic of China (PRC) or by sensationalist journalists of varying stripes inside and outside China? A powerful way to understand the contingent and variable nature of the meanings attributed to Mao, Mao Zedong thought, and the Chinese Revolution is to see the living Mao in his historical context. To do this, we avail ourselves of the skills of historiography to filter out (to the degree possible) our later concerns and to recover something of the concerns of Mao's times. Thus this book begins with context, then turns to Mao's actions in context, and finally turns to an analysis of the meanings attributed to Mao out of those contexts. The book thus seeks to present the historical Mao and explicitly juxtapose that Mao with the very significant but importantly ahistorical Maos that so deeply concern millions of people across the globe today.

The two parts of the book are organized accordingly: Part I, Mao's World, and Part II, Mao's Legacy. The first chapter gives a broad outline of Mao's life and historical significance. It signals the major points of controversy concerning Mao. It considers how we know what we know about Mao (the problem of sources) and provides a brief tour of scholarship on Mao. It ends with some notes on strategies for reading Mao as an independent thinker – the first strategy being to get a sense of the context by reading the chapters that follow.

Part I, Mao's World, offers the contexts in which Mao emerged and then operated, focusing on Mao's political lifetime, from the 1920s to his death in 1976. Chapter 2 looks at the politics and historical pressures to which Mao's generation was a part. The next three chapters tell the story of his revolutionary career in both organizational activities and writings. The next four chapters of this part look at key relationships in the political praxis that defined Mao's career (and legacy): Mao and his followers, Mao Zedong thought and his propagandists, Mao and women, and finally, Mao the man and the icon. These four dynamics include the three key social groups raised in Chapter 2 (political/military leaders, intellectuals, and peasants) and set the stage for the continuing "uses of Mao" among China's leaders, China's opinion makers, and China's dispossessed classes (e.g., workers, women, and migrants, as well as poor farmers). Part II, Mao's Legacy, turns to the meanings assigned to Mao over the past three decades since his death. This section includes chapters dealing with China's Maos, third world Maos, Western Maos, and finally, the reflections of a senior scholar from China and from Western academia, respectively, on "the significance of Mao." We provide maps, a timeline, and a selective, annotated list of further reading.

The contributors are mostly senior academic specialists on Mao and modern China studies, although I have sought to include some junior colleagues reflecting newer perspectives. Although composed predominantly of historians, this list includes both other social science and humanities disciplines and some comparative perspectives to put Mao and the Chinese case into global perspective (especially Chapter 12). Additionally, we have included varying voices (or different viewpoints): by generation of scholars, by cultural location (Europe, the United States, China), and by gender. Although this does not cover the whole range of views and perspectives on Mao, it provides an indication of the diversity of such views.

The general reader will be offered in this book an engaging introduction to this mercurial and mythic figure, as well as a surer footing and useful information for understanding what Mao did and did not do during his life and the tools by which to improve her or his own reading of Mao's writing and actions. Readers thus may become their own public intellectuals when it comes to Mao and Maoism, able to assess the "authoritative" interpretations offered by scholars, journalists, and governments today.

Acknowledgments

This book is dedicated to Stuart R. Schram, the doyen of Mao studies in the West. His work since the 1960s has shaped all our work on Mao, and whether or not we have agreed with this or that interpretation put forward by him, we have benefited from his writings and his example of careful scholarship. This book came about because Diana Lary at the University of British Columbia and Marigold Acland at Cambridge University Press conspired to hold me to my pronouncement that academics should take more effort to provide readable and reliable books on Mao and Chinese history. I thank them for doing that. The Cambridge University Press peer reviewers were helpful and demanding and improved the plan for this volume and sharpened the draft chapters. The contributors to this volume have been active participants in refining that plan and bringing you this final product. I benefited from criticism and feedback from the UBC China Studies Group, the New England China Seminar at the Fairbank Center, Harvard, the Visiting Scholars Seminar at the School of Social Work, City University of Hong Kong, and commentators at several talks that I gave elsewhere. Although several colleagues graciously reviewed parts of this book, on behalf of all the contributors, I particularly want to thank Joe Esherick for critical engagement above and beyond the call of duty and Delia Davin for irrepressible (and very helpful) editorial acumen. As ever, I am indebted to Nancy Hearst at the Fairbank Center Library, Harvard; because of her eagle eye the text is nearly error free. At UBC, the Centre for Chinese Research at the Institute of Asian Research and the College for Interdisciplinary Studies provided both a congenial home and research support, not least in the form of the services of my editorial RA, Ms. Heidi Kong, who helped with the pictures.

T.C., Vancouver, BC, July 2009

Timeline of Twentieth-Century China

1893 Mao born to a farming family in Hunan Province.

1895 China defeated by Japan in the Sino-Japanese War.

1900 Boxer Rebellion and counterattack by foreign powers.

1905 Qing Dynasty ends the civil service exams.

1911 Republican revolution; fall of the Qing Dynasty.

1912 General Yuan Shikai replaces Sun Yat-sen as president of the republic.

1913 Sun Yat-sen founds the Guomindang (GMD), or Nationalist Party.

1915–25 New Culture Movement.

1919 May Fourth Movement in Beijing opposes the Versailles Treaty.

1921 Official founding of the Chinese Communist Party (CCP) in Shanghai; Mao Zedong is one of the founding members.

1923 CCP and GMD cooperate in the first United Front; Mao then works in the GMD Propaganda Department and its Peasant Training Institute.

1925 Sun Yat-sen dies; Chiang Kai-shek eventually takes over the GMD.

1926 Northern Expedition under GMD leadership starts out from Guangzhou in southern China to reunify the country. Mao returns to Hunan to work in the countryside.

1927 Mao writes his "Report on the Peasant Movement in Hunan." Chiang Kai-shek turns against the CCP and in April massacres CCP activists. GMD forms a new national government and moves the capital of the Republic of China to Nanjing.

1930 Changsha uprising, led by Mao, fails; Mao moves to develop rural soviets.

1931 Japanese begin to occupy northeast China and will declare Manchukuo a separate country the next year. Formal establishment of the Jiangxi Soviet; Mao elected chairman of the soviet but is soon removed from top leadership.

1931–34   Nationalist government launches five "encirclement campaigns" to destroy the CCP and Jiangxi Soviet; CCP survives the first four.

1934   Communists flee the Jiangxi Soviet; the retreat becomes the Long March.

1935   Mao regains a top leadership position in the CCP at the Zunyi conference during the Long March.

1936   Communists make their new capital at Yan'an, in the northwest province of Shaanxi.

1936–47   Yan'an period, during which Mao consolidates his supreme position and develops policies that lead to CCP victory in 1949.

1937   Japan invades China, beginning World War II in Asia.

1942–44   Yan'an Rectification Movement promotes Mao's ideas and leadership.

1945   Japan formally surrenders to the Allies on September 9, ending World War II.

1945–49   Chinese Civil War between the CCP and GMD.

1949   CCP declares a new national government, the People's Republic of China (PRC), with Mao as its head.

1950   **February**: China and the Soviet Union sign the Treaty of Friendship, Alliance, and Mutual Assistance.
October: Chinese forces enter Korea, joining the Korean War.

1952   Land reform completed in most areas of China; national campaigns against corruption and bureaucratism (Three and Five Antis).

1955   First Five-Year Plan (1953–57) formally adopted to organize China's planned economy. Nationwide mass campaign to criticize two intellectuals, Hu Shi and Hu Feng.

1956   Khrushchev denounces Stalin in the USSR. Mao calls for public criticism of the CCP in the Hundred Flowers Campaign, but the response is muted. CCP holds its Eighth Party Congress in Beijing; celebrates successes of the PRC.

1957   **February**: Mao delivers his speech "On the Correct Handling of Contradictions Among the People" to boost the Hundred Flowers Campaign.
May: Hundred Flowers Campaign blooms, but with biting criticism of the CCP.
June: Anti-Rightist Movement attacks those who spoke up in the Hundred Flowers Campaign; Mao's "Contradictions" speech is published in a highly edited form.

1958   CCP adopts Mao's Great Leap Forward plan.

August: Mao's talks at Beidaihe popularize collectivization of agriculture in the people's communes.

1959   **March**: Uprising in Tibet against Chinese rule is suppressed by the People's Liberation Army (PLA).

April: Liu Shaoqi succeeds Mao as state president (Mao remains as party chairman).

August: Peng Dehuai criticizes the Great Leap Forward and is purged, showing that Mao can no longer be criticized, even by his senior colleagues.

1960   Soviet Union withdraws all experts from China. Famine deepens in China.

1961   CCP begins economic and political reforms to undo the damage of the Great Leap Forward.

1964   China explodes its atomic bomb.

1966   Cultural Revolution begins as an attack on Beijing party intellectuals but quickly spreads to the purge of senior party leaders, including, by 1967, Liu Shaoqi. Mao writes a big-character poster, "Bombard the Headquarters," to encourage Red Guard youths to attack "the four olds" and "to rebel is justified"; Red Guard terror begins.

1969   Mao declares the "victory" (that is, end) of the Cultural Revolution and supports Marshal Lin Biao as his new successor; radical policies – and urges – continue.

1971   **July**: U.S. secretary of state Henry Kissinger secretly visits Beijing.

September: Lin Biao dies in a plane crash while trying to escape Mao's secret police; he is formally denounced.

October: China joins the United Nations, leading to expulsion of Taiwan.

1972   U.S. president Richard Nixon visits China.

1976   **January**: Zhou Enlai, the highest ranking moderate in the CCP, dies.

September: Mao Zedong dies.

Map 1. China today.

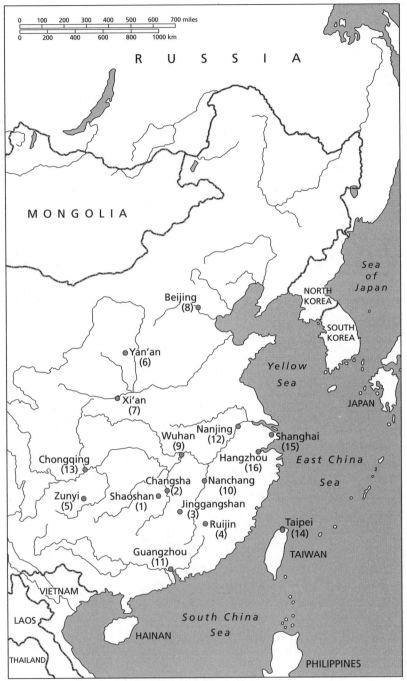

Map 2. Key locations in Mao's life.

Notes on Map 2

1. Shaoshan: Mao's Birthplace.
2. Changsha: Where Mao went to school and later worked in the Hunan Normal School. Also the site of Mao's abortive Autumn Harvest uprising.
3. Jinggangshan: The original safe haven in Jiangxi Province that Mao and others fled to after the failed uprising of 1927.
4. Ruijin: The capital of the Jiangxi Soviet.
5. Zunyi: The site of the conference in 1935 where Mao began his rise to supreme power in the Chinese Communist Party (CCP).
6. Yan'an: The communist headquarters after the Long March and throughout the war against Japan.
7. Xi'an: The site of Chiang Kai-shek's kidnapping by the northern warlords, which led to creation of the second United Front.
8. Beijing: China's capital before the collapse of the empire in 1911 and once again after the Revolution.
9. Wuhan: Birthplace of the 1911 Revolution and site of intramilitary conflict at the height of the Cultural Revolution. Also briefly twice China's capital under the Guomindang, first as they moved north before taking Nanjing and later as they fled Nanjing after the Japanese invasion.
10. Nanchang: Site of a doomed communist uprising in 1927.
11. Guangzhou (Canton): The Guomindang's headquarters after Yuan Shikai ignored the national election result in 1912. The scene of many bitter battles during the 1920s. Also the site of a short-lived commune after the communist uprising in December 1927.
12. Nanjing: Capital of China after the 1911 Revolution and again after the Guomindang established a new national government after the Northern Expedition in 1927. Site of the Rape of Nanjing after the Japanese invasion and of the puppet regime of Wang Jingwei under Japanese control.
13. Chongqing: Became the Guomindang's base during the war against Japan.
14. Taipei: The capital of the Guomindang's Republic of China from 1949 to the present day.
15. Shanghai: China's major commercial center and one of the centers of radicalism during the Cultural Revolution. The base of the radical Maoists in power in the Cultural Revolution.
16. Hangzhou: Another site of radical leftism. Site of a number of important conferences and meetings at the outset of the Cultural Revolution.

Part I
Mao's World

1 Mao, Revolution, and Memory

TIMOTHY CHEEK

I think my first impression – dominantly one of native shrewdness – was probably correct. And yet Mao was an accomplished scholar of Classical Chinese, an omnivorous reader, a deep student of philosophy and history, a good speaker, a man with an unusual memory and extraordinary powers of concentration, an able writer, careless in his personal habits and appearance but astonishingly meticulous about details of duty, a man of tireless energy, and military and political strategist of considerable genius.

Edgar Snow, Red Star Over China (1937)[1]

Psychologists of mass behavior might have an explanation for what went wrong in China in the late summer of 1958. China was struck with a mass hysteria fed by Mao, who then fell victim himself.... Mao's earlier skepticism had vanished. Common sense escaped him. He acted as though he believed the outrageous figures for agricultural production. The excitement was contagious. I was infected, too.

Li Zhishi, The Private Life of Chairman Mao (1994)[2]

Beijing relies on the [Party] Center,
Shanghai on its connections,
Guangzhou leans on Hong Kong,
The drifting population lives by Mao Zedong Thought.

Popular ditty in China among working poor, 1990s[3]

Mao Zedong has always come to us through stories. Some reflect fragments of personal experience, some seek to weave a sensible historical narrative, and some promote a myth that serves other interests. The stories began in the 1930s, and they keep coming today. The stories do not match generally because different authors seek to demonstrate different

[1] Edgar Snow, *Red Star Over China* (New York: Grove Press, reprint, 1968), p. 92.
[2] Zhisui Li, *The Private Life of Chairman Mao* (New York: Random House, 1994), pp. 276–277.
[3] "Musical Chairman," from Geremie R. Barmé, *Shades of Mao: The Posthumous Cult of the Great Leader* (Armonk, NY: M. E. Sharpe, 1996), pp. 283–284.

conclusions. Just as often, the teller has experienced or researched the story of only a small part of Mao's life. Yet each story has value for the person who would like a comprehensive sense of Mao – Who was he? Why is he so famous? Was he as wonderful as earlier reports painted him or as evil as many books claim today? What, in the end, is significant about Mao? The purpose of this book is to provide the general reader an opportunity to make sense of Mao and his role in modern Chinese history and the "socialist moment" in twentieth-century world history, as well as his continuing significance both in China and beyond. We bring the tools of academic research and scholarly discipline to bear on the events, experiences, and stories that swirl around Mao to offer a historical account.[4] We are more than a dozen scholars, old and young, Western and Chinese, male and female, representing a range of academic disciplines, and we do not tell a uniform history. In post-Mao China, one of the enduring political developments has been "pluralization" (*duoyuanhua*), and the stories in this book reflect the multiple meanings of Mao in the past and present. Indeed, it is our theme: There are multiple Maos, and to settle on one dominant image is to distort the whole.

Mao Zedong lived from 1893 to 1976. He is the most famous Chinese of the twentieth century and certainly China's most influential political leader. He is remembered as China's paramount Marxist-Leninist leader and theorist. A junior Communist Party member in the 1920s and controversial regional leader in the countryside in the late 1920s and early 1930s, by the mid-1940s Mao had become the supreme leader of China's communist movement and, in 1949, of the new People's Republic of China (PRC). The personality cult around Chairman Mao culminated in outrageous popular veneration in the turbulent Cultural Revolution in the 1960s, and his memory remains vibrant in China today. His writings continue to serve as the official doctrine of the still-ruling Chinese Communist Party (CCP), and his memory elicits strong feelings (both positive and negative) among China's diverse population, as well as students of Marxism and revolution worldwide. In the international history of communism, Mao Zedong played a key role in leading the largest communist revolution in the world outside of Russia and in his "creative developments" or "Sinification" of Marxist-Leninist orthodoxy to suit Chinese conditions, adaptations that have influenced revolutions in Asia, Latin America, and Africa. In all, Mao remains the preeminent representative of the successes and failures of Chinese revolutionary ideology and praxis.

---

4   This useful parsing of historiography into experience, history, and myth is explored in Paul A. Cohen, *History in Three Keys: The Boxers as Event, Experience, and Myth*, 2nd ed. (New York: Columbia University Press, 1998).

Mao is remembered by all as a revolutionary leader. He has been presented by his faithful followers in the CCP as the embodiment of the socialist revolution that reunited China and restored national dignity after decades of war, division, and semicolonial subjugation. It also brought the Communists to power in the new PRC in 1949. That "story" was extremely compelling – not only to a majority of Chinese over several decades at mid-century but also to non-Chinese academics trying to explain China's many social and political changes.[5] Meanwhile, Mao's competitors and enemies depicted him and the revolution he came to lead as evil and bad for China.[6] Today, more than three decades after Mao's death, it is not so simple. Even inside China, Mao's faults, the achievements of other CCP leaders, and the contributions of talented Chinese in other areas are all part of the story of China's modern revolutions.[7] In private, around China and in the Western press, even Mao's former followers reflect critically and sometimes with the outrage of the apostate on Mao and the revolution they served.[8] Meanwhile, Mao's portrait continues to overlook Tiananmen Square, taxi drivers sport Mao medallions like St. Christopher medals, and temples across China include Mao as a tutelary god in China's irrepressible popular religions.

Mao remains a very controversial and much distorted figure – not least by the infamous personality cult that climaxed in the turbulent 1960s. Mao's memory and legacy in China are still vivid for many: hated as a despot, grudgingly respected as an effective national unifier, and revered for what he is remembered as doing for China's dispossessed, particularly in contrast with the declining fortunes of many working poor in China today. This ambivalence is reflected in the opening quote from Li Zhisui, one of Mao's doctors from the late 1950s. Similarly, readers of our book do not come to Mao without assumptions. Popular and scholarly writing on Mao in English since Edgar Snow's glowing account

---

[5] Mark Selden, *The Yenan Way in Revolutionary China* (Cambridge, MA: Harvard University Press, 1971). Even those critical of Mao put him at the center of a single Chinese Revolution. See Merle Goldman, *Literary Dissent in Communist China* (Cambridge, MA: Harvard University Press, 1967), and Simon Leys, *Chinese Shadows* (New York: Viking Press, 1977).

[6] Karl A. Wittfogel, *Oriental Despotism: A Comparative Study in Total Power* (New Haven, CT: Yale University Press, 1957); Warren Kuo, *Analytical History of the Chinese Communist Party*, 2nd ed. (Taipei: Institute for International Relations, 1968); George Paloczi-Horvath, *Mao Tse-tung: Emperor of the Blue Ants* (London: Secker & Warburg, 1962); Robert North, *Chinese Communism* (New York: McGraw-Hill, 1966).

[7] This is covered in the review of Chinese and Western literature later in this chapter.

[8] There is a growing literature of reckoning from Mao's surviving followers from Yue Daiyun and Carolyn Wakeman's account of Yue's life, *To the Storm*, in the 1980s to Jung Chang and Jon Halliday's denunciation, *Mao: The Untold Story*, in 2005.

in *Red Star Over China* in 1937 has ranged from cold war denunciations to anti–Vietnam War adulation to sober assessments of contributions and failings. However, the "God Mao" and "Devil Mao" sell many
more newspapers and pop books than ponderous academic tomes on the
"Complicated Mao." *A Critical Introduction to Mao* taps that academic
knowledge and many of the leading scholars of our day to provide a
more engaging entry into the scholarly contributions to understanding
Mao and his historical significance.

This introduction is intended to prepare readers to make the most of
this book by doing three things. It gives an outline of Mao's life and contributions to China's modern revolutions and the historical significance
of his ideology, "Mao Zedong Thought." Second, it reviews the major
points of controversy concerning Mao, his role in China's twentieth-
century revolutions, and the meanings attached to Mao during his life
and today. Finally, it will prepare readers both to assess the competing
interpretations of Mao and to make their own reading of Mao's biography and writings by reviewing how we approach Mao and his role in
modern Chinese history, how we know what we know about Mao, and
what critical assessment of texts on or by Mao can tell us. It concludes
with some notes on strategies for reading Mao and writings on Mao
(including those in this book) as an independent thinker.

MAO'S LIFE OF REVOLUTION

Mao Zedong's life of revolution is a significant representative of both
Marxist and state socialist practice in twentieth-century China and of
the contributions of Chinese experience to socialist ideology and practice worldwide. Inside China, Mao is widely viewed as filling the roles of
both Lenin – generator and theorist of the revolution – and Stalin – the
harsh but effective implementer of the socialist revolution in a national
context. Since the late 1940s, Chinese in the PRC have been taught that
the Chinese Revolution found its fruition in the life, work, and writings
of Chairman Mao. The post-Mao period has brought a diversification
of the history of China's Revolution and of the contributions of many,
many Chinese to both Marxist thought and revolutionary praxis. The
story is no longer all about Mao.[9] Names such as Li Da, key theorist in
the 1920s; Liu Shaoqi, long the number two leader and key organizational
figure; Chen Boda, Mao's ideological secretary; Ai Siqi, popularizer of

---

[9]   Tony Saich, *The Rise to Power of the Chinese Communist Party: Documents and
Analysis* (Armonk, NY: M. E. Sharpe, 1996); Jeffrey N. Wasserstrom, "Mao Matters: A
Review Essay," *China Review International* 3:1 (1996), pp. 1–21.

dialectical materialist philosophy in the 1930s and 1940s; and numerous generals who developed and implemented the "people's war" have returned to history books in China and Western societies.

Making Revolution in China

Mao is but the foremost of a generation of Chinese intellectuals and activists known as the *May Fourth Generation* (for the patriotic anti-imperialist movement centering on the demonstrations in Beijing on May 4, 1919, that protested the transfer of Chinese territory to the Japanese in the Treaty of Versailles). This generation wrestled with a confusing array of Western ideas – from anarchism to pragmatism to social Darwinism, and finally, after 1917, Marxism – as a way to explain the failures of the Chinese government to resist the inroads of European and Japanese imperialism. In Chapter 2, Joseph Esherick gives a vivid social history of this generation. May Fourth intellectuals were vigorously iconoclastic, crying, "Down with the House of Confucius." They promoted major social reforms, including free marriage (as opposed to arranged), labor unions, and the adoption of the vernacular language in books and periodicals. This was their "ideological moment" in China. It was a diverse generation that sought answers to social crisis in ideology. In the 1920s, this generation divided across the political spectrum from neoconservatives seeking a Confucian revival, to political liberals hoping for democracy, to militarists seeking order, to revolutionaries seeking a new society.

Mao entered this May Fourth world from a rural community in central China. He was born and raised in Shaoshan, Xingtan County, in Hunan Province. His father was a prosperous farmer and was able to pay to send Mao to school. Thus Mao was not a peasant in the simple sense but was most emphatically a rural person who came to believe that the heart of China lay in the villages, not the cities. Mao soaked up the rich array of May Fourth translations from European and Japanese sources, including socialist and soon Russian Marxist writings. (Mao never learned a foreign language.) He chose to be a revolutionary and set off – first to Changsha (the capital of Hunan) and then to Beijing and Shanghai – to find that revolution.

Mao's career and writings can be viewed in three major stages: as a junior member of the new CCP who led the shift from an urban to a rural revolutionary strategy (1920s–mid-1930s), as the primary leader of the revolutionary party and army from the mid-1930s to the mid-1950s, and as the undisputed charismatic supreme leader of the CCP and PRC from the 1950s until his death in 1976. These three periods broadly correspond to the three chronologic chapters in this book: Chapter 3 by

Brantly Womack on Mao's move from urban radical to rural revolution-ary; Chapter 4 by Hans J. van de Ven on war, revolution, and state build-ing; and Chapter 5 by Michael Schoenhals on Mao's ruinous continuous revolutions from the mid-1950s. The CCP was officially founded in Shanghai in July 1921, and Mao attended the first congress as a regional delegate from Hunan. The new party was small and under the strong influence of Comintern advisors sent from Moscow. The tiny CCP grew by joining forces with the Nationalist Party [Guomindang (GMD)] under Sun Yat-sen in 1923. After the counterrevolution of April 1927, in which GMD forces under General Chiang Kai-shek (Jiang Jieshi) deci-mated union and Communist ranks in Shanghai and other major cities, Mao and colleagues repaired to the countryside, setting up rural soviets in southeast China. This lasted until 1934, when GMD military forces crushed the Communists and forced them on the retreat that came to be known as the Long March.

Mao had not only not been a top leader during this period but also had fallen out of favor with the Moscow-appointed Chinese leadership of the CCP. In fact, his highest party positions in the mid-1920s were in the GMD – at the Whampoa Military Academy – before the 1927 split. However, the debacle of the 1927 GMD White Terror and then the collapse of the Jiangxi Soviet in 1934 – in which urban orientation and positional warfare were shown to fail while rural orientation and guer-rilla warfare at least provided survival – provided the opportunity for Mao to gain some top positions. Over the next few years, he skillfully built a coalition of colleagues, sensible military and social policies, and a persuasive ideological corpus that confirmed him as the leader of the Chinese Revolution.

These policies were implemented in the 1940s when the CCP's capital was in the dusty Shaanxi Province market town of Yan'an in northwest China. Mao's "Introducing the Communist" (1939) named the "three magic weapons" for defeating the enemy in China's Revolution: the United Front, armed struggle, and party building. This was the begin-ning of Mao's application of the Bolshevik model to China, or the "Sinification of Marxism." It produced effective policies that catapulted the CCP to national leadership in a decade.

Internally, Mao ruthlessly eliminated his rivals for leadership and effectively streamlined and energized the party rank and file. This was accomplished most clearly in the 1942–44 Rectification Movement. Here, Mao's writings from 1936 to 1942 became the core of the CCP's "Sinification of Marxism" – the application of general Marxist-Leninist theory (in its Stalinist form) to the realities of Chinese politics and culture. At the heart of Mao's approach was the "mass line" (*qunzhong luxian*) – a broadly participatory mode of political administration that brought in the views, interests, and experiences of common working people in a fashion never stressed by Lenin or Stalin. This was not democracy. Indeed, Mao and the CCP stressed "democratic centralism" (*minzhu jizhong*) and were ruthless in suppressing dissidents, such as the left-wing intellectuals associated with the writer Ding Ling and theorist Wang Shiwei who dared to question Mao and CCP practice from an independent Marxist (and feminist) stand in 1942.

Yet this repression of dissent inside the CCP – which foreshadowed disastrously expanded versions of this tyranny in 1957 and 1966 – paralleled effective organizational and public-policy reforms, including simplified administration, armies that not only did not rape and pillage but actually paid for the food they used, and a powerful ideology that mobilized a generation of cadres to "serve the people." The lessons of this coordinated but flexible organizing have been applied to social movements elsewhere, from the Vietcong in Vietnam, to Che Guevara in Latin America, to Naxalite activists in Nepal (see Chapter 12).

Externally, Mao led his colleagues in making the CCP and their program for China look better than the only likely alternative: the increasingly corrupt Nationalist government of Chiang Kai-shek. By 1939, the GMD government presented Chiang Kai-shek as the hero of war-torn China, and the GMD began a leadership cult to establish Chiang as China's charismatic revolutionary leader. The publication of his book, *China's Destiny*, in 1943 brought Chiang's leadership cult to a crescendo. Thus the Mao cult of the 1940s was a response to this practical challenge, as well as drawing from the example of Stalin.[10]

Mao adroitly cast his public utterances in moderate terms. His 1940 essay, "On New Democracy," became widely popular among urban readers, especially youth. Although clearly a Marxist-Leninist document, Mao's program promised a long period of democratic transition on the road to eventual socialism and communism. In addition, he provided a public history of China's humiliating confrontation with European and Japanese imperialism that, using Lenin's ideas on imperialism as the highest form of capitalism, made sense of China's history and, more important, gave Chinese readers a sense of purpose, hope, and meaning.[11] In the face of

---

[10] Lyman Van Slyke, in *The Cambridge History of China*, Vol. 13: *Republican China, 1912–1949*, Part II (Cambridge, England: Cambridge University Press, 1986), p. 692.

[11] "On New Democracy," in Stuart R. Schram, ed., *Mao's Road to Power* (Armonk, NY: M.E. Sharpe, 2006), Vol. 7, pp. 330–369; the official version in his *Selected Works* was revised in many parts.

rampant corruption in GMD-administered areas and the continued misery of working and rural peoples, Mao's "On New Democracy" combined with the impressive track record of the armies and administrations under CCP rule in the 1940s to create a very appealing political platform and ideology of public service along with an organization that appeared able to deliver on these promises.

His peers certified Mao Zedong as the charismatic supreme leader at the Seventh Congress of the CCP in Yan'an in April 1945. From that time on, he was known as Chairman Mao. In the ranks of the party leadership he was, at first, restrained and practical, but all deferred to him. Externally, he was the great Father of the Revolution who could publicly proclaim in September 1949, "The Chinese People Have Stood Up!"[12] Mao's work in the new People's Republic was largely practical in the early 1950s, as this rural movement adjusted to the profound tasks of administering not only major cities but also a territory the size of Europe. The new socialist government "leant to one side" – taking on the Soviet model of a centralized command economy and joining the Soviet Union in the emerging cold war. Russian advisors guided the modern sector, and Stalin lent (but did not give) funds to help rebuild the war-torn nation. The Korean War came upon the new government almost immediately – in June 1950. This confrontation with the United States heightened the already brutal land reform and anti-intellectual political movements, as well as anticorruption campaigns, during the early 1950s.[13] Yet, life for most Chinese was better than it had been in living memory.

By 1956, the new PRC government was feeling the pains of office.[14] Wasteful bureaucratism, the limits of the Stalinist economic model, and restiveness among the working peoples and, of course, a critical intelligentsia bedeviled the CCP leadership. Khrushchev's denunciation of Stalin – communism's revered leader – in his 1956 secret speech scandalized CCP leaders. Mao at first sought to moderate application of his revolutionary approach. In 1956, he revived the Rectification Movement approach of self- and mutual criticism but extended it beyond the CCP to the educated public, inviting intellectuals and professionals to "let

[12] Mao Zedong, "Zhongguo ren congci zhan liqilaide," *Mao Zedong wenji* (Writings of Mao Zedong) (Beijing: Renmin Chubanshe, 1999), Vol. 5, pp. 342–346.

[13] Jeremy Brown and Paul Pickowicz, eds., *Dilemmas of Victory: The Early Years of the People's Republic of China* (Cambridge, MA: Harvard University Press, 2007).

[14] While some still view the early 1950s as a "golden age" of CCP rule, there were profound tensions from the early mass campaigns (the Three Antis and Five Antis), war in Korea against the United States, the violent side of land reform, and intellectual repression. The current view is a more balanced one of successes and tensions. See Brown and Pickowicz, *Dilemmas of Victory.*

a hundred flowers bloom" and to criticize the ruling CCP. This was an unprecedented act for a ruling Communist Party and was vigorously opposed by Mao's senior colleagues.

This was Mao's last great public ideological effort that had some promise of success. Because of his profound authority among his followers (see Chapter 6), only Mao could have enforced the toleration of critical public debate in a socialist state. In "On the Correct Handling of Contradictions among the People" (original text, February 1957), Mao sought to lay the theoretical basis for limited – but real – public criticism and dissent under a ruling Communist Party.[15] By defending loyal opposition to party bureaucratism and abuses of power as "contradictions among the people" in contrast to "contradictions with the enemy," Mao went further than even the most daring of the Eastern European regimes in the de-Stalinization of 1956. This promising opening to socialism with a human face was ruined by Mao's own dictatorial style and petulance. When the invited criticisms arrived in the spring of 1957, they were not to Mao's liking, so he declared the critics to be counterrevolutionary Rightists. The text of "Correct Handling" was significantly rewritten before official publication in June 1957 to make Mao look good and to ratchet back permissible discussion to the restricted scope familiar to other state socialist societies. It was a failed experiment that cost the lives and careers of half a million intellectuals and party members.

The next decade was a grim one for China and for Mao's legacy. The "Hundred Flowers" rectification of 1957 was followed by a harsh nationwide purge, the Anti-Rightist Movement. Next, Mao promoted an ambitious economic development strategy, the Great Leap Forward (1958–60), that was disastrously flawed and ruthlessly implemented. It contributed to at least 15–46 million deaths – mostly attributable to the famine – by 1961. This has to be the single greatest crime during Mao's rule of China. After a retrenchment in the early 1960s (administered by his number two, Liu Shaoqi) brought an end to the famine and began the economic recovery, Mao initiated a final effort at total revolution: the Cultural Revolution. It was designed to protect China from the dire threat of revisionism that Mao saw in the Soviet Union under Khrushchev, and China and the Soviet Union fell into an ideological split that culminated in national confrontation and fighting on the Manchurian border in 1969. Now, at Mao's behest, the CCP revived the thought reform and rural orientation of the Yan'an period but, alas, not as comedy but as a horror

---

[15] See Mao's "Speaking Notes (*Jianghua Gao*)" translated in Roderick MacFarquhar, Timothy Cheek, and Eugene Wu, eds., *The Secret Speeches of Chairman Mao* (Cambridge, MA: Council on East Asian Studies, Harvard University, 1989), pp. 131–189.

show. Mindless adulation of every utterance by Mao was represented in the "Little Red Book," *Quotations from Chairman Mao Zedong*. In all, some 4.4 billion books and pamphlets of Mao material were published in the 10 years 1966–76 (see details in Chapter 9). The social results were catastrophic – Red Guard youth gangs terrorized communities under the slogan "To Rebel Is Justified" (a Mao quote), colleagues denounced each other, universities were closed to send students and faculty to the countryside "to learn from the peasants," and individuals were subject to endless "thought investigations."[16] To the degree that the populace in China participated in this self-subjugation, the Cultural Revolution even outpaced Stalin's Russia as the closest realization of Orwellian dystopia.[17] Mao clearly allowed this to happen and saw the suffering as a necessary cost of resisting "revisionism."[18]

Mao's final revolution was, after decades of angry confrontation with American imperialism, to spring a rapprochement with U.S. President Richard Nixon in 1972 in order to outmaneuver the Soviet Union. This external pragmatism softened the already faltering chiliastic rituals of the Cultural Revolution and left China and China's ideological leaders tired and dispirited but still standing at the time of his death.

When Mao died on September 9, 1976, China was struck with grief. It was a mixed grief, combining the memory of both Mao's great contributions to the establishment of the nation, the application of socialist goals, and the realization of economic progress and his cruel persecution of intellectuals, his abandonment of the peasants, his ruinous mass campaigns, and the arbitrary dictatorship of his later years. When Mao was born, China was a failing, backward empire and the playground for competing imperialist interests. When he died, it was a respected (or feared) nation on the world scene – a nuclear power with a permanent seat on the UN Security Council and able to feed its huge population and run a modern economy. The price of this success had been high, and the credit for it belongs to thousands of hardworking Chinese, not simply to Mao. Yet Mao has come to represent the noble goals, the grand achievements, and the terrible failures of China in the twentieth century.

---

[16] Roderick MacFarquhar and Michael Schoenhals, *Mao's Last Revolution* (Cambridge, MA: Harvard University Press, 2006).

[17] This self-subjugation is poignantly portrayed in post-Mao PRC films, such as Chen Kaige's *Farewell My Concubine* (1993), Tian Zhuangzhuang's *The Blue Kite* (1993), and Zhang Yimou's *To Live* (1994) – all widely available internationally with English subtitles.

[18] See Joseph Esherick, Paul Pickowicz, and Andrew Walder, eds., *The Chinese Cultural Revolution as History* (Palo Alto, CA: Stanford University Press, 2006).

Mao Zedong Thought: Revolutionary Ideology and Praxis

Mao Zedong is known as much for his writings – his ideas, his pronouncements, his ideology – as for his actions. China's twentieth-century Revolution came from the responses of a generation of revolutionaries (and not just communists) and the ideas they generated.[19] Mao (with the help of the CCP apparatus) was able to distill these ideas into an appealing ideology that disciplined and organized that revolutionary movement. By mid-century, Mao's ideology had brought the CCP to national power and mobilized a new generation of Chinese revolutionaries. These ideological contributions of Mao Zedong are systematized in "Mao Zedong Thought" (*Mao Zedong sixiang*), which remains the official ideology of the CCP today. Post-Mao CCP authorities have made it clear that Mao Zedong Thought is the "crystallization" of the revolutionary experience of the party *and* the contributions of numerous other Chinese Marxists.[20] Mao Zedong Thought is Sinified Marxism, according to this official view. Thus it is reasonable to consider the ideological contributions of Mao as the key, but not the only, representative of Chinese contributions to Marxist thought and praxis worldwide.

In terms of philosophy, Mao's approach to Marxist analysis of society makes practice primary. It is the resolution of contradictions in material life *as experienced by individuals* that drives Maoist dialectics (the reality of contradictions in the world and how to face them). The mechanism for Maoist practical dialectics, unlike for Lenin and Stalin, is human will – individual and collective. Thus Mao is in both the humanist and idealist wings of Marxist thought, placing the superstructure over the base as the location of the motor of history (he first articulated this in 1937 in "On Contradiction"). This can be seen in Mao's transformation of "proletarian" character from a description of a social class into a virtue that can be learned by any class – through personality-transforming praxis and ideological education (i.e., through rectification). If Lenin thought only the Bolshevik Party could push forward the wheel of history, Mao held that Bolshevization could be radically internalized in the individual (albeit under the dominating guidance of a charismatic leader).

In terms of revolutionary praxis and political policy, the experience of the CCP under Mao's leadership created a variant of the Russian model that has been very influential among revolutionary movements

---

[19] A still useful account of the range of revolutionary ideas and their alternatives is Jerome Grieder, *Intellectuals and the State in Modern China* (New York: Free Press, 1980).

[20] See discussion in this chapter below on "Approaching Mao," especially note 57.

in Asia and Latin America and even today provides tools that may well be picked up again by those concerned with social change in China and abroad. First, Mao instituted the *mass line* and *mass campaigns* (*yundong*), an organized form of "democratic centralism" and mass mobilization that could be very responsive to local needs and that included the broadest actual popular consultation and participation in any communist movement. The classic example of this mass politics is land reform, which the CCP under Mao pursued from the 1930s (see Chapter 4). The dark side of the mass line was the Red Guards and the popular terror of the Cultural Revolution. Second, the CCP under Mao applied party education far more thoroughly than any other communist movement. The Rectification Movement of 1942–44 implemented the mass line by providing noble goals of public service (which distinguishes the CCP, then, from Pol Pot's Khmer Rouge), the means to inculcate those goals among administrators (party and government cadres), and mechanisms to test the level of success in their implementation. Used well, rectification provides one way to inform, guide, and control a revolutionary regime; used badly, it has led to the excesses of the Cultural Revolution and the Killing Fields. Third, Mao and the CCP consistently returned to the idea of the *United Front*, an ideological tool that allows a Bolshevik regime to share power with other social forces. The United Front is institutionalized in the PRC government and has operated ever since the 1940s (with the exception of some years in the Cultural Revolution). Building on the Soviet model of the Popular Front, the United Front was expanded to become a tool that has contributed to the longevity of the CCP in power. A good example of United Front work is the Chinese People's Political Consultative Congress that engages elites from outside as well as inside the party in both provincial and national congresses that do not make laws (the National People's Congress does that) but advises the government on policy. Fourth, Mao consistently attacked *bureaucratism*, even though his flawed efforts (and personal faults) ultimately failed to address the issue successfully. Nonetheless, the corpus of Mao Zedong Thought provides a trenchant analysis of what Milovan Djilas called the "New Class" (though not with this phrase) under socialism and justifications for using the mass line and rectification to combat the abuse of political privilege. Fifth, Mao stressed *rural issues* and the peasantry. Integrating a primary focus on the countryside into the program of a Communist Party has, perhaps, been the single most influential contribution of Chinese revolutionary praxis worldwide. Finally, Mao was straightforward about politics and favored *armed struggle*. He was a violent revolutionary and a pragmatic military leader. His writings contain hundreds of pages of practical analysis and examples of guerrilla warfare and other forms of popular violent struggle.[21] Those who have found themselves in intolerable social circumstances where local governments violently repress opposition have found Maoist military strategy compelling – from the Vietcong to the Naxalites (see Chapter 12).

There are also negative contributions or negatives to each of these six developments that are most poignantly embodied in the ideological repression of the 1957 Anti-Rightist Movement, the massive deaths of the Great Leap Forward, and the social terror of the Cultural Revolution. All were generated by the self-same Mao Zedong Thought and the CCP. Thus the legacy of Mao Zedong and his thought is deeply mixed – having led the Chinese people to "stand up" in 1949, he needlessly struck China down in two decades of avoidable human suffering (see Chapter 5). This has led some, in China and outside, to a total rejection of Mao.[22] The CCP itself has attempted selective amnesia, maintaining Mao as the font of ideological authority but refusing to address the root causes of the disasters for which he – and the party – is responsible. However, some in China today, from radical academics such as Cui Zhiyuan or Gan Yang to rural activists or popular religious practitioners, seek to draw from the ideas and practices of Mao Zedong to address the problems that have emerged since Mao's death as China globalizes.[23]

Stuart Schram, the doyen of Mao studies in the West, has long held that "the soberer elements in Mao's thought" from 1935 to 1965 constitute "a vehicle of Westernization" for China.[24] This is true if we think in terms of helping China to come to terms with the new power of the West since the mid-nineteenth century and the imperialism associated with it. Despite his tragic errors, the CCP under Mao led China from a war-torn, divided, and impoverished collection of provinces to a stable nation-state and world nuclear power. Conversely, the significance of Mao and Mao Zedong Thought for the rest of the world is the contribution of Chinese experience – both good and bad – to the wider experience of revolution, state socialism, and postsocialist reform.

[21] For a sense of the range and volume of Mao writings, see Schram, ed., *Mao's Road to Power* (10 vols.), and notes in final section of this chapter.

[22] For example, Li Zhisui, *The Private Life of Chairman Mao* (New York: Random House, 1994), or Jung Chang and Jon Halliday, *Mao: The Untold Story* (New York: Alfred A. Knopf, 2005).

[23] Mobo Gao, *The Battle for China's Past: Mao and the Cultural Revolution* (London: Pluto Press, 2008).

[24] Stuart Schram, *The Thought of Mao Tse-tung* (New York: Cambridge University Press, 1989), p. 192.

MEMORY AND MEANING: HISTORICAL
SIGNIFICANCE AND CONTESTED LEGACIES

Assessments of Mao are hotly contested – the contrast at the start of
this chapter between Edgar Snow's idealization and Li Zhisui's demoni-
zation is just the tip of the iceberg because these two views represent
the extremes. Understanding Mao or any major historical figure is tied
not only to problems of data and scholarly interpretation but also to
the "story" put forward by interested parties, particularly the nation-
state that claims ownership of that historic figure. Popular media pick
up and change these state-led story lines, and various groups of people
adopt and adapt these stories to suit their needs. No reader of this book
comes to the question of Mao innocent of impressions. The effort to
understand Mao or any topic in history thus must include at least a brief
effort to reflect on the stories we have accepted – or to which we have
reacted – up to now. Then we can turn to see how others have made
sense of Mao – from revolutionaries in the "third world" to the complex
range of groups and individuals in China today.

Mao Studies and Images of Mao Internationally

Both the academic study of Mao and popular images of Mao in
Western societies have been tied to other interests, most usually the
war of the day. Edgar Snow's glowing account in 1936 gave readers "a
Lincolnesque figure" who promised to lead China in the worldwide
fight against fascism in what became World War II. Dire accounts of
atrocities by "Chi-Coms" and "Reds" in the 1950s and 1960s spoke
to the experience of U.S.-led UN forces in the Korean War (1950–53),
America's own fight in Vietnam, and more broadly the U.S.-Soviet
struggle for dominance in the cold war. Since the 1960s, China has been
presented in scholarship and popular media in a roller coaster of ideal
images (beginning with anti–Vietnam War activists in the 1960s) and
dystopian tales (such as reports of forced abortions in the 1980s).[25] Thus
the general reader can find glowing accounts of Mao or negative reports
of the Chairman from any decade since the 1960s.

Scholarly treatments of Mao, while more surely grounded in social
science disciplines and afforded the opportunity to carry on at length in
order to explore complexity, nonetheless show the influence of broader

---

[25] For one survey of the broad outlines of China scholarship, see Timothy Cheek, "The
New Chinese Intellectual: Globalized, Disoriented, Reoriented," in Lionel Jensen
and Timothy Weston, eds., *China's Transformations* (Lanham, MD: Rowman &
Littlefield, 2007), esp. pp. 266–276.

political pressures. In 1951, Benjamin Schwartz gave the first scholarly account of Mao, and he strove to show that Mao, whatever his promises and faults, was not a puppet of Stalin and the Soviet Union.[26] While post-Mao revelations have confirmed Schwartz's initial analysis, his view was hotly contested by fellow scholars throughout the 1950s and 1960s. Most broadly, scholarship during Mao's life assumed that he was absolutely critical for understanding "China today." Whether they thought Mao a savior or a tyrant, or a bit of both, these studies tended to neglect other actors and other forces in explaining the rise and current operation of "China's Revolution." By the 1980s, revolution was off the agenda for China – especially after the dashing of hopes for a democratic revolution in 1989 – and likewise scholars have broadened their study of Mao and the CCP to other subjects. Most notably, current scholarship looks not at revolution but at modernization, not at Mao (or other leaders) but at the experience of wider groups of peoples, especially individuals who had to live through Mao's policies.[27]

The scholarship that tends to reach a broader public is biography. Stuart Schram's early biography of Mao came out as a Penguin paperback in 1966, with a second edition in 1968. It was the standard for decades and still remains a reliable story based on a careful reading of Mao's writings in historical context. There are literally dozens of scholarly biographies of Mao, most dating from the 1960s and early 1970s or from the last 10 years. Among the more recent are grand tales by Philip Short and Ross Terrill and brief introductions by Delia Davin and Jonathan Spence. Maurice Meisner has been known through his life as a sympathetic Leftist critic of Mao, pioneering the critique of Mao's failings on the basis of Mao's own ideas, and his last book, a biography for Polity Press, captures this approach. Michael Lynch provides a recent (2004) biography that tries to balance various views (indeed, his "Further Reading" on pp. 249–254 provides a fine annotated guide to writings on, about, or by Mao for the general reader).[28]

[26] Benjamin Schwartz, *Chinese Communism and the Rise of Mao* (Cambridge, MA: Harvard University Press, 1951). An early and emblematic debate occurred between Schwartz and Karl Wittfogel in the opening issues of *China Quarterly* (Nos. 1 and 2) in 1960.

[27] Wasserstrom, "Mao Matters," pp. 1–21, documents this shift in scholarship in a thoughtful review of recent studies.

[28] Stuart R. Schram, *Mao Tse-tung* (Harmondsworth, England: Penguin, 1966); Philip Short, *Mao: A Life* (New York: Henry Holt & Co., 1999); Ross Terrill, *Mao: A Biography* (Palo Alto, CA: Stanford University Press, 1999); Delia Davin, *Mao Zedong* (Stroud, England: Sutton, 1997); Jonathan Spence, *Mao Zedong* (Harmondsworth, England: Penguin, 1999); Maurice Meisner, *Mao Zedong* (Cambridge, England: Polity Press, 2007); Michael Lynch, *Mao* (London: Routledge, 2004).

Popular images of Mao and China's Revolution are shaped more by Hollywood than by Harvard. As Charles Hayford shows in Chapter 13, popular Western images derive from themes in films such as *The Good Earth* (based on Pearl S. Buck's novel) but have been driven by journalists – professionals who answer to media masters chasing the ever-elusive "top story" of the day. Edgar Snow was one such journalist, and his successors on the "China beat" have brought vivid images of Mao and China to newspapers and magazines in Western countries. Understandably, those stories have been driven by the concerns of the reading publics of *The New York Times*, *The Guardian*, or *Le Monde* more than by concerns of historical balance or complex contexts. More interesting than most academic accounts, these press reports have been more subject to the changing whims of contemporary politics. They are important because they nonetheless shape popular and political ideas about China much more than academic works. The key difference is that most scholarship will frustrate the human desire for a "clean story" – a clear line of why things happened and who's to be praised or blamed.

Mao has carried yet other meanings in what has long been called the "third world" of developing countries, many of which are experiencing rural revolutions. Alexander Cook in Chapter 12 shows that inspiration revolutionaries from India to the Philippines to Peru have taken from Mao's revolutionary writings and the example of the CCP. These "readings" of Mao are not necessarily any more accurate than pro or con journalism in New York or London, but they are significant for the social movements they fuel.

Multiple Maos in China Today

Clearly, the most important legacies of Mao are in China itself. Mao Zedong remains an enduringly manifold figure in China today, loved and hated, and used for political leverage, celebrity value, and even religious efficacy. Such multiplicity is the mark of the postmodern world, from the jumbled artifacts of globalized markets, to the Internet Balkanization of intellectual communities, to the diversity of ethnic and cultural communities in our own neighborhoods. This diversification of public and private experience in China has a further dimension: the breakup of the "directed public sphere" of the propaganda state.[29] While China is still an authoritarian state and not a democracy, no longer does the orthodoxy of the CCP dominate public discourse – writers and readers have the opportunity to explore alternate readings of Mao Zedong Thought, Marxism,

---

[29] See Yuezhi Zhao, *Communication in China: Political Economy, Power and Conflict* (Lanham, MD: Rowman & Littlefield, 2008).

or even Liberalism, and more blessedly, all have the right at present to choose not to discuss political ideology at all. Pluralization can serve, then, to remind us both of the changes in the political atmosphere in China today and of the multiple voices that thus have come to the fore representing a diversity of experience across a country that is nearly the size of the European Union and over three times as populous.[30]

There is, however, a shared theme in all the multiple Maos embraced (or excoriated) among China's diverse population: *nationalism*. Mao will always be associated with the founding of the nation (PRC) and the throwing off of imperialism. Mao did not create the revolution that would throw off foreign domination, but he did come to represent the successes of Chinese nationalism at mid-century. He captured the mission of the CCP powerfully in his 1940 essay, "On New Democracy," and that project still resonates in China today:

> Since the invasion of foreign capitalism and the gradual growth of capitalist elements in Chinese society, that is, during the hundred years from the Opium War until the Sino-Japanese War, the country has changed by degrees into a colonial, semi-colonial, and semi-feudal society. China today is colonial in the enemy-occupied areas and basically semi-colonial in the non-occupied areas, and it is predominantly feudal in both.... It is precisely against these predominant political, economic, and cultural forms that our revolution is directed.[31]

Mao captured the success of that revolution in 1949, standing on the balcony of Tiananmen and officially declaring the founding of the People's Republic of China on October 1 (see Figure 11) Just the day before, Mao coined a phrase that has stuck ever since: "The Chinese people have stood up!" This claim has endured, as the PRC has endured and, since the 1990s, prospered under the rule of the CCP. There is no more public worshiping of Mao as was seen in the Cultural Revolution, but Mao still plays a framing role in Chinese society (see Chapters 10 and 11). The interesting story, however, is the different uses to which that frame is put. Mao is used differently by the CCP, scholars, workers, and farmers (what we might call *interest groups*); in commercial culture; and finally, in the personal memories of individuals.

---

[30] This section draws from Timothy Cheek, "The Multiple Maos of Contemporary China," *Harvard Asia Quarterly* 11: 2–3 (Spring–Summer 2008), pp. 14–25.

[31] Mao Zedong, "On New Democracy" in Schram, *Road to Power*, Vol. 7, pp. 330–369; also in *Selected Works of Mao Tse-tung* published in Beijing and available online at www.marxists.org/reference/archive/mao/.

The official orthodoxy of the CCP is Marxism-Leninism–Mao Zedong Thought. Maoist orthodoxy is used by the CCP to provide the legitimacy that otherwise would come from the ballot box. The story of China's modern history as told by the party – which remains the one we saw Mao announce in 1940 in "On New Democracy" – is central to this legitimation. Whether or not various people in China believe every part of this official narrative, the basic assumptions or identity of China that the CCP presents is widely accepted. Thus we need to distinguish between the specific and general claims made in Maoist orthodoxy. Today, most people in China do not claim to follow Mao's explicit teachings, nor do they think the current party is a noble example of Mao's or anyone's ideals. Yet most people in China appear to accept the assumptions in this story about China's national identity, about the role of imperialism in China's history and present, and about the value of maintaining and improving this thing called China. Increasingly, moreover, China's middle classes accept the additional story in Maoism – the story of rising China: China was great, China was put down, China is rising again.

Politically, Maoism is the CCP's orthodoxy. It has been "enriched" by doctrinal additions from Deng Xiaoping, Jiang Zemin, and now China's current leader, Hu Jintao. The new contender for admission to the Maoist canon is Hu Jintao's theory of "Harmonious Society" (*hexie shehui*).[32] This spin on the party platform focuses on the interests of the overwhelming majority of Chinese. It shifts the burning issues confronting the interior provinces, the downtrodden, and the losers of reform to front and center. The new emphasis on "Harmonious Society," however, will remind those familiar with Latin American history of other forms of authoritarian populism. On the one hand, it draws attention to questions of social equity, but on the other hand, it also signals intolerance of dissent or "disturbances" by protestors.[33]

Intellectuals in China still deal with Mao. The pluralization of experience and views that shapes the rest of China equally affects academic and intellectual circles. No longer do writers have to praise Mao

---

[32] Liu Yunshan, "Strengthening, Expanding, and Innovating in Propaganda and Ideological Work in Accordance with the Requirements of Constructing a Harmonious Socialist Society," *Qiushi* 19 (2005), translated in FBIS-CHI (Foreign Broadcast Information Service, US Government], October 1, 2005.

[33] Peronism – the economic, political, and social ideology called *Justicialismo* (social justice) associated with the rule of Juan Domingo Peron in Argentina at mid-century – is the obvious point of comparison. See Steven Levitsky, *Transforming Labor-Based Parties in Latin America: Argentine Peronism in Comparative Perspective* (New York: Cambridge University Press, 2003).

and avoid criticism. But there are limits – still the ones broadly defined by the CCP's 1981 "Resolution on Certain Questions in the History of our Party Since the Founding of the Nation."[34] This is summed up in the popularly quoted equation: Mao's contributions equal 70 percent and failings equal 30 percent (ironically, Mao's own assessment in the 1950s of Stalin).[35] Scholars now use Mao in most cases strategically (to hammer home a point or to shield themselves from political criticism), but more important, Mao is often not used at all in intellectual debate and discussion of public issues. It is the constituent parts of Mao's thought – the nationalism, pragmatism, calls for social equity – that animate debates and serve as legitimizing themes rather than the invocation of Mao's "wisdom" per se (see Chapter 11). Indeed, it is now possible to criticize Mao in limited focus (particular policies in the past) and even to poke fun at him in the arts. There are a few writers who invoke Mao's ideals in claiming that Maoism should be restored, but these calls are a distinct minority among scholars.[36]

Scholars, of course, overlap with different social interests – from party intellectuals to academics to advocates for labor rights or environmental protection. There is a huge publishing industry on Mao – books, articles, TV shows, and study guides – that follows the paradigm set down by the CCP's Historical Resolution. The Mao craze of the mid-1990s started a new wave of biographies, reminiscences, and "when Mao and I were ..." stories. Thomas Scharping has well described this subindustry as a revival of traditional Chinese preference for personalized history focusing on the moral behavior of great men and serving "the gutsy appetite of the public for a peep show into the private lives of leaders, and the commercial instincts of a multitude of publishing houses...."[37] In the decade since, this rich flow of detail has continued – of family history, stories of Mao in different historical periods (such as Yan'an during World War II), and stories from his body guards, doctors, secretaries, interpreters, nurses, pilots, train attendants, and even dance partners. While the texts published in the 1990s tended toward

---

[34] *Beijing Review* 27 (July 6, 1981), pp. 10–39; Helmut Martin, *Cult & Canon* (Armonk, NY: M. E. Sharpe, 1983), pp. 180–231.

[35] In fact, the resolution does not give the 70/30 estimate, but the interpretation has evolved that this was its point. See Warren Sun, "On the 70/30 Estimation of Mao's Contributions" (unpublished ms). Mao's 70/30 assessment of Stalin came in 1963 in his "On the Question of Stalin" in the "Second Comment on the Open Letter of the Central Committee of the CPSU" (September 13, 1963); thanks to Delia Davin, who was in Beijing at the time.

[36] See Gao, *The Battle for China's Past*.

[37] Thomas Scharping, "The Man, the Myth, the Message – New Trends in Mao-Literature from China," *China Quarterly* 137 (March 1994), pp. 168–179.

the hagiographic, some of the newer books in the past few years have given more complexity and even shown a bit of Mao's darker side (see Chapter 11).

While popular books are presented as scholarship, the formal worlds of party ideological study and of academic research are largely separate from this popular scholarship. The CCP maintains tight control over the sources of information on Mao, from Party Archives to the oddly named Central Compilation and Translation Bureau (*Bianyiju*) that maintains privileged access to the original documents by and about Mao. Thousands of books, articles, and study guides are produced by the party school system and departments of party history at universities across China. Bibliographies of these studies run to thousands of pages for just the past decade alone.[38] These studies are about as popular as studies on theology of mainstream religions are in the West – important for the faithful and the priesthood but ignored by the general public.

Academic intellectuals use Mao in two ways. First, when speaking beyond academia to issues of public concern, they invoke different Maos to support their contending approaches toward how to "worry about China" (i.e., solve China's public problems).[39] These public intellectual debates, since the 1990s, have been notoriously contentious and have broken down on several lines, particularly "New Left" versus "Liberal."[40] For New Left intellectuals who seek to criticize contemporary Chinese society for its lack of equity and care for the poor, Mao's writings on the rights of working people and the need to control capitalists come into play. For example, in June 2007, Gan Yang made a review of the main sources of modern Chinese political culture by identifying three important strands: Confucianism, May Fourth enlightenment, and Maoist praxis.[41] So-called liberal intellectuals, who stress the need for political freedoms to promote civil society, also find recourse in the works of Mao, but in the more moderate writings of the Yan'an period, when he trimmed his sails to fit the United Front between the CCP and Chiang Kai-shek's Nationalists in the fight against Japan. For

---

[38] One of the scholars best acquainted with this CCP stream of Mao studies is Nick Knight. See in particular his collection of translations, *The Philosophical Thought of Mao Zedong: Studies from China, 1981–1989* (Armonk, New York: M. E. Sharpe, 1992) and "Contemporary Chinese Marxism and the Marxist Tradition," *Asian Studies Review* 30:1 (March 2006), pp. 19–29.

[39] See Gloria Davies, *Worrying About China: Contemporary Chinese Critical Discourse* (Cambridge, MA: Harvard University Press, 2006).

[40] For an excellent introduction and set of translations of these debates, see Chaohua Wang, *One China, Many Paths* (New York: Verso, 2005).

[41] Gan Yang, *Dushu* [Reading] (June 2007), pp. 1–6.

these scholars, citing Mao is more than a political precaution taken to keep party censors at bay. It is an effort to garner some of the remaining legitimacy Mao holds among their readers to support their contending solutions for China's problems.

China's workers and farmers are increasingly outspoken as the social consequences of reform create winners and losers. In the fight over resources that deregulation, privatization, and uncoordinated development have created, farmers, workers, and urban residents have protested and struck back. In such resistance they often invoke Mao's ideas and image to support their claims. Ching Kwan Lee gives a notable example from the northeastern province of Liaoning in China's state-owned industry rustbelt. In March 2002, some 30,000 workers from a score of factories marched in the streets carrying a huge poster of Mao Zedong. One of the participants told Lee:

> There were people singing "The Internationale": an elderly woman worker cried out loud lamenting that "Chairman Mao should not have died so soon!" ... There was a huge Mao portrait that an elderly worker took from his home, a personal collector's item. We actually had a planning meeting before and decided that we should take a Mao portrait with us, because we wanted to show the contrast we felt between the past and the present.[42]

Hundreds of other examples of workers using Mao portraits, badges, quotations on banners. and even drawings of Mao on the sidewalk outside a factory from which one has been fired (as one worker in Henan did to good effect – he got his job back) can be cited. Each instance shows a combination of using Mao to protect protestors from official violence or retribution and to shame officials into honoring what the workers see as the social contract between the socialist state and workers that has been violated under China's new economic reforms. These are "weapons of the weak," adopted by farmers and rural workers as well, as they seek to protect their homes, their farm land, and their air and water from expropriation by developers and pollution by new rural industries.[43]

In between labor agitation and pop culture lies the Internet. While party propaganda organs and scholarly journals have Web sites and even

[42] Ching Kwan Lee, "What Was Socialism to Workers? Collective Memories and Labor Politics in an Age of Reform," in Ching Kwan Lee and Guobin Yang, eds., *Re-envisioning the Chinese Revolution: The Politics and Poetics of Collective Memories in Reform China* (Palo Alto, CA: Stanford University Press and Washington, DC: Woodrow Wilson Center Press, 2007), pp. 158–159.

[43] See Kevin J. O'Brien and Li Lianjiang, *Rightful Resistance in Rural China* (New York: Cambridge University Press, 2006).

blogs (bo-ke in current parlance), it is the unofficial Web sites that shed the most light on the contemporary Chinese imaginings of Mao. These Web sites are run by individuals and groups not associated with the government. We should keep in mind, however, the constituency for this "Virtual China" – those well off enough to have a computer or pay for access at thousands of computer cafes across the country, as well as a small but vocal community of expatriate Chinese across the globe who continue to participate in Sinophone conversation (i.e., in Chinese language) on the Web while living outside China. As is the case in North America, Europe, and elsewhere, the Web both balkanizes communities of discourse and provides considerably more opportunity and freedom for the expression of a range of opinions. Chinese-language Mao Web sites aimed at the PRC public include both official Web sites (such as CCP propaganda portals to virtual museums of the Cultural Revolution) and a variety of nonofficial Web sites. Guobin Yang usefully maps out the diverse terrain of these nonofficial Web sites, which range from radical Leftist defenses of Madame Mao and the "Spirit of Daqing" (a Cultural Revolution labor ideal), to digital archives beyond the grasp of the CCP, to blogs for zhiqing – the students sent down to the countryside in the late 1960s for 3 to 10 years who now form a social group with a shared grievance: They lost their chance at education by serving Mao then.[44]

A figure as significant as Mao becomes a feature of popular culture, beyond the uses of state and discourse of elite society. As Geremie Barmé notes in his collection on this posthumous cult of Mao, for many ordinary Chinese, "Mao was representative of an age of certainty and confidence, of cultural and political unity, and above all, of economic equality and probity."[45] Not so for the youth of the 1990s, who had not experienced life in Mao's China. Rather, as Barmé gleefully notes, youth found in this new Mao cult "a politically safe idol that could be used to annoy the authorities, upset parents, and irritate teachers."[46] With this market in place, Mao's image has become a commodity item in street markets across China. T-shirts, cigarette lighters, art pieces, and bric-a-brac of all sorts sport the image of the Chairman (both as young revolutionary and older national leader). Although for some these images are

[44] Guobin Yang, "'A Portrait of Martyr Jiang Qing': The Chinese Cultural Revolution on the Internet," in Lee and Yang, Re-envisioning the Chinese Revolution, pp. 287–316.

[45] See Barmé, Shades of Mao: The Posthumous Cult of the Great Leader, p. 19. This volume provides the best summary of party efforts and popular subversions based on an extensive set of translations.

[46] Ibid., p. 48.

heartfelt, for others they are symbols of youth rebelliousness, and for many these commodified Maos signify celebrity interest rather than ideological commitment.

Another popular-cultural use of Mao is more complex: religion. Mao now joins the host of popular tutelary gods in popular religious temples across China. This is an astonishing syncretism of twentieth-century ideological politics and long-standing Chinese religious folkways. Mao's image, as many business travelers and tourists to China have seen, hangs from the rear-view mirrors of taxi drivers to ward off accidents; Mao's image has been put on ceremonial gold cash (used for the purposes of popular religion) with the words "May This Attract Wealth" or with the traditional eight hexagrams; and Mao's full image appears in these temples – both rural and in working-class urban neighborhoods – not as a political figure but as a religious figure.[47] He has become a popular god, but importantly, only one of many popular gods. As I noted before, the pluralization of public life in China defines the contemporary period. Mao allowed claims to be made that he was the only "god" in the Cultural Revolution. Now, however, Mao is embraced in the pantheon of deified human greats from ancient generals to particularly efficacious (and especially dangerous) emperors.

Not all popular-culture Maos are apolitical. Among the huge underclass of migrant workers in China – now generally estimated to be around 150 million people – Mao stands as a contrasting example with the current leadership. In popular ditties and graffiti, Mao is lionized as the advocate for the landless poor or contrasted positively with the corruption of the current party leadership – as the street ditty quoted at the start of this chapter indicates.

The uses of Mao's image and legacy just reviewed are public, sometimes collective, and usually political meanings of Mao found in China today. There exists a nearly endless set of personal Maos for those still living who experienced life under his rule or under his system in the 1970s and early 1980s. These memories are vivid, powerful, and widely diverse. They range from respect and nostalgia to anger and disgust.

One set of personal memories of Mao that is becoming publicly important is the suffering of the "sent-down generation," the *zhiqing* (or "educated youth") whom we saw using the Internet to make contact with each other. While some still honor Mao and blame local despots and cheats for ruining Mao's vision, there are many who lay the blame

---

[47] Wang Yi (under the pen-name Xin Yuan), "A Place in the Pantheon: Mao and Folk Religion," published in Hong Kong in 1992 and translated in Barmé, *Shades of Mao*, p. 195.

squarely at Mao's feet. These stories are explosive. They cannot cohabit a public space with the glorified Mao that gives legitimacy to the CCP. Thus we rarely see the expression of these tales of suffering blamed on Mao himself published in China. We do, however, see them published abroad, and they are increasing. Jung Chang and Jon Halliday's controversial and critical biography of Mao, published in English in 2005 is, if nothing else, the tip of this iceberg of pain and suffering that will have to come out at some point.[48] Maoist China has yet to face its truth and reconciliation process.

In all, Mao's memory in China today is a two-edged sword of legitimacy for the CCP: an ambivalent symbol of national pride for educated Chinese, a cool brand for middle-class youth, and a talisman of self-worth for China's disposed who have suffered under reform and globalization. Behind these meanings reside wider historical meanings of hope and despair analyzed by scholars in Western countries, as well as the inspiration Mao provided for rural revolutions in Asia, Africa, and Latin America.

APPROACHING MAO: HOW DO WE KNOW WHAT WE KNOW ABOUT MAO?

The independent reader needs more than the historical context of Mao's writings and life or a sense of how various communities have made sense of him. We also need to know how the words we read in a document come to us in order to assess how we should judge those words.[49] The most obvious point to note here is that Mao Zedong wrote in modern Chinese. Therefore, to read Mao in English is to read translations. The translations cited in this book are the best available (by the finest scholars in the field or by the official Beijing translation committee of Mao's *Selected Works*). As is always the case, these translations are interpretations: The multiple layers of meaning or suggestion in the original language often cannot be rendered – and certainly not in the same interpretative context – as the original. Short of learning Chinese, however, these serious translations are the best avenue to what Mao was thinking and saying that is available.

There is a continuing debate in Mao studies in the West over the interpretations of these texts by Mao. The general reader, however, should be

---

[48] Since Chang and Halliday's biography was first published in English, Charles Hayford considers it in Chapter 13.

[49] This is what professional historians call "source criticism." See John Tosh, *The Pursuit of History*, 3rd ed. (London: Longman, 2000).

aware of a few issues in order to mine these texts independently. Stuart Schram's basic collection of translations, *The Political Thought of Mao Tse-tung*, as well as his collection of alternate Cultural Revolution "genius" editions of Mao's works in *Mao Zedong Unrehearsed*, provide ample background, along with Roderick MacFarquhar and company's *The Secret Speeches of Chairman Mao*. In addition, Schram has produced a review of the current literature, "Mao Studies: Retrospect and Prospect" (1984), that raises problems of interpretation.[50] More provocatively, Nick Knight, another Mao scholar, challenges the reader to confront the problems of relativism and unconscious assumptions in analyzing Mao texts.[51]

In the case of Mao Zedong's writings, the general issues of interpretation are further complicated by his stature as the Great Helmsman, the Savior of the Chinese People, and the author of "Marxism-Leninism- Mao Zedong Thought," still the official ideology of the CCP. The problems in textual transmission and editing of Mao's writings most nearly resemble those of theological texts, such as biblical writings. Recent scholarship, especially in China, helps us to know which sort of Mao or Mao text we are reading.[52]

Since the advent of "Mao Zedong Thought" in the early 1940s, Mao's writings have been published in China in three kinds of collections. These may be distinguished by the intent of their editors and called "collective wisdom" editions, "genius" editions, and "historicist" editions.[53] First, beginning in 1944, volumes of the *Selected Works of Mao Zedong* (*Mao Zedong xuanji*) began to appear by the order of one or another high-level CCP institution. They were edited by committee according to a "collective wisdom" criterion: the belief that Mao

---

[50] Stuart Schram, *The Political Thought of Mao Tse-tung*, revised edition (New York: Praeger, 1969); Schram, *Mao Tse-tung Unrehearsed*, revised edition (Harmondsworth, England: Penguin, 1974); Schram, "Mao Studies: Retrospect and Prospect," *China Quarterly* 97 (1984), pp. 95–125. See also Brantly Womack's thoughtful review essay on the first five volumes of Schram's *Mao's Road to Power*, "Mao Before Maoism," *China Journal* 46 (July 2001), pp. 95–117.

[51] Nick Knight, "Mao and History: Who Judges and How?" *Australian Journal of Chinese Affairs* 13 (January 1985), pp. 121–136. Dr. Knight makes a further contribution in the July 1986 issue (no. 16) as part of a set of studies in the journal, "Mao Zedong: Ten Years After." Knight's reflections are collected in his *Rethinking Mao* (Lexington, MA: Lexington Books, 2007).

[52] For much more detail on the source criticism of Mao texts, see Timothy Cheek, "Textually Speaking: An Assessment of Newly Available Mao Texts," in MacFarquhar, Cheek, and Wu, *Secret Speeches*, pp. 75–103.

[53] These are my categories and not Chinese ones, although they correspond (in order) to the Chinese categories of official (published by the Mao Committee), unauthorized, and reference (or *yanjiu* "research") in the publication of Mao writings.

"represented" the summation of Sinified Marxism-Leninism and thus should reflect the consensus of the party leadership. That this editing relied most heavily on Mao's voluntary acquiescence and that the process was highly distorted as early as 1960 did not weaken, in the minds of the party editors, the attempt to make official Mao works a "collective" enterprise. Indeed, both Mao himself and advisors from the Soviet Union were active in this process during the early 1950s when the authoritative *Selected Works* was compiled. Second, during the Cultural Revolution and particularly at the height of the Red Guard movement in 1967, Mao writings were published by a confusing array of unnamed editors based on the belief that the Chairman was a lone genius not subject to revision by any collective leadership, least of all by a party riddled with "capitalist roaders." Finally, since Mao's death, party historiographers have published both restricted-circulation and publicly available collections of Mao writings that reflect in varying degrees a historicist urge to understand the past as it really was and to place Mao and his individual writings more firmly in historical context.

Although it makes sense to read the scholarly translations of the original versions of Mao's writings in order to understand Mao in his time and place, official (or "collective wisdom") editions are still useful. Such official versions – even though they have been more or less heavily edited from the original – are the versions that were studied by hundreds of millions of Chinese since the 1950s – as well as around the world – as the authoritative word of Mao and doctrine of the CCP.[54] Nonetheless, the reader of any Mao text that comes from one or another of his official *Selected Works* needs to keep two points in mind. First, the texts have been freely edited to conform to what the editors consider to be the needs of changing circumstances. That is, in contravention of scholarly standards of accuracy in reprinting historical documents, the texts have been altered. Many well-known studies have documented this phenomenon.[55] Among the more common changes are the deletion of positive comments about the GMD, earthy language, references to policies that did not work, and specific details. Scholars who want to research Mao's role and intentions in specific contexts therefore must

---

[54] According to Michael Y. M. Kau and John Leung, as many as 236 million copies of the first four volumes alone were published during Mao's life. Michael Y. M. Kau and John Leung, eds., *The Writings of Mao Zedong*, Vol. 1: *1949–1956* (Armonk, New York: M. E. Sharpe, 1986), p. xxvi.

[55] See Jerome Chen, *Mao Papers: Anthology and Bibliography* (London: Oxford University Press, 1970), Introduction.

seek out the original versions – which, happily, are already widely available.[56] However, for those wishing to contemplate the *impact* of the Chairman's writings on the Chinese reading public, the admittedly revised *Selected Works* versions are more appropriate because they were the versions so widely read.

Second, the reader should be aware that the official editions of Mao's writings published before his death in 1976 are considered by the CCP leadership to represent "the crystallization of collected wisdom in the CCP."[57] This has been the case since Mao Zedong Thought was officially designated as the guiding thought of the CCP in the June 1945 party constitution passed at the Seventh Congress of the CCP in Yan'an. This is the tradeoff for letting Mao speak for the party – the party can check what he says in print.[58] The current guide inside China for permissible interpretations of CCP history and, of course, Mao's writings is the "Resolution on Certain Questions in the History of Our Party since the Founding of the Nation," passed by the Central Committee on June 27, 1981.[59] Perhaps the best preliminary metaphor for the issues surrounding historicist party history writings in the 1980s, including

---

[56] Takeuchi Minoru, *Mao Zedong ji* [Collected Writings of Mao Zedong], 10 vols., revised edition (Tokyo: Hokobosha, 1971–72, 1983) and *Mao Zedong ji bujuan* [Supplements to Collected Writings of Mao Zedong], 10 vols. (Tokyo: Sososha, 1983–86). The tenth volume of *bujuan*, which is unnumbered, contains a chronology of Mao's writings. These sets constitute the most reliable edition of Mao's writings in Chinese, along with *Mao Zedong wenji* [Collected Writings of Mao Zedong], 8 vols. (Beijing: Renmin chubanshe, 1993–99), which, so far, only goes up through Mao's writings in 1957. The standard references for translations of Mao's collected works are Stuart R. Schram, ed., *Mao's Road to Power: Revolutionary Writings 1912–1949*, planned 10 vols., with seven published as of 2010 (Armonk, New York: M. E. Sharpe, 1992–), and for September 1949 to December 1957, Michael Y. M. Kau and John K. Leung, *The Writings of Mao Zedong, 1949–1976* (Armonk, New York: M. E. Sharpe, 1986, 1992).Unfortunately, the Kau and Leung volumes will go no further. The official, or "collected wisdom," edition of the *Selected Works of Mao Zedong* in Chinese and English, as edited by the CCP and published in Beijing, is widely available, with a corrected edition released for Mao's centenary in 1993. Finally, full texts of the official English version of the *Selected Works* are available on the Web at the Mao Zedong Internet Archive, http://eprints.cddc.vt.edu/marxists/reference/archive/mao/selected-works/index.htm.

[57] Locus classicus of this claim is to be found in para. 28 of the Central Committee's June 1981 resolution, "On Certain Questions" The English version can be found in *Beijing Review* 27 (July 6, 1981), pp. 10–39; para. 28 appears in the reprint in Martin, *Cult & Canon*, p. 213.

[58] See, for example, Martin, *Cult & Canon* and Joshua A. Fogel, *Ai Ssu-ch'i's Contribution to the Development of Chinese Marxism* (Cambridge, MA: Council on East Asian Studies, Harvard University, 1987).

[59] *Beijing Review* 27 (July 6, 1981), pp. 10–39; Martin, *Cult & Canon*, pp. 180–231.

those specifically on Mao's writings, is that of academic theology in the Christian and Jewish traditions, where "scientific" linguistic and historical analyses seek to contribute to a living faith.

Using these Mao texts, scholars in China and outside China try to apply the disciplines of academic research to the question of the memory and meaning of Mao. Their major contribution is to test our assumptions and improve our methods for determining what we know about Mao – most often by providing vivid historical context in which to understand particular words and actions. Chinese scholars are constrained by CCP policy but do remarkable work nonetheless (see Chapters 10, 11, and 14A). As we have seen earlier, scholars outside China, predominantly in Euro/American university circles, continue to do research on Mao and to debate his historical role, significance, and legacy. The summary of Mao's life and ideas that I gave earlier in this chapter draws on that scholarship and, I hope, reflects its main lines. The individual chapters herein also build on and extend this scholarly literature with general readers in mind. Readers, however, should not be constrained to take our word for it. This collection seeks to provide interested readers with sufficient historical context and methodologic tools to form their own informed answers to the questions of what we can know about Mao and his role in Chinese history and what significance his experience and ideas have for understanding China today, as well as the issues he sought to address.

2 Making Revolution in Twentieth-Century China

JOSEPH W. ESHERICK

With our several thousand years of accumulated ailments, where everything is contrary to the needs of the times, if we wish to change what is unsuitable and achieve what is suitable, we must overturn things from the foundations, clean things out thoroughly. Alas! Alas! This is the task of Revolution [English in original] (what the Japanese call kakumei [Chinese: geming] ...). It is the one and only way to save China today.

Liang Qichao, "Explaining 'ge,'" 1903

Why are Chinese like a sheet of loose sand? What makes them like a sheet of loose sand? It is because there is too much individual freedom. Because Chinese have too much freedom, therefore China needs a revolution.... Because we are like a sheet of loose sand, foreign imperialism has invaded, we have been oppressed by the commercial warfare of the great powers, and we have been unable to resist. If we are to resist foreign oppression in the future, we must overcome individual freedom and join together as a firm unit, just as one adds water and cement to loose gravel to produce something as solid as a rock.

Sun Yat-sen, "Three Principles of the People," 1924

Revolution is not a dinner party, or literary composition, or painting, or embroidery. It cannot be done so delicately, so gentlemanly, and so "gently, kindly, politely, plainly, and modestly." Revolution is an insurrection, the violent action of one class overthrowing the power of another.

Mao Zedong, "Report on an Investigation of the Peasant Movement in Hunan," 1927

When Mao Zedong was born on December 26, 1893, China was entering the last years of an extraordinarily successful but now obsolescent imperial system. The ruling Manchu court had presided over 250 years of relative peace and prosperity that had enabled a tripling of China's population; with its expansion into Tibet, Mongolia, and Central Asia it had doubled the extent of the empire. In the nineteenth century, however, a series of defeats at the hands of the Western powers and Japan had reversed the empire's progress, and by the 1890s, commentators were speculating on the breakup of China. The Qing dynasty, it seemed, was on the brink of collapse, not unlike the Mogul Empire in India or the Ottoman Empire in the Middle East. China was the "sick man of Asia," and the cure that twentieth-century political elites would prescribe for the country's malady was revolution. Mao Zedong certainly was China's most important revolutionary leader, but his conviction that revolution was necessary to restore China's greatness was very much a product of his time.

From the perspective of the early twenty-first century, with China now an emerging economic giant and a nuclear-armed superpower, it is easy to forget that just over a century ago this was a tottering empire ruled by a corrupt and increasingly ineffective Qing dynasty, descendants of the proud Manchu warriors who had conquered China in 1644. Although the Manchus held the central reins of power, local governance was largely in the hands of ethnic Chinese (Han) officials who qualified for office through examinations that tested their mastery of the ancient Confucian classics and respect for the precedents of imperial history. To foreign observers, it was a sleeping giant trapped by its past, and the contrast to the dynamic, forward-looking, confident China of today could hardly be more stark.

It was precisely in the years of Mao's youth that momentous changes began to rock the Chinese empire. Just a few months after Mao was born, China and Japan went to war in a dispute over influence in the Korean court. Thirty years earlier, Japan's preindustrial economy of peasant agriculture and handicraft production bore many similarities to China's, but since the Meiji Restoration of 1868, Japan had centralized power under the emperor, promoted industrial growth, modernized and greatly expanded its army and navy, instituted constitutional government, incorporated new knowledge from the West into its new nationalized education system, and proclaimed in its vibrant press a new vision of Japan's destiny as a model and guide for Asia's modernization. Still, Japan was a small island nation whose population of 42 million was but a tenth of China's. When its army and navy dealt China a series of devastating defeats on land and sea, the shock was far greater than China's earlier setbacks in the Opium Wars (1839–42, 1856–60) or the Sino-French War (1884–85). The outcome of the Sino-Japanese War was particularly disastrous: Japan seized the island province of Taiwan and by the Treaty of Shimonoseki opened up China to foreign investment in industry and mining. China's territorial integrity was now under direct threat. The European powers foresaw the potential breakup of the Manchu empire and soon launched the "Scramble for Concessions," carving out separate "spheres of influence" in which they acquired preferential rights to railway construction and exploitation of China's rich mineral deposits. Chinese patriots saw this as "carving up the melon" and warned of an imminent partition of their homeland.[1]

"The Russians are spying on us from the north and the English are peeping at us on the west; the French are staring at us from the south and the Japanese are watching us in the east. Living in the midst of these four strong neighbors, and being in the Middle Kingdom, China is in imminent peril."[2] Thus wrote Cantonese scholar Kang Youwei (1858–1927), expressing a new sense of alarm in the wake of defeat by Japan and the advance of Western colonialism among China's former tributaries in Southeast Asia. Kang helped to inspire a brief attempt at radical reform led by the Guangxu Emperor in 1898; and his most famous disciple, Liang Qichao (1873–1929), promoted these reforms at a new School of Current Affairs (*Shiwu xuetang*) in Mao's home province of Hunan.[3] However, a coup by the Empress Dowager Cixi (1835–1908) brought these efforts to an abrupt halt, driving Kang and Liang into exile, where they continued to promote their reformist program. The conservative Manchu princes who dominated the court in the next year allowed the antiforeign Boxer Uprising to ravage Christians and foreigners in northern China. By 1900, the "Great Powers" had organized an allied expedition to suppress the Boxers, drive the court from Beijing, occupy and loot the capital, and impose a staggering indemnity (to be

[1] On the Sino-Japanese War, see John Rawlinson, *China's Struggle for Naval Development, 1839–1895* (Cambridge, MA: Harvard University Press, 1967), and for an important recent revisionist view, see Allen Fung, "Testing the Self-Strengthening: The Chinese Army in the Sino-Japanese War of 1894–1895," *Modern Asian Studies* 30:4 (1996), pp. 1007–1031. A key case study of the Scramble for Concessions is John E. Schrecker, *Imperialism and Chinese Nationalism: Germany in Shantung* (Cambridge, MA: Harvard University Press, 1971).

[2] Kang Youwei on the founding of the "Society for the Study of Self-Strengthening" (*Qiangxue hui*), in Teng Ssu-yu and John K. Fairbank, eds., *China's Response to the West: A Documentary Survey, 1838–1923* (Cambridge, MA: Harvard University Press, 1979), p. 152.

[3] On the 1898 reforms, see Luke Kwong, *A Mosaic of the Hundred Days: Personalities, Politics and Ideas of 1898* (Cambridge, MA: Harvard University Press, 1984) and a contrasting view in Young-Tsu Wong, "Revisionism Reconsidered: Kang Youwei and the Reform Movement of 1898," *Journal of Asian Studies* 51:3 (August 1992), pp. 513–544. On the reform movement in Hunan, see Joseph W. Esherick, *Reform and Revolution in China: The 1911 Revolution in Hunan and Hubei* (Berkeley: University of California Press, 1976), pp. 11–19.

paid over 30 years) of 450 million silver taels, five times the annual revenue of the central government.[4] China's fate at the beginning of the twentieth century could hardly have been more perilous.

THE LATE QING NEW POLICY REFORMS

The disasters that befell China at the turn of the century at last spurred a group of powerful provincial officials to pressure the court to undertake a vigorous program of reform, which would be known as the "New Policies" (Xinzheng).[5] Following defeat by Japan in 1895 and the foreign armies' quick occupation of the imperial capital in 1900, military modernization was given the highest priority. Arsenals were built, and troops were equipped with modern rifles, artillery, and machine guns and drilled with the help of German and Japanese advisers. Military academies were established to train a new generation of officers. The most important of these was established at Baoding, south of the capital, by Yuan Shikai (1859–1916), a leading reform official who became president after the fall of the Qing. Chiang Kai-shek (Jiang Jieshi) (1888–1975), who would later lead the Nationalist Party and become Mao Zedong's rival for power throughout the 1930s and 1940s, attended Baoding before continuing his military training in Japan. The prominence of these men in modern Chinese politics is a measure of the new status that military men would enjoy in the twentieth century. The Confucian teachings of imperial China had always stressed the virtues of civilian rule, and the ideal scholar official was a silk-robed gentleman with fine calligraphy, restrained manners, and a gift for poetry. Now, in a time of national crisis, military drill was added to the school curriculum, reformers preached the virtues of militarism (junguo zhuyi), and many young men from elite families "discarded the writing brush to join the ranks" (toubi congrong). On the streets of China's cities, a military uniform became a mark of modernity and a model for both police and student dress. The development of the New Army was uneven, with Yuan Shikai's Beiyang Army in the north the largest and best trained, but recruiting young men with basic literacy, disciplining them in drills and calisthenics, teaching them the virtues of patriotism, and stressing

---

[4] On the Boxer Uprising, see Joseph W. Esherick, The Origins of the Boxer Uprising (Berkeley: University of California Press, 1987); Lanxin Xiang, The Origins of the Boxer War: A Multinational Study (London: RoutledgeCurzon, 2003).

[5] The best overview, stressing the impact of the Japanese example, is Douglas R. Reynolds, China, 1898–1912: The Xinzheng Revolution and Japan (Cambridge, MA: Harvard University Council of East Asian Studies, 1993).

their role as defenders of China created a new generation of military officers eager to play a role in determining China's destiny.[6]

The reform of education was another top priority, and here, the most dramatic step was the 1905 abolition of the imperial examination system. For centuries, Chinese men had qualified for office by passing the rigorous series of local, provincial, and national exams based on mastery of the Confucian classics. The education that had prepared young men for these exams created a literate elite with a shared sense of history and ethical principles, an indispensable basis for a common Chinese cultural identity. But the stress on rote learning and the lack of practical training in science and mathematics, on the history and geography of foreign countries, or on current affairs made the old examination system an anachronism in the modern world. Abolition of the exams broke a critical link between the gentry elite and the imperial state, and increasingly the gentry focused its attention on local initiatives.[7]

The new schools established to train China's modern elite were modeled on those of the West and Japan. Their curriculum still included plenty of classical learning and Chinese history, but it added world history and geography, basic scientific knowledge, mathematics, and physical education. Perhaps even more important were the institutional changes, for these schools departed from the more individualized master-student mentoring relations of the traditional academies and brought together large numbers of students, many of them boarding, in classes that moved as a group through the new curriculum. It was not long before these young people began to develop a student culture of their own, forming clubs and study societies and showing an increasing interest in politics. The best schools were in larger cities and provincial capitals, where a vibrant Chinese press emerged in the early twentieth century. Uniformly patriotic and generally reformist in tone, newspapers kept students abreast of changes in China and the world and encouraged them to do their part to transform and strengthen the

---

[6] Ralph L. Powell, *The Rise of Chinese Military Power, 1895–1912* (Princeton, NJ: Princeton University Press, 1955); Edmund S. K. Fung, *The Military Dimension of the Chinese Revolution: The New Army and Its Role in the Revolution of 1911* (Vancouver, British Columbia, Canada: University of British Columbia Press, 1980); Donald S. Sutton, *Provincial Militarism and the Chinese Republic: The Yunnan Army, 1905–25* (Ann Arbor: University of Michigan Press, 1980).

[7] William Ayers, *Chang Chih-tung and Educational Reform in China* (Cambridge, MA: Harvard University, Council on East Asian Studies, 1971); Benjamin A. Elman, *A Cultural History of Civil Examinations in Late Imperial China* (Berkeley: University of California Press, 2000). Elman's book is a revisionist defense of the examination system, with Chapter 11 stressing the downside of its abolition.

nation.[8] Tens of thousands of students went abroad to study, mostly to Japan, where living was cheaper and the written language easier to learn. Both the exiled reformers of 1898, such as Liang Qichao, and anti-Manchu revolutionaries were based in Japan, and through their journals, students were exposed to a wide range of radical ideas about democracy, the rights of citizens, and socialism.[9] Social Darwinist ideas of "survival of the fittest" were repeatedly invoked to support the notion that only radical change could save China from extinction.[10] When these students returned home, often to take up teaching positions in the new schools, they brought their radical ideas (as well as proscribed revolutionary pamphlets) back with them to spread among the next generation of students.

The last years of the Qing dynasty also witnessed the beginning of China's economic modernization. The Treaty of Shimonoseki permitted foreign manufacturing in China, and a number of firms were established in the foreign-administered treaty ports – mostly textile firms, food-processing firms, and water and power companies – and mining enterprises were opened in the interior. The intrusion of foreign economic power into China spurred a reasonably vigorous Chinese response. The court promoted the establishment of chambers of commerce, and provincial officials helped to finance coal and iron companies, textile mills, and other enterprises to compete with the foreign firms. Local gentry invested in these enterprises and in railway construction – especially if the state granted tax relief or guaranteed markets or high interest returns on bonds. As a result, a small business community, usually closely linked to established gentry families and supportive officials, emerged in the first decade of the twentieth century. Through the local chambers of commerce, it frequently would make its views heard on important issues of public affairs.[11]

[8] Esherick, *Reform and Revolution*, pp. 46–49; Hiroshi Abe, "Borrowing from Japan: China's First Modern Educational System," in Ruth Hayhoe and Marianne Bastid, eds., *China's Education and the Industrialized World: Studies in Cultural Transfer* (Armonk, NY: M. E. Sharpe, 1987), pp. 57–80; Paul John Bailey, *Reform the People: Changing Attitudes Towards Popular Education in Early Twentieth-century China* (Edinburgh: Edinburgh University Press, 1990). On the press, see Joan Judge, *Print and Politics: "Shibao" and the Culture of Reform in Late Qing China* (Palo Alto, CA: Stanford University Press, 1996); Barbara Mittler, *A Newspaper for China: Power, Identity, and Change in Shanghai's News Media, 1872–1912* (Cambridge, MA: Harvard University, Asia Center, 2004).

[9] Sanetō Keishū, *Chūgokujin Nihon Ryūgaku shi* [A History of Chinese Students in Japan] (Tokyo, 1970).

[10] James Reeve Pusey, *China and Charles Darwin* (Cambridge, MA: Harvard University, Council on East Asian Studies, 1983).

[11] Wellington Chan, *Merchants, Mandarins and Modern Enterprise in Late Ch'ing China* (Cambridge, MA: Harvard University Press, 1977); Albert Feuerwerker,

Perhaps the most dramatic and ultimately the most decisive of the New Policy reforms were the moves toward parliamentary governance. Japan's defeat of Czarist Russia in the Russo-Japanese War of 1904–05 was interpreted in the Chinese press as a victory of constitutional rule over autocracy. Constitutional government with an elected parliament and local assemblies gave citizens a stake in politics and thus promoted patriotic support of the nation. The Qing court dispatched a commission to study foreign constitutional models and in 1908 adopted a program of gradual progress toward constitutional rule, very much modeled on Japan. In the following year, provincial and local assemblies were elected by a very exclusive electorate, basically male members of the old gentry and wealthy individuals who were willing to declare a moderate tax obligation. Although these assemblies had only advisory powers, they typically were led by the most active younger leaders of the local elite and became powerful institutions for criticizing official corruption, promoting local economic interests, and pressuring for a more rapid institution of full parliamentary rule. Most importantly, these assemblies for the first time gave the gentry an institutional basis from which to engage in local politics. The imperial system's "law of avoidance" had prevented scholar-officials from holding office in their native provinces, a provision designed to ensure central control over local networks of vested elite interests. But the Qing's constitutional reforms began a process that greatly increased the power of local elites and provincial governments in the twentieth century.[12]

THE REVOLUTIONARY MOVEMENT

While China was undergoing dramatic social, political, and institutional change in the early twentieth century, the most important new thinking came from the exile and student communities abroad. Forced to flee in 1898 with a price on their heads, Kang Youwei and Liang Qichao traveled among overseas Chinese communities around the world but

"Economic Trends in the late Ch'ing Empire, 1870–1911," in John K. Fairbank and Kwang-ching Liu, eds., *The Cambridge History of China*, Vol. 11: *The Late Ch'ing, 1800–1911*, Part 2 (Cambridge, England: Cambridge University Press, 1980), pp. 1–69; Yu Heping, *Shanghui yu Zhongguo zaoqi xiandaihua* [Chambers of Commerce and China's Early Modernization] (Shanghai: Shanghai renmin chubanshe, 1993).

[12] Norbert Meienberger, *The Emergence of Constitutional Government in China (1905– 1908): The Concept Sanctioned by the Empress Dowager Tz'u-hsi* (Bern: P. Lang, 1980); Roger R. Thompson, *China's Local Councils in the Age of Constitutional Reform, 1898–1911* (Cambridge, MA: Harvard University, Council on East Asian Studies, 1995); Zhang Pengyuan, *Lixian pai yu xinhai geming* [The Constitutionalists and the 1911 Revolution] (Taipei: Zhongyang yanjiuyuan jindaishi yanjiusuo, 1969).

found their primary base in Japan. Both were brilliant classical scholars, and Kang Youwei had devised a particularly creative reading of Confucian texts as a justification for reform. He remained the leader of a group devoted to restoring the Guangxu emperor to power, but it was his prolific and far more imaginative disciple Liang Qichao who became the dominant intellectual of the age. Liang published a series of influential journals and wrote in a crisp, engaging style on subjects ranging from Chinese and European history and philosophy to public affairs and the reform of literature. He promoted newspapers to inform the citizenry and the modern novel as a means to spread new ideas among the reading public. He decried the lack of public concern among Chinese: "Among our people there is not one who looks on national affairs as if they were his own affairs. The significance of public morality has not dawned on us."[13] He particularly condemned China's lack of nationalism, saying that those who found comfort in China's great population should recall the fate of India and those proud of its ancient culture should look at what happened to Greece.[14] He promoted people's rights to overcome the "slavish mentality" brought about by autocratic government and a broad process of social and cultural transformation to create a "New People." At his most radical, he was unsparing in his criticism of the Qing state: "What, then, is the way to effect our salvation and to achieve progress? The answer is that we must shatter at a blow the despotic and confused governmental system of some thousands of years; we must sweep away the corrupt and sycophantic learning of these thousands of years."[15]

As growing numbers of Chinese students traveled to Japan to study and to immerse themselves in a wide range of translated texts on European history, many became obsessed with explaining Europe's economic progress and political-military power and the comparative backwardness of their own country. In 1903, one young student proposed an

[13] From "Xinmin shuo [Renewing the people]," as cited in William Theodore de Bary and Richard Lufrano, *Sources of the Chinese Tradition*, 2d ed., Vol. 2: *From 1600 Through the Twentieth Century* (New York: Columbia University Press, 2000), p. 291.

[14] *Ibid.*, p. 298.

[15] *Ibid.*, pp. 292–293. Among the many books on Liang Qichao, the best are Joseph R. Levenson, *Liang Ch'i-ch'ao and the Mind of Modern China* (Cambridge, MA: Harvard University Press, 1953); Chang Hao, *Liang Ch'i-ch'ao and Intellectual Transition in China, 1890–1907* (Cambridge, MA: Harvard University Press, 1971); Philip C. C. Huang, *Liang Ch'i-ch'ao and Modern Chinese Liberalism* (Seattle: University of Washington Press, 1972); and Xiaobing Tang, *Global Space and the Nationalist Discourse of Modernity: The Historical Thinking of Liang Qichao* (Palo Alto, CA: Stanford University Press, 1996).

extraordinary solution to the problem: revolution. His passionate pamphlet, "The Revolutionary Army," was printed repeatedly and smuggled to readers across China, becoming one of the most influential writings of its day. The message was unmistakable:

> Revolution is a universal rule of evolution. Revolution is a
> universal principle of the world. Revolution is the essence of
> the struggle for survival or destruction in a time of transition.
> Revolution submits to heaven and responds to men's needs.
> Revolution rejects what is corrupt and keeps the good. Revolution
> is the advance from barbarism to civilization. Revolution turns
> slaves into masters....

Citing the precedents of the English, American, and French revolutions, he concluded that "They sacrificed the individual to benefit the community, and they sacrificed the nobility to benefit the common people, so that everyone could enjoy equality and freedom."[16] For the audacity of this message, Zou Rong was arrested in the International Concession in Shanghai and two years later died in a Chinese prison at the tender age of 21.

Although Liang Qichao had played a prominent role in radicalizing Chinese discourse in the early twentieth century and had been influential in introducing the Japanese neologism for "revolution" (Chinese: *geming*),[17] he soon distanced himself from the new generation of revolutionaries and became an outspoken defender of constitutional monarchy as an alternative to the chaos he feared in the wake of violent revolution. His adversaries in the debates over reform versus revolution were an extremely diverse and factionalized group whose common denominator was their dedication to overthrowing Manchu rule. In 1905, they came together in a loosely organized revolutionary alliance, the Tongmenghui, under the (at least nominal) leadership of Sun Yat-sen (1866–1925).

Like so many of China's first generation of progressive thinkers, Sun Yat-sen was another man of the south. However, unlike Kang Youwei and Liang Qichao, both of whom came from distinguished literati lineages, Sun's ancestors were simple farmers, and his own road to advancement was common among natives of his home county adjacent

---

[16] Tsou Jung (Zou Rong), *The Revolutionary Army: A Chinese Nationalist Tract of 1903*, trans. by John Lust (Paris: Mouton, 1968), pp. 58–59.

[17] Chen Jianhua, *"Geming" de xiandaixing – Zhongguo geming huayu kaozheng* [The Modernity of "Geming" – An Inquiry into the Chinese Discourse on Revolution] (Shanghai: Shanghai guji, 2000), pp. 1–18.

to the Portuguese colony of Macao: he went abroad. Sailing to Hawaii as a teenager, he received most of his education in English-language missionary schools. Returning to China several years later, he continued his education in Hong Kong, studying to be a doctor before he turned his attention to politics. Very much a marginal man in his own land, Sun converted to Christianity and associated easily with foreigners – British, Japanese, French, and Americans – from whom he sought advice and financial assistance in his efforts to transform China. After several failed attempts to use anti-Manchu secret societies to carry out his revolutionary schemes, Sun turned to the students in Japan, with whom he formed the Revolutionary Alliance in 1905.[18]

There was a great deal of common ground between the reformers and the revolutionaries of the late Qing. They both sought to strengthen the nation and develop the economy in the face of Western and Japanese imperialism. They both supported basic freedoms of the press and assembly and endorsed some notion of "people's rights." The reformers thought this could be accomplished with a constitutional monarchy under the Qing, whereas the revolutionaries insisted that only expelling the Manchus and establishing a republican form of government could accomplish those ends. The revolutionaries added a social dimension to their program. Their journal spoke often of the virtues of socialism, and Sun Yat-sen affiliated his movement with the Socialist International. Most importantly, their program called for the equalization of land rights such that "the power of landlords will be wiped out from the Chinese continent" and "only self-cultivating farmers can obtain land from the state."[19] While this program for land reform was vaguely conceived and never articulated as a coherent plan of action, it was an important indication of the revolutionaries' early interest in the problems of China's peasantry and their conviction that an effective revival of China would require also a solution to the inequities of China's domestic economy.

THE 1911 REVOLUTION AND WARLORDISM

In the decade after the Boxer debacle, China seemed to be making dramatic strides in economic, military, and political reform. But by the summer of 1911, progress had stalled. A financial crisis in 1910 left the economy weakened. When it came time for the court to appoint its

[18] The best account of Sun's early career is Harold Z. Schiffrin, *Sun Yat-sen and the Origins of the Chinese Revolution* (Berkeley: University of California Press, 1968).

[19] Hu Hanmin in *Minbao* 3 (April 1906), as translated in de Bary and Lufrano. *Sources of the Chinese Tradition*, p. 319.

first cabinet, it selected a group dominated by Manchu princes. Then it nationalized the gentry-controlled railway companies and took out foreign loans to build the major trunk lines. All hopes for an orderly process toward representative government and the limitation of foreign penetration of China were dashed. When the premature explosion of a revolutionary group's bomb sparked an uprising by radicals who had infiltrated the army in the central China city of Wuchang, disaffected members of the Provincial Assembly and officers in the New Army rallied to the new revolutionary government. Within weeks of the October 10 uprising, the process was repeated in other provinces throughout China, but especially in the south. By December, Sun Yat-sen had returned from abroad, and on January 1, 1912, he was inaugurated as provisional president of the Republic of China. Despite widespread support for the new republic in the south, Yuan Shikai's Beiyang Army still held the preponderance of military power. Soon a deal was negotiated in which Yuan arranged for the abdication of the last Qing emperor, and in exchange, Sun Yat-sen ceded the presidency of the republic to Yuan.[20]

The new republic was greeted with great enthusiasm. A profusion of new political parties sprouted to contest the parliamentary elections scheduled for 1912. With the end of Qing censorship, the press blossomed. Urban residents embraced the new republic by cutting off the queues imposed by the Manchus, measuring time by the solar calendar, adopting Western dress, and celebrating national holidays with speeches, parades, and a profusion of national flags.[21] The optimism proved short-lived. In the 1912 elections, Yuan Shikai's party lost to a new Nationalist Party (Guomindang) organized by the former revolutionaries and their allies among the southern provincial elites. In response, Yuan engineered the assassination of the Guomindang's parliamentary leader and in 1914 banned the party and evicted its members from parliament. Sun Yat-sen again fled into exile, his supporters in disarray. By 1915, Yuan sought to unify the country by having himself "elected" emperor, but even his own generals refused to follow this demarche, and in the following year Yuan Shikai died in disgrace and failure.[22]

Yuan was followed as head of the central government by a succession of military men, mostly officers of his own Beiyang Army. Many

---

[20] Esherick, *Reform and Revolution in China*, pp. 143–215; Ernest P. Young, *The Presidency of Yuan Shih-k'ai: Liberalism and Dictatorship in Early Republican China* (Ann Arbor: University of Michigan Press, 1977).

[21] Henrietta Harrison, *The Making of the Republican Citizen: Political Ceremonies and Symbols in China, 1911–1929* (Oxford, England: Oxford University Press, 2000), pp. 14–92.

[22] Young, *The Presidency of Yuan Shih-k'ai*.

had their own regional power base in the provincial armies, whose sizes had expanded exponentially during the course of the 1911 Revolution. China entered an era of warlord rule that would last until 1927 and in many areas even longer. Local civil elites made deals with their military overlords to protect their own positions, foreign arms merchants profiteered by selling weapons to the warlords, and the common people were subjected to a huge expansion of miscellaneous taxes, confiscation of draft animals by armies on the move, and the periodic destruction wrought by local conflicts among feuding warlords. Mao's home province of Hunan was repeatedly victimized by rival warlords seeking to dominate the main north-south lines of communication. The national consequences of this military rule would be demonstrated dramatically in 1919.[23]

When World War I broke out in Europe, the Japanese had moved quickly to seize the German sphere of influence in Shandong province. China later joined the war on the Allied side, sending workers to man the docks and arsenals in France, expecting that as one of the victors it would recover its rights to Shandong in the peace settlement. At the Versailles Peace Conference, however, the Chinese negotiators discovered that representatives of the warlord government in Beijing had surrendered China's rights in Shandong in exchange for a Japanese loan to finance their armies. Warlordism and imperialism had combined to engineer another sacrifice of Chinese sovereignty. When news reached the Chinese public, a wave of protest swept the country, set off by a dramatic student demonstration in Beijing's Tiananmen Square on May 4, 1919. In the end, the nationwide protests forced the government to fire the offending ministers and refuse to sign the Versailles Treaty. May 4 also marked the beginning of Chinese intellectuals and students' active and direct engagement in the affairs of state and provided a new repertoire for student protest that would remain influential throughout the twentieth century.[24]

---

[23] The most important studies of warlordism in China are James Sheridan, *Chinese Warlord: The Career of Feng Yü-hsiang* (Berkeley: University of California Press, 1966); Sutton, *Provincial Militarism*; Lucian W. Pye, *Warlord Politics: Conflict and Coalition in the Modernization of Republican China* (New York: Praeger, 1971); Edward A. McCord, *The Power of the Gun: The Emergence of Modern Chinese Warlordism* (Berkeley: University of California Press, 1993); and Andrew Nathan, *Peking Politics, 1918–1923: Factionalism and the Failure of Constitutionalism* (New York: Columbia University Press, 1976).

[24] Chow Tse-tsung, *The May Fourth Movement: Intellectual Revolution in Modern China* (Cambridge, MA: Harvard University Press, 1960), pp. 84–170.

STUDENTS AND INTELLECTUALS

The May Fourth Movement did not spring from a vacuum. In the new Republic of China, colleges and universities were emerging as independent and influential breeding grounds for new ideas. In this process, Beijing University led the way, and it was no accident that its faculty and students initiated the 1919 protests. Its new chancellor, Cai Yuanpei (1868–1940), combined the prestige of the highest (*jinshi*) degree in China's imperial examination system with an education abroad in Germany, then the model for higher education throughout the world. He hired a faculty of great distinction and extraordinary intellectual diversity. The most famous were men such as Chen Duxiu (1879–1942), who was appointed dean of humanities, and Li Dazhao (1889–1927), the university librarian. These two went on to become founders of the Chinese Communist Party (CCP). Alongside them stood Hu Shi (1891–1962), an American-trained student of John Dewey, a pragmatic educator, and critic of student activism who would become China's most famous liberal intellectual. Hu Shi and Chen Duxiu were both cosmopolitan intellectuals and leaders of the New Culture Movement, which criticized the conservative and authoritarian aspects of the Confucian tradition and advocated use of the vernacular in order to spread new knowledge to a wider public. But the Beijing University faculty also included influential defenders of China's classical language and culture, and classical learning was an essential part of the university curriculum.[25]

While Beijing University certainly led the way in the early republic, it was not alone. Other important universities grew up in most of China's major cities, and teachers' colleges (normal schools) were established throughout the country. While many of the students at Beijing University came from elite families with official connections, the tuition-free normal schools attracted students of lesser means (including Mao Zedong) who then would go on to spread their new knowledge through schools in small towns of the Chinese hinterland.[26] A large number, perhaps the majority of these students were interested primarily in comfortable positions in government or education, and Beijing University students had a special reputation for dissolute lifestyles of drinking, gambling, and visits to the nearby theater and brothel

[25] Timothy Weston, *The Power of Position: Beijing University, Intellectuals and Chinese Political Culture, 1898–1912* (Berkeley: University of California Press, 2004).

[26] Xiaoping Cong, *Teachers' Schools and the Making of the Modern Chinese Nation-State, 1897–1937* (Vancouver, British Columbia, Canada: UBC Press, 2007).

district.[27] However, these universities also provided a context for personal and intellectual exploration, and what mattered far more than the idle transgressions of China's youth was the seriousness with which so many sought a new moral and political compass in an era of profound and disorienting political and social change.

The new schools and universities offered a variety of opportunities for young people to explore new directions for their own lives and for China. The faculty often consisted of young men in their thirties, and relations with students combined personal informality and intellectual rigor. At Beijing University, disciples of the anti-Manchu revolutionary Zhang Taiyan (1868–1936), a renowned classical scholar and defender of China's "national essence," emulated his practice of hosting eager students in a cramped apartment to scrutinize ancient texts and debate their contemporary meaning. At the library, Li Dazhao's office attracted large gatherings for passionate discussions of more political issues. Similarly, back in Hunan, Mao Zedong became very close to his ethics teacher, Yang Changji (1871–1920), so close in fact that regular visits to his mentor's home developed into an affair and eventually marriage to Yang's daughter.[28] Students also formed their own associations, frequently based on their county or province of origin, reflecting the continued importance of local and parochial affiliations but also the comfort of discussing in one's native dialect and sharing familiar food and drink. Over time, both social and political associations proliferated, from poetry and calligraphy clubs to choirs and glee clubs and athletic teams and hiking clubs.

A common theme in many of these new associations was the search for new ethical principles to guide both personal and political life. At Beijing University, Chancellor Cai Yuanpei led a Society for the Promotion of Morality (*Jindehui*), whose members foreswore gambling, visiting prostitutes, taking concubines, or seeking public office – this latter an indication of the ill repute into which official position had fallen under the corrupt warlord governments. In Hunan, Mao Zedong led in organizing a New People's Study Society (*Xinmin xueshe*), which took its name from Liang Qichao's essays for the reform of the Chinese people. The Hunan society required of its members "no falsity, no

[27] Weston, *Power of Position*, pp. 100–106.
[28] *Ibid.*, pp. 110–112, 160–161; Zhonggong zhongyang wenxian yanjiushi, ed., *Mao Zedong nianpu* [Chronological Biography of Mao Zedong], Vol. 1 (Beijing: Zhongyang wenxian chubanshe, 1993), pp. 16–17, 29–30, 39; Li Jui, *The Early Revolutionary Activities of Comrade Mao Tse-tung*, trans. by Anthony W. Sariti (White Plains, NY: M. E. Sharpe, 1977), pp. 15–21.

laziness, no extravagance, no gambling and no whoring."[29] Such strictures reflected the profound alienation of young people from the moral hypocrisy of the old elite. At the same time, much of their new thinking combined elements of Confucian self-cultivation with Western notions of individualism. While they sought to escape the hierarchical bonds of the old Confucian ethics, they also sought new forms of community to give social meaning to their lives. This search for community lay behind the appeal of anarchist groups to many (including Mao), for they seemed to promise liberation of the individual with a new egalitarian form of communal life.[30]

It was from these new forms of associational life and intellectual engagement that the New Culture Movement developed and spread in the first decade of the republican era. Both the universities and commercial publishing houses in Shanghai spread new ideas in a proliferation of journals, by far the most influential of which was *New Youth* (*Xin qingnian*), edited by Chen Duxiu. The "Call to Youth" which opened its inaugural issue proclaimed an iconoclastic message that inspired many and enraged others. Basing his argument on the biological principle that "in the process of metabolism, the old and the rotten are incessantly eliminated to be replaced by the fresh and the living," he proposed six principles to guide China's youth: "Be independent, not servile.... Be progressive, not conservative.... Be aggressive, not retiring.... Be cosmopolitan, not isolationist.... Be utilitarian, not formalistic.... Be scientific, not imaginative...." Each of these was argued with a series of illustrations that typically associated the positive quality with European culture and the negative with Chinese.[31] Few intellectuals were as radically iconoclastic as Chen Duxiu, but *New Youth* was widely read and enormously influential across the country, and through it and similar journals young people became familiar with a range of new ideas: Western individualism, John Dewey's pragmatism, socialism, and anarchism. Gender issues were particularly important, with condemnation of the crippling practice of female foot binding and marriages arranged by parents, and the promotion of women's education (which resulted in most colleges becoming coeducational by the 1920s). "Mr. Science and Mr. Democracy" became the rallying cry of the New Culture Movement, and while the

---

[29] Weston, *Power of Position*, pp. 143–145; Zhonggong zhongyang wenxian yanjiushi, eds., *Mao Zedong nianpu*, Vol. 1, pp. 34–35.

[30] Peter Zarrow, *Anarchism and Chinese Political Culture* (New York: Columbia University Press, 1990); Arif Dirlik, *Anarchism and the Chinese Revolution* (Berkeley: University of California Press, 1991).

[31] Chen Duxiu, "Call to Youth," in Teng and Fairbank, *China's Response to the West*, pp. 240–245.

meanings of these terms would be debated endlessly, their widespread appeal among the new intellectual class was beyond question.[32]

The intellectual searching of the New Culture Movement reflected the profound disappointment of China's educated elite in the aftermath of the 1911 Revolution. Many had been active in the revolutionary movement and believed that the end of imperial autocracy and the institution of republican governance would bring a new vitality to the Chinese nation. But the weakness and corruption of parliamentary institutions and China's descent into warlord rule left them convinced that more fundamental social and cultural changes were required. The nature of that transformation was always contested, but intellectuals never doubted that they had a particular responsibility to help chart the process. Confucian culture had always honored learning and, through the examination system, the empire had sought the ablest scholars to serve in its bureaucracy. China's modern intellectuals were heirs to this tradition of a scholar's obligation to serve the country, but they were no longer willing to do so as obedient servants to an absolutist state. The universities, the press, the new publishing houses, and the proliferation of popular and scholarly journals provided a relatively autonomous intellectual space, new sources of employment, and new forms of association from which to participate in national affairs.

The May Fourth Movement provided a moment of triumph for China's new intellectuals, but it proved brief and transitory. After 1919, the warlords in Beijing and the provinces grew increasingly harsh in their suppression of student activism, and soon, many of China's leading intellectuals fled to the safety of the foreign concessions in Shanghai or to Guangzhou (Canton), where a new revolutionary movement was growing in the 1920s. In the 1930s, under the new regime established by the Nationalist Party, China's institutions of higher learning would experience another period of growth and intellectual vitality. Still, the extent of this growth was extremely limited. In a 1934 League of Nations survey of 26 countries, China ranked last in the number of college students per unit of population, with only 0.88 student per 10,000 population, less than one-third the ratio in twenty-fifth ranked Turkey.[33] The small

[32] Chow Tse-tsung, *The May Fourth Movement*, pp. 171–196, 254–337; Vera Schwarcz, *The Chinese Enlightenment: Intellectuals and the Legacy of the May Fourth Movement of 1919* (Berkeley: University of California Press, 1986), pp. 12–145.

[33] E-tu Zen Sun, "The Growth of the Academic Community, 1912–1949," in John K. Fairbank and Albert Feuerwerker, eds., *The Cambridge History of China*, Vol. 13: *Republican China, 1912–1929*, Part 2 (Cambridge, England: Cambridge University Press, 1986), p. 396.

size of the academic community only served to enhance its elite status. By the 1930s, most professors at the leading institutions held foreign (usually American) advanced degrees, their academic journals published important articles of original research, and many intellectuals continued to speak out on national affairs. Although the Nationalist Party attempted to control the universities through a process of "partyfication" (*danghua*), the independence and critical spirit of China's intellectuals would endure through the twentieth century. Both the Nationalist and Communist parties engaged in a variety of efforts to attract, reward, coerce, and control China's intellectuals, and they would remain a group that every modern Chinese state had to contend with.[34]

THE NATIONAL REVOLUTION OF THE 1920S AND THE RISE OF LENINIST POLITICS

Following the 1911 Revolution's failure to establish a viable republican politics and Yuan Shikai's 1914 expulsion of the Nationalist Party from parliament, Sun Yat-sen was again forced into exile and a period of political eclipse. By 1917, however, he was back in his home province of Guangdong as titular head of a government formed by a group of dissident parliamentarians from Beijing and supported by local warlords. Sun's position was always precarious, and his grandiose visions for national revolution repeatedly sparked conflict with his warlord allies, on several occasions forcing Sun to flee for his life. The decisive turn in the fortunes of Sun and his party came only in 1923, with the critical assistance of the Soviet Union.

The Bolshevik Party seized power in Russia in the October Revolution of 1917 and for the next few years was preoccupied with ending the war with Germany, securing its borders, and suppressing domestic opposition. When the leaders of the Communist International (Comintern) turned their attention to China, it was in the context of Lenin's theory of imperialism. Lenin sought to explain why the class contradictions in capitalist society had failed to produce the proletarian revolution and transition to socialism predicted by Marx. The reason lay in Western bourgeois democracies' ability to purchase the support of the working class with the ill-gained profits of imperialism. Accordingly, the best way to advance socialism in the world was to attack the imperialist system at its weakest point – by encouraging anticolonial and nationalist

---

[34] Jerome B. Grieder, *Intellectuals and the State in Modern China: A Narrative History* (New York: Free Press, 1981).

movements in Asia and elsewhere. China was particularly important in this strategy both because of its size and its revolutionary potential and because its long border with the Soviet Union made a friendly government there vital to Russian security.[35]

Soviet policy toward China proceeded along a series of parallel tracks. In the Karakhan Declaration of July 1919, the USSR dramatically renounced all of Czarist Russia's claims to special rights in Manchuria, extraterritorial privileges, and indemnity payments from the Boxer Indemnity. Coming just after China's victimization by the Western powers at Versailles, the declaration immediately distinguished Soviet policies toward China from those of the imperialist powers. Russia briefly sought allies in China's chaotic warlord politics but soon focused on Sun Yat-sen as its most promising ally. It was a wise choice. Sun had spent much of his career seeking support from foreign powers, and he was always open to a promising deal. In addition, the disappointment of Versailles and the hostile attitude of the Western powers (especially Britain) toward his revived revolutionary movement left Sun more open to the anti-imperialist message of his new Russian friends.

By 1923, the basic parameters of Soviet assistance to the Chinese Revolution had been worked out. A group of Soviet advisers was sent to Canton under the leadership of Mikhael Borodin (1884–1951). Borodin helped the Nationalist Party reorganize along Leninist democratic centralist lines and expand its organization and propaganda departments. A Leninist political party required a unifying ideology, and Sun Yat-sen delivered a series of lectures to party members on the "Three People's Principles: nationalism, democracy, and people's livelihood." The lectures were hastily drafted, broadly stated, and lacking in details, but they became the basis for Nationalist Party propaganda and political education in the decades to follow. Nationalism involved restoring China to her past glory and ending the political and economic threat of imperialism. Democracy, or people's rights (minquan), was qualified with the idea that China would have to pass through a period of "political tutelage" by the Nationalist Party to prepare the people for full democratic participation. People's livelihood (minsheng) was certainly the most widely contested of the three principles. While Sun explicitly rejected Marxist notions of class struggle, he repeatedly compared this

---

[35] Allen S. Whiting, *Soviet Policies in China, 1917–1924* (New York: Columbia University Press, 1954); Alexander Pantsov, *The Bolsheviks and the Chinese Revolution, 1919–1927* (Honolulu: University of Hawaii Press, 2000).

principle to socialism and also revived his older notion of the equalization of land rights.[36]

In this era of Chinese history, as Mao Zedong would famously declare, "political power grows out of the barrel of the gun," and if Sun's new party was to be effective, it needed an army. Here Soviet assistance was absolutely indispensable. It provided financial aid, military advisers, arms shipments, and a clear model for a new institution in Chinese politics: the party-army. The officer corps of the new army was trained at the Whampoa Military Academy, where the commandant was Chiang Kai-shek, an officer trained at Baoding and Japanese military academies and a long-time member of the revolutionary party, who had established himself as Sun Yat-sen's most loyal military aide. At Whampoa, the carefully selected cadets were given solid military training (with advisers from the Soviet Red Army) and a strong dose of political education emphasizing loyalty to Sun Yat-sen and the Three People's Principles. The benefits of this well-trained, disciplined, and politically motivated army were soon evident as the cadets led a series of quick campaigns that established Nationalist Party control through most of Guangdong Province. In the longer term, the graduates of Whampoa became the core of the Nationalist power structure and loyal supporters of Chiang Kai-shek, toward whom their bond as students of a stern and respected teacher commanded unstinting allegiance.[37]

The final component of Soviet support for the Chinese Revolution was its mentoring of China's young communists. The CCP grew out of a number of disparate study societies that had emerged during the May Fourth Movement. Intellectuals' interest in Marxism blossomed in the wake of the Bolshevik Revolution. Li Dazhao penned an enthusiastic *New Youth* article, entitled, "The Victory of Bolshevism," in which he saw the Russian Revolution as "the fuse of world revolution." The new soviets of labor would replace all forms of government and "unite the proletariat of the world, and create global freedom...."[38] Li Dazhao's vision of communism resembled a chiliastic movement of global liberation in which the Chinese people, including the great masses of Chinese

---

[36] Sun Yat-sen, *San Min Chu I: The Three Principles of the People*, trans. by Frank W. Price (Taipei: China Publishing Company, n.d.) is the official English translation authorized by the Nationalist Party.

[37] C. Martin Wilbur, *The Nationalist Revolution in China, 1923–1928* (Cambridge, England: Cambridge University Press, 1984); C. Martin Wilbur and Julie Lien-ying How, *Missionaries of Revolution: Soviet Advisers and Nationalist China, 1920–1927* (Cambridge, MA: Harvard University Press, 1989).

[38] Li Dazhao, "The Victory of Bolshevism," *New Youth*, November 15, 1918, trans. in Teng and Fairbank, *China's Response to the West*, pp. 246–249.

peasants, were all part of the world proletariat. A Marxist study group grew up around Li to explore how the lessons of the Russian Revolution could be applied to China.[39] *New Youth* followed up Li's clarion call to revolution with a series of articles explaining various aspects of Marxism and socialism, and after 1920, Chen Duxiu turned the magazine into an organ of the Shanghai cell of the fledgling communist movement.[40]

By 1920, there were small groups of self-styled communist intellectuals in a half dozen cities across China, but in many of the groups the anarchist ideals of Kropotkin and utopian socialist notions were as appealing as the class struggle of Marx and Lenin. In addition, very few writings by Marx or Lenin had been translated at this time, so the understanding of Marxist theory typically was based on secondary sources, Japanese translations, or explanations by members better versed in foreign languages. Above all, these early communist study societies were groups of friends who gathered together for fellowship in their search for a solution to the oppression of the Chinese nation and the corruption and inequities of Chinese society. It was only after representatives of the Comintern contacted key members in Beijing and Shanghai in the summer of 1920 that they moved toward the formation of a national party, which was accomplished (at least in name) when 13 young intellectuals (including Mao from Hunan) representing 53 members traveled to Shanghai in July 1921 for the First Congress of the Chinese Communist Party.[41]

The first years of the CCP were not particularly impressive. The founding congress was marred by bitter disputes over intellectual work versus labor organizing and especially over the possibility of working with other parties such as the Nationalists. The Comintern representatives at the meeting were resented as imperious Europeans, and they, in turn, disdained the Chinese intellectuals as hopelessly divorced from the ranks of Chinese labor. After the conference, differences persisted in the various regional cells, and most of the anarchists and many of those best read in Marxist theory withdrew over the new party's commitment to the dictatorship of the proletariat. Local party groups vigorously resisted efforts at party centralization as they made their own efforts to reach out to the working class through night schools and the support of strike actions. A flurry of strike activity in 1922 briefly raised

---

[39] Maurice Meisner, *Li Ta-chao and the Origins of Chinese Marxism* (New York: Atheneum, 1977) is the classic and still valuable study of Li Dazhao.

[40] Tony Saich, *The Origins of the First United Front in China: The Role of Sneevliet (Alias Maring)* (Leiden: E. J. Brill, 1991), p. 50.

[41] Saich, *Origins*, pp. 43–69.

hopes for the labor movement, but the workers were largely motivated by economic issues, and when warlord tolerance for labor organizing ended with the bloody suppression of a railway workers strike in the north, optimism about the prospects for a communist-led labor movement quickly collapsed. By 1923, the party faithful had fallen to as few as 100 to 250 members.[42]

The critical turn in the fortunes of the party came when the Comintern induced it to join a United Front with Sun Yat-sen and the Nationalist Party. In the agreement that Sun Yat-sen signed with Soviet envoy Adolph Joffe in January 1923, both sides agreed that "the Communistic order or even the Soviet system cannot actually be introduced into China" and that the efforts of the two sides should be devoted to achieving national unity and independence of foreign imperialism.[43] To advance the national revolution, communists were to join the Nationalist Party as a "bloc within" – an unusual arrangement that most members of the CCP resisted as an unacceptable sacrifice of their party's autonomy. Obedience to the superior wisdom of the Comintern carried the day, however, and in the short term, the union with the Nationalist Party proved a great benefit to the CCP. Its members assumed prominent positions within the Nationalist Party establishment – Chen Duxiu heading the Propaganda Department and Zhou Enlai (1898–1976) becoming political director at the Whampoa Military Academy. Indeed, by the Second Congress of the Nationalist Party in 1926, over one-third of the congress's delegates and one-third of the party's central standing committee were communists.[44]

The most important gain for the communists, however, was the cover that Nationalist Party membership gave to their organization of the mass movement. As before, the focus of CCP organizing was among the working class. While China's industrial development was limited, World War I had provided a period of relief from foreign competition in the textile industry and also created a market for munitions-related minerals from China's mines. As a result, there was significant growth in

[42] In addition to Saich, *Origins*, the critical works on this early period of CCP history are Hans J. van de Ven, *From Friend to Comrade: The Founding of the Chinese Communist Party, 1920–1927* (Berkeley: University of California Press, 1991) and Arif Dirlik, *The Origins of Chinese Communism* (Oxford, England: Oxford University Press, 1989). A now somewhat dated classic is Benjamin Schwartz, *Chinese Communism and the Rise of Mao* (Cambridge, MA: Harvard University Press, 1951). The 1923 membership figure is from van de Ven, *From Friend to Comrade*, p. 100.

[43] The Sun-Joffe agreement is translated in full in C. Martin Wilbur, *Sun Yat-sen: Frustrated Patriot* (New York: Columbia University Press, 1976), pp. 137–138.

[44] Wilbur, *Nationalist Revolution*, pp. 32–33.

China's small proletariat in the 1910s, and the concentration of industry in a few major cities, particularly Shanghai, made the workers, once organized, an important political force in these critical nodes of China's modern economy. The nationalists had demonstrated the potency of this new political force in their support for the 1922 Hong Kong seamen's strike, which brought major disruption to shipping in the British colony. In 1925, an even broader wave of labor activism swept China in the wake of the May 30 Movement in Shanghai, when British-commanded police in the International Settlement fired on a group protesting the death of a Chinese worker in a Japanese textile mill. When the protests spread to Canton in June, troops in the foreign concession fired into the Chinese crowd, killing over 50 people. In both these protests, communist and leftist allies in the Nationalist Party experienced the power of a political movement that succeeded in harnessing the patriotic fervor of China's students and intellectuals to the workers' struggles for economic justice and decent treatment in the workplace.[45]

This same period also saw the first stirrings of the peasant movement in China, and again the protective cover of the Nationalist Party was critical. A Peasant Movement Training Institute was established in Canton, headed by the communist Peng Pai (1896–1929) and later briefly by Mao Zedong. Sun Yat-sen had long advocated a program of land rights for the peasantry, but aside from a few key leaders such as Li Dazhao and Peng Pai, CCP interest in the peasant question largely followed the Comintern's "Theses on the Eastern Problem," which declared that the agrarian question was of "greatest importance in the struggle for emancipation from the despotism of the Great Powers" and "the revolutionary movement ... must be based on the action of the peasant masses."[46] Peng Pai had significant success in organizing peasant associations (with critical help from radical students) to struggle against the landlord elite in Guangdong, and later Mao would play a critical role in the Hunan peasant movement. In both cases, however, the greatest success came only with the protection of sympathetic military forces allied with the national revolution.[47]

[45] Jean Chesneaux, *The Chinese Labor Movement, 1919–1927*, trans. by H. M. Wright (Palo Alto, CA: Stanford University Press, 1968) is the classic Marxist study of this era, now superseded by Elizabeth J. Perry, *Shanghai on Strike: The Politics of Chinese Labor* (Palo Alto, CA: Stanford University Press, 1993). For an excellent account of the May 30 incident, see Nicholas R. Clifford, *Spoilt Children of Empire: Westerners in Shanghai and the Chinese Revolution of the 1920s* (Hanover, NH: Middlebury College Press, 1991), Chapters 6–8.

[46] Cited in Saich, *Origins*, p. 136.

[47] Fernando Galbiati, *P'eng P'ai and the Hai-Lu-Feng Soviet* (Palo Alto, CA: Stanford University Press, 1985); Roy Hofheinz, *The Broken Wave: The Chinese Communist*

With the growth of the worker and peasant movements, the CCP expanded rapidly so that by the spring of 1927 it reported over 57,000 members.[48] There was, however, a tragic vulnerability to CCP success. To a large degree, it was the vision and prestige of Sun Yat-sen that had attracted Soviet aid to the revolutionary movement and held together the alliance of the Communist and Nationalist parties. When Sun died of cancer on March 12, 1925, he left no clear successor, and the next two years saw increasingly sharp conflicts between the left and right wings of the Nationalist Party, primarily over the growing influence of the CCP within the revolutionary movement. These conflicts came to a head in the spring of 1927. In the previous year, the Northern Expedition under Chiang Kai-shek had carried the Nationalist armies all the way to the Yangzi River, quickly overwhelming some warlord adversaries and absorbing others into their fold. Behind the Northern Expedition, the peasant movement grew increasingly radical in central China, and worker pickets took over the foreign concession in Hankou and prepared to take over Shanghai. Chiang Kai-shek struck first. The army and allies within the Green Gang in Shanghai turned on the workers and their leftist allies. In several days of bloody suppression, the labor movement and its communist supporters were crushed. The purge of the left quickly spread to other cities, and Mao's organization in Hunan was destroyed in the Horse Day Massacre in May. For a while, the left wing of the Nationalist Party vacillated in the struggle between Chiang and the communists, but soon Chiang emerged as the leader of the new national government established in Nanjing. By 1928, military campaigns and careful negotiation with northern warlords brought a credible semblance of national unity to China for the first time since the death of Yuan Shikai.[49]

The communist defeat in 1927 marked a major turning point in the fortunes of the CCP and the Chinese Revolution. It ended all possibility of a proletarian-based urban revolutionary movement on the Russian model. As the remnants of the CCP fled to the hinterland and the Soviet advisers were sent home, there was both the need and the opportunity

Peasant Movement, 1922–1928 (Cambridge, MA: Harvard University Press, 1971); Angus W. McDonald, *The Urban Origins of Rural Revolution: Elites and Masses in Hunan Province, China, 1911–1927* (Berkeley: University of California Press, 1978).

[48] van de Ven, *From Friend to Comrade*, p. 194.

[49] The classic and still gripping story of this period is told in Harold Isaacs, *The Tragedy of the Chinese Revolution* (Palo Alto, CA: Stanford University Press, 1961). More reliable is Wilbur, *Nationalist Revolution*. On the Northern Expedition, see Donald Jordan, *The Northern Expedition: China's National Revolution of 1926–1928* (Honolulu: University of Hawaii Press, 1976).

for the Chinese communists to chart a more independent revolutionary course. One element of that new course was clear: The party would have to develop military forces of its own. Up to this point, almost all the successes of the communist movement had relied on the toleration and protection of political and military allies within the Nationalist Party. Now it would have to build its own Red Army.

As bleak as the future of the CCP looked, we should not regard Chiang Kai-shek's victory as unqualified. The wave of political killing during the years of White Terror that followed April 1927 initiated a new level of violence in modern Chinese politics. To that point, leftist intellectuals had largely been protected by their prestigious social status and powerful local political connections. Now thousands were hunted down, arrested, tortured, and shot, and the survivors would not forget the many close friends they lost.[50] Much as he tried to blame leftist conspiracies for provoking the purge, the fact remained that Chiang had brought a definitive end to Sun Yat-sen's anti-imperialist revolution in alliance with the Soviet Union internationally and with the worker and peasant movement domestically. Although Nationalist Party propaganda under Chiang would promote a cult of loyalty to Sun Yat-sen and his Three People's Principles, many Chinese believed that the social and democratic aspects of Sun's revolutionary program had been betrayed. Sun Yat-sen's widow maintained close contacts with Chinese leftists and Soviet representatives and stood as a constant reminder of an alternative reading of Sun's revolutionary legacy. In the short run, this posed little threat to Chiang's rule, but in the longer run, these sentiments would nurture a longing for another era of united front against imperialism.[51]

---

[50] Schwarcz, *Chinese Enlightenment*, pp. 176–194. Li Jui's repeated references to martyrs of the revolution in Hunan gives a good sense of the number of close friends and colleagues that Mao lost in the purge (*Early Revolutionary Activities*, pp. 21, 65–73, 229, 313–315). For a vivid local account, see William T. Rowe, *Crimson Rain: Seven Centuries of Violence in a Chinese County* (Palo Alto, CA: Stanford University Press, 2007), pp. 245–319.

[51] The transformation of the national revolution was, of course, neither immediate nor without resistance. See R. Keith Schoppa, *Blood Road: The Mystery of Shen Dingyi in Revolutionary China* (Berkeley: University of California Press, 1995); Bradley K. Geisert, *Radicalism and Its Demise: The Chinese Nationalist Party, Factionalism, and Local Elites in Jiangsu Province, 1924–1931* (Ann Arbor: University of Michigan, Center for Chinese Studies, 2001); Joseph Fewsmith, *Party, State and Local Elites in Republican China: Merchant Organizations and Politics in Shanghai, 1890–1930* (Honolulu: University of Hawaii Press, 1985).

REVOLUTION IN THE HINTERLANDS

In the comparative literature on revolution, the Chinese case is usually treated as the classic peasant-based revolutionary movement.[52] In the sense that the CCP rose to power from bases in the countryside with an army recruited from the peasantry, this characterization is certainly correct. In the context of the time, however, it would be more accurate to say that after 1927, the CCP was compelled to pursue a strategy of revolution in the hinterlands. In the most densely populated core areas of China's broad agricultural plains, where land distribution typically was most unequal, the CCP never gained a secure foothold – although the peasant associations established under the protection of the Northern Expedition armies in the 1920s were often precisely in these areas.[53] The communist bases, organized as "soviets" in the early 1930s, were located in the isolated hill country along provincial borders, especially along the Jiangxi-Hunan border, where Mao based his movement, and the Hubei-Henan-Anhui border, where another large base was established by Zhang Guotao (1897–1979), a member of Li Dazhao's early group of Marxists at Beijing University who became a major labor organizer in the 1920s. When urban communist refugees of the White Terror fled to the hills, they linked up with young leftists from radicalized middle schools and forged alliances with bandit gangs, secret societies, and sworn brotherhoods – often from disadvantaged groups of Hakka settlers. Their movement was built more on the preexisting fault lines of intervillage, lineage, and generational conflict than along any Marxist conception of class conflict. In the early years, these bases survived and grew in part because their military rivals were poorly armed local militia forces, and regular army units were reluctant to chase small rebel bands only to see them escape across a provincial border.[54]

The hinterland base areas became a significant threat only when they linked up with scattered Red Army units that had broken away from the nationalist forces under the leadership of such CCP junior

[52] Barrington Moore, Jr., *Social Origins of Dictatorship and Democracy: Lord and Peasant in the Making of the Modern World* (Boston, MA: Beacon Press, 1967); Eric Wolf, *Peasant Wars of the Twentieth Century* (New York: Harper & Row, 1969); Theda Skocpol, *States and Social Revolutions: A Comparative Analysis of France, Russia and China* (Cambridge, England: Cambridge University Press, 1979).

[53] Roy Hofheinz, "The Ecology of Chinese Communist Success: Rural Influence Patterns, 1923–45," in A. Doak Barnett, ed., *Chinese Communist Politics in Action* (Seattle: University of Washington Press, 1969).

[54] Stephen C. Averill, *Revolution in the Highlands: China's Jinggangshan Base Area* (Lanham, MD: Rowman & Littlefield, 2006).

officers as Zhu De (1886–1976), who would become commander of the Red Army, and Peng Dehuai (1898–1974). Slowly the CCP brought a greater level of discipline and political purpose to its ragtag band of soldiers, bandits, and rural dissidents, expanding and arming the Red Army through raids on local militia units and the ill-equipped and poorly led provincial armies that were sent to attack them. Eventually, the threat of the "communist bandits" became great enough to command the attention of Chiang Kai-shek and the national government. Chiang's campaigns were frequently interrupted by challenges from rival warlords and then by the Japanese invasion of Manchuria in 1931, but by 1934, the final "extermination campaign" had driven the communists from Jiangxi and most of the other soviets to embark on the Long March that ultimately would bring them to their wartime refuge in the desolate, arid loess plateau of northern Shaanxi. Much as the Long March has been dramatized in the accounts of its survivors, in military terms it dealt a horrific blow to the Red Army, which lost roughly 90 percent of its strength in the course of the year-long retreat to the north.[55]

Once again, Chiang Kai-shek seemed to have conquered his rivals, but again the larger context revealed fatal weaknesses in his position. The Nanjing decade (1927–37) of Nationalist Party rule from its new capital on the Yangzi represented the most impressive period of economic growth and political and military consolidation that China had seen since the New Policies era of the late Qing. Major railway trunk lines were completed, highways were built, industrial growth proceeded at an impressive pace, the banking system was reformed, and China introduced its first national currency. Chiang Kai-shek strengthened his army with the help of German arms and military advisers, and as this army chased the Chinese communists through western China, central government control was extended to ever larger portions of the country. Municipal governments and modern police forces were established in major cities; urban renewal projects brought paved streets, sewers, street lights, and a new attention to public hygiene. There was a new diversity to urban culture as the Nationalists promoted a New Life Movement that has been termed "Confucian fascism,"[56] while in

---

[55] For the glorified account of the Long March, see Edgar Snow, *Red Star Over China* (New York: Grove Press, 1968), Part V; Harrison E. Salisbury, *The Long March: The Untold Story* (New York: McGraw-Hill, 1985) provides some correctives; Benjamin Yang, *From Revolution to Politics: Chinese Communists on the Long March* (Boulder, CO: Westview Press, 1990) examines the politics of the march.

[56] Frederic Wakeman, Jr., "A Revisionist View of the Nanjing Decade: Confucian Fascism," *The China Quarterly* 150 (June 1997), pp. 395–432.

Shanghai cosmopolitan urbanites went to Hollywood movies, listened to Filipino jazz bands, and danced the jitterbug.[57]

In the end, however, all this progress was overshadowed by the advancing threat of Japanese imperialism. From the time of the Meiji Restoration, imperial Japan imagined itself as the natural leader of East Asia's modern transformation, much as the United States regarded Latin America as its "backyard" and European colonialism claimed the right to carve up Africa. The 1894–95 war with China added Taiwan to the Japanese empire. Victory over Czarist Russia 10 years later brought rights to the Liaodong Peninsula in Manchuria, where the Japanese stationed a large Guandong Army, took over the Russian naval base, and built an extensive transport, mining, and economic research operation under the South Manchurian Railway Company. Korea was formally annexed as a colony in 1910, and at the outbreak of World War I, Japan pressed its Twenty-One Demands for special economic and political rights in China. When the world depression restricted European and American markets for Japanese goods, the commitment to securing its position in Asia only increased, and in September 1931, the Guandong Army fabricated the Mukden incident that led to the takeover of China's northeast provinces and establishment of the puppet state of Manchukuo under the restored last emperor of the Qing. In the following year, protests in Shanghai led to a brief Japanese occupation of much of the Chinese city and widespread destruction, but the primary Japanese advance was in the north. In an unremitting advance, the Japanese soon occupied Rehe and penetrated Inner Mongolia, then pressured the Nanjing government into accepting an autonomous zone in Hebei Province and the suppression of anti-Japanese activities there, including the former capital of Beijing.

Unremitting Japanese aggression in the 1930s sparked a wave of student protest, and the press and civic organizations called for boycotts of Japanese goods and firm resistance to the Japanese advance. But Chiang Kai-shek was convinced that his armies were not yet strong enough to roll back the Japanese, so in Manchuria he had ordered Zhang Xueliang

---

[57] On the Nanjing decade, see Thomas G. Rawski, *Economic Growth in Prewar China* (Berkeley: University of California Press, 1989); William C. Kirby, *Germany and Republican China* (Palo Alto, CA: Stanford University Press, 1984); Leo Ou-fan Lee, *Shanghai Modern: The Flowering of a New Urban Culture in China, 1930–1945* (Cambridge, MA: Harvard University Press, 1999); and *The China Quarterly* 150, Special Issue: *Reappraising Republican China* (January 1997), pp. 255–458. For an older, less positive assessment of the period, see Lloyd Eastman, *The Abortive Revolution: China under Nationalist Rule, 1927–1937* (Cambridge, MA: Harvard University Press, 1974).

(1898–2006), the local military commander and son of a northeastern China warlord whom the Japanese had assassinated in 1925, to withdraw his troops without a fight. The weakness of Chiang's response to Japanese aggression fueled widespread discontent and criticism from rival Nationalist Party politicians and warlords. What made Chiang's policy so politically poisonous was his insistence that resistance to Japan must cede priority to pacification of the communists. This gave the CCP the perfect opportunity to call for a united front against Japan, which it did with increasing clarity after 1935. There was strong public opinion in favor of just such a policy, an increasingly active student movement (with significant underground communist participation) supported it, and it soon found a willing ear in Zhang Xueliang and his Northeast Army, which had been sent to Shaanxi Province to press the campaign against the Red Army. The crisis came to a head in December 1936 when Chiang Kai-shek flew to Xi'an to put further pressure on the Northeast Army and instead found himself kidnapped by Zhang Xueliang and his allies. The Xi'an incident forced Chiang to stiffen his resistance to Japan and move toward a united front with the CCP. Less than a year later, in July 1937, a minor clash with Japanese troops south of Beijing quickly developed into full-scale war with Japan.[58]

NATIONAL RESISTANCE AND SOCIAL REVOLUTION

The 1937–45 War of Resistance against Japan created the environment in which the CCP positioned itself to sweep to nationwide victory in the Civil War that followed immediately. During this period, Mao Zedong emerged as the undisputed leader of the CCP, and a full account of his wartime policies will be found in Chapter 4. For the purposes of this chapter, what is most important is the relationship between wartime developments and the earlier history of the revolutionary movement. Most critically, the revival of the United Front (which for most of the war also involved joining the Soviet Union in a worldwide antifascist movement) once again gave the CCP the opportunity to publish newspapers (heavily censored, to be sure), propagandize, and recruit young intellectual activists in Nationalist China. Old friendships from the United Front of the 1920s were revived and cultivated, and by moderating its

---

[58] Parks Coble, *Facing Japan: Chinese Politics and Japanese Imperialism, 1931–1937* (Cambridge, MA: Harvard University, Council on East Asian Studies, 1991); Lyman P. Van Slyke, *Enemies and Friends: The United Front in Chinese Communist History* (Palo Alto, CA: Stanford University Press, 1967); John Israel, *Student Nationalism in China, 1927–1937* (Palo Alto, CA: Stanford University Press, 1966).

most radical policies, the CCP was able to make a credible claim to Sun Yat-sen's revolutionary legacy. In this United Front, however, the CCP had its own military forces, which were renamed, recognized, and for a time financed by the national government as the Eighth Route Army in the north and the New Fourth Army in central China. The CCP's insistence on maintaining full operational independence for its armies led to increasingly sharp clashes with the Nationalists, and by 1941, any effective united front had broken down entirely. Still, CCP propaganda was quite successful in blaming the Nationalists for the break and appealing for cooperation of all progressive forces in opposing Japanese imperialism.

Despite the United Front, in the early years of the war, Communist bases still were confined largely to the poor and mountainous regions along provincial borders and away from the main Japanese military forces and lines of communication. While the Nationalist forces fought a number of costly pitched battles to defend cities in the Yangzi Valley before retreating to their wartime capital in Chongqing, the smaller and weaker Communist units engaged in guerrilla actions against isolated enemy units. Gradually, however, these small harassing actions established local legitimacy for the CCP as defenders of the Chinese peasantry against the national enemy. It was only in the final two years of the war, however, after many crack Japanese units were diverted to the war in the Pacific, that large, secure bases were established including substantial stretches of the north and central China plains. As its political and military positions became more secure, the CCP increasingly pursued class-based social and economic policies of rent and interest reduction and highly progressive taxes that placed the main burden on the wealthiest families and spared the poorest altogether.[59]

These policies would be carried one step further in the radical and often violent land reform of the Civil War period. This rapid expansion of CCP power in the late stages of the war and its surprisingly

---

[59] Yung-fa Chen, *Making Revolution: The Communist Movement in Eastern and Central China, 1937–1945* (Berkeley: University of California Press, 1986); Odoric Y. K. Wou, *Mobilizing the Masses: Building Revolution in Henan* (Palo Alto, CA: Stanford University Press, 1994); David S. G. Goodman, *Social and Political Change in Revolutionary China* (Lanham, MD: Rowman & Littlefield, 2000). For classic early studies, see Chalmers A. Johnson, *Peasant Nationalism and Communist Power: The Emergence of Revolutionary China, 1937–1945* (Palo Alto, CA: Stanford University Press, 1962); Mark Selden, *The Yenan Way in Revolutionary China* (Cambridge, MA: Harvard University Press, 1971); Tetsuya Kataoka, *Resistance and Revolution in China: The Communists and the Second United Front* (Berkeley: University of California Press, 1974).

rapid victory in the Civil War seemed to confirm the central premise of China's twentieth-century revolutionary movement: The national revolution for liberation from foreign imperialism should be combined with a radical reorganization of Chinese society. In the late Qing period, that radical reorganization was understood largely in terms of empowering the people through democratic institutions. In the May Fourth era, a more thoroughgoing cultural transformation was sought to escape the hierarchical bonds of Confucian society. The 1920s witnessed Sun Yat-sen and his Three People's Principles, including strong socialist components in the principle of people's livelihood. To this mix, Marxism and the CCP added the notion of class struggle. The CCP victory in 1949 only strengthened the party's commitment to combining nation building with social transformation. But the years that followed were constantly bedeviled by the conflict between these two ideals.

3 From Urban Radical to Rural Revolutionary: Mao From the 1920s to 1937

BRANTLY WOMACK

This chapter begins the narrative of Mao Zedong's political career and covers the first half of his long life. At the end of the period covered by this chapter, Mao had become the leader of the remnants of a party that had just survived its second virtual extermination and had to adjust to the new environment and people of northwest China, as well as to the new threat of Japan. It might seem, therefore, that the "early Mao" would be interesting only as a prelude to his later career – the time when he was waiting in the wings of history's stage.

But Mao's successful leadership of China's rural revolution was not a lottery ball coughed up by chance or by deep historical processes. Essentially, the foundations of Mao Zedong's political thought were laid by 1937. Although his immediate problem in 1937 was war against Japan and consolidation of his leadership rather than class struggle in the villages, rural revolution returned as the main driver of the Civil War with the Guomindang from 1945 to 1949.

The task of this chapter is to analyze the development of Mao Zedong as a political actor from his initial socialization into the total chaos of early-twentieth-century China through his survival-driven origination of rural revolution to his reformulation of revolutionary leadership in the aftermath of the Long March. Despite the desperate situation in 1937, Mao faced his new beginning in Yan'an with a confidence built on the solid foundation of his earlier experiences.

From the beginning, Mao was not attempting to uphold an old order but rather to create a new one, and he reveled in the risk, opportunity, and glory implicit in a revolutionary enterprise. Radical politics came naturally to him, but he was neither a dreamer nor a loner. From the beginning, Mao combined theory and practice, with the heavier emphasis on practice. And even before he became a Marxist, he was convinced that the ultimate political strength was mobilized popular support. Practicality and populism led him into the Chinese Communist Party (CCP) when it was founded in 1921, but his discovery of rural mobilization put him on the fringe of the party in 1927. After the defeat and decimation of the party in 1927–30, however, the necessity of surviving in the countryside led to the emergence, by trial and error, of a program for rural revolution. The Long March ended Mao's initial experimentation with rural revolution in 1934, but it put him in a position of general leadership in the CCP, and in 1936–37, he had to reformulate his personal lessons of rural revolution into a general line for leading the CCP in the war against Japan.

Although theory and practice were never far apart for Mao, the development of Mao's thinking was the most important thread of the period covered by this chapter. Rather than presenting this period as the roots of his later activities, I will trace the interaction of Mao's environment, his thinking, and his actions as they occurred, ending with his reflections and generalizations of 1937. The key source will be Mao's writings as collected in the first six volumes of Stuart Schram, ed., *Mao's Road to Power*, because these reflect both the development of his thought and his perception of his environment. As you will see, though, the interaction of theory and practice has been a key characteristic of Mao's development from the beginning.

MAO BEFORE MARXISM

Mao was born in 1893, and he came to intellectual consciousness during a desperate renaissance in China. The old was decisively dead, the new was yet to take shape, and youth was the bearer of whatever future China might have. Unlike the European renaissance, it was not a prolonged period of reinvigoration of the present through discovery of the past. Rather, it was a confrontation with total crisis caused by the collapse of traditional China at the hands of superior Western power. Mao was shaped by the confusion and chaos of his times as well as by the sense of mission and freedom of his generation.

Three fundamental intellectual tensions were created by compressed intellectual modernization. First, there was the tension between the radical rejection of the Chinese past and the persisting reality of being Chinese. Alongside excoriating root-and-branch self-condemnations of Chinese culture and the Chinese personality would be fervent calls for transformation of self and country.[1] China was weak and backward, and therefore, all must choose between

---

[1]   Wolfgang Bauer, *China und die Hoffnung auf Glück* (Munich: Hanser Verlag, 1971), pp. 453–507.

self-transformation and extinction. Second, there was the tension between the images of the West as model and the West as menace. Western imperialism and China's humiliation were made possible by "Mr. Science" and "Mr. Democracy."[2] Five hundred years of modern Western history and thought had been so recently opened to Mao's generation that from Shakespeare to Rousseau to Spencer it was telescoped into an intense experience of wonder and admiration, and yet the most modern were the first to leap up in outrage at the indignities presented to China. Already in 1905 there were student demonstrations against American restrictions on Chinese emigration and property ownership in Changsha, the capital of Mao's inland home province of Hunan.[3] Third, new youth of China were freed from the bonds of particularism and ritual, but the total freedom of the individual was combined with an overwhelming sense of universal responsibility. The sense of community membership remained despite the removal of traditional content. The individual was glorified, but not absolute individualism. Given China's situation of total crisis, one might say that the new youth were liberated but not empowered.

Mao Zedong was a creature of his personal experiences as well as of his background. It is clear from his famous autobiographical interview with Edgar Snow that many of his early formative moments were not the products of vicarious participation in abstract or national concerns but rather resulted from immediate personal encounters.[4] To be sure, other biographers have noted that Mao embellished his revolutionary roots and neglected aspects of his family life that must have been quite important at the time.[5] Mao begins his story with his conflicts with his father at the age of 10, but because of his mother's difficulties with pregnancies, he was raised from ages two to eight as part of a four-generation family at his maternal grandmother's house in the adjoining county.[6] It is quite possible that this early experience away from home, along with his mother's sympathy, gave him a sense of self vis-à-vis his father that

---

[2] Benjamin Schwartz, *Chinese Communism and the Rise of Mao* (New York: Harper, 1967; first edition: Cambridge, MA: Harvard University Press, 1951), pp. 7–27.

[3] *Hunan Jin Bainian Dashi Jishu* [A Record of Major Events in Hunan for the Past Century] (Changsha: Hunan Renmin Chubanshe, 1959).

[4] Edgar Snow, *Red Star Over China* (New York: Grove Press, 1973; first edition: New York: Random House, 1938), Part 4.

[5] Stuart Schram, *Mao Tse-tung* (Baltimore, MD: Penguin, 1966); Philip Short, *Mao: A Life* (New York: Henry Holt, 1999); Lee Feigon, *Mao: A Reinterpretation* (Chicago, IL: Ivan R. Dee, 2002); Siao-yu, *Mao Tse-tung and I Were Beggars* (New York: Collier, 1957).

[6] Xiao Yanzhong, *Juren de Tingsheng* [Genesis of a Colossus] (Beijing: Guoji Wenhua Chuban Gongsi, 1988), pp. 24–25.

made possible his domestic rebellions. Perhaps it also contributed to the adventurous self-confidence that Mao displayed from the beginning.

Clearly, Mao's rural roots contributed to a distinctive south-country style that was notable throughout his career.[7] Mao's country manners were not simply a later affectation. It is clear from Snow's account that Mao's earthiness was remarkable even in the primitive situation of Bao'an in 1936, when Mao was still a "gaunt, rather Lincolnesque figure."[8] But it is too easy for Western observers to leap from Mao's peasant crudeness to the assumption that he was, or wanted to be, a country bumpkin with his back turned to modernity. As Xiao Yanzhong argues, Mao's background more accurately would be called "rural" (*nongjia*) rather than "peasant"(*nongmin*).[9] In contrast to the West, where the "bourg" of bourgeois culture was definitely urban, in traditional China, the cultural line between city and countryside was not so finely drawn. Mao's education began the way it would have begun in the city, if he were lucky enough to get one at all. The major rural-urban cultural divide emerged in the twentieth century as cities became the loci of novelty and cosmopolitanism. A bright, adventurous, and rebellious boy like Mao did not want to be left out of such excitement, so he moved to the county town of Xiangxiang in 1910 and to Changsha in 1911 at the age of 17. Although he returned home for an extended sick leave in 1925, Mao did not move back to the countryside until forced to do so by Jiang Jieshi (Chiang Kai-shek) in 1927.

In Changsha, Mao saw his first newspaper and became more aware of current events in China and the world. He also read broadly in the Hunan provincial library. But in tandem with the intellectual side of his explorations was an even more important practical experimentalism. Inspired by the 1911 Revolution, he joined the army for six months. He witnessed the decapitated bodies of Hunan's first nonimperial governors, nine days in office, lying in the street. He became a physical fitness fanatic. He spent a summer roaming around Hunan with a friend. Mao's applications to enter a law school, a police school, a soap-making school, and a commercial school are evidence of practical adventurousness applied to a newfound plethora of urban opportunities. It is strange to think that if Mao's English had been better, he might have ended up as a merchant in Changsha.[10]

---

[7] For a good collection of lurid examples, see Short, *Mao: A Life*, p. 22.
[8] Snow, *Red Star Over China*, pp. 90–94.
[9] Xiao Yanzhong, *Juren de Tingsheng*, pp. 26–27.
[10] Snow, *Red Star Over China*, p. 143.

In March 1914, at the age of 20, Mao became part of the third preparatory class of the Hunan First Provincial Normal School, and in the fall he entered the school's eighth class.[11] He graduated in June 1918. During his time at Hunan First Normal, Mao underwent an intellectual transformation that is documented in the first volume of *Mao's Road to Power*. Before proceeding to the analysis of his earliest works, however, we should consider Mao's social development during these years.

The two main threads of Mao's practical activities during his time at Hunan First Normal were increasing levels of organization and politicization. School pals had been important to Mao before moving to Changsha, but in September 1915, Mao published an advertisement inviting "young men interested in patriotic work" to get in touch, and in November he was elected secretary of the Student Association of First Normal. In October 1917, Mao was elected general manager of the student association and began to organize night classes for workers. Despite his successful organizing within the student association, Mao and his friends decided to form an additional, more elite group. The New People's Study Society (*Xinmin xuehui*) first met on April 14, 1918.[12] In contrast to the 60 persons who attended the October meeting of the student association, only 12 persons were present at the founding meeting of the study society. The society was not intended to become a large organization. New members required introductions from 5 people, and by 1920, the study society had 20 members in Changsha, 18 in France, and 9 elsewhere.[13]

In its organization as well as its ideology, the New People's Study Society opens a window on Mao's pre-Marxist politics. It was a hybrid between traditional Chinese organizations and values and the modern inspirations coming from the West. In late 1920, Mao provided rather intimate and informal reflections on the society's first three years, in which he gave three reasons for its founding.[14] First, members wanted to improve their own personal qualities and felt that friends and mutual aid were essential. Second, the national currents of new thought and new literature led to the "sudden realization that it was all wrong to lead a quiet and solitary life, and that, on the contrary, it was necessary

---

[11] Zhonggong zhongyang wenxian yanijushi, ed., *Mao Zedong Nianpu* [*Mao Zedong Chronology*], Vol. 1 Beijing: (Zhongyang Wenxian Chubanshe, 1993), p. 15.

[12] According to the diary of Xiao San, Mao gave April 17 as the date of the meeting; *ibid.*, p. 35.

[13] Stuart R. Schram, *Mao's Road to Power: Revolutionary Writings, 1912–1949* (Armonk, NY: M. E. Sharpe, 1992—), Vol. 2, pp. 18–34.

[14] *Ibid.*, pp. 18–19.

to seek an active and collective life." Lastly, Mao noted that most of the members were students of Yang Changji and that Yang had emphasized continual striving for self-improvement.[15]

Of course, neither Mao's activities nor those of the study society were limited to moral and intellectual self-improvement. Indeed, a list of Mao's activities might sound as scattered as his applications to various training programs in 1912 – physical education, workers night school, a work-study program to France, a province-wide bookstore, a newspaper, and a citizen movement to oust the governor of Hunan. Mao paid close attention to the feasibility of his proposed actions as well as to their importance, and by and large, all of them were quite successful. Mao was definitely a "can do" person or, more precisely, a "can mobilize" person. His approach to his key audience of potential participants was not "This is what I think. Follow me." It was rather "Here is an urgent, common problem. Here is what we can do right now that will make a difference."

As Stuart Schram observes in his introductory essay to Volume 1 of *Mao's Road to Power*, Mao's politics before 1920 evolved from support for exemplary traditional rulers to a commitment to radical political transformation.[16] However, his school activities make clear that his earlier views were not symptoms of complacency or caution. At the end of his first academic year at Hunan First Normal, Mao was actively involved in a student movement to dismiss the principal because of a ten-dollar surcharge on student fees. Along with 17 others, Mao was threatened with dismissal but was saved by the intervention of his teachers. The principal was dismissed in July.[17] Clearly, Mao was not a risk-avoider driven to radicalism by desperation. Rather, he was a risk-taker and an activist, born into turbulent times and bred to self-assertion, who came to believe that the only feasible action was radical transformation.

In general, Mao's politics in the earliest phase of his extant writings (1912–17) are dominated by a concern to establish effective order. This is particularly evident in his 1912 essay, "How Shang Yang Established Confidence by the Moving of the Pole."[18] For anyone familiar with Mao's later career, the most striking feature of this essay is

---

[15] Yang, Mao's posthumous father-in-law, had died earlier in the year, but the tribute to his influence was undoubtedly sincere. Yang was certainly the single most important intellectual and practical influence on Mao during his school years.

[16] *Mao's Road to Power*, Vol. 1, p. xxxiii.

[17] Zhonggong zhongyang wenxian yanjiushi ed., *Mao Zedong Nianpu*, Vol. 1, pp. 17–18. In 1951, Mao invited the principal (Zhang Gan张干) to dinner at Zhongnanhai.

[18] *Mao's Road to Power*, Vol. 1, pp. 5–6.

his disparagement of the Chinese people and his praise for the ancient Legalist statesman Shang Yang. However, there is underlying continuity. The essay is founded on a grave concern about the weakness and disorganization of China. The essay is conservative in that it holds up a traditional figure for emulation, but it is not in any sense a defense of the current regime against threatening forces of reform. The message is that China is in such dire straits that basic confidence in effective government must be restored. Good laws are not enough because "at the beginning of anything out of the ordinary, the mass of the people always dislike it."[19]

Mao's emphasis on physical education in 1916–17 was not just an expression of personal predilection and a response to the immediate problems of Hunan First Normal but also a quite direct approach to solving the problem of China's weakness. "A Study of Physical Education," published in China's top progressive journal, opens with the line, "Our nation is wanting in strength; the military spirit has not been encouraged."[20] But the main emphasis of Mao's essay is not on the benefits China would reap if only everyone would exercise. Rather, he relentlessly emphasizes every reader's need for physical improvement. Each must move from understanding to action. There is clearly a harmony between the strength of the community and the strength of the individual, and Mao's attention has shifted away from the problem of establishing order to the more basic and individual task of building muscle and strengthening will. The nonpolitical tone of the essay implies neither complacency nor despair about China. Certainly China is not ready for tasks that demand strength, but with exercise, the weak can become strong. As Mao states with double emphasis, "There is only movement in heaven and earth."[21]

Mao's marginal comments on Friedrich Paulsen's *System der Ethik*, translated by Cai Yuanpei, comprise the most important new text in the last 30 years for the understanding of Mao's intellectual development. Despite the contextual limitations imposed by the format, a distinctive picture emerges of Mao's intellectual personality in the winter of 1917–18, when he was in his final year of studies at Hunan First Normal. Mao's shift of attention to the individual that is already evident in "A Study of Physical Education" is completed in the notes, and in the process, Mao gives a remarkably intimate picture of himself.

[19] *Ibid.,* p. 6.
[20] *Ibid.,* p. 113.
[21] *Ibid.,* p. 118.

Of course, Mao's notes on Paulsen are neither an independent nor a complete expression of his own thought. Paulsen's text sets the agenda. If Mao had been commenting on *The Communist Manifesto*, the train of his thought would have been different. Nevertheless, it is clear that Mao's notes are not merely impulsive reactions to the paragraph that he is reading (some include references to subsequent text), and more important, Mao develops a view of the individual and morality that is distinct from Paulsen's presentation. Paulsen sets the theme, but Mao plays some of his own music. After reading Paulsen, Mao wrote an essay entitled, "The Energy of the Mind," unfortunately lost, that he himself cites as his major intellectual effort at this time.[22]

The attractiveness of Paulsen to Mao and to Mao's teacher, Yang Changji, was based on Paulsen's sustained attention to the moral situation of the individual. Paulsen's message is neither radical nor novel by Western standards. On the contrary, it is a careful and rather practically minded reconstruction of the rational basis for a mainstream morality that is centered on the self but acknowledges the ethical high ground of altruism. To Europeans recently freed from the constraints of tradition, Paulsen attempted to provide an individual moral compass that still pointed in roughly the same direction as church and state had.[23] In content, style, and purpose, Paulsen's text was neo-Kantian and the opposite of Nietzsche.

In the Chinese setting, Paulsen's text served to provide a rational and individual-based foundation for moral problems, but the novelty and challenge were considerably greater, and the traditional moral content was different. In the West the refounding of reality on the experiences of the individual had been going on since Descartes and Francis Bacon, whereas in China the sudden collapse of the Confucian world had made Mao's generation individuals by default. Moreover, the fundamental orientation of Paulsen's morality, like that of Kant, was a secularized Protestantism that stressed the relationship between the individual and universal principles rather than the particular relationships of persons in community – the three bonds – stressed by Chinese ethical traditions. In effect, Mao's comments on Paulsen show an enthusiastic acceptance of an individualist refoundation of morality combined with a critique of Paulsen's separation of individual and society.

Mao certainly is enthusiastic in his discovery of the individual:

There is no higher value than that of the individual.... it can be said that the value of the individual is greater than that of the

---

[22] Snow, *Red Star Over China*, p. 146.
[23] Brantly Womack, "Mao Before Maoism," *China Journal* 46 (July, 2001), pp. 95–118.

universe. Thus there is no greater crime than to suppress the individual or to violate particularity. Therefore our country's three bonds must go, and the churches, the capitalists, monarchy, and the state constitute the four evil demons of the world.[24]

But Mao's rhapsody on individualism takes a quite different turn from Paulsen's. In the same comment, Mao continues:

> Furthermore, a group is an individual, a greater individual ... the individual, society, and the state are individuals. The universe is also an individual. Thus, it is also possible to say that there are no groups in the world, only individuals.

The discerning reader may note some difficulties with Mao's line of thinking, but more important for an understanding of his intellectual development is the fact that his notions of individual and society are still fused. When Mao sings the praises of selfishness and criticizes altruism, he is not promoting a Nietzschean antisocial egoism or even, like Bernard Mandeville or Adam Smith, the indirect social benefits of self-centered behavior. Rather, he does not accept the boundary between self and other that is implicit in Paulsen's praise for other-regarding behavior. From Mao's perspective, the magnanimous person does not serve others but rather operates from a larger sense of self. "To pretend to be benefiting others," says Mao, "when really acting in self-interest is a great falsehood. To extend self-interest to the greater self of benefiting all mankind, ... this is to go from a small truth to a great truth."[25] In his 1920 reflections on the New People's Study Society, Mao repeatedly uses the expression, "the individual and the whole human race" (*geren yu quan renlei*) with the same implication that the good of the individual and of the whole are the same.

If Mao's individualism did not (necessarily) imply a privileging of the person over the group, then what did it mean? It was, as the title of his lost essay, "The Energy of the Mind," suggests, a discovery of the transformative power of the will rather than a reduction of society to autonomous units. China's situation of total crisis was deepening, and Mao's last school year was about to end early because a warlord army was billeted in the school. Mao's scope of feasible activities was reduced to raising relief funds for Changsha citizens and organizing the study society's work-study program in France. The larger meaning of such activities, though, which were so petty compared with the problems of

---

[24] *Mao's Road to Power*, Vol. I, p. 208.
[25] *Ibid.*, p. 202.

China, had to be found in the capacity of will (individual or collective) to transform reality.

Mao's personal excitement about being born into an age of chaos can be glimpsed in the following:

> The great actions of the hero are his own, are the expression of his motive power, lofty and cleansing, relying on no precedent. His force is like that of a powerful wind arising from a deep gorge, like the irresistible sexual desire for one's lover, a force that will not stop, that cannot be stopped.[26]

From a very self-confident person with plenty of willpower in his final year of school, this praise of the hero amounted to choosing a nontraditional career.

Mao became more involved in national radical currents as a result of his trip to Beijing and Shanghai in 1918–19, and he returned to Changsha just in time to take a leading part in Hunan's May Fourth activities. The movement had two profound but contradictory effects on Mao's politics. At first, the excitement of popular demonstrations producing an immediate impact on China's politics stimulated Mao's wildest dreams of immediate transformation, and these were expressed in eloquent essays in a publication he edited, the *Xiang River Review*, in the summer of 1919. However, the movement collapsed almost as quickly as it arose, leaving few visible effects. Mao then lowered his political sights to the ground at his feet and became intensely involved in daring but nonrevolutionary campaigns to expel the governor of Hunan and to establish provincial self-government.

The first paragraph of the Manifesto of the *Xiang River Review* conveys Mao's optimism and enthusiasm:

> Since the great call for "world revolution," the movement for the "liberation of mankind" has pressed forward fiercely, and today we must change our old attitudes toward issues that in the past we did not question, toward methods we would not use, and toward so many words we have been afraid to utter. Question the unquestionable. Dare to do the unthinkable. Do not shrink from saying the unutterable. No force can stop a tide such as this; no one can fail to be subjugated by it.[27]

Here, the great-souled but individual hero of the notes on Paulsen morphs into the collective consciousness, will, and action of the great

[26] *Ibid.*, pp. 263–264.
[27] *Ibid.*, p. 318.

union of the popular masses. Mao argues that all political strength is based on unions of people, and since the exploited always outnumber the exploiters, they will prevail if only they become conscious of their unity and strength. Consciousness is the key because even the soldiers of the oppressors are themselves oppressed, and their bullets "will turn to mud" at the sound of the great shout of the people.[28]

By the time of Mao's last issue of the *Xiang River Review* in August, high hopes for social transformation had already ebbed. Mao never criticized the May Fourth Movement, and it had been a turning point in the politicization of himself, of his comrades, and of China as a nation. However, its failure brought a fundamental shift in the expectations and content of his politics, although not in his general values and direction. His journalism now focused on current problems rather than grand schemes of transformation. He wrote a series of incisive critiques of the situation of women in China, but his most notable public activity was opposition to the governor of Hunan, Zhang Jingyao, and after Zhang's ouster came Mao's promotion of Hunan self-government. Meanwhile, Mao and the New People's Study Society were busy building the Cultural Book Society, a bookstore with province-wide reach, and Mao designed it to be a model undertaking, stressing public service and transparent operations.[29] Somewhat later, Mao founded the Hunan Self-Education College with similar attention to the details of enlightened business administration.

Mao's proposals for Hunan self-government differed in two important respects from his later politics. First, he made some rather dramatic arguments for the independence of Hunan. Mao's Hunanese roots remained evident to his last days, but this is the only time that he suggested an option of independence for a heartland province of China.[30] Second and more important, the thrust of his popular mobilization was the establishment of democratic reforms – a constitutional assembly based on universal suffrage. This was quite radical in its mode of presentation as well as its content, as the following contemporary account from the *North China Herald* makes clear:

> The document [the proposal for a constitutional convention] was the work of three men, Mr. Long of the *Da Gong Bao*, Mr. Mao of

[28] *Ibid.*, p. 380.

[29] Brantly Womack, *The Foundations of Mao Zedong's Political Thought* (Honolulu: University of Hawaii Press, 1982), pp. 24–27.

[30] By contrast, national self-determination by ethnic groups was included in the 1924 Manifesto of the Guomindang, and Mao spoke in favor of it in the 1930s. Katherine Palmer, "Mao Zedong and the Sinification of China's Minority Policy," *Southeast Review of Asian Studies* 17 (1995).

the First Normal School, and Mr. Peng, a bookseller.... of the 430 signatories, about 30 were said to be connected with the press of the city; perhaps 200 were teachers or men of the scholar class; about 150 were merchants; and, say, 50 were working men. It is interesting that not only were working men invited to sign but that representatives of their class stood side by side with some of the most cultured men in the city as members of the deputation of 15 which took the document to the governor.... There can be no doubt that the eyes of China are fixed on Hunan at this juncture.[31]

This aim was not in contradiction to the "great union of the popular masses," but the goal was political change rather than utopian transformation. The results were disappointing. When the incoming governor, Tan Yankai, felt threatened by the calls for constitutional democracy in Hunan, he disbanded the demonstrators.

MAO AND THE REVOLUTIONARY PARTY, 1921–27

Mao's correspondence with the members of the New People's Study Society residing in France presents a remarkably clear picture of his decision to become a communist.[32] His two best friends, Cai Hesen and Xiao Zisheng, were on different sides of a dispute among the French members of the study society concerning its future path, and they wrote to Mao arguing their cases. Cai argued for communism, whereas Xiao argued for "a moderate revolution, a revolution with education as its instrument."[33] Mao was careful to emphasize the common points of the proposals, and he praised some aspects of Xiao's proposal, but he decisively favored an active revolutionary party. Education was an inadequate revolutionary method because the educational systems are controlled by the current elite and, in any case, interests, not knowledge, dictate opinions. Mao conceded that communism was not as attractive as the alternatives: "[M]y present view of absolute liberalism, anarchism, and even democracy is that these things sound very good in theory, but are not feasible in reality."[34] Feasibility, then, was the primary attraction of communism. It provided a guide for meaningful action in the present nonrevolutionary era, and it had an achievable target that was part of a world revolution.

[31] "Provincial Home Rule in China: Every Province Its Own Master," *North China Herald*, November 6, 1920; cited in Short, *Mao: A Life*, p. 108.

[32] *Mao's Road to Power*, Vol. 2, pp. 5–14.

[33] Quoted by Mao in *Mao's Road to Power*, Vol. 2, p. 8.

[34] *Ibid.*, p. 11.

Mao continued to be active in the New People's Study Society and in various projects begun before his conversion to communism, but two new concerns increasingly demanded his attention. First, Mao became involved in labor organization. Although he had run a night school for workers even before the founding of the study society, now he was organizing unions throughout Hunan and becoming involved in a series of strikes. Hunan was not a leading industrial (or urban) province, but it was a leader in labor organizing before 1923 – owing largely to Mao's efforts. Mao's other major activity was CCP organization. He was one of the founding participants in the CCP's first congress in 1921, and Hunan supplied one-fifth of the delegates to that founding meeting. By the time of the second congress the following year, Hunan was one of the three largest provincial organizations, after Shanghai and Guangdong.[35] Mao was the clear leader of the Hunan CCP organization and secretary of the party committee, as well as general secretary of the All-Hunan Federation of Labor Organizations.

It is clear that when Mao joined the CCP in 1921, he did not simply become a bullet in someone else's organizational weapon. The appeal of communism was that it provided a general ideological and organizational framework for activities and general purposes to which he was already committed and to which he remained committed. As a successful provincial leader, he brought more to the CCP than he received.

The massacre of railway workers by the northern warlord Wu Peifu on February 7, 1923, swiftly turned the tide of the labor movement, and paradoxically, it also increased Mao's subordination to the CCP and the CCP's subordination to the Comintern. Thus ended Mao's career as leader of the radical fringe of the Hunan elite, and he moved to Shanghai in April to take up the practical (and assigned) tasks of running the CCP's Central Committee. Shortly afterwards he became involved in the liaison between the CCP and the Guomindang (GMD). Thus also ended the CCP's dreams of an autonomous power base and therefore its resistance to the Comintern's demands for a united front. Meanwhile, Sun Yat-sen had been experiencing unrelated setbacks in Guangzhou, and so the stage was set for collaboration.

Mao was not a happy bureaucrat, even for a revolutionary united front. Although biographers have questioned whether Mao's lengthy withdrawal to Hunan in 1925 was due to politics as well as illness, a more appropriate interpretation might be that the frustration of purely

---

[35] Tony Saich, ed., *The Rise to Power of the Chinese Communist Party: Documents and Analysis* (Armonk, NY: M. E. Sharpe, 1996), pp. 27–28.

party politics was the source of debilitating stress that required months of seclusion and recovery.[36] Physically and mentally, it seems likely that early 1925 was the lowest point of his adult life thus far. To the extent that Mao's withdrawal was political, it was not the sidestep of a political climber who had missed a rung on the ladder of success but rather the implicit questioning of whether what could be done at the current, nonrevolutionary moment was really worth doing.

A forceful new answer to the question, "Why keep going?" emerged from Mao's rural vantage point on the great upsurge of the May Thirtieth Movement. The upheavals in Shanghai and Guangzhou that awakened the proletarian hopes of his colleagues in the CCP resonated not only in Changsha but also even in Mao's isolated home in Shaoshan. From the rural heartland, Mao could see the potential of a truly national revolution, one based on mobilization of the overwhelming majority of China's population. This differed considerably from the idea of revolution based on successful party politics or even of revolution led by the urban proletariat. From Mao's new perspective, the legitimacy of a national revolution – and the legitimacy of a revolutionary party – depended on mobilization of the peasantry. His focus shifted from the most progressive to the most numerous class.

Energized by his reorienting experiences in Hunan, Mao returned to party politics in Guangzhou with a mission. Mao's emphasis on the peasantry did not contradict the public stance of the United Front and of individuals, especially Peng Pai, who had organized peasants, but clearly he now took more seriously the mobilization of peasantry than either the GMD or the CCP had previously. Mao's new emphasis was on the necessity of peasant mobilization, and his enthusiasm and expertise quickly won him leading roles in the rural work of the United Front. The preparations for the Northern Expedition were heating up, and as the balance of power began to shift in Guangdong and later in Hunan and Fujian, peasant associations sprang up that clearly supported the cause of national revolution. As Mao became more involved in peasant mobilization, his belief in the centrality of the peasant movement grew. As long as peasant mobilization contributed to the early dynamism of the Northern Expedition and to the destabilization of enemy warlords, it was lauded by the United Front. However, since the success of the Northern Expedition attracted warlord allies, and peasant associations continued to destabilize the countryside now under GMD control, both the GMD and the CCP leaderships began to consider the peasant

---

[36] Schram, *Mao Tse-tung*, p. 78.

movement out of control. At this point, at the end of 1926 and for the first half of 1927, Mao felt increasingly torn between organizational discipline and peasant mobilization, and he chose peasant mobilization.

In January 1927, Mao conducted an on-the-spot investigation of the peasant movement in five Hunan counties through which the Northern Expedition had just passed, and when he returned to Guangzhou, he wrote one of the most remarkable essays of his career, the "Hunan Report."[37] If it is taken as a foretelling of the rural revolution culminating in 1949, then it is a soaring and successful prophecy. If it is taken as what it claimed to be, namely, an analysis of the peasant associations that emerged in the course of the Northern Expedition and a prediction of their strength, it is as much an illusion as Mao's May Fourth expectations. Mao admitted to Snow that even if the CCP had supported the peasant associations and had pursued an aggressive land policy, it would not have prevailed against counterrevolution.[38] This remarkably honest admission is a measure of the distance between the enthusiasm of the "Hunan Report" and the sober realities of rural revolution after 1927.

The difference between the "Hunan Report" and Mao's earlier writings derives from the change of situation created by the explosive development of peasant associations. As the Northern Expedition began to move forward in the latter half of 1926, the peasant question changed from one of general revolutionary strategy to the practical question of whether the peasant associations should be reined in or encouraged. The CCP leadership, and especially Chen Duxiu, its first "paramount leader," reasoned strategically from the importance of a political victory to the necessity of maintaining the United Front and further to the wisdom of preventing radical peasant actions from disrupting the thrust northward. The scattered and uncontrollable actions of the peasant associations could not defeat the warlords opposing the Northern Expedition, but they could disrupt the United Front. The question of what was actually happening in the countryside was urgent for the entire leadership, and Mao went to Hunan in his capacity as chief expert on the peasants for both parties.

The "Hunan Report" is written in the first person, and it fully uses the empirical authority Mao gained from lengthy and extensive investigations. With a self-confidence undoubtedly increased by his thus far

[37] "Report on the Peasant Movement in Hunan," in *Mao's Road to Power*, Vol. 2, pp. 429–464; also Mao Zedong, *Selected Works of Mao Tse-tung*, Vol. 1 (Beijing: Foreign Languages Press, 1965), pp. 23–59.
[38] Snow, *Red Star Over China*, p. 164.

successful predictions concerning the revolutionary potential of the peasantry, Mao makes his famous claim:

> In a very short time, in China's central, southern and northern provinces, several hundred million peasants will rise like a mighty storm, like a hurricane, a force so swift and violent that no power, however great, will be able to hold it back. They will smash all the trammels that bind them and rush forward on the road to liberation. They will eventually sweep all the imperialists, warlords, corrupt officials, local tyrants and evil gentry into their graves. Every revolutionary party and every revolutionary comrade will be put to the test, to be accepted or rejected as they decide. There are three alternatives. To march at their head and lead them? To trail behind them, gesticulating and criticizing? Or to stand in their way and oppose them?[39]

In essence, Mao's claim here and in the detail of the report is that the spontaneous organization of the peasant associations is sufficient, both in its strength and in its internal sense of direction, to transform all of China's villages. The "revolutionary parties" are thus secondary to the revolution itself, and they must run to catch up. From the point of view of a party bureaucrat such as Zhang Guotao, Mao had gone native.[40]

The resonance between the "Hunan Report" and the "Great Union of the Popular Masses" of 1919 is striking. Both show a confident expectation of imminent transformation as a result of spontaneous mass action. The overwhelming majority will, in fact, overwhelm. Both documents attribute the will and energy of the masses to their experience of oppression by the exploiting minority. Both reduce the role of organization to mass mobilization. Although Mao does not abandon the CCP or return to advocating anarchism, a new revolutionary moment clearly has arrived in which organization is secondary to mobilization.

The changes in Mao's thinking over the previous eight years are also apparent. Organization is present, even if it is secondary. The "Hunan Report" is a report, not a manifesto, and the target audience is not the masses but the "revolutionary party." The implicit urban/cosmopolitan bias of the *Xiang River Review* has been replaced by a rural/localistic focus. Most important, the "great shout together" is now a class struggle

---

[39] Mao Zedong, *Selected Works*, Vol. 1, pp. 23–24.

[40] Chang Kuo-t'ao (Zhang Guotao), *Autobiography of Chang Kuo-t'ao*, Vol. 1 (Lawrence: University of Kansas Press, 1971), pp. 596–615. For his part, Mao thought that there was a "hint of something counterrevolutionary" in the attitude of the center toward the peasant associations.

in which the leitmotiv is *jiao wang guo zheng* (proper limits must be exceeded in order to right a wrong). Not only do the masses know the crimes of their targets and exact just vengeance, but in general violence against the former ruling class is the necessary birthmark of the new society rather than a taint of the old. Instant enlightenment has been replaced by self-education through revolutionary action. But the educator was himself on the eve of a hard lesson. Nevertheless, Mao's rural reorientation of 1925–27 was crucial to his subsequent adjustment to revolutionary base areas, and in time the "Hunan Report" looked prophetic for rural revolution, although not the one Mao experienced and analyzed in 1927.

SURVIVAL AND THE EMERGENCE OF RURAL REVOLUTION, 1927–34

In the six months after Mao's enthusiastic report, the United Front and the peasant associations had collapsed, and the CCP had become a tattered remnant of its former self. Two basic facts must be underlined concerning the reversal of fortunes. First, the CCP had been dealt a mortal blow. It had lost 90 percent of its membership in clashes with Jiang Jieshi and various warlords and had been reduced to scattered, furtive remnants in cities and various rural areas. Its ambitions had been shattered, and its ideology of cosmopolitan, proletarian revolution had no further hope. Marxism literally became an academic question, with attention shifting away from current politics to university research on Marxist interpretations of China's ancient history.[41] Survival seemed unlikely, success unthinkable. Had the CCP never reemerged as a significant factor in Chinese politics, its demise now would be considered inevitable.

The second basic fact is that the new paradigm of rural revolution arose from the practical struggle for survival. Necessity was the mother of the CCP's reinvention. Mao's earlier enthusiasm for peasant mobilization helped to prepare the way for rural revolution, but it was constant adjustment to the needs of survival in a hostile environment that eventuated in a new paradigm of revolution.

After a series of defeats in the summer of 1927, Mao led a remnant of supporters to the rugged Jinggang Mountains on the border of Hunan and Jiangxi provinces, where he teamed up with two left-leaning local

---

[41] Arif Dirlik, *Revolution and History: The Origins of Marxist Historiography in China* (Berkeley: University of California Press, 1978).

bandits. For the next 15 months, Mao played cat and mouse – as the mouse – with local forces and with various directives and emissaries from the Central Committee.[42]

"Political power grows from the barrel of a gun." This realization of August 1927 provided the focus of Mao's initial survival efforts. Running, hiding, and shooting were new skills for him. As he succeeded in day-to-day survival, he wondered about the longer term. By October 1928, Mao figured out that even though all the elite, from the central GMD government to the local landlords, wanted to exterminate the communists, his enemies were unorganized and fighting among themselves. By locating its bases in border areas, the CCP could take advantage of its rivals because they could not coordinate their attacks. Mao had to be very cautious about risking military assets in confrontations but very active in creating opportunities for surprise and harassment. As Mao and his co-commander, Zhu De, famously put it in May 1928, "The enemy advances, we retreat. The enemy camps, we harass. The enemy tires, we attack. The enemy retreats, we pursue."[43] At this point Mao was not arguing for rural revolution but rather for the strategic utility of rural bases.

Almost as dangerous to Mao as his enemies were the conflicting directives from the CCP's leadership. They were concerned that Mao was becoming too military-oriented, too peasant-based, and possibly too soft in pursuing class struggle. On the last point they need not have worried. Mao organized execution squads against landlords and used "red terror" to expand his mountain base. The other concerns were real, and to some extent Mao shared them. It was easy for men with guns to slip into the habits of warlordism or banditry, and it was virtually impossible to recruit proletarians in primitive rural areas. Strengthening CCP organization and criticizing the "purely military viewpoint" addressed the problems but could not solve them. In any case, however, Mao had to put his own survival above obedience to distant superiors.

The events of 1930 caused Mao's reorientation from prolonged survival in rural areas to a new paradigm of protracted rural revolution. On the one hand, party center–inspired attempts to use the Red Army to attack and occupy Nanchang and Changsha, the respective provincial capitals of Jiangxi and Hunan, were disastrous failures. On the other hand, the original Jinggangshan base was too small for the growing

---

[42] Stephen Averill, *Revolution in the Highlands: China's Jinggangshan Base Area* (Lanham, MD: Rowman & Littlefield, 2006).

[43] *Mao's Road to Power*, Vol. 3, p. 155.

army, so at the beginning of the year Mao moved most of his force to southern Jiangxi and by the end of the year had established a sizable new base area that soon was rechristened the "Jiangxi Soviet." Failure in the cities and success in the countryside persuaded Mao that the ultimate goal of national revolution should not be pursued by lurking in the countryside and waiting for the "revolutionary moment" but rather by expanding the rural bases to encircle the cities from the countryside. In a word, this was rural revolution, something quite different from either Marxist theory or Russian experience, though, of course, Mao did not emphasize the difference.

Rural revolution required an economic base capable of sustaining a military force, a political structure appropriate to a dispersed and poor population, and military tactics using the advantage of local support. The economic challenge required a serious investigation of actual conditions in the base area and a retargeting of land reform. Mao himself conducted detailed surveys of such matters as the price of chickens and the concrete effects of the revolution on various families, and he told his subordinates, "No investigation, no right to speak!" There was a subtle shift in rural class struggle from destroying the old exploiters toward how to mobilize an "overwhelming majority" to sustain production. Effective mobilization required a more favorable policy toward middle peasants and a less hostile attitude toward rich peasants than Mao promoted initially. In politics, the new emphasis was on avoiding alienation from the masses because mass support was the basic resource of the revolution. This required, in turn, a flat organization that avoided bureaucratism and was mass-regarding in its activities.

In military terms, rural revolution required Mao to develop guerilla tactics for protracted conflict. Yes, political power grows from the barrel of a gun, but how do guns grow? Like the political structure, the rural military had to minimize its distance from the people. A pyramid had to be built, with a broad base of ordinary people helping out with related tasks such as storing food and watching roads, a militia that stayed at home and raised its own food, and a smaller mobile force that was the military spearhead. Since the pyramid could not move, the military would be most effective if it could "lure the enemy in deep" into the base area. There local knowledge and support would enable the Red Army to retreat when it was weak and strike when it was strong.

One problem with luring the enemy in deep was that it endangered the population of the base area, and this contributed to a bloody internal struggle in Jiangxi between Mao and the local party organization in the new base. The local leaders opposed Mao's harsh policies against rich peasants and his strategy of not defending the boundaries of the base area. The confrontation was complicated by the existence of a secret antiparty organization, and it led to mass executions of thousands.[44] The "Futian Incident" exposed an undercurrent of brutal harshness in Mao's revolution. However, in the long term, "red terror" undercut the potential of mass mobilization and endangered the success of the revolution.

Ironically, Mao's success as a military leader and consolidator of the Jiangxi base area led to his removal from army command by late 1932. Mao's success in Jiangxi drew the attention of Jiang Jieshi, who launched a series of "encirclement and suppression" campaigns against the Jiangxi Soviet. These were massive undertakings. The first, in late 1931, involved 100,000 troops, and the second and third followed quickly, with 200,000 and 300,000 troops, respectively. Considering that the Red Army's strength was around 30,000 and that the Normandy Invasion of June 1941 involved 156,000 troops, Mao's successful defense against these attacks was an impressive accomplishment. However, his refusal to use his troops in more ambitious urban attacks as demanded by the Central Committee was sharply criticized, and as the central leadership began to move from Shanghai to Jiangxi in 1932, they pushed Mao aside as a military and party leader and put him in charge of administering the base area, now elevated to the status of the Central Soviet of the Chinese Soviet Republic.

Mao, who had just settled his accounts with localistic opposition in the "Futian Incident," himself became the local leader despised for his lack of proper Bolshevik leftism. Mao remained a troublesome subordinate, although not a rebellious one. He remained a vigorous advocate for guerrilla warfare, and even after he was removed from command, the Red Army used his tactics to defeat the fourth encirclement and suppression campaign in 1933, to the displeasure of the returned students from the Soviet Union, the so-called 28 Bolsheviks, who now controlled the CCP. The shift of Mao's rural policy from class struggle to mass mobilization also excited their suspicion and criticism. Now Mao was criticized for being soft on rich peasants and not pursuing class struggle to the end, the same crimes for which he executed people the previous year.

Despite or perhaps because of Mao's removal from military leadership, his responsibilities as chairman of the soviet government led

---

[44] Stephen Averill, "The Origins of the Futian Incident," in Tony Saich and Hans van de Ven, eds., *New Perspectives on the Chinese Communist Revolution* (Armonk, NY: M. E. Sharpe, 1995), pp. 79–115.

to an innovation in rural revolution almost as important as guerrilla warfare. He was now in charge of administering a population of 3 million people – not a lot by Chinese standards, but enough to require multiple layers of officials and more formal methods of rule than in the old base areas. Moreover, increased demands were placed on administration by military incursions, the increasingly effective blockade, Red Army recruitment, and most important, the disruptions caused by the revolution itself. The survival of the CCP now depended as much on the effectiveness of sustaining the base areas as it did on military success.

Had Mao called in Western consultants at this point, they probably would have suggested greater efficiency in administration – more professionalism, better record-keeping, and so forth. And indeed, he did try one Western-style solution, a local-level election campaign to "breathe out the stale and breathe in the fresh." After more than a year, Mao had to admit that "not a single county has completed the electoral process," and he judged that "this election campaign has been a complete failure."[45] Instead of a Weberian bureaucracy or elections, Mao institutionalized mass mobilization by inventing the mass campaign.

Mao's innovation was launched under inauspicious circumstances. In February 1933, he was put in charge of a Land Investigation Movement, which was supposed to uncover hidden landlords and rich peasants and thereby raise more money. Mao was concerned that the movement would further disrupt rural life and reduce production. Therefore, he planned a general movement that would combine the goals of land reform, production, and army recruitment and would begin with an eight-county pilot program.[46] The broader movement then could be launched with a summary of the successes of the model counties. After the high tide of mobilization, the final phase of consolidation began to summarize experiences and to correct mistakes. In December 1933, Mao inspected two model localities, and their most impressive successes were not in numbers of class enemies uncovered but rather in increased productivity despite large numbers of army volunteers.[47]

The Land Investigation Movement of 1933 set the pattern for later base-area governance in the Yan'an era and still later in the People's Republic of China. However, Mao's subtle transformation of the movement from yet another top-down Stalinist campaign to purify class ranks into a mass campaign that integrated and maximized

---

[45] *Mao's Road to Power*, Vol. 4, p. 335.
[46] Womack, *Foundations of Mao Zedong's Political Thought*, pp. 161–172.
[47] *Mao's Road to Power*, Vol. 4, pp. 584–640.

participation was the last straw for the 28 Bolsheviks. From January 1934, Mao was removed from all leadership positions, and a new, harsh Land Investigation Movement was launched. Mao's concluding speech at the Second Congress of the Chinese Soviet Republic was expected to be his swansong, and so it is particularly interesting for the lessons that he drew from his Jiangxi experience. The basic idea of the talk is expressed as follows:

> Our central task at present is to mobilize the broad masses to take part in the revolutionary war, overthrow imperialism and the Guomindang by means of such war, spread the revolution throughout the country, and drive imperialism out of China.... If our comrades really comprehend this task and understand that the revolution must at all costs be spread throughout the country, then they should in no way neglect or underestimate the immediate interests, the well-being, of the broad masses. For the revolutionary war is a war of the masses; it can be waged only by mobilizing the masses and relying on them.[48]

With this realization, Mao's own understanding of the dynamics of rural revolution had completed a cycle from the initial perception of the importance of rural revolution in the "Hunan Report" seven years earlier, to the sobering military lessons of how to survive as a localized, weak power, to a realization that mass support is not a categorical derivative of class struggle but rather a political process in which the CCP's identification with the masses was a policy objective rather than a presumption. At 41 years of age, with the cane of the 28 Bolsheviks around his neck, he could not have imagined an opportunity to make use of this insight. But the cane of the fifth encirclement and suppression campaign was around their necks, and eight months later the Jiangxi Soviet was abandoned.

PARTY LEADERSHIP AND THE FORMULATION OF "MAOISM"

Facing the fifth encirclement and suppression campaign in 1934 would have been a challenge for the best generals; it was a disaster for the Stalinists. Over 500,000 troops were involved on the GMD side, supported by air power, and Jiang Jieshi employed a new siege-like strategy of slow advances with rings of blockhouses. Advised by Otto Braun,

---

[48] *Ibid.*, p. 716; Mao Zedong, *Selected Works*, Vol. 1, p. 147.

a German Comintern agent with some military background, the CCP shifted from guerrilla tactics to positional defense and experienced heavy losses. Meanwhile, a noncommunist army in neighboring Fujian Province rebelled against Jiang and proposed an alliance with the CCP. Negotiations were begun, but the CCP vacillated on whether to support the rebels, and there was no substantive action before defeat of the rebellion. With the distraction of the Fujian rebellion out of the way, the full force of the GMD could resume strangulation of the base area.

Secret plans to abandon the base area were decided in May, and the expeditionary force of 86,000 moved out in October. The exit went smoothly, but by the end of November, the GMD caught up, and the Communists lost half their strength while crossing the Xiang River. The Long March was off to an inauspicious start. With the discrediting of the 28 Bolsheviks, Mao began to emerge first as the military commander and gradually as the major political leader of the CCP. However, the circumstances of the Long March, the anti-Japanese war, and the new base areas in northwestern China required of Mao a comprehensive strategic rethinking.

The first business of the Long March was survival in the new context of an army on the run.[49] It was Mao's military survival skills that returned him to leadership, not his insights into rural revolution. Officially, the Long March was the "march north to fight Japan," but the Red Army was well aware of its weakness, and it was searching for a safe haven. It skirted around China's heartland, through rugged terrain occupied by ethnic minorities, and cast about for a remote base close to the Soviet Union. But a chance capture of some newspapers provided information about a communist base in northern Shaanxi Province, so Mao's part of the Red Army headed there. The Long March ended on October 22, 1935, and eventually, the base area expanded to include the town of Yan'an.

Mao was no longer on the run, but his force of less than 10,000 was weak and located in a far corner of northwestern China. Interviews with foreign journalists, most notably Edgar Snow, were an important part of reestablishing the CCP as a national political force.[50] Fortunately for Mao, the GMD force tasked with exterminating him in his new location was the Manchurian army of Zhang Xueliang that had been driven from its homeland by the Japanese. Mao's calls for an anti-Japanese

---

[49] Harrison Salisbury, *The Long March: The Untold Story* (New York: Harper & Row, 1985).

[50] Snow, *Red Star Over China*; see also *Mao's Road to Power*, Vol. 5.

United Front fell on fertile ground. Zhang became lax in his anticommunist mission, and when in December 1936 Jiang Jieshi made a personal appearance in Xi'an to upbraid him, Zhang kidnapped Jiang and held him until he promised to fight Japan. Although Jiang wavered after his release, the Japanese attack known as the "Marco Polo Bridge Incident" in July 1937 confirmed the beginning of a national war against the Japanese invasion.

The outbreak of the anti-Japanese war faced Mao with his most profound reorientation since retreating to the countryside in 1927. However, instead of the concrete problem of survival, Mao now faced a more theoretical problem. What was the relevance of his rural revolutionary experience in Hunan and Jiangxi to the new situation of national war against Japan?

The first problem of reorientation was that of military strategy. How relevant was guerrilla warfare, with its base in class struggle and land reform, to fighting an enemy not rooted in the local class structure and with a modern army? Mao's most comprehensive answer was given in a series of major military writings beginning with "Problems of Strategy in China's Revolutionary War (December 1936)." Not surprisingly, Mao argues that rural resistance would be the key to the defeat of Japan because Japan would be overextended in its occupation of China. But Mao was acutely aware that military struggle had entered a new stage, and he urged the Red Army to be alert to situational changes. As he put it, "China's anti-Japanese guerrilla warfare has broken out of the bounds of tactics to knock at the gates of strategy.... Such extensive as well as protracted guerrilla warfare is quite new in the history of wars...."[51] The Red Army therefore should expect to make mistakes but should be quick to learn from them. Meanwhile, the shift of target to an alien enemy required suspension of the class struggle in the villages and a shift to a patriotic United Front.

The problems of leading the CCP's strategic shift led Mao to three interrelated conceptual innovations, each of which had roots in his earlier thinking but hitherto had not been clearly formulated. The first was the primacy of practice. In facing the new situation, Mao urged the Red Army to look to reality, not to books. Correct leadership was situationally appropriate leadership, not dogmatically derived leadership. The second was the unity of opposites. In presenting pairs of concepts such as "strategic offensive" and "strategic defensive," Mao gave his commanders an intellectual framework that was perhaps useful in understanding

---

[51] "Problems of Strategy in the Anti-Japanese War," in *Mao's Road to Power*, Vol. 6, p. 394.

a situation but nonprescriptive as to what to do. Because opposites could transform into each other, a commander could not look at the categories and find the pigeonhole for his current problem. Lastly, the idea of primary and secondary contradictions allowed Mao to argue that while class struggle had been appropriate when the principal contradiction was between the CCP and the GMD, a United Front was appropriate now that war with Japan had become the principal contradiction.

In the summer of 1937, Mao abstracted these ideas and combined them with ideological readings to give lectures on philosophy at the Anti-Japanese Military and Political College in Yan'an. In all, Mao presented 110 hours of lectures and stayed for discussions – clearly he took these philosophical matters seriously.[52] This was Mao's most sustained effort at articulating his basic thinking since his notes on Paulsen 20 years earlier. Mao did not emphasize his innovation by distinguishing himself from the Marxist classics or from current Soviet and Chinese communist philosophy. On the contrary, he emphasized the scientific character of Marxism-Leninism. Nevertheless, the point of these philosophical efforts was not to fit China into familiar patterns but to justify the primacy of practice and the complexity of reality. Universal truths existed in Marxism-Leninism, but appropriate leadership in concrete situations could not be deduced from them.

Mao's position of general leadership of the CCP was acknowledged by the Soviets in September 1938, and his talks and writings were already supplying the central leadership with a rationale for reorientation of the CCP toward war with Japan. His personal effort to readjust to the new situation was at the same time the authoritative general line. Mao's thinking became the beginning of "Mao Zedong Thought," the CCP's new orthodoxy. Despite the emphasis of his 1937 philosophical works on the primacy of practice, the need for investigation and experimentation, and the changeability of contradictions, it can be said that they mark the watershed between the active evolution of Mao's own thinking and the more fixed and authoritative role of Mao Zedong Thought.

CONCLUSION

Had Mao died in 1937, he probably would be remembered today as a folk hero of rural revolution in China because by this time he had made a major contribution to its organization and reality. Ironically, he would

---

[52] See Nick Knight, ed., *Mao Zedong on Dialectical Materialism* (Armonk, NY: M. E. Sharpe, 1990).

be less remembered for his intellectual development or for his thinking, and yet the learning process of the first half of his life provided the foundation for his successful leadership of the Chinese Revolution. Mao's youthful thinking had a more distant and problematic relationship to his post-1949 leadership – where was the primacy of practice in the Great Leap Forward? And how could the person who once opposed "book worship" of even the communist classics tolerate the worship of the "Little Red Book" in the 1960s? The dogmatic excesses of the later Mao would not have been possible without the pragmatic populism of the early Mao, but they seem a world away.

4 War, Cosmopolitanism, and Authority: Mao from 1937 to 1956

HANS J. VAN DE VEN

To call Hitler evil may well be true and morally satisfying. But it explains nothing.

Ian Kershaw, *Hitler: 1936–1945 Nemesis*, p. xvii.

On November 29, 1937, a Soviet plane landed in a blizzard in Yan'an, the communist capital in the northern Shaanxi wasteland. On board were Peter Vladimirov, Moscow's new representative to the Chinese Communist Party (CCP); Kang Sheng, the CCP Central Committee's representative to the Communist International (Comintern), who would go down in history as the Chinese communists' most loathsome spy chief; and Chen Yun, the architect of the post-Mao economic reforms and at the time the Central Committee's representative to Xinjiang warlord Sheng Shicai.

The most important passenger was Wang Ming (alias Chen Shaoyu), who had been in Moscow since 1931. The mission's arrival meant the beginning of a struggle for power between Wang, representing an internationalist Moscow-oriented tendency in the CCP, and Mao Zedong, calling for the Sinification of revolution. Mao would prevail before a year had passed, but he focused a good part of his attention in the remaining years of World War II on wringing Wang Ming–type communist cosmopolitanism from the CCP. World War I had generated powerful opportunities for globalizing forces because its horrors had led to widespread disenchantment with bourgeois-dominated nation-states. World War II shut down these opportunities while arming national liberation movements. In transforming the CCP during the 1937–45 Sino-Japanese War from a defeated, demoralized, and divided party oriented toward Moscow into an organization with a strong ethos, a clear sense of a separate Chinese identity, and a powerful army, Mao domesticated, militarized, and nationalized revolution in China.

World War II led to similar developments in Vietnam with Ho Chi Minh, in Indonesia with Sukarno, in Korea with Kim Il-Song, and in

Yugoslavia with Tito. National liberation movements during World War II constructed new social, political, and military formations as they worked to establish mastery over their own futures. Hostile to Western culture and forms of social and economic organization, they insisted on authentic national pathways toward modernity. While Mao restored national pride, there was a cost. Shortly after the establishment of the People's Republic of China (PRC), just when China needed all possible foreign investment, advice, expertise, and especially trade, Mao isolated the country after he clashed with the Soviets and set out to prove that China could make a breakthrough to a new socialist modernity on its own. The result was the disasters of the Great Leap Forward and the Cultural Revolution.

COMMUNIST GLOBALIZATION IN THE INTERWAR YEARS

The original appeal of Marxism-Leninism in China as in Europe and elsewhere drew on communist cosmopolitanism. The horrors of World War I were perceived to have exposed the folly of nation-states and their blinkered and self-interested bourgeois elites. International networks based on communist globalization were important to the CCP in the 1920s and beyond.[1] Dutch communist Henricus Sneevliet, alias Maring, who had led the Sarekat Islam in the Dutch East Indies, helped to found the CCP in 1921. Soviet emissary Adolph Joffe convinced Sun Yat-sen to accept Soviet aid on the condition that he would cooperate with the Chinese communists. Mikhail Borodin, alias Mikhail Gruzenberg, was the representative of the Comintern, established in 1916, to the political regime that Sun Yat-sen then established in Canton. Vasily Blyukher led the Soviet military team that trained its military forces.

After the first United Front ended in 1927 in disaster for the Chinese communists, the Comintern sent Yakov Rudnik and Tatyana Moiseenko to establish a new secret liaison department in Shanghai to funnel documents and money to the CCP and other communist parties in East and Southeast Asia. Following their arrest in 1931, the "Noulens Affair" – referring to the aliases the two used – became a major international affair. H. G. Wells, Albert Einstein, Henri Barbusse, Madame Sun Yat-sen, and others established a defense committee to plead their

---

[1] For a new history of the founding of the CCP emphasizing its international linkages, see Ishikawa Yoshihiro, *Chugoku Kyosanto Seiritsu Shi* (Tokyo: Iwanami Shoten, 2006).

case.[2] The Sorge Spy Ring also functioned out of Shanghai before moving to Tokyo.[3] Shanghai was a magnet for Western progressives drawn to the Revolution in China. Freda Utley, Edgar Snow, Agnes Smedley, Anna Louise Strong, and Rewi Alley made their way to China in the 1930s, as would George Hatem, an American physician of Lebanese descent who would become one of Mao's doctors.[4]

Initially, Paris, a magnate for left-wing revolutionaries, bohemians, and writers from across the world in the 1920s, had attracted many young Chinese revolutionaries, including Deng Xiaoping. Others went to Germany, Britain, or America, such as economist Chen Hansheng, who gained an M.A. degree at the University of Chicago and a Ph.D. at Berlin University. As the links with Moscow strengthened, Moscow became the destination of choice. Liu Shaoqi, the CCP's number two until his death during the Cultural Revolution, was among the first eight students to go to Moscow in 1920 after having studied Russian with the wife of Grigory Voitinsky in Shanghai.[5] Following the establishment of Sun Yat-sen University in Moscow in 1925, many other Chinese communists followed, including Zhang Wentian, Bo Gu, and Wang Ming, all of whom had stellar careers in the CCP.

These international networks came under strain in the 1930s. In China, they first were damaged by the Nationalist Party seizure of power and the perhaps fortuitous but nonetheless significant successes of Western colonial powers to disrupt them. The arrest in 1931 of Gu Shunzhang, the communist spy chief, and the Noulenses was a first blow.[6] Gu revealed many CCP addresses in Shanghai, forcing CCP decision-making bodies and leading communists to move out of Shanghai to the Jiangxi Soviet headed by Mao Zedong. Communications and travel became more difficult. Although relations between the Shanghai group and Mao were strained, in part because of Mao's ruthless purge of local Jiangxi communists,[7] the differences were papered over as the Jiangxi Soviet faced a series of determined nationalist onslaughts.

---

[2] Frederick Litten, "The Noulens Affair," *China Quarterly* 138 (June 1994), pp. 492–512.

[3] Charles Willoughby, *The Sorge Spy Ring* (New York: Dutton, 1952).

[4] Edgar Porter, *The People's Doctor: George Hatem and China's Revolution* (Honolulu: University of Hawaii Press, 1997).

[5] Lowell Dittmer, *Liu Shao-ch'i and the Chinese Cultural Revolution* (Berkeley: University of California Press, 1974).

[6] Ma Zhendu, *Guomindang Tewu Huodong Shi* [History of GMD Intelligence Activities] (Beijing: Jiuzhou Chubanshe, 2008), pp. 62–73; F. Litten, "The Noulens Affair".

[7] Stephen Averill, "The Origins of the Futian Incident," in Tony Saich and Hans van de Ven, eds., *New Perspectives on the Chinese Communist Revolution* (Armonk,

Communist cosmopolitanism suffered from the emergence in the early 1930s of intellectual misgivings about the New Culture Movement's rejection of Chinese traditions. Chen Boda, Ai Siqi, Zhou Yang, Zhang Ruxin, Chen Hansheng, He Ganzhi, and Yang Song were communist writers, historians, and scholars who had emerged in the highly literate environment of the lower Yangzi, with its rich traditions of scholarship, education, reading, conversation, and argument.[8] Many had traveled abroad, and most stayed in Shanghai until its occupation by Japan in November 1937. As the Japanese threat loomed ever larger, and as Soviet policy seemed increasingly to serve the interests of the Soviet Union, they called into question the New Culture Movement's extreme rejection of the Chinese past, seeking to locate in it domestic Chinese resources for resistance and revolution.

Qu Qiubai, the "tender-hearted communist" who ousted Chen Duxiu in 1927 as CCP secretary general and was executed in 1935,[9] argued for a new vernacular for written Chinese to be based on the spoken Chinese of urban workers rather than the form espoused during the New Culture Movement, which featured long sentences, foreign loan words, and complicated grammatical constructions.[10] Chen Boda, who made key contributions to the development of "Mao Zedong Thought," argued that Marxism-Leninism should not be slavishly adopted from abroad but developed so that it could be both Chinese and Marxist.[11] Chen called for the integration of "Marxist theory with the practical politics of China."[12] Zhou Yang espoused a "national defense literature" based on national forms.[13]

Communist cosmopolitanism also weakened because of Soviet foreign policy ruled by a fear of a two-front war with Germany in the West and Japan in the East. The result was the infamous 1939 Molotov-Ribbentrop pact between the Soviets and the Germans. In Asia, Stalin's policy aimed at drawing the Japanese into a Chinese quagmire. Believing that the marginalized Chinese communists were too weak to form

---

NY: M. E Sharpe, 1995), pp. 79–115; Chen Yung-fa, "The Futian Incident and the AB League," *Republican China* 9:2 (1994), pp. 1–47.

[8] Raymond Wylie, *The Emergence of Maoism: Mao Tse-tung, Ch'en Po-ta and the Search for Chinese Theory, 1934–1945* (Palo Alo, CA: Stanford University Press, 1980), p. 99.

[9] Hsia Tsi-an, *Gate of Darkness* (Seattle: University of Washington Press, 1969).

[10] Paul Pickowicz, *Marxist Literary Thought in China: The Influence of Chü Chü-pai* (Berkeley: University of California Press, 1981).

[11] Wylie, *Maoism*, pp. 22–23.

[12] *Ibid.*, p. 30.

[13] *Ibid.*, pp. 23–24.

the basis for a serious resistance movement to Japan in China, Stalin decided to support the Nationalists. During the December 1936 "Xi'an Incident," he forced the Chinese communists to disgorge Chiang Kai-shek (Jiang Jieshi), whom they and the warlords Zhang Xueliang and Yang Hucheng had imprisoned. Soviet diplomatic measures tested the faith of those who looked toward Moscow for guidance, even if that faith proved as tenacious in China as it did in Europe and elsewhere.

THE RETURN OF WANG MING

Stalin dispatched the delegation including Wang Ming, Kang Sheng, and Vladimirov to Yan'an in November 1937 to secure a more fulsome CCP commitment to the United Front and the War of Resistance, which had begun in July 1937. By November, the Japanese had steamrollered over the Beijing-Tianjin area and had seized Shanghai after a three-month-long battle. Japanese forces were advancing toward Shanxi and the Nationalist capital at Nanjing. The CCP in China had joined the United Front and had accepted Chiang Kai-shek's leading position in the resistance but refused to put its own forces at serious risk. Shortly after the outbreak of war in Shanghai, at an enlarged Politburo meeting on August 22–25 Mao had insisted that Communist forces should engage only in limited guerrilla warfare in the Japanese rear. The meeting's resolution expressed doubt about the Nationalists' ability to lead the war effort.[14]

The war posed difficult choices for the CCP. Questions abounded: Was Chiang Kai-shek fully committed to war against Japan? Would he not simply use the opportunity to waste the forces of his domestic opponents, the warlords as well as the Communists?[15] If Chiang won and drove the Japanese out of China or, more likely, was able to bring them to the negotiating table, the Guomindang (GMD) would be seen as the savior of China. At the same time, if the Communists stood aside at this moment of deep national crisis, their reputation would suffer, as in fact it did.

Comintern policy called for broad left-wing movements against the fascist threat rather than just communist revolutions. This policy was a hard sell in China because the Nationalists and Communists had been fighting each other since 1927, with five Nationalist extermination

---

[14] "Resolution of the CC (Central Committee) on the Current Situation," in Tony Saich, ed., *The Rise to Power of the Chinese Communist Party* (Armonk, NY: M. E. Sharpe, 1996), pp. 791–792, and "Three Telegrams from Mao Zedong on the Issue of Guerrilla Warfare [September 1937 and April 1938]," in *ibid.*, pp. 792–794.

[15] Saich, ed., *Rise*, p. 669.

campaigns having succeeded in driving the Communists from their central China bases in the 1931–34 period. Yet Wang fell in with Comintern policy when he called for a United Front with the Nationalists from 1935. The CCP's delegation with the Comintern that year issued the August 1 Manifesto for this purpose. Mao's Long Marchers back in China must have been astonished. Their number had dwindled from 100,000 to less then 10,000.

Days after his arrival in China, Wang succeeded in convening a Central Committee meeting. He argued that the key question was "how to achieve the victory of the War of the Resistance." In this moment of national crisis, he maintained, the CCP should gear all its actions to supporting the United Front: "[R]esistance is above everything and everything should serve the United Front."[16] In a pointed attack on Mao, he stated, "[S]ome comrades do not understand the United Front and want to wreck it."[17]

Wang's call for greater commitment to the United Front had traction within the CCP. Several participants at the meeting made self-criticisms.[18] One Mao critic, Ren Zhuoxuan, had been a long-time CCP member but joined the GMD during the war. He drew an analogy between Mao and Li Zicheng. At the end of the Ming Dynasty, Li had raised a peasant army and overthrown the Ming but had thereby created the opportunity for the Manchus to seize Beijing and establish the Qing Dynasty that lasted from 1644 until 1912.[19] Ren implied that Mao's lukewarm attitude toward the war might well end Nationalist rule but could lead to a China under lasting Japanese control.

Wang Ming's December 1937 Central Committee meeting changed leadership arrangements. While Mao, forced to agree that "we underestimated the changes in the GMD after the beginning of the War,"[20] continued to preside over military affairs. Wang Ming assumed responsibility for United Front affairs, whereas Zhang Wentian, who also had spent considerable time in Moscow, managed party matters. A Yangzi Bureau to be located in Wuhan would lead the CCP in the south. Its members were Xiang Ying, Zhou Enlai, Bo Gu, and Dong Biwu, most of whom had international experience. A preparatory committee was established to convene a new party congress to articulate new policies and make more drastic leadership changes.

[16] Ibid., p. 796.
[17] Jin Chongji, ed., *Mao Zedong Zhuan 1893–1949* [Biography of Mao Zedong, 1893–1949] (Beijing: Zhongyang Wenxian Chubanshe, 1996), pp. 506–507.
[18] Ibid., p. 511.
[19] Wylie, *Maoism*, p. 143.
[20] Jin, ed., *Mao, 1893–1949*, p. 507.

Developments on the ground quickly ended Wang Ming's challenge to Mao's leadership. In April 1938, a much hyped victory at the Battle of Taierzhuang in northern China had briefly electrified the country, but Japanese forces defeated the Nationalists shortly afterwards at Xuzhou. Chiang Kai-shek succeeded in preventing their immediate march on Wuhan by blowing up the Yellow River dikes. The flood inundated large areas and stopped the Japanese in their tracks, but at huge cost to Chinese life and property. The Japanese regrouped quickly, and during the summer the Japanese armies advanced along both shores of the Yangzi River toward Wuhan, which fell in October 1938. China sank into pessimism because the future looked bleak. The Nationalists retreated to Chongqing in the far west to continue their resistance from the agriculturally rich but isolated province of Sichuan. Others returned to their home regions. The United Front continued, but what Chinese communists refer to as the "first high tide of friction" between the CCP and the GMD welled up in the fall of 1939.

The capitulation on October 25, 1938, of Wuhan effectively spelled the end of Wang Ming's challenge to Mao. Wuhan was to have been China's Madrid, that is, the place where opponents of the Japanese – communists, nationalists, and warlords – would come together to make a common stand against Japan. For a while, it seemed to work. The CCP Central Committee met for its Sixth Plenum from September 29 to November 6, 1938, just as the battle for Wuhan raged. The plenum opened with Wang Ming and Mao Zedong sounding relatively harmonious. Yet, when Wuhan fell, Mao turned on Wang. He characterized his approach to the United Front as selling out to the GMD, insisted again that the CCP had to retain independence of military command, and demanded that its forces restrict themselves to limited guerrilla operations in the Japanese rear. He denied that the CCP should abandon covert activities during the war. Wang, Mao stated, had focused exclusively on the cities and had neglected the countryside and the peasantry, who were the real basis for revolution in China.[21] Returning from Moscow, Wang Jiaxiang, then the CCP representative with the Comintern, relayed an oral message from Georgi Dimitrov, its Bulgarian head, sanctioning the policies that the CCP had followed toward the United Front from the beginning of the war, thus declining to support Wang Ming's attack on Mao. He announced that the Comintern approved Mao's leading position in the CCP. Wang Ming could not but acknowledge that "the party must unite under Mao Zedong's leadership."[22]

---

[21] Mao Zedong, "On the New Stage," in Saich, ed., *Rise*, p. 813.
[22] Jin, ed., *Mao, 1893–1949*, p. 625.

THE RECTIFICATION MOVEMENT

Yet Mao would pursue Wang Ming with unremitting enmity from then until 1945, when the "Resolution of the Central Committee of the CCP on Certain Historical Questions" made Wang responsible for all the disasters that had befallen the CCP since 1931 and anointed Mao as China's own "Communist Great" who had rescued the party by correctly applying the general truths of Marxism-Leninism to the unique situation in China.[23] Wang was for Mao a straw man to drive through his Sinified form of Marxism-Leninism and the domestication of Communist Revolution. During 1942–44, Mao orchestrated the Yan'an Rectification Movement that aimed at instilling his vision into the CCP by having all party members engage in study sessions of, besides writings by Lenin and Stalin, his own and write criticisms and self-criticisms. They also were asked to analyze the history of the CCP using party documents selected by Mao to learn how the "dogmatism" of Wang Ming had generated a "deviationist" political line that had hugely damaged the CCP until Mao had rescued it at the 1935 Zunyi conference.

Power certainly was one of Mao's concerns. He used the Rectification Movement to make himself the supreme ruler of the CCP. A major step was reached in this process in 1943, when the Central Committee readjusted leadership arrangements. Mao was made chair of the Politburo that decided all major issues in between Central Committee meetings. A Secretariat made up of Mao, Liu Shaoqi, and Ren Bishi handled daily affairs, with Mao having the final say on all issues discussed by the Secretariat.[24] Because the Politburo rather than the Secretariat was responsible for setting general policy, Mao had not yet quite achieved full control, but at the 1945 Seventh Party Congress, Mao became chair of the Politburo, the Central Committee, the Central Committee Secretariat, and the Military Council. In the report accompanying the new party constitution that enshrined Mao Zedong Thought as the guide for Revolution in China, Liu Shaoqi hailed Mao as not only "the greatest revolutionary and statesman in Chinese history but also the greatest theoretician and scientist," whose development of Marxism had produced a guide for "the national democratic revolution in the colonial, semi-colonial, and feudal countries in the present period."[25] By 1945, Mao Zedong's power was overwhelming.

---

[23] "Resolution of the CCP CC on Certain Historical Questions," in Saich, ed., *Rise*, pp. 1164–1179.
[24] Jin, *Mao 1893–1949*, p. 649–650.
[25] Saich, ed., *Rise*, p. 1190.

The story of the fight against Wang Ming and the Rectification Movement is important in helping us understand how Mao inspired but also subordinated and even cowed strong and capable figures in the CCP. Some became loyal and even fanatical supporters of Mao, others ready supplicants, and yet others simply afraid, knowing the high cost of even loyal opposition. And as Mao's hold on power strengthened over subsequent decades, the consequence was that no one was able to stand up to Mao even when he adopted a path in the late 1950s that, although inspired by a grand vision for a Chinese socialist modernity, could only bring ruin.

The Rectification Movement was about much more, though, than Mao's drive for supreme power. Mao sought to develop and instill a unique Chinese revolutionary path. It had concrete prescriptions for military, political, and cultural policies. They included (1) a disciplined party rallied around Mao Zedong Thought; (2) large base areas in the countryside with a tight administrative apparatus (usually in border regions between provinces); (3) administrative organs and mass organizations in which the CCP had a controlling influence but which also drew in the broader population; and (4) people's warfare, characterized by reliance on guerrilla operations in the enemy rear by an army firmly under party control. Communist armed forces consisted of local militia, a higher level of armed units able to operate away from their home areas for a short period of time, and finally, the People's Liberation Army itself, which grew from a few divisions to a force of 1 million regulars during the war.[26]

CCP strategy during the war also included flexible participation in the United Front, always with the proviso that the Red Army would not concentrate on positional warfare, something from which it departed only during the One Hundred Regiments offensive of August 1940 to January 1941 and then only to a limited degree and apparently without Mao's blessing.[27] Rent- and interest-reduction measures, rather than land confiscations, were to demonstrate the benefits of CCP rule to the vast majority of people without alienating an excessively large number of

---

[26] A good overview of the CCP during World War II is Lyman Van Slyke, "The Chinese Communist Movement during the Second World War," in Denis Twitchett and John Fairbank, eds., *The Cambridge History of China*, Vol. 13, Part 2 (Cambridge, England: Cambridge University Press, 1986), pp. 609–722. An important recent contribution is Gao Hua, *Hong Taiyang Shi Zenyang Shengqide? Yan'an Zhengfeng Yundong de Lailong Qumai* (How the Red Sun Rose: The Origins and Development of the Rectification Movement) (Hong Kong: Chinese University of Hong Kong Press, 2000).

[27] In reality, this was a dispersed and fragmented offensive. See Lyman Van Slyke, "The Battle of the Hundred Regiments: Problems of Coordination and Control during the Sino-Japanese War," *Modern Asian Studies* 30:4 (1996), pp. 979–1005.

large land owners.[28] Bureaucratically, the CCP sought to develop small government that interacted in a mobilizational way with the population it governed. "From the masses, to the masses" was the formula that encapsulated the idea that governors and the governed would engage with each other in a constant process of dialogue. While the mass line did not at all imply some form of popular democracy or an aversion to firm government, it did envision a process whereby the governed could criticize their masters to prevent the emergence of an exploitative bureaucracy divorced from and even oppressing a people it was supposed to lead toward modernity.

If these were the concrete aspects of Mao's revolutionary path, the struggle against Wang Ming also was a drive to instill a sense of Chinese distinctness and of separation between China and international communism. By insisting that the path that Lenin had forged in the Soviet Union was not immediately replicable in China, Mao argued that Marxism-Leninism had to be thoroughly domesticated before it could be made useful for China. Culturally, Mao called for a literature and art that China's farmers could understand and that derived from China's past traditions in folk songs, village plays, calendars, music, and posters. The use of these may well have played a considerable role in the CCP's mobilizational success in part because it provided a way to link the CCP's Revolution with China's salvationary traditions.

Ideologically, the origins of the Rectification Campaign drew on a series of articles Mao wrote after the Long March. These included "Strategy in Opposing Japanese Imperialism," "The Question of Strategy in the Chinese Revolutionary War," "On Practice," "On Protracted Warfare," and "On the New Stage." In part intended to demonstrate that Mao was not merely very good at leading peasant armies and also to provide an alternative to the Chiang Kai-shek cult that the GMD was manufacturing, these contained many of the policy prescriptions mentioned earlier but also offered a theoretical defense for maintaining that Revolution in China would have to take a local Chinese form.

Mao made his strongest claims to theoretical innovativeness in lectures he gave in July and August 1937 at the Red Army University, later renamed the Central Party School. These lectures, of which one version of the notes is available, were published as two articles, "On Practice" and "On Contradiction," in 1950 and 1952. In "On Practice," Mao articulated a Marxist theory of cognition that stressed that knowledge

---

[28] Besides Van Slyke, "The Chinese Communist Movement," see also Mark Selden, *The Yen'an Way* (Cambridge, MA: Harvard University Press, 1971).

arose as people used concepts to understand the concrete situation in which they found themselves and then sought to formulate general principles to guide action. Mao wrote that "the most important question in Marxist philosophy ... is to change the world with this knowledge of the principles of the objective world."[29] Neither merely following foreign examples, which Mao termed "dogmatism," nor simply acting without reflecting on the general principles behind phenomena, that is, "empiricism," could lead to effective practice. In "On Contradiction," Mao argued that all phenomena had contradictions, that in each set of contradictions one was central, and that this one had a universal as well as a particular aspect. Only by identifying the main contradiction and grasping its universal and its particular aspects could effective forms of action be evolved. This meant, as Mao pointed out, that Lenin's theory of revolution could only be valid for one place and one time, even if Lenin's revolutionary praxis also had transcendental significance. To develop a sound policy for the Revolution in China, the Chinese communists would have to do their own thinking. These articles created the basis for claiming that the Chinese Revolution was different from the Soviet one but that this did not mean that it violated Marxism-Leninism.

The 1942–44 Rectification Campaign had its pragmatic side. The rapid expansion of the CCP, its mass organizations, and its armed forces during the first years of the war fueled fears that the party might be undermined from within. Mao Zedong noted in a telegram to General Peng Dehuai that 90 percent of its 800,000 members had joined after the beginning of the War of Resistance.[30] According to Mao, while that expansion was good, the many arrivals from urban coastal areas had no experience of the countryside and were unfamiliar with the CCP's policies. Rectification was "a struggle between proletarian and petit-bourgeois ideologies" aimed at compelling these new members to give up their former lifestyles, make them become acquainted with rural conditions, and accept party discipline – and to weed out infiltrators and spies.[31]

The interpretation of the party's own past was a key aspect of the Rectification Campaign. Already in October 1939, Mao had raised this as an issue by stating that at the Zunyi conference the CCP had begun to adopt a correct political line. This was a denial of Wang Ming's stance, which held that the policy of Bolshevization he had introduced at the

[29] Jin, ed., *Mao, 1893–1949*, p. 447.
[30] *Ibid.*, pp. 624–625.
[31] *Ibid.*, p, 639, quoting "Mao Zedong zai Zhongyang Xuexizu Fayan Jilu [Record of Mao Zedong's Speeches at the Central Study Group]," May 28, 1942.

Fourth Plenum of the Sixth Central Committee in December 1930 had marked that point. In March 1940, Wang republished *Fighting for the Further Bolshevization of the Chinese Communist Party*, noting in the Foreword that this piece was important to educate new party members. In response, Mao published his reports on rural investigations conducted between 1930 and 1933 to demonstrate that he had always based his policies on a Marxist-Leninist analysis of concrete conditions in China.[32] He collected materials from the CCP's history, which he presented to an expanded Politburo meeting of September 1941. The collection formed the evidence for Mao's argument that dogmatism and empiricism had been the cause of a political line since the Fourth Plenum that had led to the defeat of the Jiangxi Soviet. At the meeting, Mao also stated that the Zunyi conference had not merely adjusted military strategy but also had ensured that Wang Ming's erroneous ideological line had not been able to damage the CCP further. To counter the obvious point that in that case the Rectification Campaign was not necessary, Mao added that "the poison of subjectivism still exists."[33]

The rapid development of educational, publishing, and internal vetting organs formed the institutional foundation for Rectification. Since it became more difficult in the course of the 1930s for revolutionaries from across the world to travel to Moscow, from 1935 on the Comintern urged communist parties to establish their own educational institutions. The CCP established the Central Party School, the Marxism-Leninism Institute, the Anti-Japanese Military and Political University, the Lu Xun Academy of Arts and Letters, and the Academy of Natural Sciences.[34] Public and secret journals proliferated. In August 1941, the CCP established a Central Investigation Bureau to gather military and political intelligence, whereas the Central Organization Department served as a human resource department that generated assessments of its members to inform assignments. The Social Department, under the leadership of Kang Sheng, interrogated, arrested, and imprisoned or executed suspect party members.

The Rectification Movement began at the top and then gradually expanded down the institutional hierarchy. At an enlarged Politburo meeting in September 1941, Bo Gu (alias Qin Bangxian) – who had

[32] This collection would become *Liuda Yilai* [Since the Sixth Congress], published internally in 1950 and 1980 by the Office of the Central Committee of the CCP. The collection *Zhonggong Zhongyang Wenjian Xuanji* [Selection Documents of the CCP Central Committee] (Beijing: Central Party School, 1989–92) is based on this.

[33] Jin, ed., *Mao, 1893–1949*, p. 631.

[34] Wylie, *Maoism*, pp. 59–60.

studied at Sun Yat-sen University in Moscow, was an ally of Wang Ming, and had been CCP secretary general between 1932 and 1935 – stated in a self-criticism that "I was one of the main persons responsible for the errors made in the years between 1932 and 1935. We ... simply transferred to China some dogmas from the construction of socialism in the Soviet Union. Party resolutions were often simply copied from the Comintern."[35] A Central Research Group with Mao as its chair was formed to spearhead Rectification. Mao's speech, "Rectify the Party's Work Style" at the Central Party School in February 1942 marked the formal beginning of Rectification.[36] More than 10,000 cadres were put through Rectification in its first wave.[37]

Rectification provoked powerful responses and stubborn resistance, which, in turn, triggered a tough party crackdown, as the infamous Wang Shiwei case illustrates. A researcher at the Marxism-Leninism Institute, Wang had been at loggerheads throughout 1941 with Li Weihan (alias Lo Mai), its Maoist head, arguing that the adoption of traditional Chinese art forms would lead to subversion of the Marxist-Leninist content of the message.[38] In the spring of 1942, Wang published a criticism of life in Yan'an, fulminating against the privileged access of high cadres to food, clothing, medicine, and women. He also posted "Arrow and Target" as a wall poster that criticized Li Weihan in a waiting room of the Central Research Institute and at a busy marketplace. It drew huge crowds.[39] Wang's acts asserted a claim to moral independence for artists, defined as the duty of the artist to expose problems wherever he or she found them, and resisted the nationalization of Marxism-Leninism. Wang was dragged through numerous criticism sessions and eventually arrested and tortured. When the Nationalists drove the Communists from Yan'an in 1947, Wang was executed.

Mao convened the Yan'an Forum on Literature and Art between May 2 and 23, 1942. He insisted that artists in Yan'an must serve the CCP and adopt its standpoints; that they should produce work for workers, peasants, soldiers, and cadres in the base areas; and that they should employ artistic forms drawn from China's past. He depicted Yan'an's intellectuals as deeply corrupted by their prewar urban lifestyles: "They must change their ideologies and emotions; they must transform themselves. Without this, nothing will be achieved."[40]

[35] Jin, ed., *Mao, 1893–1949*, p. 632.
[36] *Ibid.*, p. 637.
[37] *Ibid.*, p. 638.
[38] Wylie, *Maoism*, pp. 147–149.
[39] Jin, ed., *Mao, 1893–1949*, p. 646.
[40] *Ibid.*, p. 642.

A year later, the campaign entered an even darker stage. The Central Committee issued "On Further Developing the Rectification Movement." It stated that the tasks of the movement were "the rectification of non-proletarian thinking among cadres and the elimination of counter-revolutionaries hidden in the party."[41] According to Mao, "Rectification is party cleansing in the ideological arena; the investigation of cadres is party cleansing in the organizational arena." Kang Sheng was put in charge of this phase of the campaign. Kang maintained that the first phase of Rectification had exposed the "counter-revolutionary ideological poison" of many members and that Wang Shiwei had led a conspiracy by a "five member Anti-Party Clique." He insisted that all confess their "evil" tendencies so that they then could become real Chinese:

> Why does the Communist Party make so much effort to rescue you? Simply because it wants you to be Chinese, and not be cheated into serving the enemy. Those of you who have lost your way, be conscious, take a firm decision, repent to the party, and cast off the special agent's garb ... and put on Chinese clothes.[42]

During the so-called rescue campaign, torture and executions became acceptable means in the party's hunt for supposed counterrevolutionaries after Kang Sheng claimed that in Yan'an alone there were 1,400 spies.[43]

The Rectification Campaign was many things. Mao used the struggle against the blind imitation of the Soviet example that Wang Ming supposedly represented to establish his supreme power in the CCP. It was a process used by Mao and his supporters to discipline the CCP around a single vision and gear it to work within a single set of policies toward the aim of achieving revolutionary victory. It also was a dispute about past history and future direction. But what I have sought to emphasize here is that the Rectification Campaign suppressed the globalizing and internationalizing strain in communism. The pathways that had been forged in the interbellum period were broken up not only because during the war practical problems made travel and international communication more difficult but also because Mao and his followers were bent on Sinifying Marxism-Leninism. As Kang Sheng stated, the party wanted its members "to be Chinese."

[41] Ibid., p. 652.
[42] David Apter and Tony Saich, *Revolutionary Discourse in Mao's Republic* (Cambridge, MA: Harvard University Press, 1994), p. 289.
[43] Jin, ed., *Mao, 1893–1949*, p. 653.

THE DEMISE OF COMMUNIST GLOBALIZATION
IN THE EARLY YEARS OF THE PRC

On the evening of September 25, 1949, Mao Zedong convened a meeting in Zhongnanhai, the eastern part of the Forbidden City housing the communist leadership, to prepare for ceremonies to mark the establishment of the PRC a week later. In the 10 years before they arrived at this extraordinary moment, about to declare the founding of a new state, much had happened. Japan's best effort had failed to bring the Nationalists or the Communists to their knees, despite numerous military campaigns, a terror bombing campaign against cities in unoccupied China that lasted two years, and the "Three All" – Burn All, Kill All, Loot All – campaign against communist base areas. While the United Front between the Nationalists and the Communists had lasted for the duration, three periods of "friction" illustrated that even during the War of Resistance the two parties could not work together.

After the Japanese surrender on August 15, 1945, efforts to forestall civil war rapidly failed despite American mediation. While the Communists rushed to occupy Manchuria, which the Soviets had occupied in the last weeks of the war, the Nationalists' return from Sichuan Province to their prewar bases in China's coastal areas was hopelessly mismanaged. Inflation, corruption, score settling between stay-behinders and returnees, and continued malaise in the international trading order prevented the reconsolidation of GMD power. The expectations for a fairer social order and a better life, without the injustices, grinding poverty, and social inequalities of prewar days, ran high in China as elsewhere. The Nationalists could not meet these longings for a new start. While in the first phase of the 1946–49 Civil War, Nationalist armies defeated Communist forces, by 1948 the tide had turned decisively. In three massive campaigns in Manchuria and northern China in late 1948 and early 1949, the Communists defeated their Nationalist opponents. Nationalist resistance crumbled, and Chiang Kai-shek moved his remnant forces to Taiwan.

In attendance at the Zhongnanhai meeting were CCP members such as Zhou Enlai, the writer Mao Dun, and the poet-politician Guo Moruo, as well as eminent nonparty figures, such as educationalist Huang Yanpei, economist Ma Yinchu, painter and calligrapher Xu Beihong, and overseas Chinese magnate Tan Kah Kee. The topic of discussion was the choice of a national flag and anthem for the People's Republic of China. Mao favored a red flag with five golden stars because "it represents the strong unity of our revolutionary people."[44] The "March of the Volunteers," with lyrics by the playwright Tian Han and music by Nie Er, was chosen as China's national anthem. Composed in 1935 as tensions with Japan had mounted, it became widely popular during the war. Guo Moruo objected to the line "The Chinese nation faces its moment of greatest peril," suggesting instead "The Chinese people are now emancipated." The original wording was retained after Zhou Enlai argued that the words remained apt; the CCP's victory inevitably would increase imperialist hostility toward China.[45] Six days later at 3 o'clock in the afternoon, some 300,000 people in Tiananmen Square sang "The March of the Volunteers" while the five-starred flag rose up a flagpole as the PRC was inaugurated.

Just before this, Mao Zedong had declared that China would "lean to one side," by which he meant that it would side with the Soviet Union. The Chinese economy was in chaos. China needed the mantle of Soviet protection against possible hostile powers such as the United States and Japan, as well as Soviet material aid and expert advice to develop its economy and build up an industrial base without which modernization would be impossible. The Sino-Soviet Friendship Treaty of February 1950 and creation of the Soviet bloc in Eastern Europe held the promise of a postwar revival in communist globalization centered on the Soviet Union. But this moment soon passed, and Mao would strike out on his own to push through a breakthrough to modernity independent of the Soviet Union. Tensions that had been building up between China and the Soviet Union since the mid-1950s became public at a 1960 Congress of the Romanian Communist Party when Chinese and Soviet delegates engaged in a verbal slinging match.

In 1949, the PRC faced two immediate and hugely difficult problems: The first was how to stamp violence out of Chinese society, and the second was how to halt rampant inflation and restore the economy. By introducing a new currency, confiscating hoarded goods, closing banks and stock exchanges, and adopting a wage-point system for city workers that tied salaries to the price of a basket of essential commodities, inflation was under control by 1950. The rapid restoration of railroad lines and waterways with the help of the People's Liberation Army (PLA) to ensure supplies to Shanghai, Tianjin, Beijing, and other cities also helped to dampen inflation. No doubt some very tough action

---

[44] Quoted from a record of the meeting. Pang Xianzhi and Jin Chongji, ed., *Mao Zedong Zhuan, 1949–1976* (Beijing: Zhongyang Wenxian Chubanshe, 2003), pp. 4–5.
[45] *Ibid.*, p. 5.

by the PLA, as it occupied newly liberated areas, imposed martial law, and rounded up bandits, as well as during the land reform campaign of 1950–52 when land and property of large landlords and rich peasants were expropriated, was necessary to remove the weapons from Chinese society. China's new rulers were inheritors of the tough, even ruthless pragmatic strain in Chinese politics that, for instance, also had come to the fore during the Taiping Rebellion a century earlier – when Confucian generals showed no mercy in the suppression of the rebellion, razing Nanjing to the ground – and did so again in 1989 during the Tiananmen Square demonstrations.

But they were also revolutionaries, impatient to change their country, establish a new economic, social, and political order, and restore national pride. As important as changing class relations and hence ownership of land, factories, and businesses was cultural change. Opium smoking was prohibited, as was concubinage, child marriage, and foot binding. Supposedly backward religious practices were proscribed, as were many festivals and ceremonies. Instead, people were made to gather for political discussion meetings and mass rallies. Such proscriptions went hand in hand with monumentalist building programs, such as the laying of the first railroad and bus bridge over the Yangzi River at Wuhan, the construction of large dams and hydroelectric plants, and the building of reservoirs, canals, and dikes.[46] China became a country of blue ants as fashionable dress, haircuts, and popular forms of entertainment such as banqueting and Chinese opera went out and workmanlike Mao clothes became ubiquitous. The new China was to be clean in mind, in bodily practices, and in social and private behavior – rather than dirty, selfish, and corrupt as foreigners had so long said China to be.

The impatience to construct a Chinese socialist modernity drove the CCP to increasingly radical measures. Just before the founding of the PRC, Mao had argued in "On the People's Democratic Dictatorship" that the "people" included the urban working class, the peasantry, the petit-bourgeoisie, and the national bourgeoisie. Only the large landowners and GMD reactionaries were identified as "enemies," but even these were to be accommodated. If revolutionary impatience made it unlikely that this moderate stance would hold for long,[47] the Korean War (1950–53) would accelerate the lurch toward breakthrough development.

[46] Judith Shapiro, *Mao's War Against Nature: Man and the Environment in Revolutionary China* (New York: Cambridge University Press, 2001).

[47] Yang Kuisong, "The Evolution of the Chinese Communist Party's Policy on the Bourgeoisie, 1949–1952," *Journal of Modern Chinese History* 1:1 (August 2007), pp. 13–30.

After the U.S. intervention in Korea, Mao Zedong insisted against considerable opposition within the CCP leadership that the PRC should dispatch Chinese People's Volunteers to fight alongside their North Korean comrades to forestall an imperialist victory on the Korean peninsula. Mao feared that the Americans would not stop at China's borders but would broaden the war to overthrow his regime. Intervention in Korea presented China's armed forces and administrative organs with an entirely new challenge: how to supply its troops in Korea with food, clothing, blankets, arms, and ammunition over very long distances. In the past, PLA units had essentially lived off the land. While the government's purchases fueled an economic boom, it also led to corruption and fraud as government and party officials colluded with private businesses. The Korean War generated a panic about internal traitors and spies believed to have been left behind by the Nationalists in preparation for a return to the mainland. In 1951, the CCP initiated Rectification-style campaigns to combat these two problems.

Even before the founding of the PRC, the CCP had established revolutionary universities to retool urban managerial and entrepreneurial elites by having them study Mao Zedong's writings and CCP policy. The regime in these hardened as the twin fears about corruption and internal traitors intensified. Those sent to revolutionary universities, who may have numbered hundreds of thousands, if not a million people, were compelled to write confessions and participate in criticism meetings. In 1951, the CCP began three interlinked campaigns: the Savings Campaign and the Three and Five Anti Campaigns. The Savings Campaign required government organs to produce accounts of their assets to uncover illegal earnings over the past couple of years. Many had no doubt laid in stocks of grain, precious metals, cooking oil, and foreign currency during the last years of the Civil War to deal with high inflation and the coming transition to a new government. The Three Anti Campaign against Corruption, Sloth, and Bureaucratism in government, army, and party organizations was pressed after it emerged that hundreds of high-level party members, including many with stellar pre-1949 revolutionary careers, had taken millions in bribes.[48] Raiding the reserves of government organs also helped to defray the cost of the intervention in Korea. In the spring of 1952, this campaign turned into a witch-hunt against so-called big tigers and little tigers, defined according to the amount of their illegal gains. Mao declared that the tigers

---

[48] Pang and Jin, ed., *Mao, 1949–1976*, pp. 216–218.

were "... enemies who betrayed the people. If we don't uncover and punish them, they will do endless damage."[49]

The fear was that government and party corruption would create a basis for bourgeois restoration. The Five Anti Campaign against Bribery, Tax Evasion, Fraud, False Reporting, Cheating on Government Contracts, and Stealing Secret Economic Information targeted merchants and businessmen in China's large- and medium-sized cities. The national bourgeoisie was no longer an ally who could help with the rebuilding of the Chinese economy but an enemy. "No capitalist is clean,"[50] CCP leaders declared. The CCP had to "fight off the violent counter-attack of the bourgeoisie."[51]

The human cost of these campaigns was high. The requirement to inform on family, friends, and acquaintances and the pressure to finger tigers tore up human networks. Suicides were common. The economic cost was huge. During the spring of 1952, many government bureaucracies, especially those dealing with financial issues, trade, and taxation, became paralyzed.[52] Output of consumer products dropped to 30 percent, whereas production of industrial materials fell to 15 percent. Many private companies closed, and construction workers were thrown into unemployment. In some cities, food riots broke out. By 1953, the campaigns had to be reined in.

In the wake of the collapse of the "New Democracy" model for the social and economic development of China, the CCP adopted an approach that depended on government control of agriculture to extract financial resources from rural production to finance industrial investment in urban areas. Mao Zedong was deeply committed to and even obsessed with heavy industry. In June 1954, he stated, "[T]oday we are able to produce tables and chairs, tea cups and pots, we can grow food, and even grind flour and manufacture paper, but we cannot make one car, one airplane, one tank, or one tractor."[53] In March 1955, he declared, "[W]e have arrived at a new stage in history. We must ... in a couple of decades complete the basic industrialization of the country ... and catch up or surpass the most advanced capitalist countries of the world."[54]

[49] *Ibid.*, p. 213.
[50] Quoted in Yang, "Evolution of CCP Policy," p. 24.
[51] *Ibid.*, quoting "CCP CC Directive on First Developing the Five Anti Movement in Large and Middle Cities," pp. 53–54.
[52] Pang and Jin, ed., *Mao, 1949–1976*, ed., pp. 213–215.
[53] *Ibid.*, p. 273.
[54] *Ibid.*, p. 285.

The First Five-Year Plan, valid for the 1953–57 period, depended on central procurement and distribution of agricultural production, especially grains, to finance investment in capital goods production. Already in 1950 the PRC had centralized fiscal authority to curtail spending by provincial and local governments. In 1952, a State Statistical Bureau and State Planning Committee were established, and a large number of vertically organized industrial ministries were formed to control industrial development.[55] In the countryside, land reform in 1949 and 1950 had broken the power of landlords. In the following years, first the introduction of Mutual Aid Teams, which pooled labor, and then Agricultural Producer Cooperatives, in which peasants shared all property and were paid according to their labor, increased the party-state's control over the countryside, although it also fit visions of a socialist future.[56]

This approach was heavily indebted to Soviet economic models, expert advice, engineers, loans, and capital goods. Initially, the plan seemed to work. National income grew at nearly 9 percent annually, industrial output grew at 18.9 percent, and life expectancies jumped from 36 to 57 years. Urban housing standards improved as a result of the building of 100 million square meters of living accommodation, and urban incomes rose 40 percent (as opposed to an increase in living costs of 10 percent).[57] Yet the countryside suffered: Grain output in 1953 grew at only 2.5 percent and at 1.6 percent the next year, failing to keep pace with population growth. Cotton production in 1954 fell by 9 percent.[58] The shock discovery resulting from the 1953 census that China's population at nearly 600 million was far larger than previously assumed, plus a rapidly increasing birth rate, added to the sense that if something radical was not done, the disappointing economic growth, especially in the countryside, might lead to disaster.

Mao's relations with Stalin had never been comfortable. He had told Edgar Snow in 1936, who had asked whether a CCP victory would lead to some form of merger with the Soviet Union, "[W]e are not fighting for an emancipated China to turn the country over to Moscow."[59] Mao had found discussions with Stalin in Moscow in late 1949 and early 1950

---

[55] Nicholas R. Lardy, "Economic Recovery and the 1st Five-Year Plan," in Twitchett and Fairbank, eds., *Cambridge History of China*, Vol. 14, Cambridge, England: Cambridge University Press, 1987), pp. 158–160.

[56] Fredrick C. Teiwes, "Establishment and Consolidation of the New Regime," in *ibid.*, p. 110.

[57] Lardy, "Economic Recovery," pp. 155–156.

[58] *Ibid.*, p. 161.

[59] Stuart R. Schram, "Mao Tse-tung from 1949 to 1976," in Twitchett and Fairbank, eds., *Cambridge History of China*, Vol. 15, (Cambridge, England: Cambridge University Press, 1991), p. 54.

difficult and had persisted only "out of consideration for the interests of socialism."[60] In the early 1960s, Mao looked back to the early years of the PRC and remarked. "[W]e copied almost everything from the Soviet Union," showing "weakness – a lack of creativity and lack of ability to stand on our own feet."[61]

In 1956, Mao was angered when without prior notification the gaffe-prone and occasionally boorish Nikita Khrushchev denounced Stalin's personality cult and Stalin's crimes during the purges of the 1930s. Mao Zedong, too, was critical of Stalin, especially of the way he handled internal dissent and class struggle, had intervened in the Chinese Revolution with uneven success, and had failed to treat him as an equal during his first visit to Moscow. But Mao also opposed Khrushchev's denunciation of Stalin, arguing that Stalin had been 70 percent good.[62] Mao worried about Khrushchev's switch in economic policy in favor of the production of consumer goods, his relaxation of domestic suppression, his failure to consult about international issues, and his search for peaceful coexistence with capitalist countries. Combined with irritation at the behavior of some Soviet advisors in China, serious difficulties in the relationship had emerged.

The relationship ruptured completely when Mao Zedong abandoned the Soviet model and opted for a Chinese way with the Great Leap Forward – a push to achieve socialism politically, culturally, and economically in one giant leap. Before this, Mao attempted to demonstrate that the PRC could deal with internal dissent and social conflict better than the Soviets. Following the rapid success of land reform and collectivization but also after a revolt against the Soviets in Hungary in 1956 and Khrushchev's denunciation of Stalin's purges, Mao insisted that the CCP should "Let a hundred flowers bloom and let a hundred schools of thought contend." The resulting storm of antiparty criticism led to a quick reassertion of controls. Mao also began the Great Leap to remake China into a shining socialist society with an industrial base larger than Britain's and a proud, energetic, public-minded people. All of society was reorganized into semiautonomous communes of about 5,000 families each. Commune members were to live in dormitories, eat in cafeterias, and work according to a common work plan. If a utopian fever first took hold, hunger and famine soon dispelled the notion that self-reliance and revolutionary fervor alone could produce a new future. Even if Mao's stature was diminished for some time, his power

[60] *Ibid.*, p. 56.
[61] *Ibid.*, p. 57.
[62] *Ibid.*, p. 59.

nonetheless was so certain that it would take his death to end China's isolation and make it possible for China to reengage with the world – to the benefit of many.

CONCLUSION

Lenin believed the arrival of modernity in Russia was prevented by blockages that could be removed only by revolution. By the turn of the twentieth century, England had long industrialized, and Germany, France, the United States, and Western Europe generally had quickly caught up, but Russia and other Eastern European countries had stagnated. At a time when belief in the struggle for survival of the fittest was widespread, Lenin concluded that a violent and rapid breakthrough was needed to remove the blockages standing in the way of the takeoff of modernity in Russia. The hierarchical Leninist Party, organizing and commanding the party membership as the German General Staff coordinated German armed forces, was his tool to achieve that breakthrough. Mao may have departed from orthodox Marxism-Leninism by insisting that the Chinese Revolution had to go through the countryside. But after 1949, the CCP returned to the cities, and Mao then searched for a way to make the breakthrough that Lenin too had longed for. No matter how thoroughly Mao Sinified Marxism-Leninism, he remained in that sense a Leninist at heart.

Mao miscalculated not only in believing that China could make a rapid transition to a Chinese socialist modernity in one big push. In the circumstances of the cold war and the deepening split with the Soviet Union, he sought to demonstrate that China could achieve a Leninist breakthrough without foreign assistance or advice and even in complete isolation. As soon as he came to power, Deng Xiaoping reopened China's doors. For all the manifold differences with the globalization of the interwar period, its vitality, dynamism, creativity, movement, and energy returned almost immediately.

This hints at the possibility of a broader historical perspective. During the seventeenth and eighteenth centuries, the great Qing monarchs Kangxi, Yongzheng, and Qianlong created a strongly centralized Qing Empire that conquered vast new areas, almost doubling its territorial size. From the early nineteenth century, for reasons still to be fully fathomed, although the drainage of the country's silver stock was an important factor, the Qing armies weakened, social problems led to distress and rebellion, and regionalization undermined Beijing's control. Beset as well by Western imperialism, the center failed the hold. Warlords established virtually independent satrapies during the Republican period. Mao's Sinification of Marxism-Leninism; his insistence on China, China, China in all things; and his centralization of power (be it in his own hands) led to the reunification of China. Whether that will last or not – Beijing is fading once more – there is no doubt that this is an important part of his legacy.

The two decades between 1937 and 1956 formed the defining period in Mao's life. It began just after the defeat of the Jiangxi Soviet and the Long March and ended on the eve of the Great Leap Forward. Largely because of Mao, the CCP not only had kept together during World War II but also had devised an effective rural strategy to achieve power. By insisting that China was different from the Soviet Union and that Chinese communists would have to think for themselves and stand on their own legs, Mao had restored pride. But the turn to autarky and isolation, no matter how understandable in the context of World War II and against the background of widespread lack of self-belief and even self-hatred, would prove disastrous when during the cold war Mao Zedong went all out for a Leninist breakthrough.

5 Consuming Fragments of Mao Zedong: The Chairman's Final Two Decades at the Helm

MICHAEL SCHOENHALS

Every people puts its own scent on its food, and it accepts change only if it can conceal the change from itself, by smothering each novelty in its scent. Optimism about change, whether in politics, economics or culture, is only possible if this premise is accepted.

Theodore Zeldin, *An Intimate History of Humanity*, 1994[1]

Nikita Khrushchev was not to Mao's taste. The Chairman of the Chinese Communist Party (CCP) showed no craving for *gulyáskommunizmus*. He hungered for something ... er ... different. In the remarkable art film *The Ming Tombs Reservoir Fantasy* from 1958 (in which Mao appears briefly in person), we are served a sampling of what it may have been.[2] Set in 1978, ten years after the liberation of Taiwan, with New China well into the "higher phase of communist society [when] ... all the springs of co-operative wealth flow more abundantly," the film has young revolutionaries gathering in the shade of a tree from the branches of which grow bananas, apples, pears, loquats, *lizhi* ... and living among farmers who each rear an average of 365 pigs a day to meet some of the dietary needs of a population that has found a cure for cancer (massive quantities of Turfan grapes) and whose members live to the ripe old age of well past a hundred.[3] It is a unique record of the utopia of Mao's Great Leap Forward, a sweet Chinese dream of plenty.

Poverty, Mao had argued a few months prior to the shooting of *The Ming Tombs Reservoir Fantasy*, gave rise to a powerful desire for

I wish to thank Jie-Hyun Lim and the Research Institute of Comparative History and Culture, Hanyang University, for organizing and inviting me to the Sixth International Conference on Mass Dictatorships (Seoul, June 2008), at which a version of this chapter was first presented.

[1] Theodore Zeldin, *An Intimate History of Humanity* (London: Harper Perennial, 1994), p. 95.
[2] *Shisanling shuiku changxiangqu*, based on a play by Tian Han, directed by Jin Shan, and produced by the Beijing Film Studio.
[3] Karl Marx, *Critique of the Gotha Programme*. Available at www.marxists.org/archive/marx/works/1875/gotha/cho1.htm.

change (*bian*).[4] Perhaps the blandest of words expressing the act or instance of becoming different, "change" was in Mao's conceptual universe intimately related to epistemology – knowledge, as understood by him, both stimulating and feeding on change. In 1958, after two years of digesting the implications of its direction in the Soviet Union since the Twentieth Congress of the Communist Party of the Soviet Union (CPSU) and its progress in China since the forced abortion of the "Socialist Upsurge" of 1956 (aka the First Leap Forward), Mao set about to pursue change barely distinguishable from chaos. Chaos came with "the immense advantages of chaos," he was to assert in 1964, and it was on this very point that Mao's evolutionary thinking was in fact cutting-edge. As Stuart Kauffman's and Christopher Langton's research has since suggested, being "on the edge of chaos ... provides the greatest evolvability."[5] It was away from an oppressive past by way of an imperfect present that Mao sought *at any cost* to evolve China into a communist society. For fellow revolutionaries of his own generation satisfied with anything less than living on the border of disorder, he had only contempt. Pride in progress was fine, but contentment was revisionist! On the first day of the year 1976, his last at the helm of the CCP, China's radio stations broadcast a poem in which Mao's communist roc interrupted a revisionist sparrow salivating over the prospect of piping hot potatoes and beef in the land of plenty, telling her, "Quit farting! Look, the world is being turned topsy turvy!"[6]

In what follows, Mao's reflections on the subjects of change and knowledge bulk up a chronocollage of the final two decades of his life – from the Great Leap Forward and the nightmare famine that followed to the "Four Cleanups" and successive "revolutions within the Chinese revolution."[7] Taking my cue from Richard J. Parmentier's *The Sacred Remains* and being aware of how ideology undoubtedly seasons *all* sources, I make no attempt at straining out false consciousness in order to lay bare a "raw truth" behind the dissimulation of Mao's extant *oeuvre* but seek instead to uncover in the metaphors of the man the principles

---

[4] *Jianguo yilai Mao Zedong wengao* (Manuscripts of Mao Zedong Since the Founding of the Nation) (Beijing: Zhongyang wenxian chubanshe, 1992), Vol. 7, p. 178.

[5] Edward O. Wilson, *Consilience: The Unity of Knowledge* (New York: Alfred A. Knopf, 1998), pp. 88–90. See also www.edge.org/3rd_culture/kauffman03/kauffman_index.html and www.santafe.edu/research/publications/workingpapers/93–06–040.pdf; accessed February 9, 2008.

[6] I was there. I heard the broadcast; *Jianguo yilai Mao Zedong wengao* (Beijing: Zhongyang wenxian chubanshe, 1996), Vol. 11, p. 466.

[7] See the title of John K. Fairbank and Roderick MacFarquhar, eds., *The Cambridge History of China*, Vol. 15: *The People's Republic*, Part 2: *Revolutions Within the Chinese Revolution 1966–1982* (Cambridge, England: Cambridge University Press, 1991).

of his ideological flavoring, coloring, and texturizing.[8] The visceral effectiveness of Mao's ideas always rested on the appeal of the metaphors he chose to work with. To recognize this is not altogether different from what students of creative writing learn to do early on: "Sensory details, telling details, the 'divine' detail, this is where the truth lies.... Fact: We had dinner at 6 p.m. Detail: We had dinner of roast chicken, boiled red potatoes, corn on the cob, and tomatoes. It was a little early for the corn...."[9] The reader be forewarned: This is not a paper in the literary or cultural vein, albeit that in its chosen methodology it attempts a transfer from one meaning to another through a personal operation based on impressions that the reader must experience for himself or herself.[10]

WHERE DO CORRECT IDEAS COME FROM?

Without the participation of intellectuals, victory in the revolution is impossible.

Mao Zedong, December 1, 1939

Much has been written about the broader political and historical context in which Mao's ideas ended up, in one form or another, on paper. Rather fewer attempts have been made to capture the intimate circumstances under which he produced what eventually became "Mao Zedong Thought." In recent years, however, the memoirs of former bodyguards and personal staffers have begun to throw fascinating new light on how some of Mao's most fertile ideas emerged after a prolonged process during which Mao, it turns out, was remarkably vulnerable.

Li Yinqiao, a former bodyguard of Mao's, recently fleshed out considerably the context that students of Mao Zedong Thought had to contend with in the past. The time: autumn of 1947. The place: northern China countryside. Mao, Li recalled, had been sitting at his desk, poring over maps, occasionally consulting the *Cihai* encyclopaedia and a dictionary, now and then grabbing his pen making notes, jotting something down. Li recalled:

Suddenly the CCP Chairman frowned and moments later grabbed some paper and headed for the door. I hurried along behind him. In the doorway he informed me: "I need to relieve myself. Bring along

---

8   Richard J. Parmentier, *The Sacred Remains: Myth, History, and Polity in Belau* (Chicago: University of Chicago Press, 1987), p. 2.

9   See www.judyreeveswriter.com/truth_in_details.htm; accessed January 2, 2008.

10   Slightly abbreviated definition of "metaphor" lifted from Bernard Dupriez, *A Dictionary of Literary Devices* (Toronto, Canada: University of Toronto Press, 1991), p. 276.

a shovel and help me dig a hole." I quickly grabbed a shovel and flashlight and, staying right behind Mao Zedong, headed out into the wild yonder on the outskirts of the village.[11]

Having dug a hole for Mao, Li stood by, keeping a watchful eye on the surroundings. Done, Mao turned to him on the way back and asked: "Tell me, when do you think is the best time to reflect upon a problem [*sikao wenti*]?" Li suggested that perhaps it was when lying in bed. "Wrong!" said Mao, moving closer to Li in the dark: "I'll tell you, it's when you shit. The best time to contemplate things [*xiang shiqing*] is while you're taking a shit."[12] Needless to say, ethnographic information of this sort forces historians to consider alternative readings of part of the CCP canon, most notably Mao's 1963 essay entitled, "Where Do Correct Ideas Come From?" in which he had asked: "Where do correct ideas come from? Do they drop from the skies? No. Are they innate in the mind? No. They come from social practice, and from it alone."[13]

Rather than dismiss the information leaked by Li Yinqiao as just so much rubbish, we need to let it feed our imagination – our thinking about Mao, about his politics, and about the nature of his relationship with the men and women around him. Marshal Lin Biao, prior to his demise in 1971, was described as Mao's "most outstanding pupil," although about *what* he learned from his teacher that earned him the epithet we know precious little. In the case of Premier Zhou Enlai – described in 1968 as "Chairman Mao's close comrade-in-arms and outstanding pupil" – we know rather more, thanks to the disclosures of *his* personal staff.[14] That the ingredients of Zhou's politics always differed from Mao's is well known, but in his epistemologic practice the Premier was by the mid-1950s no less Maoist than the Chairman. A personal secretary of his between 1949 and 1957 has since revealed that Zhou's toilet was referred to by herself and her colleagues as the First Office (*di yi bangongshi*), and it was here that, every morning, the Premier would reflect long and hard on problems and contemplate matters of state, as well as sign off on government decrees and occasionally even hold closed-door high-level meetings. In an interview with a Beijing University historian published under the title "Are the Common People

---

[11] Sun Mingshan, ed., *Lishi shunjian III* [A Moment in History III] (Beijing: Qunzhong chubanshe, 2004), p. 191.

[12] *Ibid.*, p. 192.

[13] *Jianguo yilai Mao Zedong wengao* (Beijing: Zhongyang wenxian chubanshe, 1996), Vol. 10, pp. 299–300.

[14] Chongqing gongren bianjibu, ed., *Yi Mao zhuxi weishou de wuchanjieji silingbu wansui* [Long Live the Proletarian Headquarters Headed by Chairman Mao] (Chongqing, 1968), pp. 304–305.

of Beijing Able to Get Vegetables Like These?" a man who served as one of Zhou's bodyguards from 1945 to 1968 described a visit to the busy First Office by a senior colleague of Zhou's. Not only did Zhou not object to the visitor who burst in unannounced but even had him pull up a chair to talk policy. "My business is finished," the visitor is said to have remarked as he left. His visit "left a very deep impression on me," Zhou's former bodyguard remembered.[15]

GREAT LEAP

The zeal for revolution and for construction that the people are showing in 1958 is higher than at any time in the past.

Mao Zedong, January 16, 1958

In his lecture notes "On Dialectical Materialism," Mao had observed in 1937 how "If you want knowledge, you must take part in the practice of changing reality. If you want to know the taste of a pear, you must change the pear by eating it yourself."[16] Twenty years later, at a November 1957 Meeting of the Representatives of the Communist and Workers' Parties of Twelve Socialist Countries in Moscow, Mao picked up the same theme, commenting thus on the hitherto fruitless attempts of socialism's enemies to change socialist reality: "If it were not for the Soviet Union, we would probably all be swallowed up by the other side. Of course, by this I do not mean to say that without the Soviet Union the socialist countries would all be swallowed up and digested by imperialism and all their peoples would perish."[17] Mao's crucial point here was one of strategy: Knowledge could be acquired only gradually and change not be effected all at once. "Strategically," Mao elaborated, still in Moscow that same week, in front of delegates representing some 64 communist and workers' parties, "we take the eating of a light meal lightly, we are sure we can manage it. But when it comes to the actual eating, it must be done mouthful by mouthful: you cannot swallow an entire banquet at one gulp. This is called the piecemeal solution and is known in military writings as destroying the enemy forces one by one."[18]

---

[15] Cheng Hua, ed., *Zhou Enlai he tade mishumen* [Zhou Enlai and His Secretaries] (Beijing: Zhongguo guangbo dianshi chubanshe, 1992), pp. 178, 381.

[16] Stuart Schram, ed., *Mao's Road to Power: Revolutionary Writings 1912–1949* (Armonk, NY: M. E. Sharpe, 1992—), Vol. 6, p. 606.

[17] Michael Schoenhals, "Mao Zedong: Speeches at the 1957 'Moscow Conference,'" *Journal of Communist Studies* 2:2 (June 1986), p. 113.

[18] *Ibid.*, p. 120.

On his return to China, Mao appears to have found that "the piece-meal solution" had begun to taste tired. Why, we may never know – but rather than seek to revive it, he chose to throw it onto the proverbial compost heap of history. Changing reality from its imperfect present into an altogether new communist form had, after the Moscow visit, acquired a rare urgency. Of course, compared with not all that long ago, parts of China by 1958 *already* had been changed beyond recognition. In Mao's own words, "We've consumed the large end [*datou chidiaole*], the bureaucrat-capitalist class. Should the small end, the national bourgeoisie, attempt to resist, it would be powerless to do so."[19] But it was as if Mao saw his old recipe for success as ripe for radical change. In a *People's Daily* editorial, Mao held out the prospect of an irresistible new dessert in the form of "bountiful economic fruit" that "entirely in accordance with the laws" would be awaiting those who were prepared to join him in attempting to do more "faster, better, and more economically."[20]

Knowledge of how to proceed was far from easy to come by: "All knowledge is acquired in the course of difficulties and setbacks," Mao would lament in front of his political secretaries.[21] Where epistemology intersected with development strategy, scaling down while simultaneously increasing numbers seemed initially to resolve the conflict Mao had identified in Moscow. Taking the notion of small as beautiful to its extreme, Mao in May 1958 expressed admiration for an unlikely agent of change: "There are certain microbes called germs who, though small in size, are in some sense more powerful than men. They have no superstition and are full of energy. They strive for greater, faster, better, and more economical results and for the upper reaches. They respect no one and fear neither heaven nor earth."[22] The enemies of progress and of communism were, meanwhile, viewed by Mao as subject to an evolution that made them increasingly vulnerable to germs, to decomposition, to rot. In 1961, Mao would compare them to "ghosts"; in 1958, he still envisioned them as tigers, albeit made of cellulose, of meat, of coagulated soy milk.[23] Elaborating, Mao put the following on paper

[19] *Du* Sulian zhengzhi jingjixue jiaokeshu *shehuizhuyi bufen de tanhua jilugao* [Record of Some Conversations on the Section Devoted to Socialism in the Soviet Textbook on Political Economy] (Beijing, 1975), p. 226.

[20] Michael Schoenhals, *Saltationist Socialism: Mao Zedong and the Great Leap Forward 1958* (Stockholm: Föreningen för orientaliska studier, 1987), pp. 40–43.

[21] *Du* Sulian zhengzhi jingjixue jiaokeshu *shehuizhuyi bufen de tanhua jilugao*, p. 359.

[22] *Mao Zedong sixiang wansui (1958–1959)* [Long Live Mao Zedong Thought (1958–1959)] (N.p., 1967), p. 55.

[23] *Jianguo yilai Mao Zedong wengao* (Beijing Zhongyang wenxian chubanshe, 1996), Vol. 9, p. 426.

during a Central Committee plenum near the end of 1958: They were "real tigers who devoured people, devoured people by the millions and tens of millions," but if they had not already, they would in the end all of them without fail change into "paper tigers, dead tigers, bean-curd tigers. These are historical facts. Haven't people seen or heard about these facts?"[24]

FAMINE

This man-made disaster is not one our enemies have created, but one we have created ourselves.

Mao Zedong, December 30, 1960

By the end of the summer of 1959, it seemed increasingly unlikely that China would get a good taste of communism in the near future: The tree in *The Ming Tombs Reservoir Fantasy* was growing none of Mao's "bountiful economic fruit"! With alarming frequency, the Ministry of Public Security's top secret *Public Security Work Bulletin* and *Public Security Intelligence* told, instead, of ever more severe domestic food scarcities. If this was the onset of communism, a lot of ordinary Chinese privately admitted, they craved none of it. One report quoted a senior "democratic personage" in Beijing as saying, "[I]n the villages, the suffering is terrible: while they [the CCP] speak day in and day out of ever bigger harvests, what the people have to eat becomes less and less with each passing day."[25] Mao's urging to fellow CCP Politburo members, at the end of a particularly confrontational July 1959 meeting about what was going wrong and who was to blame, had a sharp and caustic poignancy: "Comrades," he said in an agitated state at the end of what Roderick MacFarquhar has characterized as a "brilliant debating performance," "you should analyse your own responsibility and your stomach will feel much more comfortable if you move your bowels and break wind."[26] Mao's words did little to turn the situation around, however. Nobody would, in the weeks and months that followed, "feel much more comfortable." At a meeting of senior party leaders at the end of 1960, Mao commented on the "communist wind" by saying that "unless there is a degree of suffering, a degree of pain, [people] will never learn a lesson."[27]

---

[24] *Jianguo ylai Mao Zedong wengao*, Vol. 7, pp. 610–613.

[25] *Gong'an qingbao* (Public Security Intelligence) 4 (January 23, 1960), p. 2; 29 (March 26, 1960).

[26] Roderick MacFarquhar, *The Origins of the Cultural Revolution 2: The Great Leap Forward 1958–1960* (New York: Columbia University Press, 1983), pp. 218–221.

[27] http://tieba.baidu.com/f?kz=82661598; accessed February 17, 2008.

Between 1959 and 1961, large parts of China were in the grip of a famine that ended up taking an estimated 20 to 30 million lives.[28] "Ample food and clothing will not drop from the skies!" Mao was quoted as saying in the *Fujian Daily* in the summer of 1961, as if to admit that he had by then run out of "correct ideas" that might at this stage improve the lives of the tired, poor, and starving.[29] And so, with none of it dropping from the skies, ordinary Chinese went looking for food elsewhere. The class enemy, no less opportunistic than the energetic germs that Mao had paid tribute to in 1958, did not hesitate to go *up* the food chain: In Hubei, according to a report in *Public Security Work Bulletin*, a family of thieves and robbers running a hostel in the isolated mountains of Badong County had killed and consumed no less than six passing travelers in the winter of 1959.[30] And in April 1960, the Xinhua News Agency's top secret *Internal Reference* had carried news of how

> statistics from eleven counties and municipalities in Gansu, the Ningxia Muslim Autonomous Region, and Guizhou, tell of seventeen cases of "cannibalism" [*chi renrou*—lit. "eating human flesh"] since the beginning of the year. Of these cases, eleven occurred in Gansu, and three each in Ningxia and Guizhou. The seventeen cases involved the slaughter and murder of fifteen individuals (of whom three were young children) and the excavation and consumption [*juechi*] of sixteen corpses. The altogether twenty-two offenders involved in these cases included eleven rich-peasant, landlord, counterrevolutionary, or bad elements; two members of reactionary sects; two middle peasants; three poor peasants; one petty trader; and three housewives.[31]

As the report's wording indicates, these were not the kinds of practices that the communist ideal of an all-consuming revolution endorsed, which is not to say that grassroots officialdom never ever indulged in something similar. In Guangdong's Lianping County, police officers had on one occasion in the early 1950s "without asking for permission executed two people and without considering the impact this might have permitted the masses to cut them up and take pieces of flesh with them

[28] Li Chengrui and Shang Changfeng, "Sannian kunnan shiqi fei zhengchang siwang renkoushu yanjiu shuping [Survey of Research into the Number of Abnormal Deaths During the Three Bad Years]," unpublished conference paper, Yan'an, 2007, p. 14.

[29] *Fujian ribao*, July 29, 1961. Reprinted in and here quoted from *Mao zhuxi yulu suoyin* [Index to Quotations from Chairman Mao] (N.p., 1970), p. 272.

[30] *Gong'an gongzuo jianbao* (Public Security Work Bulletin) 21 (March 11, 1960), p. 10.

[31] *Neibu cankao* 3032 (April 14, 1960), p. 25.

home."[32] During the Cultural Revolution (when, coincidentally, the slogan "There is class struggle at the pointed end of the chopsticks!" was described in *Red Flag* as a "very simple and plain, very vivid" example of the "language of the masses"[33]), the brain and tongue and heart and testicles of counterrevolutionaries were on a handful of rare occasions eaten in the wake of executions in remote parts of Qiaojia County in Yunnan and Wuxuan County in Guangxi.[34]

Ordinary Chinese in 1960 and 1961 were forced to go down the food chain – to eat flowers, leaves, roots, bark, seeds, and bulbs. Nowhere to be seen were Mao's pears and the sweet taste of knowledge they provided; mushrooming, instead, were "substitute foods" from which too big a bite could prove as lethal as did political ignorance. Mao – who himself went on a vegetarian diet in October 1960 – had always maintained that "to attempt to cover the objectively existing poisonous weeds with mud and dirt and in this way prevent them from appearing" was "idiotic" and showed "no understanding of the tactics of class struggle." Confident in the common sense of ordinary people, he had announced at the beginning of the Great Leap Forward that "[t]he party is convinced the masses have the capacity to distinguish the poisonous weeds and to conquer the poisonous weeds."[35] But was his confidence realistic? This is an example of what *Public Security Work Bulletin* had to report in November 1960:

> When the urban residents of Ji'nan in Shandong and Wuhan in Hubei visit the [rural] suburbs in search of substitute foods [*daishipin*], they grab whatever they can get their hands on. More than 2,000 people come each day to the fields surrounding the two production brigades of Wuhan's Dai Mountain [People's] Commune to scavenge for vegetables.... As of recently, large numbers of workers and urban residents from the cities of Ji'nan and Qingdao in Shandong Province visit the surrounding rural areas daily in search of edible wild plants. They take whatever they can find.[36]

---

[32] Yiting [pseud.], "Wushi niandai Guangdong zhenfan [The Suppression of Counterrevolution in Guangdong in the 1950s]," *Tianya wangwen* [Net Articles from Remote Corners of the World]. This three-part study was posted on the Hainan Web site *Tianya* on October 8, 2007 (when the author downloaded it in full) but has since been removed by the PRC Cyber Police.

[33] *Wenzhang xuandu (pinglunwen bufen)* [Selected Readings (Critiques Section)] (N.p., 1970), p. 4.

[34] Roderick MacFarquhar and Michael Schoenhals, *Mao's Last Revolution* (Cambridge, MA: Harvard University Press, 2006), p. 259.

[35] *Jianguo yilai Mao Zedong wengao*, Vol. 7, pp. 93–94.

[36] *Gong'an gongzuo jianbao* 80 (November 18, 1960), p. 5.

Widespread food poisoning occurred where Mao's confidence proved misplaced. "Since October," a ministerial report on November 5, 1960, explained, there had been "5,404 known cases of food poisoning from eating the Siberian Cocklebur Fruit" in the cities of Taiyuan and Changzhi in Shanxi Province alone. In Tangshan, Qinhuangdao, Changli, and Yutian in Hebei Province, the fruit (actually a herb, poisonous when digested in large quantities, used in traditional Chinese medicine to dispel wind and damp) had "in early October poisoned an estimated 7,900 persons and claimed the lives of thirty-four."[37]

Yet some of the worst suffering in actuality, if not in memory, had limited natural causes. As an investigation conducted by a Ministry of Public Security task force in 1962 discovered in the province of Qinghai:

> Because the scope of attack has been excessive and large numbers of people have been offended these past years, close to 300,000 died in the province as a whole, and the masses show signs of displeasure. Add to this that in quite a few regions, the food grain available to the peasants is only half a *jin* while in some places social order is no good, and there is even the possibility of unrest.[38]

What sort of criminally misguided Great Leap Forward was it that managed to terminally "offend" 0.3 million Qinghai residents? What kind of punitive "communism" was it that fed people but half a *jin* of grain per person per month?

It takes a leap of the imagination to find the key. Publication of the "brutal, obscene and disgusting" (this is its author William Burroughs' own characterization of it) novel *Naked Lunch* in the United States in 1962 prompted, in due course, a Massachusetts court to ask if the title "relates to capital punishment"? Testifying on behalf of *Naked Lunch*, Allen Ginsberg responded, "No, no. It relates to nakedness of seeing, to being able to see clearly without any confusing disguises, to see through the disguise." A full naked "lunch," Ginsberg asserted, would in this case correspond to "a complete banquet of all this naked awareness." Ginsberg said he understood *Naked Lunch* to point at "the number one World Health Problem, which, he [Burroughs] feels, is this tendency on the part of – the tendency in a mechanized civilization for very few people to get control of enormous amounts of power."[39] In China,

---

[37] *Gong'an gongzuo jianbao* 73 (November 5, 1960), pp. 4–5.

[38] *Gong'an gongzuo jianbao* 14 (April 29, 1962), p. 10. The original recipient of my copy (no. 234) of this now declassified top secret report has written in pencil next to the casualty figure, "14.4% of the entire population." A *jin* is about one English pound.

[39] William S. Burroughs, *Naked Lunch* (New York: Grove Press, 1966), pp. xxi–xxv.

punishment, nakedness, health, and the concentration of power were meanwhile intersecting in ways that showed Burroughs to have been remarkably perceptive:

On 1 October [1960], Liao Jun, general [party] branch secretary in Zhuanghou brigade, Gushi township, Suichang County, Zhejiang Province, announced at a meeting of cadres at and above the rank of team leader and at a mass meeting of members of the Guanling production team to celebrate National Day that "petty thieves have no sense of shame. Merely to hang them up and beat them doesn't do the trick. You also have to remove their clothes, their trousers, strip them naked." In accordance with his instructions, altogether eleven members of the masses (five males, six females) in the brigade subsequently ended up having their clothes removed and being paraded naked through the streets. Six of them were members of the Guanling production team. On 2 October, the middle peasant Zheng Lifa (aged 28) had been caught stealing nine corn ears and was taken to the brigade where the [party] branch secretary Zheng Yanhuo told four militia members at a mass meeting to remove all of Zheng Lifa's clothes and put him on public display for over an hour.... On 5 October, the poor peasants from the same team Ye Aichai (female, aged 47), Xu Genlan (female, aged 55), and Zhou Moying (female, aged 60) each took two, three *jin* of corn ears and when Zheng Yanhuo found out he immediately sent the militia to remove their clothes and parade them naked through the streets. On their knees, Ye and the others pleaded for mercy while members of the masses, one after the other, asked Zheng to show forgiveness. But he insisted on their removing all of their clothes and furthermore ordered Zhou Moying to bang a gong while walking naked up front, militia escort following close behind, for one *li* and a half. Afterwards, Ye Aichai was so devastated with shame she wanted to kill herself, but her husband managed to talk her out of it. On 9 October, the woman Chen Jinjuan (aged 18) was spotted by the head of the brigade as she took three corn ears growing by the roadside on her way home from the production brigade where she had bought some cooking oil. He immediately insisted on fining her eight yuan, money which she was unable to produce. When she pleaded for mercy, crying, he refused to give way and demanded she take off her clothes and leave them as collateral instead. She was only able to return home after her family had turned up with another set of clothes for her to wear.[40]

COMING CLEAN

Some leading comrades ... have puffed up the arrogance of the bourgeoisie and deflated the morale of the proletariat. How poisonous! Viewed in connection with the Right deviation in 1962 and the wrong tendency of 1964 which was "Left" in form but Right in essence, shouldn't this make one wide awake?

Mao Zedong, August 5, 1966

Nakedness is next to cleanliness, and "Clearly, cadres had to be clean if they were to carry conviction," Rod MacFarquhar has concluded from his analysis of famine realities in *The Origins of the Cultural Revolution*.[41] Since the "banquet of all this naked awareness" of 1959–61 indicated that large numbers of powerful CCP cadres were in fact *not* "clean," a drastic remedy needed to be devised. Though Mao and his colleagues eventually would split over just how to proceed, there was initial agreement on what the remedy was to entail. Mao announced that the gist would be "cadres, relying on the poor and lower middle peasants, washing their hands and taking baths."[42] Peng Zhen explained in an extended discourse on the subject that "leading comrades will be taking a preliminary bath. It's been well over ten years since they last did this.... It's better to take an early bath than a late bath, and even a belated bath is better than no bath at all.... For years, Chairman Mao has been proposing that we wash our faces every day."[43]

Though Mao spoke of their needing to wash their hands, he did not mean that cadres were to disclaim responsibility for their actions. As one contemporary source had it, "[We] must stress and point out in particular that the aim of the bath is to overcome any and all thinking and behavior *not conducive to socialism*."[44] They were meant to act as role

---

[40] *Gong'an gongzuo jianbao* 81 (November 23, 1960), p. 5.

[41] Roderick MacFarquhar, *The Origins of the Cultural Revolution 3: The Coming of the Cataclysm 1961–1966* (New York: Columbia University Press, 1997), p. 341.

[42] *Mao Zedong sixiang wansui (1960–1967)* [Long Live Mao Zedong Thought (1960–1967)] (N.p., 1967), p. 51.

[43] Zhonggong zhongyang zuzhibu bangongting, ed., *Zuzhi gongzuo wenjian xuanbian 1963 nian* [Selected Documents on Organization Work from the Year 1963] (Beijing, 1980), p. 103.

[44] *Shanxi sheng Wenshui xian Macun Shangxian dadui shehuizhuyi jiaoyu yundong juti jingyan huibian* [Collected Concrete Experiences from the Socialist Education

models for ordinary Chinese who might themselves also have been in one way or another tainted. CCP Vice Chairman Liu Shaoqi suggested that "once the cadres have taken a bath and really given themselves a thorough cleansing, the masses will naturally follow and take a bath too. It need not take too long, a few days should do it."[45] The reality of the "Four Cleanups" – as the remedial cleansing became known – was relayed in texts such as a report from Di County in central Shanxi entitled, "Some Impressions Gained from Organizing Rural Grass-Roots Cadres to Wash Their Hands and Take Baths," which spoke of how "according to their positions and duties, the nature of their problems, their attitudes being good or bad, etc. research was conducted into the scope of cadres needing a bath and the methods of bathing. As a norm, brigade cadres would wash themselves in the brigade, team cadres would wash themselves in the team, while party and league cadres would wash inside the organization."[46] The starved peasant women from Zhejiang mentioned earlier had been forced to walk naked down the village street because they had stolen two, three *jin* of corn ears each; in Di County, three of four commune cadres "needed to take baths" when it turned out that the total "value of what they had eaten and taken that exceeded their share was 249, 128 yuan."[47] Hereupon, "in the course of bathing, they confessed to having stolen 2,300 *jin* of grain and expressed their resolve to show through action their repentance."[48]

PURGING THE ENTIRE SYSTEM: THE CULTURAL REVOLUTION

Before the movement, a lot of people kept saying they were ill and needed expensive drugs and rest, maybe seven or eight months a year. When the Cultural Revolution began, their illnesses disappeared.

Mao Zedong, October 5, 1968

Movement in Macun and Shangdian Brigades in Wenshui County, Shanxi Province] (Beijing: Zhonggong zhongyang Huabeiju xuanchuanbu, 1964), p. 16.

45 *Pipan ziliao: Zhongguo Heluoxiaofu Liu Shaoqi fangeming xiuzhengzhuyi yanlun ji* [Criticism Material: Collected Counter-revolutionary Revisionist Utterances by China's Khrushchev Liu Shaoqi], Vol. 3 (Beijing: Renmin chubanshe ziliaoshi, 1968), p. 598.

46 *Guanyu zhaokai gongshe sanganhui zuzhi ganbu xishou xizao de jige cailiao* [Some Material on Convening Meetings of Three Levels of Commune Cadres for the Purpose of Bringing Cadres to Wash Their Hands and Take Baths] (Taiyuan: Zhonggong Shanxi shengwei nongcun siqing bangongshi, 1965), p. 26.

47 *Ibid.*, p. 23.

48 *Ibid.*, p. 24.

The very orderliness that Mao saw emerge in the "Four Cleanups" made him concerned. Signs of a rethink of the initial remedy began to appear as time passed. A crucially important programmatic document circulated in January 1965 as CCP Central Document *Zhongfa* [1965] 26 hinted in vague terms at what Mao was contemplating and where he might be going next. It signaled a decreased concern with external cleanliness overall in that it stated clearly that work team members "don't necessarily have to be all that 'clean.'"[49] "The class content of purity is different in different societies. There are so-called pure officials in capitalist societies as well," Mao told Chen Boda three days after Chen had presented him with an early draft of the document, "and they are all big tycoons."[50]

What Mao had in mind or was reflecting on was not disclosed beforehand. As Roderick MacFarquhar and I have noted elsewhere, Mao played his cards very close to his chest, pursuing a "deliberate opaqueness" that kept even some members of his inner circle in the dark.[51] Hence there remained, well into the autumn of 1966 when the "Four Cleanups" drew to a close nationwide, something ambiguous about much that was being said: Even statements made by Mao's "most outstanding pupil" could be interpreted simultaneously as presaging more of the same *and* as foreshadowing something completely different. Compare the following:

> I don't mean to say that all [powerholders] must take their
> trousers off in front of the masses.... [But] when standing in
> front of the masses, should we adopt a posture that involves
> making a thorough self-criticism and an equally thorough self-
> denunciation – comparable to pouring water off a steep roof –
> by taking our trousers off? Or should we adopt the posture
> of organizing some of the masses to protect us? If we adopt a
> posture of thoroughly denouncing ourselves, dispense with our
> nauseating airs, and take our trousers off, then we shall succeed
> in mobilizing the broad masses to denounce us and turn the spear
> of attack against us.[52]

Unless they managed to intuit something very different from Mao's behavior, members of Lin's audience plausibly and rationally could

---

[49] *Shejiao wenjian* [Socialist Education Documents] (Lanzhou: Zhonggong Gansu sheng-wei nongcun shejiao bangongshi, 1965), p. 65.

[50] *Mao Zedong sixiang wansui (1960–1967)*, p. 124.

[51] MacFarquhar and Schoenhals, *Mao's Last Revolution*, pp. 47–48.

[52] *Lin Biao wenxuan* [Selected Works of Lin Biao], Vol. 2 (Xi'an: Xi'an yejin jianzhu xueyuan geming weiyuanhui xuanchuanbu, 1967), p. 391.

interpret his words as simply describing the runup to "taking a bath" and cadres "giving themselves a thorough cleansing." And there were numerous precedents that suggested just that.

The possibility that to "take our trousers off" might be a prelude to something very different did not dawn on many until the end, which is not to say that from a position of hindsight one cannot already discern where things were moving, for example, in the CCP's counterrevisionist discourse on *gulyáskommunizmus*. In the Soviet Union, in the words of Liu Shaoqi, "Large contingents of bourgeois intellectuals have come to the fore that are seen as having grown up on socialism. While in their mother's womb and while on mother's milk, that which they consumed was socialism's milk. So, we ask, do they still count as bourgeois intellectuals? They may not count as such, but in actuality they are!"[53] Truly consequential impurities, in other words, would for the duration be on the inside. "Like the Monkey King" in *Journey to the West*, Mao eventually would be quoted as saying, they provoked "counterrevolutionary activities" in the belly after having penetrated it by way of clever use of "military tactics." In some cases, "conceit, self-complacency, lack of vigilance and absorption in the day-to-day job to the neglect of politics on our part as revolutionaries" might even allow them to "penetrate our liver."[54] Unless this slow process of *internal* absorption was interrupted and reversed well before it had run its full course, the effect (as the Soviet case showed) ultimately would be full-blown revisionism.

None had a better command of Mao's metaphors than the men who at one time or another had served him as ghost writers and/or alter-ego "theorists." They could produce a discourse that was for all practical purposes as much Mao as Mao's own. It is hence as the emulation and near-perfect simulation of the CCP Chairman's thinking that we must read and understand the following assertion by Hu Qiaomu (style editor of Mao's *Selected Works*) dating from the time of the "Four Cleanups" and describing a very different process to which "take our trousers off" was *also* a perfectly appropriate prelude. In 1970, Mao's brief and cryptic order, "Expel waste matter," would be duly included in the People's Liberation Army's (PLA's) massive 2,200-page *Index to Quotations from Chairman Mao* (the entry, sourced to *Red Flag*, read *in full*: "Expel waste matter … ");[55] in what follows, Hu Qiaomu elaborates on the why

[53] Zhonggong Shanghai shiwei bangongting geming zaofandui, ed., *Liu Shaoqi zai gedi sanbu de xiuzhengzhuyi yanlun huibian* (Collection of Liu Shaoqi's Three Revisionist Utterances) (Shanghai, 1967), p. 226.

[54] *Mao Zedong sixiang wansui (1949.9–1957.12)* [Long Live Mao Zedong Thought (1949.9–1957.12)] (N.p., 1967), pp. 51–55.

[55] *Mao zhuxi yulu suoyin*, p. 2004. Ellipsis points as in original.

and wherefore of what Mao *really* expected the cadres to do with their trousers down:

> Here is a kind of social phenomenon consisting of feces produced by socialist society in a manner similar to man's having to eat and defecate every day. If man does not defecate, there will be a reshuffle [*gaizu*] in his internal organs. Once he has eaten, man needs to defecate, which is of course a bother, since it involves a waste of time as well as of paper. On the other hand, it is not a bad thing either, since unless we defecate, how do we rid ourselves of the waste matter? Societies are like that, [like people] they also have to defecate, which is not a bad thing. Once this truth has been made clear to people, it will no longer appear strange to them. Of course, differences in essence as well as process distinguish defecation by socialist societies from defecation by capitalist or feudal societies.[56]

The Cultural Revolution, the name that Mao would give his grand experiment, would subject the CCP and officialdom to a purge of unprecedented ferocity.

A REVOLUTION IS NOT A DINNER PARTY

Maybe in a few more years, we'll have yet another revolution.

Mao Zedong, n.d. [1973]

"A revolution is not a dinner party," the *Quotations from Chairman Mao* had the CCP Chairman musing. By the autumn of 1968, the organ of the CCP Central Committee, *Red Flag*, was quoting him in an editorial as saying (in words officially described as "embodying extremely profound dialectics") that "If we don't expel waste matter, don't absorb fresh blood, the party will have no vitality."[57] The editorial, drafted by Yao Wenyuan, contained an entire paragraph dissecting the waste matter Mao had in mind and listing its components – politically suspect "elements" of one kind or another.[58]

The first Cultural Revolution was to leave many CCP members more than satisfied: Mao's successors were unable to stomach even the mere thought of a second one or, even worse, successive revolutions "every seven to eight years" as Mao now and then threatened. One of

---

[56] *Tantan baozhi gongzuo* [On Newspaper Work] (Beijing: Xinwen yanjiusuo, 1978), p. 55.

[57] *Hongqi* 4 (October 14, 1968).

[58] Ibid.; *Jianguo yilai Mao Zedong wengao* (Beijing Zhongyang wenxian chubanshe, 1998), Vol. 12, p. 580.

the last occasions on which he elaborated on the dialectic of change and epistemology was, as far as we know today, the CCP's Ninth National Congress in April 1969, at an informal predinner conversation on April 11 with the congress Secretariat and regional delegation leaders. No complete official transcript of what was said on that day has since been declassified by the CCP, yet historians have at present no less than five different *unofficial* transcripts of it, all of them equally authoritative in the sense of being rough stenographic records taken down either by someone who was present or someone who heard a tape recording of Mao and his "comrades in arms" speaking.

Prior to taking a short break, Mao had explained why it was imperative "for our comrades to be thoroughly familiar with our party's historical experiences, in order to avoid repeating past mistakes."[59] After the break, he had begun to speak again but quickly found himself interrupted by Kang Sheng. Transcript 1 notes that it was Kang's interjection that prompted Mao to elaborate as follows:

> A person has to eat and he has to shit. After all, he cannot only eat and not shit. There has to be a process of digestion between eating and shitting. Dialectics expresses itself by way of a process. Infants, right after they're born, will both eat and shit. If we only remember to eat, and not remember to shit, how's that going to work? After all, one cannot wait until the moment one has to shit to dig a pit. At any given period, there's always a principal contradiction.[60]

Vintage Mao Zedong Thought, one might at first be inclined to believe. Transcript 2, however, complicates the ascription of direct (1969) authorship to Mao of this passage by suggesting that the speaker was Kang, interrupting Mao and apparently summarizing what Mao had said in Yan'an decades earlier about the importance of correctly digesting experience. Transcripts 3 and 4 are almost identical in their syntactic imperfections, both possibly suggesting Kang *was* at least partially responsible for what was being recorded.

On the basis of the likely intent of the person(s) providing a variant text of Mao's, Timothy Cheek some two decades ago defined the

---

[59] Pang Xianzhi and Jin Chongji, ed., *Mao Zedong zhuan 1949–1976* [Biography of Mao Zedong 1949–1976] (Beijing: Zhongyang wenxian chubanshe, 2003), pp. 1550–1551.

[60] "Mao zhuxi jianghua: 4 yue 11 ri xiawu 4 dian 30 fen dao 6 dian [Chairman Mao Talks: from 4.30 to 6 p.m. on 11 April]," in *"Jiuda" ziliao huibian* [Collected Materials on the "Ninth Congress"] (Ji'nan: Ji'nan tieluju Ji'nan chelianggu 5.7 zhongxue, 1969), p. 5.

stubbornly persistent conceptual category of the "genius edition."[61] It basically assumes that the provider (typically one of the best minds of a generation starving to recreate the syntax and measure of the Chairman's prose)[62] regarded Mao as a "lone genius not subject to revision by any collective leadership" and looked on editorial tinkering with the Chairman's word the same way Jack Kerouac had looked on ex post facto alterations of his own: "Once God moves the hand, you go back and revise it's a *sin!*"[63] If we apply Cheek's categories to the five different records of what Mao is meant to have said at the Ninth National Party Congress, it would at first appear as if they all fall squarely within the "genius" category. Nothing appears to have been done to them to enhance the *form* for the sake of making the content more intelligible. At the same time, however, the fifth record actually manages to fuse the "genius" with a rather impudent category – the *"homogenized 'collective wisdom'"* that Cheek for some reason hesitates to call by its rightful name, the *Antimao*.[64] Transcript 5 makes a powerful case for treating Mao's knowledge as collective, reproducing as it does a kind of conversation, in the middle of which Mao very pointedly even downplays his own role:

> (*Revered Kang [Sheng]*: The Chairman said already a long time ago that after all, you can't work and sleep or eat and relieve yourself simultaneously. He said in Yan'an that at any one time, there is always one that is the major one.) I didn't say that in Yan'an. (*Revered Kang*: The Chairman said it numerous times while discussing dialectics, that there has to be a process, that we relieve ourselves when we've eaten, that like infants sucking the breast, they eat and shit at the same time.) (*Everybody laughs*) It's only when we have to shit while our troops are on the march that we dig a pit, some of us even digging one ourselves. (*The Premier*: We make mistakes, not remembering to dig a pit.) (*Xu Shiyou*: Once

---

[61] Timothy Cheek, "The 'Genius' Mao: A Treasure Trove of 23 Newly Available Volumes of Post-49 Mao Zedong Texts," *Australian Journal of Chinese Affairs* 19/20 (January–July 1988), pp. 318–319. Personally, I think Cheek got it wrong, but as Stuart Kauffman put it, "Definitions are neither true nor false; they're useful or useless" (see www.edge.org/3rd_culture/kauffman03/kauffman_index.html), and Cheek's definition is nothing if not useful.

[62] Cf. the lines from *Howl* not reproduced in Umberto Eco, "Intertextual Irony and Levels of Reading," in *Umberto Eco on Literature* (Orlando, FL: Harcourt, 2002), pp. 212–235.

[63] Quoted in Charles E. Jarvis, *Visions of Kerouac*, 2d ed. (Lowell, MA: Ithaca Press, 1974), p. 7.

[64] Cheek, "The 'Genius' Mao," p. 327.

in the barracks, we would no longer be digging.) The barracks have segregated our military from the workers and peasants and that is not a good thing, though of course not having any of it would not be good, the common people would resent that as well.[65]

Who *are* historians to say that it was *not* exchanges like this one that the CCP Central Committee had in mind when, with Mao dead and gone, it insisted that "numerous outstanding party leaders made important contributions to the formation and development of Mao Zedong Thought"?

And so we return to the men and women on Mao's personal staff and security detail. Young Miss She from the PLA worked for two and a half months for Mao in Wuhan in 1964; the record has it that the other women in her detail were flush with envy when she received her assignment. Her officially sanctioned account of what it entailed (duly censored for political correctness and published by a prestigious arm of the official CCP history establishment three decades later) has it that she "provided Chairman Mao with boiled water, tidied his bed, cleaned his room, washed his bathtub, and flushed his toilet for him." Of their conversations, a poignant snippet survives. Miss She: "To be able to serve the Chairman makes me really happy!" Mao: "Really? You serve me and I serve the people."[66] No official resolution on party history drives it home with greater punch, no academic scholarship at Harvard or Beijing University can really afford to be that blunt in describing the deal between Mao and *800,000,000 – The Real China*. Because, does that one intimate sound bite not say, "I serve you a revolution, and you clean up the mess when I'm done"?

---

[65] "4 yue 11 ri xiawu 5 shi zhi 6 shi ban de jianghua [Talk from 5 to 6.30 p.m. on 11 April]," in *Mao Zhuxi zai Zhongguo gongchandang di jiu ci quanguo daibiao dahui shang de zhongyao zhishi* [Chairman Mao's Important Instructions at the Ninth National Congress of the CCP] (N.p., 1969), p. 7.

[66] Zhonggong Hubei shengwei dangshi ziliao zhengbian weiyuanhui, ed., *Mao Zedong zai Hubei* [Mao Zedong in Hubei] (Beijing: Zhonggong dangshi chubanshe, 1993), p. 318.

6 Mao and His Followers

FREDERICK C. TEIWES

To me Mao was like God, I believed that he was not only the great leader of the Chinese people, but also the great leader of people throughout the world. I feared the day when he would no longer be with us. I really hoped there'd be a scientific breakthrough that would enable young people like us to voluntarily give up a year of our lives to add a minute to his.

> Dai Qing, adopted daughter of Marshal Ye Jianying, recalling the sentiments of young princesses and princes of the party and other urban youth at the onset of the Cultural Revolution in 1966[1]

The general attitude of the masses [during the 1976 Tiananmen crisis] was anger at the unfair treatment of [Premier] Zhou Enlai, antipathy toward the [Politburo] radicals, and difficulty in comprehending the government's behavior. But it is hard to describe sentiment toward Mao himself. There was dissatisfaction and anger over his support for the "gang of four" and the treatment of the Premier, but at the same time a continuing deep faith in Mao.

> A businessman's recollection concerning his experiences as a young factory worker who regularly visited Tiananmen Square, January–April 1976[2]

Chairman Mao's great feats are enduring. Chinese history has proved that ... only Chairman Mao could have led us to victory. Without Chairman Mao, there would be no new China. [His] ... greatness cannot be overestimated.... Chairman Mao was not without shortcomings and mistakes. Yet they are insignificant when compared to his great feats.... [It is wrong to say that, like Stalin], he had [only] 70 percent achievements and 30 percent mistakes.

> Deng Xiaoping's comments during the central work conference preceding the Third Plenum, November 25, 1978[3]

---

[1] From the film, *The Gate of Heavenly Peace*, produced and directed by Richard Gordon and Carma Hinton (Canberra, Australia: Ronin Films, 1996).

[2] Interview, January 2005.

[3] Yu Guangyuan, *Deng Xiaoping Shakes the World: An Eyewitness Account of China's Party Work Conference and the Third Plenum (November-December 1978)*, ed. by Ezra F. Vogel and Steven I. Levine (Norwalk, CT: EastBridge, 2004), p. 77.

From the founding of the People's Republic of China (PRC) in 1949, Mao Zedong was the unavoidable leader of the entire Chinese population. Given the totalitarian nature of the emerging system, virtually all members of the body politic became the Chairman's followers, willingly or not, with varying degrees of enthusiasm. For many, particularly at the higher reaches of the political system, following Mao involved intense fealty – for them the Chairman was the central legitimizing figure who gave meaning to their lives. More broadly, for the vast array of major social groups, Mao was a revered figure who could not be challenged even though attitudes varied in intensity and over time. Writing in a broader context on charismatic leadership, Andrew Walder pointed to Mao's exceptional relationship with the Chinese populace: "[Of all the cults created by official propaganda in ideological regimes], only the cult of Mao Zedong appears to have had genuinely charismatic, not manufactured, qualities – and then only for a brief period ... and only among certain [participants in] the movements."[4] Describing and explaining the complex nature of Mao's leadership are the tasks of this analysis.

This chapter explores the relationship of Mao to his various followers, examining changes in his leadership style and methods and variations and developments in the responses of different groups in China's political structure. Particular attention is given to the Chairman's relations with his top leadership colleagues, an area where the evidence is most suitable for sustained argument. Groups covered more sporadically include somewhat lower-ranking figures, including important quasi-confidants, intellectuals (covered more systematically in Chapter 7), rank-and-file cadres and party members, the energized Red Guard youth of the Cultural Revolution, and broad sections of the "masses," particularly the peasantry. Apart from the difficulty created by the very scope of the followers considered, variations within groups and the episodic and limited nature of the data make generalizing about broad sections of society somewhat problematic. Beyond this is the problem of the many millions of Chinese who, by virtue of "bad" class backgrounds or personal treatment during Mao's repeated campaigns, harbored grievances against the regime, including hatred of the Chairman. By necessity, these citizens were found within larger groups of his followers, and they, too, receive attention.

My approach is chronological, starting with the consolidation of Mao's leadership in the 1940s and then following the tortuous post-1949

---

[4]   Andrew G. Walder, *Communist Neo-Traditionalism: Work and Authority in Chinese Industry* (Berkeley: University of California Press, 1986), p. 130.

road of Mao's early successes and later disasters. I conclude by analyzing why, as illustrated by the quotations at the start of this chapter, Mao retained, to the very end, significant, if declining, loyalty, obedience, and reverence from not only his leadership colleagues but also other key groups and the "masses."

THE SAVIOR EMERGES: MAO AND THE PARTY, 1941–49

By the early 1940s, Mao had emerged as the unchallenged leader of the Chinese Communist Party (CCP). Rather than attaining that status at the Zunyi conference during the Long March in 1935, as officially claimed, a gradual accumulation of power unfolded. Zunyi restored Mao as a significant party leader, but largely in the military sphere based on his criticism of the failed strategies of the Moscow-oriented Returned Student faction. The political ideas and Soviet ties of this group continued to have influence and were reinforced by the return from Moscow of its leading figure, Wang Ming, at the end of 1937. A tense political struggle between Wang and Mao developed that was largely settled in late 1938 in Mao's favor as a result of the achievements of his base-area strategy and, ironically, Stalin's message that Mao should be the party's leader. Mao's position strengthened significantly thereafter with the canonization of his views as "Mao Zedong Thought," the official ideology that all party members studied as sacred texts during party Rectification in 1942–44, the formal decision to give Mao the determining voice in CCP councils in 1943, and the installation of a new Maoist leadership at the Seventh Party Congress in 1945.[5] All of this was in the context of the successes of Mao's revolutionary policies, successes that in 1945 were far from complete but which far surpassed anything imaginable in the dark days of the early 1930s. As further unimaginable successes unfolded in the 1946–49 Civil War, Mao's status and authority grew accordingly.

While the increasing success of Mao's revolutionary strategies was central to his emerging position, his persona also was a major factor for his fellow leaders and others in the Yan'an base area who had contact with him. Mao seemed to combine the talents of a political thinker, philosopher, general, poet, and perhaps even a Chinese sage, someone with the grand vision and practical skills that held out hope for achieving the

---

[5] See Frederick C. Teiwes with Warren Sun, *The Formation of the Maoist Leadership: From the Return of Wang Ming to the Seventh Party Congress* (London: Contemporary China Institute Research Notes and Studies, 1994), pp. 3–23.

promised land of a new China. American Sidney Rittenberg, who came to Yan'an, joined the CCP, had personal contact with Mao, stayed for 35 years, including two stints in the Chairman's prisons, yet remained loyal throughout, summarized the impact of the Yan'an Mao: "When I was with Zhou [Enlai], I felt I was with a real friend, a comrade. With Mao, I felt I was sitting next to history. With Zhou I felt warmth. With Mao, awe."[6]

If revolutionary successes were the core factor in sustaining awe among Mao's followers, it was further bolstered by Mao's calculated building of his Marxist-Leninist bona fides and the indoctrination of the party from the top down in his "thought." Mao's Marxist-Leninist theorizing may not have reached any great heights, and he relied on Chen Boda, later his secretary and perhaps, to the extent anyone truly qualified, a confidant, to assist with the ideological niceties. But it was the practical thrust of Mao's approach, his shaping of Marxism-Leninism (the arrow) to make it relevant to hitting the target of the Chinese Revolution, that gave Mao Zedong Thought its power and gained the support of party leaders and ordinary cadres alike. It is indicative of the breadth of Mao's support by this point that a leader of the Returned Student faction, Wang Jiaxiang, was the first person to coin the phrase "Mao Zedong Thought" as the party's formal ideology. And it is instructive that, at a much lower level, Rittenberg became "almost a blind follower" of Mao in his prison cell after studying "On Protracted War," a thesis focusing on the political-military situation rather than abstruse Marxist theory. The paradox was that Mao's pragmatic ideology was indoctrinated as an almost biblical text, allowing no challenge to its basic principles. The further irony was that both the pragmatism of the doctrine and its unyielding indoctrination furthered Mao's cause.

A feature of Mao's leadership that had great benefit for both his personal standing and the party's larger cause was his emphasis on party unity. From a strategic perspective, only a unified organization stood any chance against the superior forces of the Japanese and Guomindang (GMD). In terms of party sentiment, there was revulsion over inner-party struggles in the early 1930s that involved killings and torture of communists. Although having contributed to such excesses during the bloody Futian incident in 1930–31, Mao now advocated a new "organizational line" that abjured the "ruthless struggles and merciless blows" of the earlier period.[7] But Mao was not abjuring the use of coercion in

6   Sidney Rittenberg and Amanda Bennett, *The Man Who Stayed Behind* (New York: Simon & Schuster, 1993), p. 77. Rittenberg (p. 449) lists the qualities cited here save for that of sage.

7   See Frederick C. Teiwes, *Politics and Purges in China: Rectification and the Decline of Party Norms 1950–1965*, 2nd ed. (Armonk, NY: M. E. Sharpe, 1993), pp. 48ff.

the very real struggle against spies who had infiltrated the party, and the so-called rescue movement produced a nasty outbreak of torture and imprisonment in 1943. This was a result of Politburo member Kang Sheng's cruel methods, but Mao bore ultimate responsibility owing to his excessive assessment of the dangers facing the party. Yet Mao quickly backed off this approach, pushed aside and effectively demoted Kang, and formally apologized to the party even as his genius was proclaimed in CCP propaganda.[8] On the whole, Mao lived up to his new organizational line in Yan'an, earning further loyalty from his followers.

At the top, rather than advancing over the broken bodies of opponents, as often claimed, Mao emphasized party unity in various respects: moderate treatment of former political opponents,[9] eschewing appointing a Politburo made up of his own closest supporters, drawing widely on talent and representatives of different party constituencies to staff key positions, and presiding over a flexible and consultative policy process that devolved responsibility as required by a decentralized war situation, and where policies could be argued by Mao's colleagues even as he retained the final say. Many in the emerging leadership had stood on different sides of various issues from Mao in the pre-Zunyi period. But Mao's posture toward such figures was inclusive. Zhou Enlai, an early 1930s opponent, became the third-ranking leader of the party, albeit only after extensive self-criticism of his earlier errors. Meanwhile, the new number two leader and presumptive successor, Liu Shaoqi, was enormously talented, represented the party underground, was closest to Mao in ideological outlook, and yet lacked close personal ties to him. The loyalty of such followers, all drawn to Mao by his revolutionary accomplishments, was further enhanced by the recognition of their abilities and constituencies that he shrewdly gave.

The lengthy criticism and self-criticism of Zhou Enlai and other leaders notwithstanding, the harshest aspects of the rectification process were reserved for lower-level party members, particularly aspiring revolutionary intellectuals drawn to Yan'an during the anti-Japanese war and intoxicated by Mao's vision of an independent, strong, and egalitarian China. As in other respects, the recollections of Sidney Rittenberg illuminate the exacting psychological process these recruits to the revolution encountered: "The first thing to do was to take stock

[8]   See Teiwes with Sun, *Formation*, pp. 52–59.
[9]   Even in the struggle against Wang Ming and the Returned Students in Yan'an, Mao combined destroying their position ideologically with allowing them to continue in lesser positions as testimony to his magnanimity. See *ibid.*, pp. 14, 16–17, 51–52, and the discussion in Chapter 5 of this book.

of my life, and looking back over my past I could see how [the party] might have suspected me. I had been halfhearted and wavering.... From that vantage point, [the party's treatment of me was] reasonable and ... offer[ed] me a rare opportunity for self-training and transformation." The pressures of study, criticism, and self-criticism subdued Rittenberg and the vast proportion of others subjected to rectification through a combination of rational argument, manipulating the desire to belong to the revolutionary community, and outright fear. Rittenberg experienced nightmares featuring a threatening Mao, yet he emerged from prison all the more convinced of the Chairman's genius.[10]

Outside of Yan'an and the top party leadership, more distant groups of Mao's followers formed in this period. In the villages of northern China as the CCP's programs of rent reduction and land reform took hold, peasant activists identified with the cause of the party and its leader. As the Civil War unfolded and GMD corruption became increasingly intolerable, many urban Chinese looked favorably on the promise of the communists and formed positive opinions of the CCP leader they knew little about. Many with suspect class backgrounds decided to stay rather than flee with the GMD, unsuspecting of what lay ahead under a communist dictatorship. The hopes for a new China had created a huge pool of potential followers for the party and Mao on the eve of the new regime.

THE EMPEROR PRESIDES: EARLY SUCCESSES, 1949–56

With establishment of the PRC, Mao had truly achieved the status of emperor, and the founding emperor of a new dynasty at that. This is not the facile conclusion of outside observers; the comparison has been made by Mao himself, other top-level leaders, and Chinese of all stations (for contemporary Chinese reflections on this status, see Chapter 10). Clearly, a new level to his already unchallengeable authority within the CCP had been created, and that authority extended to the entire society as the new regime consolidated its power. The period up to the Eighth Party Congress in 1956 only increased that authority as the CCP attained its core goals: firm control over society, rapid economic growth, concrete benefits to key social groups, and the socialist transformation of the political and economic structure. In broad measure, these successes mirrored the desires of the populace for national unity and dignity, peace after more than two decades of war, good social order, and a modicum of prosperity.

[10] Rittenberg and Bennett, *Man Who Stayed Behind*, pp. 152–153, 158ff, 162.

While Mao was the ultimate authority who unilaterally made some of the most controversial decisions, in some respects his overall performance in these years can be considered more as that of a chairman of the board rather than as the fountainhead of new policies. In large part this was due to the consensus, fully shared by Mao, on the need to follow the Soviet model of development and state organization. It also was due to Mao's recognition of his limitations, notably in economic policy, where he largely ceded control to Premier Zhou and the Politburo's economic czar, Chen Yun, and more broadly to his commitment to maintaining the consultative style and emphasis on party unity of the Yan'an years. Yet Mao grasped firmly those areas he knew best, foreign policy and rural policy, as well as the overall direction of the new regime. Thus the two clearest examples of overriding the consensus position of his colleagues were the decision to enter the Korean War in 1950 and to speed up the pace of agricultural cooperativization in 1955. Importantly, in both cases, Mao's decisions were viewed in the contemporary context as successes, as yet further evidence of his unmatched strategic brilliance.[11]

Mao's ongoing commitment to party unity and a form of collective leadership further nourished the strong support he had received from his top-level followers, but they were in tension with the imperial power of the emperor. While party unity was broadly reflected in the reelection of nearly all 1945 Politburo members at the Eighth Party Congress, one event put stress on party unity and raised doubts about Mao's commitment – the Gao Gang affair of 1952–54 that ended with Gao's suicide. This affair remains mysterious in important respects, but a thumbnail sketch is that Mao was unhappy with Liu Shaoqi and Zhou Enlai over their perceived caution regarding the transition to socialism, expressed his unhappiness in several private conversations with Gao, and Gao proceeded to take soundings about replacing Liu and/or Zhou with key party leaders, including Chen Yun and Deng Xiaoping. Chen and Deng eventually reported Gao's approaches to Mao, and the Chairman turned on Gao, accusing him of damaging party unity. Gao was not purged, with Mao holding out a lesser but still significant regional post, but the humiliated Gao chose suicide. Mao's motives are unclear: Was he truly trying to get rid of Liu and/or Zhou but foiled when Chen and Deng voiced their concerns, or did he have some lesser objective? In

---

[11] See Frederick C. Teiwes, "The Establishment and Consolidation of the New Regime, 1949–57," in Roderick MacFarquhar, ed., *The Politics of China The Eras of Mao and Deng* (New York: Cambridge University Press, 1997), pp. 12, 56ff.

any case, the affair indicates two things. First, when forced to choose, Mao opted for party unity over upsetting the arrangements of Yan'an. Second, the exceptionally cautious behavior of other leaders, including the hesitation of Chen and Deng to approach the Chairman, indicates their perception of his absolute authority. There is little to suggest that they would have resisted had he chosen to proceed with the removal of Liu or Zhou.[12]

The tensions of the Gao Gang affair notwithstanding, the consultative process continued at the highest level with Mao's Politburo and sub-Politburo colleagues prepared to make forceful policy arguments. The outstanding case occurred in 1955 on the issue of the speed of cooperativization. The relevant point is not that others, notably Liu Shaoqi, pushed a cautious pace of development from the start of the year but that Rural Work Department head Deng Zihui continued to argue for this view even as Mao's preference for a faster rate of growth became apparent in the spring. After disputing the issue with Mao a second time, Deng's colleagues in the Rural Work Department were astonished that he dared to "offend Chairman Mao merely over hundreds of thousands of cooperatives." Mao rejected Deng's advice, subjected him to criticism as a "right deviationist," but Deng retained his position. While it turned out to be a foolhardy act, Deng's behavior suggests his belief that the Yan'an understandings still applied.[13] That this was a more general view among Mao's top-level followers is suggested by the actions of Zhou Enlai a year later. In May 1956, Zhou approached Mao to argue against his decision to increase investment despite an almost unanimous Politburo preference for a more restrained policy, and after a temper tantrum, Mao agreed.[14] This incident demonstrated not only Mao's responsiveness to rational argument but also the willingness of his colleagues to make a case to him even after the Gao Gang episode and Deng Zihui's rebuff. The delicate balance between bending to Mao's awesome authority and articulating what they believed was in the interests of the country was high in the consciousness of Mao's top-level followers throughout this successful period.

[12] See Frederick C. Teiwes, *Politics at Mao's Court: Gao Gang and Party Factionalism in the Early 1950s* (Armonk, NY: M. E. Sharpe, 1990), pp. 6, 93ff, 116–120, 143, 149–153.

[13] See Frederick C. Teiwes and Warren Sun, eds., *The Politics of Agricultural Cooperativization in China: Mao, Deng Zihui, and the "High Tide" of 1955* (Armonk, NY: M. E. Sharpe, 1993), pp. 6–21.

[14] See Frederick C. Teiwes with Warren Sun, *China's Road to Disaster: Mao, Central Politicians, and Provincial Leaders in the Unfolding of the Great Leap Forward, 1955–1959* (Armonk, NY: M. E. Sharpe, 1999), pp. 26–29.

Larger groups of followers credited Mao and the party with overcoming corruption, crime, unemployment, inflation, prostitution, illiteracy, and other seemingly intractable problems, successes in what came to be regarded as something of a golden age. Beyond appreciation of these achievements, there was a sense of hope for the new China. Party intellectual and distinguished writer Liu Binyan recalled a time when "[f]or a while everyone felt good ... and look[ed] to the future with optimism.... [T]he early 1950s were easy years, and safe years.... People weren't forced, most agreed willingly."[15] A further insight is conveyed by post-Mao nostalgia for the 1950s as a period of national vibrancy, egalitarianism, and shared suffering. While such memories overstate the reality, they capture a broad contemporary sentiment. Part of this was due to the sense of "easy years" recalled by Liu Binyan, something difficult to reconcile to intense political campaigns, controlled executions, and suicides. In any case, various interviewees recall being unaffected by many campaigns, whether owing to the fact that their particular sector was not targeted or to the comparative moderation of movements in their individual work units. Yet another factor was the concrete benefits received by key groups, notably industrial workers, who gained not only jobs in the expanding economy but also status as the working class that was notionally the master of the new system, and the bulk of the peasantry, who benefited from land reform.

In this popular support for the system, Mao was inseparable from the party. Although Mao's personality cult tapered off somewhat after 1952, throughout the period the propaganda apparatus brought stories of Mao's greatness to schools, factories, government offices, and villages. The precise view of the Chairman varied by situation. For example, peasants in northern China villages who had been active in the revolutionary upheaval of the 1940s were undoubtedly more likely to see Mao as their hero than those elsewhere who had CCP rule imposed on them after 1949.[16] Others less tied to the revolutionary experience accepted Mao without question, as in the case of an ordinary trade union cadre who remembers finding it hard to think of Mao except as the emperor, a very good emperor who had brought dignity to the nation. Yet she noted a difference in these "down to earth" years that set them apart from later periods: While no doubts were felt toward Mao, who was deeply

---

[15] Liu Binyan, *Two Kinds of Truth: Stories and Reportage from China*, ed. by Perry Link (Bloomington: Indiana University Press, 2006), pp. 2–3.

[16] See Edward Friedman, Paul G. Pickowicz, and Mark Selden with Kay Ann Johnson, *Chinese Village, Socialist State* (New Haven, CT: Yale University Press, 1991).

honored, there was no religious fervor toward him in her circle.[17] Clearly, there were doubts and worse about Mao in the huge Chinese body politic, as became apparent in 1957 during the Hundred Flowers Movement, but these were a side current. Much as there was little resistance to the new regime, Mao's status as a good emperor was well entrenched as the period came to an end at the time of the Eighth Party Congress.

"THE FIRST EMPEROR OF ANY DYNASTY WAS ALWAYS SEVERE AND BRILLIANT,"[18] 1957–65

Peng Dehuai's comment at the time of the seminal 1959 Lushan conference that saw Mao's furious rejection of Peng's criticism of the Great Leap Forward and Peng's subsequent dismissal as minister of defense pointed to a significant change in Mao's leadership style from the party's halcyon days of 1956. In contrast to the successes of 1949–56, China now embarked on a series of policies that resulted in failures of varying magnitude, policies where Mao had major responsibility. Yet Mao's virtually single-handed driving of policy as the headstrong emperor only began with the Great Leap Forward from late 1957. Before that, the Hundred Flowers Movement that saw unanticipated and unprecedented criticism of the party and the harsh, debilitating crackdown of the Anti-Rightist Campaign that followed were largely consensus positions, although Mao was the initiator in both cases. In contrast, during the Great Leap Forward, the rest of the leadership was dragged along by Mao and was at best cautious or clumsy in seeking to modify policy disasters – disasters leading to somewhere between 15 and 46 million peasant deaths. The Chairman changed course only when he could no longer deny the evidence and then retreated to the "second front,"[19] leaving the task of cleaning up the mess to Liu Shaoqi, Zhou Enlai, and others. Despite claims to the contrary, this did not mean the slightest diminution of Mao's authority, and he periodically intervened to change policy, most notably in 1962 when he called a halt to the retreat from the Great Leap and introduced "class struggle" as the organizing concept of political life. But the emperor was now remote, more distant from his colleagues, and more elusive in his meaning than ever before. In this context, he

---

[17] Interview, April 2007.

[18] See *The Case of Peng Teh-huai, 1959–1968* (Kowloon: Union Research Institute, 1968), pp. 36, 427.

[19] The idea of dividing the leadership into "two fronts," under which Mao would exert ultimate control from the "second front," whereas other leaders on the "first front" assumed responsibility for the daily administration of the party and state.

began to ruminate over events and personalities that led to the Cultural Revolution.

The seminal events in Mao's relations with his colleagues were the Nanning conference at the outset of the Great Leap in January 1958 and the July–August 1959 Lushan conference when Mao turned on Peng Dehuai and launched a new campaign against "right opportunism." At Nanning, Mao pressed his vision of rapid economic development, a vision that gained wide support within society, enthusiastic backing from sections of the party, and strong support from various top leaders – most notably Liu Shaoqi and Deng Xiaoping. However alluring the appeal of rapidly achieving prosperity and national strength, though, Mao's methods undermined any semblance of "collective leadership." Mao launched the new program in tandem with strong criticism of Zhou Enlai, Chen Yun, and other responsible officials for the cautious economic policies of 1956–57, notwithstanding his approval at the time. Zhou, Chen, and others were forced to engage in self-criticisms at Nanning and subsequent meetings. The contrast to 1956 could not have been greater. Rather than being able to approach Mao to argue economic policy, Zhou was now denied the right to address economic issues – it was truly a case "where no one could say anything different." As events unfolded in the heady days of this period, leaders competed to meet Mao's demands, often against their better judgment, as seen in the June explosion of the 1958 steel target when various central and local leaders visited the Chairman and repeatedly raised projections to the ludicrous extent of doubling annual production in 1958. Meanwhile, others put their doubts aside and came to believe in the Leap as fantastic reports of achievements rolled in.[20]

The pressure engendered by Mao further inhibited his colleagues from raising the problems that became apparent in fall 1958. Consequently, it was Mao who first addressed these matters at the end of the year, pointing to the need to reduce unrealistic targets and generally cool the movement down. But the Chairman was unwilling to question the basic policies of *his* Great Leap, and different leaders, particularly provincial leaders, took different tacks on how to proceed, some strongly pressing ahead. Mao's ambivalence was reflected in his unwillingness to confront directly the hotheads in the provinces, but as the Lushan conference approached, he appeared to be setting the stage for a further retrenchment of the Leap.

[20] See Teiwes with Sun, *China's Road to Disaster*, Chap. 3 and Appendix 2.

Mao's receptivity to more cooling down appeared confirmed in the early stages of the meeting, but when Peng Dehuai wrote his letter of opinion providing a wide-ranging critique of the movement, Mao was deeply offended. Peng's effort was a clumsy misreading of Mao's psychology: Whereas Peng's aim was to prod Mao into taking further steps in the direction he had already signaled, the Chairman interpreted it as a personal challenge. Other leaders attempted to calm the situation to no avail as Mao insisted on Peng's dismissal and began the new lurch to the left. Apart from the disastrous policy consequences, what dismayed the assembled audience at Lushan from the Politburo level, notably Zhang Wentian who made a systematic plea for inner-party democracy, to provincial leaders, to Mao's own secretaries, Li Rui and Hu Qiaomu (quasi-confidants able to speak to Mao much more freely than top leaders), was Mao's arbitrariness. Mao himself pointed to this in an emotional comment: "[You say] I have reached Stalin's later years, [am] despotic and dictatorial, ... [and] no one dares to speak up in front of me." Mao had seriously damaged his prestige, but nobody opposed his actions, and the country descended into accelerated crisis.[21]

By spring 1960, reports of starvation began to reach the party center. As in 1959, Mao again gave conflicting signals, combining calls to deal with problems with a reendorsement of basic Great Leap policies, before finally taking the initiative in calling for a change of course in November. With a clear direction set by Mao, other leaders, most notably Liu Shaoqi, implemented a far-reaching retreat over the next year and a half. By early 1962, as the crisis deepened further, even more extensive policy changes, including toleration of individual farming, were undertaken, whereas at the 7,000 cadres conference in January Mao made his first significant self-criticism since Yan'an. Clearly, there was considerable bitterness among those present, and one Politburo member, Peng Zhen, suggested that even Mao had made mistakes, but there was no political challenge or even significant criticism. That Mao's authority was unaffected quickly became clear when he reacted to what he saw as unprincipled retreat, particularly in the dissolution of agricultural collectives, and forced key policy reversals in the summer of 1962. Most telling was Deng Xiaoping's quick retraction of his just articulated slogan, "It doesn't matter if a cat is black or [white] as long as it catches the

---

[21] See *ibid.*, p. 168, note 133 and Epilogue 1; Teiwes, *Politics and Purges*, pp. liii–liv, 319. In a 1993 interview, Li Rui explained the Chairman's secretaries' comparative lack of constraint as reflecting their lower status and thus absence of a perceived threat, and emphasized Hu Qiaomu's forceful advocacy to Mao.

mouse," as soon as he sensed Mao's changed attitude. Despite other leaders' deep policy misgivings, there was no opposition to the Chairman's altered course.[22]

While Mao had adjusted course in the summer of 1962, there was no clarity as to what this meant. Although exhorting the party to "never forget class struggle," the dislocations caused by the Great Leap were too dire for any marked shift to the left, and Mao carefully distinguished between "class struggle" and "work," declaring that the former should never disrupt the latter. With Mao now retreating to the "second front," his top colleagues faced a vexed situation. Despite their efforts to meet Mao's objectives, and in the great bulk of cases he approved their actions, on occasion he criticized sharply, always forcing a bureaucratic response. Perhaps the most revealing case concerned the drafting of the third five-year plan in 1964. After carefully reviewing and adjusting the plan in accord with their perception of Mao's wishes, Liu, Zhou, and the planners were astonished by his angry reaction that labeled their efforts as "practicing [GMD ideology]." In a display of raw power, the Chairman not only forced changes in the document but also sidelined the State Planning Commission, creating a "small planning commission" of more junior officials to take over the planning function. In this context, Mao's top followers had to put up with unpredictability and uncertainty as they carried out their tasks. On Mao's part, he began to question the reliability and loyalty of those colleagues, particularly Liu Shaoqi, but in the post-Lushan period, there were relatively limited changes in the top-level leadership until the Cultural Revolution.[23]

If life for top-level and lower party leaders was made difficult by Mao's ambiguous and changeable positions, things were much worse and began to deteriorate earlier for other followers. Intellectuals and ordinary citizens suffered in 1957 as a result of the Hundred Flowers and Anti-rightist developments. The accumulated discontents of life in the PRC were initially broached tentatively in response to Mao's invitation to criticize the party, but they eventually burst forth following repeated prodding. Even then, most criticisms hewed to topics authorized by the regime, but an indeterminate, although undoubtedly limited, number savagely attacked the party and, in apparently even lesser numbers, Mao. But the critical change that would cast a

---

[22] See Teiwes with Sun, *China's Road to Disaster*, pp. xxiv–xxvii and Epilogue 2; and Roderick MacFarquhar, *The Origins of the Cultural Revolution 3: The Coming of the Cataclysm 1961–66* (New York: Columbia University Press, 1997), pp. 157–158 and Chap. 7 *passim*.

[23] See Teiwes, *Politics and Purges*, pp. xxxvi–xliv and Chap. 11.

pall for decades was the Anti-Rightist Campaign, a harsh onslaught causing widespread fear among intellectuals, ordinary party members, and cadres generally. For many, there was a clear distinction between earlier movements that, however nasty, somehow passed them by and the intense struggles of 1957. In a not untypical memory, a low-ranking cadre recalls the Anti-Rightist Campaign as creating personal instability because for the first time she was afraid.[24] Yet a common recollection is of having no doubts concerning Mao, including believing even more strongly in the Chairman. The result was particularly striking in the case of Liu Binyan: "[My] 'rightist' label shocked me but did not make me doubt Mao. Even though I thought the charge was a mistake, I peered inside myself to see if there was some problem Mao could see that I had missed."[25] The thinking of Yan'an remained deep.

A much vaster group of Mao's followers, the peasants, was even more sorely tested by the Great Leap Forward. Initially, peasants were strongly attracted to the Leap vision, although massive propaganda and coercive pressures played their roles as well. This was well put by one Chinese observer: "[The peasants] responded to Mao's dream for a prosperous China.... With his blueprint, [Mao] inspired the people, especially the peasants who believed [that he] ... would lead them out of their wretched lives of bare subsistence and poverty. [So], ... half out of enthusiasm, half out of fear, and not without misgivings, the peasants [followed his Great Leap policies]."[26] The true test came as enthusiasm for promised bounty was overtaken by the reality of starvation. It is impossible to grasp the peasant response comprehensively, particularly because the extent of the famine varied from place to place. Certainly there was peasant resentment and, in limited areas, outright rebellion. Internal party documents record bitter attacks, for example, peasants and soldiers recruited from the villages asking whether Mao was willing to let people starve. More striking, and suggesting more widespread resistance, are the prison memoirs of Yang Xiguang, the famous Cultural Revolution radical who authored a devastating attack on the regime in 1968 and was jailed as a result. Based on conversations with fellow inmates from the countryside, Yang reports the formation of significant underground "counterrevolutionary organizations," hatred of Mao, and speculation among peasants that the dynasty was on the verge of collapse.[27]

[24] Pamela Tan, *The Chinese Factor: An Australian Chinese Woman's Life in China from 1950 to 1979* (Dural, NSW, Australia: Rosenberg Publishing, 2008), p. 75.

[25] Liu Binyan, *Two Kinds of Truth*, p. 7.

[26] Tan, *Chinese Factor*, pp. 87–88.

[27] See Teiwes, *Politics and Purges*, pp. 346–347; and Yang Xiguang and Susan McFadden, *Captive Spirits: Prisoners of the Cultural Revolution* (Hong Kong: Oxford University Press, 1997), pp. 139, 224, 280–281.

But there was another, seemingly more widespread peasant reaction to the dire situation. Overall, it appears that the regime and Mao remained legitimate in rural areas. In a northern China village that had been active in the revolutionary struggle and whose leaders considered the Chairman their savior, peasant faith was shaken but not broken. Some held that while Mao was truly great, they didn't have enough to eat. The inclination was to blame bad local officials, to believe the best of Mao, and – in a theme echoed in other groups – to conclude that if only Mao knew the situation he would again save them. More broadly, a partially passive peasantry apparently retained their faith in the party and Mao, much as urban people accepted the propaganda line that problems were due to natural disasters and Soviet perfidy. Arguably, the situation is best captured by the recollection of a provincial leader at the time, Shanxi's Tao Lujia, who marveled at the peasants' tolerance: "They were so accepting, no one thought to rob the granaries [despite the emerging famine]."[28]

As conditions began to improve in 1962, such tolerance apparently diminished underground counterrevolutionary activity and enhanced Mao's continuing acceptance by the peasantry, so deep was his image after a decade plus of official propaganda. The degree of enthusiasm varied, with rural youths and peasants in some relatively well-off villages believing the Socialist Education Movement's propaganda on the power of Mao's Thought on the eve of the Cultural Revolution, whereas peasants in poor regions complained about the Great Leap losses and reportedly showed minimal affection toward Mao.[29] Meanwhile, various urban groups continued to follow Mao, often rationalizing that others must be responsible for recent disasters. If this was without great passion, such passion would soon be aroused.

"TO REBEL IS JUSTIFIED [EXCEPT AGAINST MAO]," 1966–71

The Cultural Revolution and the extent of Mao's intent to reshape the leadership, shake up the bureaucratic system, and "revolutionize" society came as a surprise to everyone – the leaders attacked and purged, the general populace, and even radicals such as Yao Wenyuan, who was

[28] Friedman, Pickowicz, and Selden, *Chinese Village, Socialist State*, pp. 240, 272–273; Jasper Becker, *Hungry Ghosts: China's Secret Famine* (London: John Murray, 1996), pp. 309ff; and interview with Tao Lujia, July 1997.

[29] Anita Chan, Richard Madsen, and Jonathan Unger, *Chen Village: The Recent History of a Peasant Community in Mao's China* (Berkeley: University of California Press, 1984), pp. 74–93; and interview with work team member sent to central China villages in 1964–65, May 2007.

secretly enlisted by Mao to pen the first shot of the movement. The startling innovation of Mao's mid-1966 call to rebel against an ill-defined but subsequently expanding "bourgeoisie within the party" had the effect of breaking the hitherto sacred link of the party and its Chairman. As time went on, Mao's own understanding of the movement evolved, and by the start of 1967, he endorsed the destruction of the party organization. With the collapse of party control, chaotic mass turmoil from below caused extensive disruption to the economy and society and a significant loss of life over the two years to mid-1968. During this period, Mao observed developments from Olympian heights, alternately issuing directives to curb or encourage radicalism, but despite inserting the PLA as the ultimate organ of power in lieu of the party, he never provided clear authority to bring matters under control. When he finally became fed up with destructive mass violence in 1968, Mao initiated the most severe topdown repression since 1949 to restore order, particularly the murderous "cleansing of class ranks" campaign in the latter part of 1968 and 1969.

Beyond surprise, leaders at the Politburo level and in other highranking positions were uncertain as to the movement's meaning and the implications for themselves. After conducting the initial phase of the movement in Beijing universities with standard work team methods, Liu Shaoqi was startled to receive Mao's severe criticism when the Chairman returned to the capital in July 1966. The next month, Liu offered a self-criticism in a "voice belong[ing] to a man who was bewildered, ... adrift in a sea not of his making," and by October when he stood on the rostrum at Tiananmen, Liu's face was etched in fear.[30] Others at somewhat lower levels had faced the uncertainty earlier, drawing different conclusions. Playwright Wu Han, the target of Yao Wenyuan's first shot, like many others, thought that this would be another rectification movement where, after criticism, everything would be all right. But others drew much more alarming conclusions. Both Deng Tuo, Wu's colleague in the Beijing municipal apparatus, who also came under harsh criticism for his writings, and Tian Jiaying, Mao's secretary, who had used the secretaries' relative lack of constraint to present the Chairman with unwelcome views in 1962, saw a much bleaker future, knew it was impossible to repudiate Mao and undoubtedly had no desire to do so, and opted for suicide as a way out in the spring of 1966.[31]

---

[30] Rittenberg and Bennett, *Man Who Stayed Behind*, pp. 312–313, 329.

[31] See Teiwes, *Politics and Purges*, pp. lx–lxi, 460–464; Timothy Cheek, *Propaganda and Culture in Mao's China: Deng Tuo and the Intelligentsia* (Oxford, England: Oxford University Press, 1997), p. 283; and Teiwes with Sun, *China's Road to Disaster*, pp. 224–227.

The guessing game continued throughout 1966–71, with the Chairman's colleagues attempting to divine his intent at critical junctures – and often getting it wrong. A major case in point was the so-called "February adverse current," a meeting in February 1967 when a number of old leaders confronted the new Cultural Revolution group, led by Mao's wife, Jiang Qing, to complain about the excesses of the movement. While treated by Mao as an attack on *his* Cultural Revolution, the senior figures present thought they had an opening in Mao's recent criticism of Jiang's excesses. But everyone understood the overwhelming authority of Mao, and when he came down on the radicals' side, opposition melted away. Equally revealing of the need to be in tune with the Chairman were Zhou Enlai's efforts to protect other top leaders, something he only did within his understanding of Mao's wishes, and would crudely abandon when necessary. Thus, despite early efforts to provide some protection for Liu Shaoqi, when Mao determined that Liu was a traitor in 1968, Zhou scrawled on the relevant document, "Traitor Liu deserves execution." In this case of gross historical injustice, no one of significance offered the slightest objection.[32]

In personnel terms, the Cultural Revolution was devastating both to individuals and to previous patterns of leadership selection. Only seven full members of the 1956 Politburo were reelected in 1969, and of those, only Zhou, Ye Jianying, and Li Xiannian (plus Lin Biao) were active figures. The bulk of the Politburo was filled by "establishment beneficiaries" of the Cultural Revolution, lower-ranking party officials who could not have reasonably expected promotion to the top body on pre-1966 standards, and by radicals from the margins of the system. Moreover, many party leaders were treated abysmally, marched through the streets in dunces' hats, physically abused, and otherwise humiliated. And from the Politburo itself, Liu Shaoqi, He Long, and Peng Dehuai died at least in part because of mistreatment. Beyond this, there was a bizarre personal twist in Mao's handling of top leaders. While Liu, "the number one capitalist roader in the party" was hounded to a miserable death, Deng Xiaoping, "the number two capitalist roader," while also removed from office, was protected from harm on Mao's orders. Deng, like Lin Biao, had long been a personal favorite and was even considered

[32] See Frederick C. Teiwes and Warren Sun, *The Tragedy of Lin Biao: Riding the Tiger During the Cultural Revolution, 1966–1971* (London: C. Hurst & Co., 1996), pp. 72–79; and Sun Wanguo [Warren Sun], "Gu you Dou'e, jin you Lin Biao [There Was Dou'e in the Past, There Is Lin Biao in the Present]," in Ding Kaiwen, ed., *Chongshen Lin Biao zuian* [The Lin Biao Case Reassessed] (Hong Kong: Mirrorbooks, 2004), p. 164.

by Mao in 1967 as a replacement for Lin in view of his successor's poor health.[33]

Apart from bad health, Lin Biao's selection as successor in August 1966 illustrates the strangeness of Mao's relations with his top-level followers. Lin was reclusive, had no record or much interest in domestic politics, and above all did not want the position, but he could not refuse. Mao's motives undoubtedly included his favoritism toward his respectful younger colleague, Lin's recent (but hardly unique) role in promoting the Mao cult, and a calculation that as a revered PLA marshal, Lin would guarantee that the army would uphold the Cultural Revolution. Particularly strange was Lin's overall passivity during the movement, providing little apart from occasional *moderate* inputs and adhering to the principle of "in our work, we do no more than follow in [Mao's] wake."[34]

But Lin soon learned that given his inability to control members of his own household, this could not shield him from Mao's shifting attitudes during the fractious politics of the period. The decisive turning point was the summer of 1970 Lushan meeting, when, growing out of conflict between civilian radicals headed by Jiang Qing and a military group marshaled by Lin's wife, Ye Qun, and bizarrely focusing on Lin's advocacy of Mao's genius and whether Mao should be state president, Mao ruled in favor of Jiang Qing and demanded self-criticisms from Lin's supporters. Over the last year of his life, Lin did little more than seek to make amends, but Mao refused to see him. Meanwhile, a group of military officers headed by Lin's 24-year-old son, Lin Liguo, met secretly to discuss incoherent plans to overthrow Mao, in all likelihood without Lin's knowledge. With Mao pressing for a showdown, Lin and family fled China in September 1971, only to die in a plane crash in the Mongolian desert. Mao was not elated, instead suffering a physical and emotional downturn, one undoubtedly caused by dismay that a close favorite would flee, no matter how threatened he may have felt.[35]

Arguably, the most telling aspect concerning Mao's followers at the leadership level and throughout the party apparatus is that not only was there virtually no resistance to the purge of Liu Shaoqi and other elite figures, but also no evidence (leaving aside the dubious case of the very young Lin Liguo) of leaders opposing Mao to protect themselves.

[33] See Frederick C. Teiwes and Warren Sun, *The End of the Maoist Era: Chinese Politics During the Twilight of the Cultural Revolution, 1972–1976* (Armonk, NY: M. E. Sharpe, 2007), pp. 19–20, 25, 66ff.

[34] Teiwes and Sun, *Tragedy*, p. 1 and *passim*.

[35] See *ibid.*, pp. 134–160; and Teiwes and Sun, *End of the Maoist Era*, pp. 31–32.

There was much maneuvering, attempts to form protective networks, and assertions of loyalty to the Chairman, but once Mao placed someone in the suspect camp, there was no rejoinder except to wait for his review of the person's case. This was not simply a prudent reading of political realities; it also reflected a deeply held sense of Mao's historic position. A case in point was the January 1972 funeral of Marshal Chen Yi, a revolutionary hero and foreign minister on the eve of the Cultural Revolution who had been strongly attacked during the movement. When Mao unexpectedly turned up at the service in his pajamas, Chen's wife attempted to apologize for Chen's faults, but Mao rejected her efforts and praised the marshal. The family's reaction was one of pride and gratitude. Chen's contributions to the communist cause, after all, were now validated by the man who made the revolution.

If the Cultural Revolution had largely been a searingly negative experience for the top leadership and party apparatus more broadly, the impact on society generally was more mixed and variable as events unfolded. Clearly, a wide range of factors shaped the reactions of subgroups within larger categories – class designations, economic situations and opportunities, tensions between activists and others, and intraorganization political networks, among others. Inevitably, attitudes toward Mao varied greatly, but with great devotion and fanaticism in at least some groups as a burgeoning cult, an appealing antibureaucratic message, and the mobilization of grievances became staples of incessant propaganda.

The leading edge of the Cultural Revolution onslaught was provided by student Red Guards who, along with rebel groups in official organizations, were enveloped in "a trance of excitement and change." In attacking party leaders and "bourgeois authorities," these excited youths took inspiration from Mao's often vague pronouncements, generally believing the sanctity of his words and making serious efforts to figure out what they meant. Often these efforts resulted in rationalizations of the interests of specific Red Guard factions, and as the movement splintered, contending factions confronted each other with dueling Mao quotations, a situation in which both sides were sincere, technically correct because each used exact quotations, and driven to self-righteousness in the belief that they had Mao's backing. Such self-righteousness fueled bloody clashes, with each faction proclaiming loyalty to the Chairman. Even when faced with questions such as how Liu Shaoqi could have consistently carried out a wrong line without Mao knowing, doubts were ignored by rebels, who believed it impossible that Mao could make a mistake. More broadly, as one college student at the time later recalled, she worshipped Mao above everything and observed that this was typical of her "pure and innocent" generation.[36]

Worship led to extreme behavior, whether in pitched battles between rebel groups, brutal attacks on defenseless "black elements," or severing family ties. Belief merged with religion, as seen in the fervor of the young, whereas older cadres recall still believing in Mao, but in a measured way. The rituals of the time reinforced the religious atmosphere, with loyalty dances to the Chairman and reports directed to his photo (for more on Mao the Icon, see Chapter 9). Mao, previously a hero, had become a god. But more than religious piety was involved; as in many religions, fear accompanied belief. A graphic illustration occurred in the home of a Shanghai journalist as a child. When Mao's portrait accidentally fell off the wall, his terrified mother fell to her knees before it, begging forgiveness.[37] Yet, for all the extremity of the period, there were striking continuities with the previous capacity of the system to generate belief, anxiety, and self-doubt. In a southern China village, a disgraced local Red Guard responded to psychological pressure in a manner eerily similar to Rittenberg at the dawn of the PRC and Liu Binyan during the Anti-Rightist Campaign: "I still believed in Mao Zedong. So I was afraid that perhaps my own thoughts were wrong.... I truly felt ashamed of my faults."[38]

Such behavior, of course, was not universal, and significant disillusionment and cynicism set in as the Cultural Revolution ground on. One factor was growing perceptions that the movement was a barely comprehensible leadership struggle where the masses were being used by Mao. Endless strife also fed disengagement, whereas those deeply involved in ongoing factional battles increasingly acted more as calculating participants than as true believers. While undoubtedly many continued to love Mao regardless, by the end of the 1960s, others had lost faith or even had developed hatred for him, whether owing to exposure to particularly brutal acts, the destruction of a relative, or simply the conclusion that Mao's great project was a charade rather than a genuine revolution.[39] But arguably more indicative of "public opinion" than either ongoing devotion or hidden hatred toward Mao were the

[36] See Fulang Lo, *Morning Breeze: A True Story of China's Cultural Revolution* (San Francisco, CA: China Books & Periodicals, 1989), p. 98; and Feng Jicai, *Ten Years of Madness: Oral Histories of China's Cultural Revolution* (San Francisco, CA: China Books & Periodicals, 1996), p. 102.

[37] Tan, *Chinese Factor*, p. 131; and interview, November 2002.

[38] Chan, Madsen, and Unger, *Chen Village*, p. 158.

[39] See Lo, *Morning Breeze*, pp. 52, 134–135; and Yang and McFadden, *Captive Spirits*, pp. 102–103.

attitudes of the less engaged, nonactivists in various units and the so-called bystander faction of youths. Such people were disenchanted with the Cultural Revolution, but the evidence suggests that on the whole they continued to believe in Mao, even if they no longer believed in anything else, and, in a familiar pattern, when considering responsibility, blamed the Chairman's subordinates.[40] Belief and fear contributed to this, along with Mao's historic achievements and the drumbeat of incessant propaganda. Yang Xiguang perceptively captured the mix of these factors by observing that not only were most of his fellow inmates afraid to oppose the Chairman, but "almost no one dares to *doubt* Mao, even privately."[41]

FRAIL IN BODY, SHIFTING ATTITUDES, ABSOLUTE AUTHORITY, 1972–76

The Lin Biao affair marked a turning point. Whether or not it was directly responsible for Mao's deteriorating health, by early 1972, his condition was so parlous that a special Politburo team was set up to monitor his progress. This situation continued to late 1975, when Mao's health took a decided turn for the worse, and in the summer of 1976, he fell into a virtual coma until his death in September. Mao's declining health contributed to his farther distance from his leadership colleagues, seldom seeing Politburo leaders and relying on relatives to convey his instructions. Equally significant, the shock of Lin's apostasy encouraged Mao to intensify moves to rebuild party and government organizations and curb "ultraleft" behavior. Realizing that the demise of his successor caused serious doubts about the Cultural Revolution, he moved to save *his* movement by addressing its problems. Mao claimed that the Cultural Revolution had "70 percent achievements, 30 percent mistakes," and for much of the period, he focused on correcting the 30 percent mistakes.[42] The essence was achievements, however, and whenever he believed rectifying problems threatened the essence of the movement, he called a halt, most notably in late 1975 with the result that Deng Xiaoping, who had been recalled and given the assignment of righting the situation, was removed from office a second time. These shifting policies further diminished Mao's credibility, with the shabby treatment of Zhou Enlai after his death in January 1976 and the April

---

[40] Chan, Madsen, and Unger, *Chen Village*, pp. 148, 156–157; and interview with middle school student of the period, May 2007.

[41] Yang and McFadden, *Captive Spirits*, p. 115 (emphasis added).

[42] See Teiwes and Sun, *End of the Maoist Era*, pp. 3, 11–12, 26ff, 96–97.

Tiananmen incident protesting that treatment resulting in a new low point in Mao's popular standing. Yet throughout these last years Mao was obeyed, no leadership figure challenged his erratic behavior, and the massive problems caused by his legacy were left for resolution after his passing.

Mao's reshaping of the Politburo in 1973 created a diverse leadership group and a new dynamic, one that, in contrast to the bitter attacks on established leaders in 1966–68, was restrained by the Chairman's repeated calls for unity even as ongoing conflict reflected his two-sided approach of correcting Cultural Revolution excesses while upholding its spirit. A limited core of old revolutionaries consisting of Zhou, Ye Jianying, Li Xiannian, and Deng Xiaoping played key roles in managing the party-state. But almost equally important were the younger "establishment beneficiaries" of the Cultural Revolution whose socialization in the party apparatus meant that their policy preferences and instinctive respect were directed to the old guard. Significantly, these "beneficiaries" had all been well known by Mao before 1966, thus providing him with trusted subordinates. In contrast, apart from his wife, Mao had little personal knowledge of the core radical group, the so-called gang of four. Most dramatic was the young former factory official and Shanghai rebel leader, Wang Hongwen, who astonishingly was selected as Mao's successor in 1973. In sum, even allowing for the independent revolutionary prestige of Zhou and Deng, the post–Lin Biao leaders all owed their position to Mao – and were unquestioningly loyal to him.[43]

Mao's relations with this eclectic group were further complicated by his personal preferences and preoccupations, as seen strikingly in his treatment of Zhou and Deng. Although Zhou was never purged, it was the younger, twice-dismissed Deng, the student to Mao's teacher, who was always the favorite, whereas Mao regarded Zhou with envy for his large domestic and international prestige and with disdain as politically and ideologically weak. Simply put, although relying on Zhou for the crucial task of U.S.-China rapprochement, Mao treated the Premier abominably, subjecting him to severe criticism on tenuous charges and forcing him to suffer such criticism while in pain with terminal cancer. Deng, in contrast, earned Mao's glowing praise as well as his delighted excitement ("I knew he would") when he learned that Deng had joined in the humiliation of Zhou in late 1973.[44]

---

[43] See *ibid.*, pp. 12–14, 93ff, 601.
[44] See *ibid.*, pp. 19–23, 132ff.

Mao's deeply personal attitudes extended to the radical camp. The key figure was Jiang Qing. For all of Mao's criticisms of the political excesses of the "gang of four," in fact, they were overwhelmingly directed at Jiang personally. The paradox is that Jiang's "special status" as Mao's wife not only inhibited criticism of her by other leaders but also infused the Chairman's own attitudes. He made it clear that she was not to be attacked; "not opposing Jiang Qing" was a condition of Deng's return. Nevertheless, while they had not lived together for many years, much of Mao's critical attitude carried an overlay of marital tensions.[45]

As had been increasingly the case since the early 1960s, the over-arching problem for leaders of all stripes was to correctly understand Mao's often ambiguous intent. The most graphic case occurred in 1975 when the most systematic, if still guarded, effort to correct the 30 percent faults of the Cultural Revolution was undertaken by Deng. As in all shifts to either the "right" or "left" in 1972–76, the new direction originated with Mao. What was different in 1975 was both the range of corrective measures Mao endorsed and the extent of the authority he gave to Deng to carry out the new course. But the issue remained of just how far Mao wanted Deng to go, as reflected in the question posed by Chen Yun to Deng at the time: "Did you accurately get Chairman Mao"s pulse [i.e., understand his meaning] or not?" Deng confidently answered that he had but was astonished in the fall when Mao turned against him for ignoring the Cultural Revolution. Significantly, the doubts had not been put in Mao's mind by the Politburo radicals. Instead, they origi-nated in the complaints of the Chairman's nephew, Mao Yuanxin, that Deng's measures were undermining the Cultural Revolution. That Mao took more notice of his young relative than the "gang of four" suggests not only greater access but also a willingness on Mao Yuanxin's part to press his case that was arguably similar to that of the Chairman's sec-retaries in earlier periods. In any case, from October 1975, Mao Yuanxin became the Chairman's liaison to the rest of the leadership, exercising enormous influence in the process.[46]

Throughout this last period of Mao's life, although the political fear of being out of tune with his wishes was as strong as ever, there was an amelioration of life-and-death fear within the elite, at least for the time being. This was due in part to the experience gained during 1966–68. Then leaders were in a panic over unprecedented attacks; now they were better prepared to endure radical criticism during leftist upsurges. But

[45] See *ibid.*, pp. 14, 190–192, 212–213.
[46] See *ibid.*, pp. 3, 374ff, 387, 399ff, 476ff, 597ff.

the key factors were not only that Mao had banned physical attacks on leaders but also that he was seemingly adhering to traditional rules, in particular by rehabilitating cadres and thus making amends for Cultural Revolution excesses. Rehabilitations unfolded with increasing scope in 1972–75, with Mao both initiating the process and vetting each case. While the picture was complicated by a real fear of what might happen after Mao's death if the "gang of four" seized control, there also were expectations, akin to those of Wu Han in 1966, that even a critical Chairman would forgive mistakes, and things would be okay after criticism and self-criticism. A case in point was Minister of Education Zhou Rongxin. Despite pointed attacks in the fall of 1975, Zhou refused to believe that his case was serious, departed on an overseas trip without much concern, and even after returning concluded that at worst he would be demoted to ambassadorial status. He was mistaken (he died of his heart condition while under political attack in April 1976), but nearly all people of his station avoided serious consequences during the radical upsurge of 1976.[47]

The most constant feature of Mao's relations with his elite followers was their acceptance of his absolute authority, something seen dramatically in the last year of Mao's life even as his actions endangered moderate leaders. His removal of Deng was unchallenged by Deng or anyone else. No one questioned the accuracy of the Chairman's directives as relayed by Mao Yuanxin. While there was considerable elite unhappiness with the arrangements for Zhou Enlai's funeral, Mao's determination to keep these as limited as possible was obeyed. When popular resentment broke out on Tiananmen Square, no one in the top leadership supported the mass sentiments, the Politburo was determined to uphold Mao's prestige, and his directive for a forceful but nonlethal clearing of the square was strictly carried out. And even after Mao slipped into a coma in late July, his political line was unquestioned, and despite fears about the actions of the "gang of four," as part of his Politburo team, they were untouched while he lived. Graphic examples of elite loyalty to Mao came with the reactions of two of his quasi-confidants at the time of his death. Wang Li, the young radical who accompanied Mao on his 1967 tour at a key point in the Cultural Revolution but was later imprisoned, wept at the news from his cell. Meanwhile, Hu Qiaomu, ousted in 1966, returned to work in 1975 as an expert who could interpret Mao's meaning but, again heavily criticized as a "rightist" in 1976, was denied official status at Mao's funeral. It was a bitter blow as he stood among

---

[47] See *ibid.*, pp. 419–423, 431–432, 455–456, note 177, 611ff.

the masses at Tiananmen mourning the man he had served for so long and so closely.[48]

In comparison with the elite, there was greater erosion of Mao's standing in the broader public in 1972–76, although it is difficult to avoid the conclusion that overall he retained the status of legitimate emperor at his death. If the Lin Biao affair shocked even senior members of the leadership, it had a disorienting effect among ordinary communists and cadres, intellectuals, and social groups more broadly. While many had been able to suppress doubts concerning Mao's ignorance of Liu Shaoqi's counterrevolutionary activities, the revelation that his personally anointed successor planned to assassinate the Chairman was much harder for people from various walks of life to rationalize. As one disillusioned party intellectual put it, she "became aware that something was fundamental wrong with the system in which [she and her party intellectual husband] ... had believed so devotedly." But what is striking is evidence that many people did not extend their disillusionment to a rejection of Mao. Some retained admiration by excusing him as old and sick; others concluded that the Politburo radicals – not Mao – were responsible for continuing "leftist" excesses; and still others proclaimed deep feeling for Mao even as they attacked the Cultural Revolution.[49] For many it took the events of late 1975 against Deng to destroy their hope that Mao had turned away from radicalism. According to Liu Binyan, "I began to doubt Mao then. People like me started turning our hopes toward what might happen after Mao died."[50]

Worse was to come with the insensitivity to public opinion over Zhou's death and the 1976 Tiananmen incident. These events finally drove many people in various groups to lose their remaining faith in the Chairman. By this time, the widespread discontent with radicalism spilled over into ill-feeling toward Mao. While the discipline of the system restricted public opposition, people were more willing to vent their opinions among themselves, with anger over the treatment of Zhou finally leading people to say what they were thinking. And, of course, obvious if allegorical attacks on Mao at Tiananmen in April were what most worried the leadership. In this unhappy atmosphere, aware citizens awaited Mao's death, some hoping it would come soon.

---

[48] See *ibid.*, pp. 382, 405, 413ff, 435ff, 475ff, 553; and Roderick MacFarquhar and Michael Schoenhals, *Mao's Last Revolution* (Cambridge, MA: Belknap Press, 2006), p. 442.

[49] See MacFarquhar and Schoenhals, *Mao's Last Revolution*, pp. 338–339, 350ff.

[50] Liu Binyan, *Two Kinds of Truth*, p. 8.

While the decline in Mao's standing among his followers in society is clear, an overall assessment must be speculative. Undoubtedly many millions remained in thrall of fundamentalist faith in Mao. While sobbing and wailing at his death may have been pro forma for many, for many others it reflected immersion in the Mao myth that encompassed personal revolutionary experience and benefits from Mao's regime. The depth of the religious and fear-enhanced worship that remained was illustrated shortly before the Chairman's death following the Tangshan earthquake when a village youth looked for his mother but, seeing both her and a bust of Mao, rescued the bust first before turning to help his mom.[51] Yet perhaps the general public attitude is best captured by the second quotation at the start of this chapter: Despite widespread dismay at his recent politics, Mao remained a figure that was difficult to deny. Yet, what is striking is the apparent lack of emotion in many circles at the Chairman's passing – loyalty was still there, but feeling was fading. This is tellingly revealed by Sidney Rittenberg's recollection of his second stint in Mao's prisons. Whereas Zhou's death had produced genuine grief from Rittenberg, fellow inmates, and prison personnel, the reaction to Mao's passing was cold. Rittenberg recalled his own puzzling reaction: "I couldn't understand my reaction. In my mind, Mao was the most important man in the world, wise, gifted, philosophically sound, strategically masterful.... His death was much more serious than Zhou's.... And yet I could not produce a single tear when news came of Mao's death."[52] Many Chinese would have experienced a similar reaction at the end of decades of loyalty to the Chairman.

EXPLAINING THE LOYALTY OF MAO'S FOLLOWERS

Despite the disasters of his last two decades and fading faith in the Chairman, many diverse citizens, including those with personal hatred for Mao, believe that at the end of his life and after his death Mao's prestige was still high with the peasants and lower orders generally. This was clearly a factor, along with personal loyalty, leading Deng and other leaders to continue to uphold his banner on the political, as opposed to policy, level. Down to this day, Mao and the PRC are inseparable.

What explains the enduring loyalty of virtually all of Mao's top colleagues, the great bulk of party officials, and probably the majority within almost all social groups? In the broadest terms, this loyalty reflected a

---

[51] Feng, *Ten Years*, p. 98.
[52] Rittenberg and Bennett, *Man Who Stayed Behind*, p. 427.

combination of belief, fear, and moral authority. Over Mao's last two decades, belief diminished, whereas fear increased, but belief remained a major factor to the end, and both factors were linked to the moral authority of Mao as the father of the country, the leader who gave meaning to elite lives, was venerated in many villages for destroying old evils and ending chaos, and the omnipresent emperor who most people believed was concerned with the good of the nation. Belief was generated by a combination of real achievements and a potent national myth. Many concrete gains came in the period to 1956 – peace and social order, a modicum of prosperity, rapid economic construction, employment opportunities for the expanding working class, and economic and political benefits for the poor peasantry from land reform. But the enduring national myth was more important, the narrative of overturning an exploitative social system, liberating the people, creating social equality, and, above all, expelling the foreign powers and restoring China's national dignity. In both official propaganda and popular consciousness, Mao was at the center of this narrative, and as actual achievements were overtaken by great tragedies, his followers in the elite and society increasingly looked back to that formative myth in order to rationalize their continuing loyalty. Thus, as chaos spread, a perplexed Red Guard recalled Mao's successes in defeating the Japanese and GMD, concluding: "He is our greatest hero [and] must want to do something good ... in launching the Cultural Revolution."[53] Similar rationalizations concerning his good intentions supported belief in Mao for the remainder of his days.

The national myth also was a communist myth, and loyalty to Mao likewise was furthered by the deeply held belief that he was advancing China toward a classless society. This was most palpable for the elite and party intellectuals, but it also affected many ordinary communists and cadres. Such ideological commitment also contributed to support for such wild ventures as reaching communism in a few short years during the Great Leap or frontally attacking "bourgeois" phenomena during the Cultural Revolution. Beyond general or specific support, however, ideological commitment facilitated psychologically induced anxiety as individuals sought inclusion in the sacred community. The acceptance of Mao was necessary not only to avoid punishment but also to appease one's own sense of guilt and make sure that one was morally in tune with the infallible leader of the revolution.

An even stronger force influenced society from top to bottom – Chinese political culture. People from many walks of life cite Chinese

---

[53] Lo, *Morning Breeze*, p. 68.

culture as an explanation for loyalty to Mao. One recurrent theme is the proclivity to submit to authority, particularly to strong leaders of which none were more worthy of obeisance than the founding emperor of a dynasty. Mao, of course, exemplified a "severe and brilliant" first emperor, but as Shanghai critic Li Jie has observed, he further came to embody the "sage emperor so dear to the hearts of the Chinese."[54] Part of the cultural preconception is that any emperor should be, and generally is, a benevolent, upright ruler who is concerned with the overall good of the realm rather than self-interest. Thus, when things go wrong, fault is instinctively assigned to subordinate officials, and throughout the Mao era, many believed that if only the Chairman knew, matters would be righted.

For all Mao's real and mythic achievements and the deeply supporting patterns of Chinese culture, the esteem in which he was held by his vast range of followers was also deliberately constructed. The totalitarian propaganda state, as one interviewee put it, meant that virtually from birth he assimilated the idea of Mao as a great leader. This was not only the result of incessant (if varying intensity) media propaganda, but it also was incorporated in everyday life – in schools, work units, and neighborhood organizations. Crucially, obeisance to Mao was linked to the state's coercive apparatus and the party's political campaigns that added psychological pressure and fear to the mix. Such pressure not only affected committed communists like Rittenberg and Liu Binyan, even school children resolved their anxieties by identifying with Mao. A former ordinary cadre recalled, while each successive movement made her wonder, Mao's standing was a delicate matter best left unaddressed – she was brainwashed, didn't dare question Mao even to herself, and survival increasingly became her only concern. Arguably, the most potent aspect of the propaganda state was its monopoly of ways to look at the world. Recollections repeatedly point to the absence of arguments for resistance, the lack of any alternative framework for judging events, and the inability to think independently. As Yang Xiguang observed of his fellow inmates, on the whole they were unable to escape the system's mental bondage, with "few people [able to] even know what [a rightist critic] is talking about," and as noted previously, "almost no one dares to doubt Mao, even privately."[55]

---

[54] See Geremie R. Barme, *In the Red: On Contemporary Chinese Culture* (New York: Columbia University Press, 1999), pp. 321–322.

[55] Feng, *Ten Years*, p. 12; Yang and McFadden, *Captive Spirits*, pp. 36, 115; and interviews with sources cited in notes 2 and 17.

For all the preceding reasons, there was a remarkable degree of loyalty, even reverence, toward Mao, where his right to rule was either actively supported or passively accepted. For broad social groups, notwithstanding dissidents within various strata and growing doubts as Mao's era proceeded, by and large his considerable prestige remained. A former cadre who, in the last months of Mao's life, found herself in sympathy with a colleague being attacked for wishing he would die, nevertheless, at the Chairman's death still was of the opinion that he "had been a great man but had exceeded the limit."[56] Similarly, committed party intellectuals only gradually lost faith in the Chairman toward the end of his life and beyond, as in Rittenberg's case, as he remained loyal after his release from prison before painstakingly coming to the view that Mao's "tragic hubris" had caused great damage yet could not completely eclipse his outstanding achievements.[57] Further up the political structure, important elite members who became significant post-Mao reformers could not disassociate themselves from Mao. In 1979, liberal *People's Daily* editor-in-chief Hu Jiwei reacted with incredulity that his loyalty could be doubted: "Who would oppose Chairman Mao after participating in the revolution for so many years?"[58]

Hu's remark pointed to Mao's real achievement in winning the revolutionary struggle, the very factor that produced the greatest loyalty from the Chairman's top leadership colleagues. As reflected in Deng's comment at the start of this chapter, Mao's achievements could not be denied; his brilliance, in their view, had created the unimaginable victory that gave validation to their life endeavors. Owing to the victory of the real revolution of 1949, Mao Zedong not only was obeyed, but he also was forgiven for grave errors that damaged China, the CCP, and these leading followers who had sometimes suffered grievously despite unbending loyalty to their leader. It was a moral obligation that could not be denied.

---

[56] Tan, *Chinese Factor*, p. 245.

[57] Rittenberg and Bennett, *Man Who Stayed Behind*, pp. 434ff, 449.

[58] Hu Jiwei, "Report on a Series of Struggles in the Top Echelons of the CCP" (September 13, 1979), *Zhengming* [Contention], August 1, 1980, in FBIS – People's Republic of China, August 15, 1980, p. U2.

Figure 1. Mao giving a report to cadres in front of his cave home in Yan'an, 1942. Photographer Wu Yinxian gave this the title, "Builder of a New Cause." © Wu Yinxian/ChinaStock.

Figure 2. Mao posing for an official photo, Yan'an, 1945. © Wu Yinxian/ ChinaStock.

Figure 3. Red Army generals Peng Dehuai (*right*) and Zhu De in Wuxiang, Shanxi, around 1939–40. © ChinaStock Collection.

Figure 4. "Chongqing Talks Begin": US envoy Patrick Hurley brings Mao (to his right) and Zhou Enlai (to his left) to Chongqing to negotiate with the Nationalist government at the end of World War II in 1945. Guomindang General Zhang Chunzhong is at far left; Wang Jie of the CCP is at the far right. © Wu Yinxian/ChinaStock.

Figure 5. Mao with Stalin in Moscow, December 21, 1949, during negotiations of the Sino-Soviet friendship treaty. © ChinaStock Collection.

Figure 6. Mao with Deng Xiaoping, 1959. © Hou Bo/New China Pictures/ ChinaStock.

Figure 7. Family gathering of Mao Zedong in 1962, with his second son, Mao Anqing, at left, and daughters-in-law, Shao Hua, second from left, and Liu Siqi, third from right. Couple at right are not known. © Lu Houmin/ChinaStock.

Figure 8. Mao with party leaders at the 7,000 Cadres Conference of January 1962 that faced the failures of the Great Leap. From left to right: Zhou Enlai, Chen Yun, Liu Shaoqi, Mao, Deng Xiaoping, and Peng Zhen. © Lu Houmin/ChinaStock.

Figure 9. *Red Star over China* – wood cut of Mao in *Resistance Weekly*, June 22, 1937 (personal copy). For analysis of these propaganda images of Mao, see Chapter 9.

Figure 10. Mao and Stalin in Beijing's *People's Daily*, February 15, 1950, presenting Mao the same size as the Soviet leader (personal copy).

Figure 11. *The Founding of the Nation*, Dong Xiwen's famous poster of Mao speaking from the top of Tiananmen at the Founding Ceremony of the People's Republic of China, October 1, 1949. This version from 1964. Collection International Institute of Social History, Amsterdam [e13–960].

人民公社好

我们的伟大领袖毛主席，在大跃进的一九五八年巡视大江南北。

Figure 12. *People's Communes Are Good!* Poster extolling the Great Leap Forward using a photo from one of Mao's inspection tours of the new People's Communes in 1958. Poster from New China News Agency, 1969. Collection International Institute of Social History, Amsterdam [e13–552].

Figure 13. Image of the "Iron Woman" as engineer, 1953. Caption reads: "Study the Fighting Spirit of the Red Army's Long March. Conquer Nature to Build the Fatherland." Collection International Institute of Social History, Amsterdam [e15–832].

Figure 14. *The Three Loyalties* – to Mao, his Thought, and his Revolutionary Line. From the Cultural Revolution (*ca.* 1968). Denounced as "modern superstition" in post-Mao China, this loyalty to Mao and the party engulfed the nation in the 1960s. Here, a godlike Mao appears out of the sun in his signature military uniform above jubilant workers, peasants, and soldiers carrying a huge sunflower with "Loyalty" and various quotations from Mao and the banner, "Long Live Chairman Mao!" Collection International Institute of Social History, Amsterdam [e15–506].

Figure 15. Unofficial photos of Mao in a Red Guard broadsheet from the Cultural Revolution, *ca.* 1967 (personal copy).

毛 主 席 去 安 源

一九二一年秋，我们伟大的导师毛主席去安源，亲自点燃了安源的革命烈火。

Figure 16. *Chairman Mao Going to Anyuan*. A mythologized image of the young Mao heading off to famous labor strikes in the 1920s. Poster from 1968. Collection International Institute of Social History, Amsterdam [e12–703].

7 Mao, Mao Zedong Thought, and Communist Intellectuals

HUNG-YOK IP

It has been said that Mao Zedong always disagreed with his intellectual comrades. In his career, he clashed with many leading revolutionaries in terms of ideology formation and/or policymaking. He caused irreparable damage to educated revolutionaries through his anti-intellectual stance. By looking into his ideological development, culminating in what is conventionally dubbed "Mao Zedong Thought,"[1] I argue that despite his conflicts with many communist intellectuals,[2] Mao shared with them similar concerns and ideas. In so doing, I shall analyze his theorization about the role of communist intellectuals in the Revolution. This dimension is chosen for two reasons. First, it is most germane to Mao and his colleagues because they always assumed that they were members of this coterie. And second, Mao and other communist thinkers drew on their experiences to contemplate what they as the educated revolutionary elite should do in order to accomplish their mission of

I must express my appreciation to Delia Davin and Joseph Esherick for reading this chapter, correcting its mistakes, and improving its presentation. Timothy Cheek, who asked me to write this chapter and then edited it with great care, deserves special thanks.

[1] The term "Mao Zedong Thought" was invented in 1943. To analyze it, I basically use Takeuchi Minoru, ed., *Mao Zedong ji* [Collected Writings of Mao Zedong] (Tokyo: Hokubosha, 1972), based mainly on the 1944 and 1947 versions of *Mao Zedong xuanji*, but importantly, Takeuchi's team compares these "collective wisdom" versions of Mao's thought to the original publications (and to later changes in the 1950s editions of Mao's *Works*). These "collective wisdom" collections refers to sets of Mao's writings edited by party authorities who assumed that Mao's ideas represented Sinicized Marxism-Leninism and enjoyed the consensus of CCP leadership. See Timothy Cheek, *Mao Zedong and China's Revolutions: A Brief History with Documents* (New York: St. Martin's Press, 2002), pp. 37–38. In this chapter I use *Mao Zedong ji* in conjunction with Stuart Schram's translations in *Mao's Road to Power: Revolutionary Writings, 1912–1949* (Armonk, NY: M. E. Sharpe, 1992—).

[2] I adopt basically the CCP's pre-1949 definition of intellectuals: Revolutionary intellectuals in the communist Revolution were those who had received at least a high school education or its equivalent. See Hung-yok Ip, *Intellectuals in Revolutionary China, 1921–1949: Leaders, Heroes and Sophisticates* (London: Routledge: 2005).

revolutionizing China. As a result, Mao's discussion on revolutionary intellectuals reflects the themes defining Mao Zedong Thought.

This chapter is divided into three sections. First, to show that communist intellectuals laid the foundation for Mao Zedong Thought, I shall examine the ideological milieu of the communist Revolution: I focus on how revolutionary intellectuals contemplated their own role in the Revolution generally and in the rural Revolution especially in view of Mao's largely rural career. Second, I analyze how Mao theorized revolutionary intellectuals' performance in the mass-based Revolution, resonating with the communist ideological milieu, and systematizing and vigorously promoting those ideological themes he shared with other leading revolutionary intellectuals. And finally, I conclude with my reflections on the significance of Mao Zedong Thought.

THE IDEOLOGICAL MILIEU: ANTIELITIST ELITISM

Chapter 2 has given us a sense of the broader ideological world in which Mao operated. Here I want to emphasize that Mao wrote in an ideological milieu characterized by revolutionary intellectuals' antielitist elitism. On the one hand, they occupied the elite position, expanding on the masses' shortcomings and insisting on their privilege to possess the knowledge of historical destiny. On the other hand, though, they celebrated the masses' importance as historical subjects and critically dissected intellectuals' imperfections.

Imperfect Leaders Leading the Imperfect Masses

Communist intellectuals' antielitist elitism existed from the onset of the Revolution.[3] In 1921, together with a group of young radicals, Shen Dingyi (1883–1928), a 1911 revolutionary who joined the communist cell in Shanghai in 1920, took the initiative to organize a peasant movement in his native village, Yaqian, located in Xiaoshan County of Zhejiang Province. Interacting with local peasants, he asserted his own elitism: "I want to plan ... for you so as to help free you from all kinds of suffering."[4] For him, his leadership was necessary because, uneducated,

---

[3] For politically concerned intellectuals' complex views on the masses and especially the peasantry in Republican China, see Maurice Meisner, Li Ta-chao and the Origins of Chinese Marxism (Cambridge, MA: Harvard University Press, 1967); Arif Dirlik, The Origins of Chinese Communism (New York: Oxford University Press, 1989); Han Xiaorong, Chinese Discourse on the Peasants 1900–1949 (Albany, NY: State University of New York Press, 2005).

[4] Shen Dingyi, "Shui shi ni de pengyou? [Who are your friends?]," in Zhonggong Zhejiang shengwei dangshi ziliao zhengji yanjiu weiyuanhui and Zhonggong

the peasants could not become modernized without his village school. More deplorably, in his analysis, the local masses were weak in class consciousness, showing the most unfortunate propensity to "make friends with the capitalists" and "treat their own kind as enemies." They were, naturally, unable to launch a revolution.[5] Therefore, Shen showed no hesitation in reserving for revolutionary intellectuals such as himself a prophetic voice projecting the destiny of history. He made it crystal clear that the elite, but not the masses, was entitled to define the course of historical transformation: Treating rent resistance and rent reduction as preliminary targets of the communist Revolution, he told the peasants unequivocally that the ultimate goal of the Revolution was to abolish private property.[6]

However, Yaqian intellectuals' elitism was coupled with their anti-elitist stance. Working at a time when revolutionary ideology in China was not yet Leninist or Bolshevized, Shen Dingyi told the peasants, at least rhetorically, that revolutionary intellectuals' leadership was transitory: "Self-determination is the only method you can use in order to survive."[7] More important, he quickly became aware of his limitations as an intellectual and reformed himself in order to communicate – hence lead – the peasants more effectively. According to Keith Schoppa, he spoke in the local dialect in speeches delivered to the peasants and wore the clothes of the farmers.[8] Young radicals working under his auspices, too, were imbued with the spirit of self-evaluation. Wang Guansan, one of them, admitted his own ignorance of local conditions and needs, as he documented a peasant's response to his plea for supporting education for rural children: "The school is far away from our home.... Moreover, whenever I ask him what he learned from the school, he replies: 'Here is one cat, and there are two cats.'" Although he set out to remove ignorance of the rural area, he came away feeling embarrassed about how little he knew about the local folks.[9]

The Yaqian radicals' campaign was short-lived, but antielitist elitism had a life of its own. It evolved quickly, as seen in the case of Peng Pai,

---

Xiaoshan xianwei dangshi ziliao zhengji yanjiu weiyuanhui, eds., *Yaqian nongmin yundong* [The Yaqian Peasant Movement] (Beijing: Zhonggong dangshi ziliao chubanshe, [1921] 1987), p. 16.

[5] *Ibid.*, pp. 14–15.

[6] Shen Dingyi, "Nongmin zijue [Self-Determination of the Peasants]," in *Yaqian nongmin yundong*, p. 20.

[7] *Ibid.*

[8] Keith Schoppa, *Blood Road: The Mystery of Shen Dingyi in Revolutionary China* (Berkeley: University of California Press, 1995), p. 103.

[9] Wang Guansan, "Jiating fangwenji [My Visits to Peasant Families]," in *Yaqian nongmin yundong*, p. 46.

who launched the Haifeng Peasant Movement in Guangdong (1922–29). On his return from Japan, Peng founded the Haifeng County General Peasant Association in 1923 before joining the Chinese Communist Party (CCP) the next year. Like Shen Dingyi, he was an elitist leader, believing that leading the socialist Revolution was the prerogative of the intellectuals because "they have the chance to receive a better education and are more knowledgeable."[10] In his famous report on the Haifeng Peasant Movement, he detailed local peasants' defects, expanding on their lack of class consciousness and insufficient education.[11] However, mirroring Shen, he chose not to celebrate his authority but concentrated on the importance of the peasants' self-emancipation: In 1923, after the peasants had forced the local authority to release some activists from the county prison, he encouraged them: "This success has nothing to do with Peng Pai's ability.... [Our] comrades' release from prison is the result of your struggle to help and save yourselves."[12] Moreover, he shared the Yaqian intellectuals' understanding that self-reform was necessary if he wanted to communicate with and guide the peasants successfully. Writing to a good friend in the early 1920s, he described how he "de-intellectualized" himself: He threw away his fashionable attire and gave up his comparatively refined linguistic style.

However, Peng Pai strengthened the elitist part of his antielitist elitism in the latter half of his political career. In the late 1920s, as a member of the Central Committee of the CCP, Peng worked with a leading core that was remaking its organization into a Bolshevik-style party. He celebrated peasant independence no more when he delivered a speech in 1927, two days before he founded the Haifeng Soviet: "The party leads us to rise up and overthrow the reactionary government and the reactionary army. The party also guides us to kill all the local bullies and bad gentry."[13] Whereas Shen Dingyi organized a rent reduction and resistance movement while dreaming of socialism, Peng Pai in late 1927 eagerly anticipated an imminent transition to socialist Revolution while implementing the program of land redistribution. He quickly

---

[10] Peng Pai, "Shui yingdang chulai tichang shehui zhuyi? [Who Should Promote Socialism?]," in *Peng Pai wenji* [The Works of Peng Pai] (Beijing: Renmin chubanshe, [1922] 1981), p. 9.

[11] Peng Pai, "Haifeng nongmin yundong [Report on the Haifeng Peasant Movement]," in *Peng Pai wenji* ([1926] 1981), pp. 101–186.

[12] *Ibid.*, pp. 174–175.

[13] Peng Pai, "Zai Haifengxian gongnongbing daibiao dahui kaimushi shang de yanshuo [The Opening Address of the Peasant-Worker-Solider Conference in Haifeng]," in *Peng Pai wenji* ([1927] 1981), p. 281.

dismissed ordinary peasants' interest in land as "petit bourgeois."[14] Even hired farm laborers, whom he called "the rural proletariat," must, in his view, follow the example of urban workers. More important, aside from stressing party leadership over the peasantry, Peng also accepted the CCP's domination over revolutionary intellectuals. In 1926, lecturing to some educated revolutionaries, he accentuated revolutionary intellectuals' subordination to the party, advising that to help the party develop the rural Revolution, they must be modest and patient when dealing with the peasants. In other words, before his execution by the Guomindang (GMD) in Shanghai in 1929, Peng's praxis of self-reform, rooted in his decision to shake off the influence of his intellectual identity, had morphed into party-defined rules for educated revolutionaries.

Antielitist elitism changed significantly in the 1920s, when communist intellectuals assessed their leadership in various rural communities. But both Yaqian intellectuals and Peng Pai signified revolutionary intellectuals' awakening to the importance of their own honest self-examination, self-reform, and willingness to move beyond their own intellectual-ideological universe to integrate their revolutionary theory into Chinese reality.

Insufficient Political Commitment

Antielitist elitism also emerged as revolutionary intellectuals pondered another important issue – their political commitment. Although radical intellectuals argued that class background determined loyalty to the socialist cause, they did not think highly of peasants' revolutionary commitment. For instance, the Yaqian intellectuals observed that many peasants failed to evolve into staunch defenders of revolutionary interests. Decades after the movement, Yang Zhihua, who once worked for Shen Dingyi, recalled: "After [the government suppression], the peasants were frightened, and thus we could only perform our duty as village teachers." And Peng Pai recorded that peasant activists became passive once they encountered family opposition. In fact, only after Peng had helped them to resolve this family problem did they feel reinvigorated with their revolutionary work![15] By assessing the peasants' political commitment, revolutionary intellectuals in a sense assumed their own superiority as revolutionaries who, though always coming from problematic class backgrounds, were still qualified to judge the masses. In

---

[14] Peng Pai, "Gunong gongzuo dagang [An Outline of Training Hired Hands]," in *Peng Pai wenji* ([1929] 1981), p. 319.

[15] Yang Zhihua, "Yang Zhihua de huiyi [Yang Zhihua's Recollection]," in *Yanqian nongmin yundong* ([1956] 1987), p. 81; Peng Pai, "Haifeng nongmin yundong," p. 117.

fact, they sometimes stressed explicitly their stronger political commitment. Fang Zhimin, a revolutionary leader active in Jiangxi, was arrested by the GMD in 1934. Imprisoned, he wrote an autobiography, recollecting his involvement in a training program in Geyang, Jiangxi, and highlighting his revolutionary zeal, which no peasant and worker activists could surpass: "I became more and more excited as I talked. But some peasant and worker comrades who attended the class could not bear this kind of intensive training. They told me: 'You are so spirited that we are no match for you.'"[16]

In validating their (superior) commitment, however, revolutionary intellectuals still faced a stumbling block they had put in front of themselves – their own antielitism. Since the early 1920s, they had grappled with their own imperfection, which, in their own view, was by no means confined to their urban frills and ignorance of rural society. They also critiqued themselves for their own impure political commitment. Writing to the leader of the Socialist Youth Corps, Deng Zhongxia, who began his career by joining the communist study group in Beijing, rigorously attacked young radical intellectuals in 1923: "Influenced by their education, they talk about various kinds of 'isms'.... Psychologically, they ... hate any kind of restraints, love to build their reputation ... and do not have the courage to confront death."[17] Soon the CCP imposed the derogatory labels of "bourgeois" or "petit bourgeois," both connoting insufficient commitment, on revolutionary intellectuals. By the late 1920s, the party leadership was deeply entrenched in the view that intellectuals were not trustworthy. After the failure of the first United Front, the new CCP leadership heaped scorn on previous leaders' intellectual identity, and intellectuals were regarded as "dangerous elements."[18]

To prove their political devotion against the backdrop of antielitism, revolutionary intellectuals contended that one's endeavor to perfect one's political caliber – one's struggle to overcome one's flaws – marked political dedication. In their view, the willingness to go through self-criticism, especially the earnestness to confront one's petit bourgeois nature in general and impure commitment in particular, was a powerful

---

[16] Fang Zhimin, "Wo congshi geming douzheng de lüeshu [A Brief Account of My Revolutionary Struggle]," in *Fang Zhimin wenji* [The Works of Fang Zhimin] (Beijing: Renmin chubanshe, [1935] 1985), p. 55.

[17] Nanjing Yuhuatai lieshi lingyuan guanlichu shiliaoshi, *Yunhuatai geming lieshi shuxinxuan* [The Letters by the Martyrs Executed at Yuhuatai] (Nanjing: Jiangsu renmin chubanshe, 1983), p. 80.

[18] He Bochuan, *Shan'ao shang de Zhongguo: Wenti, kunjing, tongku de xuanze* [China in Crisis: Problems, Predicaments, and Painful Choices] (Guizhou: Guizhou renmin chubanshe, 1988), p. 509.

testimony to their revolutionary passion. Wu Xianyou (?–1928), who joined the CCP in 1926 as a high school student, wrote to criticize his younger brother who was aspiring to become a revolutionary: "Your petit bourgeois mentality has led to ... egotistic heroism.... You are indolent, never interested in work and study." Only through self-reform could the young man cure his disease of insufficient commitment: "You must cleanse yourself of all the bad habits to become a true proletarian.... We must brush aside our self-interests ... – this is the proletarian spirit."[19] At the end of his life, Fang Zhimin implored his intellectual comrades to follow the true "Bolshevik spirit" by undertaking self-criticism, recalling the mistakes some revolutionary leaders had made in the campaign to remove counterrevolutionaries (e.g., the purges in the Jiangxi Soviet covered in Chapter 3). According to him, reluctance to engage in self-criticism reflected one's insincere attitude toward the Revolution. And by linking self-improvement to the Bolshevik spirit, Fang defined the practice of self-criticism as an institutional and moral obligation of all party members.

Feeling their inadequacy in mass mobilization, communist intellectuals conceptualized self-reform as their effort to enter into Chinese reality. The theory on praxis of self-reform was enriched as, observing their own petit bourgeois and bourgeois nature, they advocated the struggle for a kind of political devotion unimpeded by one's problematic social background. They laid the foundation for future developments in Mao Zedong Thought, which became known for this promotion of the Sinification of Marxism, individual self-transformation, and intense personal political dedication.

MAO ZEDONG I: ANTIELITIST ELITISM AND THE PEASANTRY

Struggle for Survival

While his revolutionary life unfolded mainly in China's countryside, Mao never doubted that the Chinese Revolution should be a proletarian revolution. He was by no means a peasant revolutionary.[20] While some scholars point out that Mao had identified the problem of the

---

[19] Wu Xianyou, "Gei didi de xin [A Letter to My Younger Brother]," in Zhongguo qingnian chubanshe, ed., *Geming lieshi shuxin xubian* [Second Volume of Letters by Revolutionary Martyrs] (Beijing: Zhongguo qingnian chubanshe, [1927] 1983), pp. 35–36.

[20] For a cogent analysis of this fact, see Nick Knight, *Rethinking Mao: Explorations in Mao Zedong's Thought* (Lexington, MA: Lexington Books, 2008), pp. 67–115.

peasantry as "most important" as early as 1923 (see Chapter 14), others think that though of peasant origins, he did not recognize the peasants' revolutionary potential until he worked with the peasants in Shaoshan in 1925.[21] After the total defeat of the 1927 peasant uprising in Hunan and the decimation of the urban CCP by Chiang Kai-shek's GMD forces that April, Mao moved to Jinggangshan and founded a military base there. In 1931, the Chinese Soviet Republic was established. However, because of his clashes with Li Lisan and Wang Ming, Mao was marginalized by the party's core leadership.

At this stage in his career, Mao contemplated how revolutionary intellectuals could win the peasants' support to survive. In 1927, he had celebrated the peasants' radical agency in his famous "Hunan Report," quoted in Chapter 3. To a certain degree, I agree with Womack that Mao intended to represent the peasants' spontaneous organizations as sufficient in transforming China. I would argue, however, that although Mao consciously spotlighted the peasants' power in shaping China's historical destiny, he still revealed a reluctance to grant the peasants too much independence. His report displayed a tendency – which was much less visible in Shen's and Peng Pai's writings – to limit peasant independence. While he predicted that the peasants would take the initiative to reject the clan structure, the authority of gods, and patriarchy, he also assumed that their bottom-up program of social-cultural change was only of secondary importance: "[S]uch attacks have only just 'begun' and there can be no thorough overthrow of all three until the peasants have won complete victory in the economic fight." Moreover, he emphasized the commanding role of the revolutionaries: "[O]ur present task is to lead the peasants to put their greatest efforts into the political struggle, ... [and] the economic struggle should follow immediately."[22] To be sure, it seems that he granted the peasants as much independence as Shen Dingyi or Peng Pai did because he told other radical intellectuals that "[a]ll revolutionary parties and all revolutionary comrades will stand before them [the peasants] to be tested, to be accepted or rejected as they decide." But he in fact warned his intellectual comrades about the danger of being marginalized by the peasantry in the making of

[21] Pang Xianzhi and Jin Chongji, ed. *Mao Zedong zhuan 1893–1949* [The Biography of Mao Zedong 1893-1949] (Beijing: Zhongyang wenxian yanjiushi,1996), pp. 107–112; Edgar Snow, *Red Star over China* (New York: Grove Press, 1961), pp. 159–160.
[22] Mao Zedong, "Hunan nongmin yundong de kaocha baogao [Report on the Peasant Movement in Hunan]," in Takeuchi Minoru, ed., *Mao Zedong ji* ([1927] 1972), pp. 1, 237; trans. in Schram, *Mao's Road to Power*, Vol. 2, p. 454.

history, challenging them to metamorphose into deserving leaders: "To march at their head and lead them? Or to stand opposite them and oppose them? Every Chinese is free to choose."[23]

Since Mao fully realized that revolutionary intellectuals, who were unfamiliar with peasant culture, were essential for the rural revolutionary project, he entreated them to connect with the masses. He argued, like the Yaqian group and Peng Pai, that they must undertake self-reform. But he spoke more harshly of intellectuals' snobbishness. In the "Hunan Report," he mocked himself and many others: "[W]hen I was going to school and saw that the peasants were against the 'foreign-style school,' I, too, used to identify myself with the general run of 'foreign students and teachers' and stand up for it, feeling always that the peasants were 'stupid and detestable people.'"[24] Now he emphasized that revolutionary intellectuals could reform themselves: According to him, after living with the rural folks in 1925, he became concerned about how much foreign-style education was divorced from rural conditions: "The texts used in the rural primary schools were entirely about urban things and unsuited to rural needs. Besides, the attitude of the primary school teachers toward the peasants was very bad and, far from being helpful to the peasants, they came to be disliked by the peasants."[25] As Mao worked in rural areas as both a GMD and a Communist cadre,[26] but not as a revolutionary organizing the peasantry in his own capacity, he moved beyond the focus on intellectuals' self-reform to press for the party's self-assessment and self-improvement. As early as 1925, he expressed his view: "We are all members of the revolutionary party, all leaders of the masses, all guides of the masses. We cannot but ask ourselves, however, do we have the capacity?"[27] Reflecting on the party's techniques of self-perfection, Mao argued for the importance of

---

[23] Mao, "Hunan nongmin yundong de kaocha baogao," p. 208; trans. in Schram, *Mao's Road to Power*, Vol. 2, p. 430.

[24] Takeuchi Minoru, *Mao Zedong ji*, Vol. 1, pp. 246–247; trans. in Schram, *Mao's Road to Power*, Vol. 2, p. 462.

[25] *Ibid.*

[26] During the first United Front of 1923–27, CCP cadres, such as Mao, also were registered in the Guomindang and Mao in 1925–27 was a leading cadre in the Whampoa Military Academy of the GMD. This dual registration of cadres ended with the violent split between the CCP and the GMD in April 1927.

[27] Mao Zedong, "Zhongguo shehui ge jieji de fenxi [An Analysis of Various Social Classes of Chinese Society]," in Takeuchi Minoru, *Mao Zedong ji*, Vol. 1 ([1926] 1972), p. 161; trans. in Schram, *Mao's Road to Power*, Vol. 2, p. 249. Schram follows the dating of this article from its original publication in December 1925 in the journal *Geming*; see his note on p. 249.

revolutionary intellectuals' objective and accurate assessment of reality. While he by no means rejected Marxism-Leninism as an analytical tool for the Chinese communists' dissection of reality, he believed that one's experience-based knowledge of peasant society should provide the foundations for particular policies.

The evolution of Mao's land policy shows how his policymaking was steered by this belief in experiential knowledge. In response to the deteriorating relationship between the GMD and the CCP, Mao adopted the aggressive agenda of nationalization in the summer of 1927.[28] And when he drafted the Jinggangshan land law in late 1928, he specified that all land would go to the Soviet government, and peasants only had the right to use it. This, in Hsiao Tso-liang's analysis, was equivalent to land nationalization.[29] Nevertheless, Mao later stipulated a more moderate land law in Xingguo, agreeing that the Soviet would, after confiscating the public land and the landlords' land, distribute it among the peasants. In the second half of 1930 and 1931, Mao stated clearly that the CCP should recognize the peasants' land ownership.[30]

Although Hsiao Tso-liang argues that Mao intended to follow the suggestions of the Communist International (Comintern),[31] it must be noted that Mao himself justified these changes by drawing the party's attention to rural conditions. In February 1931, he wrote to the Jiangxi Soviet government to clarify why he now endorsed the practice of private property: "In the past the land belonged to the soviet and there was a strong sense that the peasants had only the right to use it. In addition, the land was divided up over and over again, ... thus making the peasants feel that the land was not their own and that they had no right to do as they wished with it.... The situation is very bad."[32] Mao believed that he went beyond orthodox socialism to support land redistribution.[33]

---

[28] Mao Zedong, "Resolution on the Peasant Question," in Schram, ed., *Mao's Road to Power*, Vol. 2, pp. 467–471.

[29] Hsiao Tso-liang, *The Land Revolution in China 1930–1934: A Study of Documents* (Seattle: University of Washington Press, 1969), p. 20.

[30] Shi Shunjin, "Dangzai yijiu erqi zhi yijiu sanyi nian diquan zhengce de zhuanbian [The Changes of the CCP Policies on Land Revolution from 1927 to 1931]," in *Dangshi yanjiu* [Research on Party History] 3 (1981), pp. 45–46.

[31] Hsiao, *Land Revolution*, pp. 6, 20.

[32] Takeuchi Minoru, *Mao Zedong ji*, Vol. 4, p. 19.

[33] Lenin was in favor of having a quid pro quo with the peasants. During the October Revolution, Bolsheviks sanctioned land seizures and expected the peasantry to support the cities and the army. See John Channon, "The Peasantry in the Revolution of 1917," in Edith Rogovin Frankel, Jonathan Frankel, and Baruch Knei-Paz, eds., *Revolution in Russia: Reassessments of 1917* (New York: Cambridge University Press, 1992), pp. 111–124.

Debating land policy with the Li Lisan group in 1931, he admitted that equal land distribution "was not socialist ideology" and was "poor peasant ideology." But it could, he insisted, serve as a powerful revolutionary dynamic, crucial in "shattering the feudal system and moving [China] towards socialism."[34]

Mao failed to win over Li and soon had the misfortune of being criticized by the Returned Student group – Wang Ming and his acolytes – for his deficient class consciousness. But still in 1933, he was told to take charge of a social survey intended to root out rich peasants and landlords who disguised themselves as ordinary peasants.[35] If the party leadership was determined to brush aside Mao's land policy, it still saw value in Mao's meticulous investigation of rural conditions.

Contending for National Leadership

After the Long March (1934–35), Mao slowly rose to power, finally becoming the chairman of the Politburo and the Secretariat in 1943 (see details in Chapter 4).[36] But the challenges he faced also were onerous. Whereas the onset of the Sino-Japanese War in 1937 caused a national crisis, the GMD was a formidable force that the CCP had to deal with. In addition, he was thinking about how to enhance his own authority in the revolutionary community, whose membership rose rapidly from around 40,000 in 1937 to more than 800,000 by 1940.[37] While Mao intended to educate new peasant and worker members who were illiterate and abusive, he found young CCP members of the intellectual class more problematic. Young intellectuals who flocked to Yan'an were undisciplined, critical, and ignorant of peasant culture. And they were, according to Gao Hua, attracted to Mao's competitor for party leadership at the time, Wang Ming.[38] To train and discipline his party, Mao decided

---

[34] Mao Zedong, "Resolution on the Land Problem of the Joint Conference of the General Front Committee and the Jiangxi Provincial Action Committee," in Schram, *Mao's Road to Power*, Vol. 3, p. 564.

[35] Schram, "Introduction: The Writings of Mao Zedong 1931–1934," in Schram, *Mao's Road to Power*, Vol. 4, p. xxvii.

[36] Lee Feigon, *Mao: A Reinterpretation* (Chicago: Ivan R. Dee, 2002), pp. 67–81.

[37] *Ibid.*, p. 80.

[38] See Gao Hua, *Hong Taiyang shi zenyang shengqi de: Yan'an zhengfeng yundong de lailong qumai* [How the Sun Rose in the East: The Origins and the Development of the Yan'an Rectification Movement] (Hong Kong: Chinese University Press, 2000), p. 265. This claim may be debatable, if we take into account the fact that Wang himself found it virtually impossible to rival Mao inside the party leadership. But at the same time, Gao's claim is not entirely unlikely in the sense that students and young intellectuals may have been impressed with Wang's eloquent display of his knowledge of Marxism-Leninism.

to launch the Rectification Movement (1942–44), in which he required party members' self-transformation but mainly targeted intellectuals.

The theme of antielitist elitism was dominant before and during the Rectification Campaign. In 1939, to recruit patriotic intellectuals for the goal of national resistance, he hailed intellectuals as the "vanguards" of China's Revolution.[39] And he did not intend to depart from this position in the early 1940s because, aware of intellectuals' ideologically incorrect ways but appreciative of their real and possible contributions to the CCP, he demanded intellectuals' self-reform. One central message in the Rectification Movement was that intellectuals could reshape their nation only by being united with the masses. In order to bond with the masses, Mao told educated revolutionaries, they must objectively investigate reality, especially rural reality. And in order to penetrate into reality, he instructed revolutionary intellectuals further, they must learn from the masses, recognizing their own naïveté and absorbing the masses' localized knowledge rooted in real life, and accept the masses as heroes.[40]

These ideas did not break new ground. However, his criticism of radical intellectuals was crude and at odds with his proclaimed intention of making the movement as mild and as gentle as "breezes and drizzle,"[41] an objective derived from his disapproval of the CCP's harsh treatment of intellectuals in the 1920s and of fellow cadres in the 1930s (i.e., the Futian incident and similar purges), as well as from his recently developed theory on the new democratic revolution – expounded in the essay "On New Democracy" in 1940 – which necessitated support from various parties and classes. When he delivered his influential rectification speech at the Central Party School on February 1, 1942, he scoffed at intellectuals for their bookish learning: "... [A] book cannot walk, and you can open and close a book at will; this is the easiest thing in the world to do, ... much easier than it is for him [a cook] to slaughter a pig. He has to catch his pig.... [T]he pig can run.... [H]e slaughters him ... the pig squeals.... A book placed on a desk cannot run, nor can it squeal." He then ridiculed some snobbish intellectuals' false pride in their mastery of Marxism: "'Your dogma is no use,' or 'your dogma is less useful than excrement.' We see that dog excrement can fertilize the field and

---

[39] Mao Zedong, "Speech at the Meeting in Yan'an in Commemoration of the Twentieth Anniversary of the May Fourth Movement," in Schram, *Mao's Road to Power*, Vol. 7, p. 73.

[40] *Ibid.*

[41] Chen Yung-fa, *Zhonggong geming qishinian* [Seventy Years of History of the CCP], Vol. 1 (Taipei: Lianjing chuban shiye gongsi, 1998), p. 372.

man's can feed the dog. And dogmas? ... Of what use are they?"[42] By ridiculing those dogmatists blindly believing in the universal significance of Marxism, he contended that Chinese revolutionaries must strive to forge their own – a Sinicized – version of Marxism on the basis of both Marxist perspectives and Chinese conditions.[43]

Because of these flaws in their standpoint, communist intellectuals were pressed to undertake self-criticism. According to Chen Yung-fa and others, the Rectification Movement made educated cadres suffer and, in fact, was met with their resistance. Not only did revolutionary intellectuals feel uneasy about castigating themselves, but they also seized the opportunity to express their discontent with high-level cadres' privileged status in Yan'an.[44] What is worth noting, however, is that since they were well disposed to embrace antielitist elitism, which had been an established feature of New Culture and the communist milieu, most intellectuals did not find Mao's critical examination of their problems fundamentally objectionable. As Yi-tsi Mei Feuerwerker points out, Yan'an intellectuals were psychologically and intellectually prepared to accept the downgrading of their own status.[45]

By enhancing nonintellectual cadres' quality, and especially by reforming revolutionary intellectuals, Mao was confident about the success of his remade party, which institutionalized cadres' vigilance for their own weaknesses and was attentive to the voices from the grass roots. Such sensitivity to the people was the famous mass line, which he elucidated in the Politburo resolution of June 1, 1943. This document, also entitled, "The Method of Leadership," states: "[C]orrect leadership ... means taking the views of the masses ... and subjecting them to concentration ..., then going to the masses with propaganda and explanation in order to transform the views of the masses, and seeing that these [views] are maintained by the masses and carried over into their activities."[46]

---

[42] Mao Zedong, "Zhengdun xuefeng dangfeng wenfeng [To Correct the Incorrect Trends of Our Study, Party, and Literature]," in Takeuchi Minoru, *Mao Zedong ji*, Vol. 8 ([1942] 1972), pp. 70–75; trans. in Boyd Compton, *Mao's China: Party Reform Documents, 1942–44* (Seattle: University of Washington Press, 1952), pp. 16–22.

[43] Knight, *Rethinking Mao*, pp. 197–216.

[44] Chen Yung-fa, *Yan'an de yinying* [The Shadow of Yan'an] (Taipei: Institute of Modern History, Academia Sinica, 1990); also see Chen Yung-fa, *Zhonggong geming qishinian*, p. 373. Merle Goldman famously highlighted this conflict 40 years ago in *Literary Dissent in Communist China* (Cambridge, MA: Harvard University Press, 1967).

[45] Yi-tsi Mei Feuerwerker, *Ideology, Power and Text: Self-representation and the Peasant Other in Modern Chinese Literature* (Palo Alto, CA: Stanford University Press, 1998), p. 111.

[46] Mao Zedong, "Zhongong zhongyang guanyu lingdao fangfa de jueding [Resolution of the Central Committee of the Chinese Communist Party on Methods of

Yet Mao was so proud of the CCP's correct leadership, characterized by the mass line, that he sometimes quite ironically wrote without a shred of respect for the peasants' agency. In 1944, discussing the backwardness of rural areas, he encouraged revolutionary intellectuals to educate the masses. He adopted the language of the mass line, imploring them to be patient. But, in his view, patience was not waiting for the masses' spontaneous awakening. Party guidance was essential: "[The leaders and cadres] should not do anything until their efforts to educate the people successfully awaken the masses."[47] In addition, although he gave up the moderate wartime policy of rent reduction and readopted the policy of land redistribution to win the peasants' support for the CCP during the Civil War, Mao sounded less tolerant toward the rural masses' nonsocialist yearning for land. In 1949, as he contemplated the future of communist China, he gave prominence to the CCP and proletariat, calling them the leading forces of new China. Thinking about the construction of a socialist economy, Mao was very concerned with the peasants' nonsocialist ideology and therefore emphasized: "The serious problem is the education of the peasantry." He also forecast: "[T]he socialization of agriculture ... will require a long time and painstaking work."[48]

MAO ZEDONG II: ANTIELITIST ELITISM AND LITERATURE AND THE ARTS

The Importance of Popularization

Pondering what the revolutionary elite should do so that they could unite with the masses for the success of the Revolution, Mao also emphasized antielitist elitism in the domain of literature and the arts. His vision was that communist cultural workers must change themselves to serve the masses for party leadership but also should help to improve the masses' uncultivated artistic taste. As noted by Kirk Denton, Paul Pickowicz, Liu Kang, and others, before the Yan'an Forum on Literature and Art, radical intellectuals such as New Culture thinkers and Qu Qiubai had long struggled with the question of how they could create

Leadership]," in Takeuchi Minoru, *Mao Zedoing ji*, Vol. 8, pp. 27–28; trans. in Compton, *Mao's China*, p. 179; Mark Selden, *China in Revolution: The Yan'an Way Revisited* (Armonk, NY: M. E. Sharpe, 1995), p. 213.

[47] Mao Zedong, "Wenjiao tongyi zhanxian fangzhen [United Front Policy in Culture and Education]," in Takeuchi Minoru, *Mao Zedong ji*, Vol. 9 ([1944] 1972), p. 136.

[48] Mao Zedong, "Lun renmin minzhu zhuanzheng [On the People's Democratic Dictatorship]," in Takeuchi Minoru, *Mao Zedong ji*, Vol. 10 ([1949] 1975), p. 302; also see *Selected Works of Chairman Mao*, Vol. 4 (Beijing: People's Publishing House, 1961), p. 419.

cultural products accessible to the masses.⁴⁹ However, popularization was far from the main theme as radical intellectuals reflected on literature and the arts or pursued cultural enjoyment. Ding Ling emphasized in the early 1940s that cultural professionals should imbibe but improve the language of the people in order to write what others feel but cannot express.⁵⁰ In the revolutionary decades, communist intellectuals, famous or inconspicuous alike, wrote poetry that was beyond the comprehension of the masses. Of course, Mao had been known as a good poet, enamored of the beauty of traditional-style poetry, and those who settled in Yan'an showed an immense interest in perfecting the sound effect of their dance music. The overwhelming majority of the communist cultural professionals were not consciously committed to popularization.⁵¹

Mao was resolute to confront the issue of communication between radical intellectuals and the peasants. Although until 1941 he still preferred a "two-track" approach to literature and the arts, incorporating both elite and popular culture in the communist milieu,⁵² he soon switched to a more populist position, emphasizing the importance of appealing to peasants, workers, and soldiers. In 1942, he criticized a cultural professional who exhibited his knowledge of archaic Chinese characters when writing anti-Japanese slogans: "A few years ago I saw the following slogan at the top of the Yenan [Yan'an] city wall, 'Workers and Peasants Unite and Gain Victory in the War of Resistance.' The thought behind the slogan is not at all bad, but in the expression *kung jen* [*gongren*], the second stroke in the character *kung* [*gong*] was not written straight – it turned two corners. And to the character *jen* [*ren*], three short strokes were added on the right foot." He then teased this

---

⁴⁹ Kirk Denton, *The Problematic of Self in Modern Chinese Literature: Hu Feng and Lu Ling* (Palo Alto, CA: Stanford University Press, 1998), p. 57; Paul Pickowicz, *Marxist Literary Thought in China: The Influence of Ch'u Ch'iu-pai* (Berkeley: University of California Press, 1981), p. 225; Liu Kang, *Aesthetics and Marxism: Chinese Aesthetic Marxists and their Western Contemporaries* (Durham, NC: Duke University Press, 2000), p. 71.

⁵⁰ Ding Ling, "Zuojia yu dazhong [The Writer and the Masses]," in *Ding Ling wenji* [The Works of Ding Ling], Vol. 6 (Changsha: Hunan renmin chubanshe, [1940] 1984), p. 15.

⁵¹ Yao Tie, "Yan'an zhongyang dangxiao de wenhua shenghuo [The Cultural Life in the Yan'an Central Party School]," in Yan'an zhongyang dangxiao zhengfeng yundong bianxiezu, ed., *Yan'an zhongyang dangxiao de zhengfeng xuexi* [The Rectification Studies of the Yan'an Central Party School] (Beijing: Zhonggong zhongyang dangxiao chubanshe, 1989), p. 195.

⁵² Liu Kang, *Aesthetics and Marxism*, p. 85; Timothy Cheek, *Propaganda and Culture in Mao's China: Deng Tuo and the Intelligentsia* (New York: Oxford University Press, 1997), p. 95.

calligrapher, "His probable object was to make sure that people would not read the slogan. Otherwise it would be very difficult to explain."[53]

In his "Talks at the Yan'an Forum on Literature and Art" in May 1942, echoing his comments in the "Hunan Report," Mao revealed his own mental struggles: "I started off as a student at school, and at school I acquired student habits.... I felt that intellectuals are the only clean people in the world, and that workers, peasants, and soldiers were in general rather dirty.... [But after joining the Revolution] I came to feel that ... the cleanest people are workers and soldiers."[54] He then critiqued those communist cultural workers who refused to sympathize with the masses: "[W]hen it comes to workers, peasants and soldiers, these people don't have any contact with them ... and are no good at describing them.... They don't like their emotions, their manner, or their budding literature and art.... Sometimes they like these things, too, either out of curiosity or because they want to decorate their own work with them."[55] Just as he mocked bookish intellectuals congratulating themselves on their knowledge of Marxism, he jeered at cultural professionals contemptuous of the masses' cultural taste and needs: "These comrades still have their backsides on the side of the petit bourgeoisie."[56] Communist cultural professionals must, he implored, "see to it that their thoughts and feelings undergo transformation and reform." "Otherwise," he was sure, "nothing they do will turn out well or be effective."[57]

More than obvious was his view that popularization was the most pressing task. How else could the masses be mobilized? In addition, Mao also made clear his intention to use popularization to support party leadership. When he rebuked cultural professionals featuring revolutionary intellectuals in their own works, he quickly pointed out what they should do: "Many comrades place more emphasis on studying the intelligentsia and analyzing their psychology; their main concern is to show their side of things ... instead of guiding the intelligentsia from petty bourgeois background and themselves as well towards closer contact

53 Mao Zedong, "Fandui dangbagu [In Opposition to Party Formalism]," in Takeuchi Minoru, *Mao Zedong ji*, Vol. 8 ([1942] 1972), p. 96; trans. in Compton, *Mao's China*, p. 41.
54 Mao Zedong, "Zai Yan'an wenyi zuotanhui shang de jianghua [Talks at the Yan'an Forum on Literature and Art]," in Takeuchi Minoru, *Mao Zedong ji*, Vol. 8 ([1942] 1975), p. 116; trans. in Bonnie S. McDougall, *Mao Zedong's "Talks at the Yan'an Conference on Literature and Art"* (Ann Arbor: Center for Chinese Studies, University of Michigan, 1980), p. 61.
55 *Ibid.*, p. 123; trans. in McDougall, *Talks*, p. 66.
56 *Ibid.*
57 *Ibid.*, pp. 116–117; trans. in McDougall, *Talks*, p. 61.

with workers, peasants and soldiers, to take part in their struggles, to show how things are with them and educate them."[58]

Raising Standards

However, Mao's antielitist elitism was more complex than the theme that communist cultural workers must lower themselves for the masses and ultimately for the party's successful leadership. It also meant communist cultural professionals' mission to elevate the masses' artistic and cultural level on the basis of popularization.

Despite his caustic attack on intellectuals' petit bourgeois preoccupation with good taste, Mao refused to reject the idea of cultural refinement. He expressed his appreciation of good art in his "Talks at the Yan'an Forum": "We must absorb these things in a discriminating way, using them as models from which we may learn what to accept or what to reject.... It makes a difference to have this model, the difference between being civilized or vulgar, crude or refined, advanced or elementary."[59] In addition, Mao also argued that popularization not only laid the foundation but also would create the demand for raising standards. In his speech given at the Yan'an Forum, he predicted: "The people demand material that can reach a wide audience, but they also demand high standards....Here raising standards, like reaching a wider audience, is a popular concern."[60] In the "Talks," he also said: "If their material [popularized cultural products] stays constantly on the same level month after month and year after year, invariably consisting of the same old stock-in-trade like 'The Little Cowherd' or 'man, hand, mouth, knife, cow, sheep,' then what is there to choose between the people who prepare the material and the audience they are reaching?"[61]

Interestingly, Mao contended that the party should please not only the nonelite but also the revolutionary elite, which was drawn to refined art and worked industriously for the Revolution. Definitely not the kind of person rejoicing in "The Little Cowherd," he was aware of his intellectual comrades' desire for aesthetic enjoyment. At the Yan'an Forum, he admitted: "Cadres are the advanced elements among the masses, who have generally already completed the kind of education currently offered to the masses. Their ability to absorb things is higher than the masses, so that material intended for wider audiences among the masses at their present level, such as 'The Little Cowherd,'

[58] *Ibid.*, p. 122; trans. in McDougall, *Talks*, pp. 65–66.
[59] *Ibid.*, p. 127; trans. in McDougall, *Talks*, p. 69.
[60] *Ibid.*, p. 129; trans. in McDougall, *Talks*, p. 71.
[61] *Ibid.*

cannot satisfy them. Literature and art on a higher level are absolutely essential for them."[62]

By integrating the idea of raising standards into his speeches promoting popularization, Mao reserved some space for cultural professionals to create and perform works more engaging for them than a simple, popular drama. By analyzing the evolution of the communist theater from staging peasant *Yangge* opera to producing large-scale plays, David Holm argues that communist cultural workers elevated the standards of popularized art to prove the correctness of Mao's idea that "'little sprouts' could grow to become big trees." He views this evolution as force-paced.[63] This interpretation is accurate. For instance, when cultural professionals at the Lu Xun Arts Academy decided to produce *The White-Haired Girl* to celebrate the CCP's upcoming Seventh National Congress, they had to do everything in a rush, writing the script, discussing and revising it, and rehearsing it simultaneously. He Jingzhi, who wrote the script, recalled that from January to April in 1943, he worked relentlessly to write and revise in response to how things went in rehearsals.[64] And yet those force-paced projects allowed cultural professionals to affirm their artistic leadership. Reminiscing on the past, those involved in the production of *The White-Haired Girl* expanded on how they refined the character of Xier, the heroine of the piece. They respected the masses' input and infused her with a defiant spirit lacking in her original image. In their recollections, though, they still appeared to be leaders, evaluating, incorporating, and improving what they learned from the masses.[65]

More important, while cultural professionals worked for popularization throughout the 1940s, they eagerly awaited their turn to pursue good fine art. For instance, the Resistance Troupe, which was founded in 1939 in the Jin-Cha-Ji border region and moved to Beijing in 1949, was deprived of the privilege to create large-scale works and, in fact, had to perform simple programs all the time. Its members pined for the opportunity to learn from the "big sprouts." And the scriptwriters

---

[62] *Ibid.*, p. 130; trans. in McDougall, *Talks*, p. 72.

[63] David Holm, *Art and Ideology in Revolutionary China* (Oxford, England: Clarendon Press, 1991), p. 320.

[64] Zhang Geng, "Huiyi `jianghua' qianhou `luyi' de xiju huodong [The Theme in Luyi Before and After Mao's Forum]," in Ai Ke'en, ed., *Yan'an wenyi huiyilu* [Recollections of Yan'an Cultural Activities] (Beijing: Zhongguo shehui kexue chubanshe, [1962] 1992), p. 181; He Jingzhi, "Baimaonü de chuangzuo yu yanchu [The Creation and Performance of the White-Haired Girl]," in Ai Ke'en, *Yan'an wenyi huiyilu*, pp. 224–225.

[65] Zheng Geng, "Huiyi," pp. 182–183; Shu Qiang, "Nanwang de Yan'an yishi shenghuo [The Unforgettable Cultural Life in Yan'an]," in Ai Ke'en, *Yan'an wenyi huiyilu*, p. 199.

of the troupe cherished complexity and sophistication. Finally, in the late 1940s, they felt gratified because they were allowed to stage "big plays."[66] Indeed, communist intellectuals pursued with enthusiasm cultural refinement in the process of popularization. Many described their excitement when they prepared themselves for performing politically correct pieces that they thought were aesthetically impressive. In the 1940s, many educated radicals admired Xian Xinghai's *Yellow River Cantata*. When the art teams in the Central Jiangsu Military Zone collaborated to perform it, they "formed a choir, whose members were relatively well-trained singers." Choir members listened to leading cadres' introduction to the history of the masterpiece. Everyone took the performance seriously. According to an insider, "[The authorities] explained for us the characteristics of all the movements of the Cantata. They insisted on our minute attention to the emotions contained in each movement.... Rehearsals lasted for several hours every day, and yet no one complained."[67]

To sum up, Mao's antielitist elitism in literature and the arts marked the most important program of cultural engineering in the communist Revolution. It did not begin with Mao, and it did not alienate revolutionary intellectuals completely, even though they might not have wanted to pursue popularization on their own. Intellectually, antielitist elitism made sense to them. Emotionally, they were to some extent allowed to do what they loved – raising standards and pursuing better art – under the constraints of popularization. In my view, what is noteworthy is not how Mao clashed with revolutionary intellectuals itching for sophistication but how he was able to garner their services and to grant satisfaction, though limited, to those who may have found sheer popularization ideologically correct but artistically unrewarding.

MAO ZEDONG THOUGHT III: ANTIELITIST ELITISM AND POLITICAL COMMITMENT

Unlike Fang Zhimin and his kind, Mao Zedong was not a revolutionary leader who liked declaring fervently his own political emotions. Still, he played a crucial role in developing the theme of antielitist

[66] Hu He, "Shijian zhong xuexi de shinian – dui Kangzhan jushe xiju chuangzuo de huiyi [Ten Years of Learning from Practice – My Recollection of the Resistance Troupe]," in Zhongguo jiefangjun wenyi shiliao bianjibu, ed., *Zhongguo renmin jiefangjun wenyi shiliao xuanbian: Jiefangjun zhanzheng shiqi* [Literature and the Arts of the PLA: The Civil War], Vol. 2 (Beijing: Jiefangjun chubanshe, 1989), pp. 714–719.

[67] Tang Jingxiong, "Yi Suzhong junqu shouci yanchu 'Huanghe de hechang' [My Recollection of the First Performance of the Yellow River Cantata in the Military

elitism in communist writings addressing the issue of revolutionary commitment.

In "The Great Union of the Popular Masses," Mao in 1919 represented New Culture or May Fourth activists as a group highly dedicated to the betterment of nation and society. On the surface, he included people from all walks of life – peasants, workers, women, and so forth – into the concept of the masses, encouraging them to act: "[T]he world is ours, the state is ours, society is ours. If we do not speak, who will speak? If we do not act, who will act?"[68] But the ornate passage preceding this statement indicates clearly that he identified students as the group that fomented the movement of the masses: "[T]he May Fourth movement has broken out. Its banner has advanced southward, across the Yellow River to the Yangzi. From Guangzhou to Hankou, many real-life dramas are enacted; from Lake Dongting to the Min River, the tide rises even higher. Heaven and earth are aroused by it, the wicked are put to flight by it! Ha! We know it! We are awakened!"[69]

As Mao consciously applied a class-based perspective on Chinese society in the 1920s, he sounded more critical of the intellectuals. In "An Analysis of All the Classes in Chinese Society," written in 1925, he showed his distrust of what he called "high-level intellectuals": As he saw it, corporate managers, overseas Chinese students, college professors and students, and lawyers, all dreaming to rise to the top echelon of the bourgeois class, would never support the Revolution. As for the petit bourgeoisie, including "low-level intellectuals" such as high school students and teachers, they would support radical change only when the high tide of the Revolution arrived.[70] In 1929, in contemplating party members' problems at the Gutian conference, he concentrated on the problematic nature of the petit bourgeoisie who worked for the CCP: One of their flaws, he said, was "individualism" – their selfishness that lured them to focus on their own feelings, needs, and pleasure and to disregard the interests of the oppressed and the party.[71]

Zone of Suzhong]," in *Zhongguo renmin jiefangjun wenyi shiliao xuanbian: Jiefangjun zhanzheng shiqi*, Vol. 1 ([1987] 1989), pp. 319–320.

[68] Mao Zedong, "Minzhong de da lianhe [The Great Union of the Popular Masses]," in Takeuchi Minoru, *Mao Zedong ji*, Vol. 1, p. 66; trans. in Schram, *Mao's Road to Power*, Vol. 1, p. 386.

[69] *Ibid.*

[70] Mao Zedong, "Zhongguo shehui ge jieji de fenxi," pp. 161–174; trans. in Schram, *Mao's Road to Power*, Vol. 2, pp. 249–262. Schram follows the dating of this article from its original publication in December 1925 in the journal *Geming*; see his note on p. 249.

[71] Mao Zedong, "Zhongguo gongchandang hongjun disijun dijiuci daibiao dahui jueyi an [Draft Resolution of the Ninth Congress of the Chinese Communist Party in

But if Mao had by the late 1920s developed the view that intellectuals, including those siding with the CCP, were not always reliable, he still assumed that revolutionary intellectuals should be given the superior position to gauge – and to develop policies on – the issue of political loyalty. In 1933 he helped the CCP to set up guidelines on the Red Army's defection cases, specifying what constituted forgivable and unforgivable disloyalty and what kinds of penalties defectors should receive.[72] In so doing, he positioned himself as a well-informed and better-trained revolutionary – in short, a revolutionary intellectual who knew better than those he judged. As such, he confirmed intellectuals' leadership role in the realm of political emotions.

In the Yan'an period, the CCP leadership certainly took care to commemorate the masses who sacrificed for the Revolution. The party, for instance, honored Liu Hulan, a peasant girl who died for the CCP in the 1940s. Her life was enacted in an opera, which premiered in 1948. And since the CCP leadership intended to unite people of various backgrounds for the ideal of new democracy, revolutionary leaders did not hesitate to voice their admiration for radical intellectuals. Luo Ruiqing, the vice chancellor of the Resistance University in Yan'an, praised students flocking to the revolutionary headquarters: In his view, they abandoned "their original comfortable lifestyle" in order to join the Revolution.[73] While he may have attempted to woo these young men and women, his statement nevertheless helped nurture intellectuals' confidence in their own superior political commitment, for what was implied in it was a difference between revolutionary intellectuals and the masses: Whereas educated radicals gave up a great deal for the noble course of the CCP, the masses struggled to end their own oppression.

In this context, Mao time and again sang the praise of politically "progressive" intellectuals' commitment to change. In one of the articles he wrote for the Rectification Movement, "The Reconstruction of Our Studies," he paid tribute to radical intellectuals as a group: "While the Chinese people have experienced deep adversity during the past hundred years, outstanding personalities have struggled and sacrificed,

---

the Fourth Red Army]," ([1929] 1975b), in Takeuchi Minoru, *Mao Zedong ji*, Vol. 2, pp. 88–90; trans. in Schram, *Mao's Road to Power*, Vol. 3, pp. 203–205.

[72] Mao Zedong, "Guanyu hongjunzhong tupao fenzi wenti [Policy on Deserters]," in Takeuchi Minoru, *Mao Zedong ji*, Vol. 4, pp. 121–122.

[73] Luo Ruiqing, "Kangri junzheng daxue de guoqu yu xianzai [The Past and Present of the Resistance University]," in *Shaanbei qingnian xuesheng shenghuo* [Student Life in Shaanbei] (Washington, DC: Center for Chinese Research Materials, Association of Research Libraries, [1938] 1970), p. 52.

stepping forward to take the places of those who have fallen, groping for the truth which would save the nation and the people." He
then emphasized: "The story is both sad and glorious." Moreover,
he did not forget to place this in historical perspective, highlighting
that these outstanding historical actors' ardent pursuit of the truth
culminated in the communist movement, which promised to lead
to China's rebirth.[74] In 1949, writing "On the People's Democratic
Dictatorship," Mao also drew attention to intellectuals' love for and
crucial contributions to China: "From the time of China's defeat in
the Opium War of 1840, Chinese progressives went through hardships
in their quest for truth from the Western countries.... It was through
the Russians that the Chinese found Marxism."[75] His praises should
not be dismissed as a mere rhetorical device used to please intellectuals. Not only had Mao viewed students as the vanguards of the
Revolution, but he also considered himself an intellectual. His glorifi-
cation of progressive intellectuals was, to say the least, to some extent
genuine.

This is not to say that Mao failed to note the masses and ordinary
soldiers' political devotion. In 1944, he himself delivered a eulogy to a
soldier who had died while working for the party. What he said, inspired
by the great historian Sima Qian, was quoted innumerable times by the
Red Guards decades later: "Sacrificing one's life for the people is weightier than Mount Tai."[76] More important, in Mao's works, admiration for
radical intellectuals and his unfavorable antielitist view of them exist
side by side. The *Rectification Documents*, first published in Yan'an in
the 1940s and republished in 1950, include Mao's "Oppose Liberalism"
from 1937. Mainly addressing those from student backgrounds, Mao
attacked "liberalism," blasting some revolutionaries' insufficient commitment to the Revolution and calling on them to amend their ways
so as to work hard for the Revolution. He said, "The source of liberalism is the egotism of the petty bourgeoisie, which places the interests
of the individual first and the interests of the Revolution second. It is
as a result of this that liberalism is produced in thought, politics, and

---

[74] Mao Zedong, "Gaizao women de xueyi [The Reconstruction of Our Studies]," in
Jiefangshe, ed., *Zhengfeng wenxian* [Documents of the Rectification Movement]
(Shanghai: Xinhua shudian, [1941] 1950), pp. 48–56; trans. in Compton, *Mao's China*,
pp. 59–60.

[75] Mao Zedong, "Lun renmin minzhu zhuanzheng," pp. 292–294; trans. in *Selected
Works of Mao Zedong*, Vol. 4, pp. 412–443.

[76] Mao Zedong, "Wei renmin de liyi ersi, shi si you zhongyu Taishan [Death for the
People Is Weightier than the Tai Mountain]," in Takeuchi Minoru, *Mao Zedong ji*,
Vol. 9 ([1944] 1975), p. 111. I use but alter the translation a little.

organization."[77] Therefore, he, like Fang Zhimin, encouraged revolutionary intellectuals to rely on self-reform, based on self-criticism, to prove their devotion.

In the Rectification Movement, revolutionary intellectuals did precisely that. In addition to admitting their ignorance of – and inability to appeal to – the masses, they also critiqued their own class-based personality by reflecting on their family upbringing. In other words, they analyzed how their families conditioned them to be impure revolutionaries. For example, Zhu Ming, a woman revolutionary who came from a large landowning family in Anhui and arrived at Yan'an in 1938, talked about her own family: "In the past few years, I always told others in Yan'an that I came from a bourgeois family." She then quickly confessed that her background was much worse than just being bourgeois: "[I]n fact, my family is a solid member of the landowning class which also engages in capitalist ventures." Others did the same. Liu Baiyu was a young writer who had established himself before his relocation to Yan'an and had joined the CCP in 1938. In his self-criticism, he identified himself as someone who came from a declining feudal family. As a result, he said, his inner world was a "petit bourgeois kingdom."

Sometimes these revolutionary intellectuals' self-criticisms were gender-specific. Growing up female in a landowning capitalist family, Zhu Ming confessed, she received all the training necessary for a proper upper-class young lady. And in that process, she learned to set herself apart from women of more modest background: "Young ladies were told to be gentle, tender, and reserved.... We must not laugh aloud.... But we must keep our good posture whenever we sit and stand. Otherwise we would be criticized for acting like 'those girls from small families.'" But finding fault in themselves, revolutionary intellectuals spotted gender-neutral problems as well. Male and female intellectuals alike lambasted themselves for their egotism and expressed gratitude to the party that pressed them to face the "ugly" side of their souls.

However, most paradoxically, in their confrontations with themselves, revolutionary intellectuals also showed off what they were proud of – their political commitment. By exposing her unclean mentality and accentuating her determination to change herself, Zhu Ming in a sense displayed her earnestness to become a better revolutionary: "I always wanted to stand above the laboring masses. But now I want to become an ox working for the masses." To prove his unwavering loyalty to the

---

[77] Mao Zedong, "Fandui ziyou zhuyi [In Opposition to Liberalism]," in *Zhengfeng wenxian* ([1937] 1950), pp. 162–165; trans. in Compton, *Mao's China*, p. 186.

Revolution and the CCP, Liu Baiyu revised his critical autobiography quite a few times. Another young intellectual, Yang Li, painstakingly listed his own crimes rooted in his "petit bourgeois tail": "Caring too much about status and power, I intend to use my ability to seek self-expansion in the party.... I was always longing for attention.... If I felt ignored, I regarded the party as cruel and indifferent. I was not interested in reforming myself so as to serve the party better."[78]

Granted, no outsider can appraise these revolutionary intellectuals' sincerity, but, as David Apter and Tony Saich point out, Yan'anites always have expressed fondness for their Yan'an experience, emphasizing that they felt empowered by the Rectification Movement.[79] Indeed, it is true that they gained something important as they castigated themselves to accentuate their political passion: Believing in their superiority vis-à-vis the masses, and using their antielitist self-analyses to show their intention of perfecting their political performances as revolutionary leaders, they created themselves as an elite who fought wholeheartedly for the Revolution.[80] Mao Zedong Thought provided them with the means to make themselves into such leaders.

CONCLUSION

The CCP understood the party's legitimacy in Gramscian terms,[81] grounding the party's authority in its alliance with, and efficacious responses to the needs of, the people. Constructed in the communist ideological milieu, the antielitist elitism of Mao Zedong Thought helped to build – in truth, contributed greatly to – the party's legitimacy.

---

[78] Zhu Ming, "Cong yuanlai de jieji jiefang chulai [To Liberate Yourself from Your Own Class]," in Yan'an zhongyang dangxiao de zhengfeng xuexi, Vol. 1 ([1944] 1988), pp. 255–281; Liu Baiyu, "Wo de rensheng zhuanzidian" [The Turning Point of My Life], ibid., Vol. 1, pp. 132–139; Yang Li, "Zai na shi wo feiyue de difang [The Place Where I Soared]," ibid., Vol. 1 ([1943] 1988), p. 118.

[79] David Apter and Tony Saich, Revolutionary Discourse in Mao's Republic (Cambridge, MA: Harvard University Press, 1994).

[80] For how young people in the post-1949 regime competed to show their love for the Revolution, see Susan Shirk, Competitive Comrades: Career Incentives and Student Strategies in China (Berkeley: University of California Press, 1982). Its conclusion has a summary of how cooperation coexisted with competition. See pp. 165–181.

[81] Gramsci defines a hegemonic leadership as one in which a group – for instance, the Jacobins – leads others as kindred and allied groups. See Antonio Gramsci, Selections from the Prison Notebooks of Antonio Gramsci (New York: International Publishers, 1971), p. 78. The CCP declared that as a proletarian party it fought together with and for all the oppressed in China or even around the world, although it defined differently the oppressed at various stages of the communist Revolution.

Sinicized Marxism, together with the mass line, articulated systematically the party elite's intention of shaping their revolutionary party into a supreme historical agent always self-reflective. This historical agent was, in their imagining, capable of developing correct political lines by measuring and addressing basic wants that emerged from Chinese reality, a reality composed predominantly of the Chinese people. Mao's insistence on self-reform and self-criticism, buttressed by his forceful and even brutal approach to institutionalizing them, enabled the CCP to represent its organization as one blessed with effective techniques for its members' and especially its leading echelon's self-transformation, without which the search for a correct line was not possible.[82] It can be said, therefore, that Mao Zedong Thought was essential for the CCP's self-invention as a "Leninist phenomenon," defined by Kenneth Jowitt as a paradoxical mode of operation blending charisma with rationality.[83]

But it was precisely by working inside communist intellectuals' tradition of antielitist elitism and by conveying so powerfully what they wanted that Mao caused suffering to many of his intellectual comrades. When he chastised intellectuals for their inability to understand, communicate with, and help the masses, or when he focused on how their egotism undermined their political passion, some intellectuals might have felt reluctant to undertake self-criticism, but they as a group could not resist his demand for their self-reform. Simply put, when the top leadership of an authoritarian party pressed for changes that were unassailable in both ideological and pragmatic terms, the situation did not encourage others to question his decision, however unreasonable.

In the post-1949 period, antielitist elitism remained significant for top party authorities. At the early stage of the communist regime, though apprehensive about intellectuals' class backgrounds and ideological dispositions, the CCP needed their knowledge and training, deemed indispensable for the party's task of national reconstruction on all political, economic, and educational fronts. Therefore, ideological remolding campaigns based on the Yan'an rectification model started almost immediately in the 1950s. But antielitism did not subside and, according to many observers and insiders, reached unprecedented heights during

---

[82] I do not mean to suggest that antielitist elitism was the only source of Mao's Sinicized Marxism, mass line, and other ideas. I just mean that it was a significant source shaping these themes.

[83] Kenneth Jowitt, *New World Disorder: The Leninist Extinction* (Berkeley: University of California Press, 1992).

the Cultural Revolution. Mao at that time pressed intellectuals to give up their specialized professional knowledge to learn from the masses. While overwhelmingly antielitist, Mao still reserved in his thought a spot, however small, for the prestige of learning. In his well-publicized conversation with Red Guard leaders on July 28, 1968, he encouraged them to emulate Engels, who "had only stayed in the university for one-and-half years" and "studied natural science not at any school but all by himself at the British Museum." He then also drew their attention to Gorky's limited education. Critiquing bookish learning, Mao did not intend to promote a leadership ignorant and anti-intellectual. As a matter of fact, by spurring the Red Guards to imitate eminent radical intellectuals, Mao aspired for a revolutionary elite who were the best kind possible in his ideological universe: Their stunning accomplishments were not to be outdone by bookish intellectuals, not to mention ordinary workers and peasants.[84] But this part of his thinking was eclipsed by the ruthless antielitism he held during the Cultural Revolution (see Chapter 5).

Other leading communist intellectuals also adhered to antielitist elitism as they explained their policies and ideological positions. Conflicting with Mao in the late 1950s and early 1960s, Liu Shaoqi insisted that his economic policy was the "correct" mass line because he was the one who really listened to and relied on the masses and freed himself from the ideological constraints of Marxism to understand reality.[85] When the CCP reevaluated Mao's role in history and pointed out his mistakes in the post–Cultural Revolution period, as Nick Knight argues, it still honored the great helmsman's incorporation of Marxism into Chinese conditions. Even the current Communist leadership seems to bring into play antielitist elitism to impress Chinese citizens. For instance, when Hu Jintao made his Chinese New Year pilgrimage to Jinggangshan in 2009, he vowed to follow through on the Jinggangshan principle (Jinggangshan jingshen), defined by the CCP's leading core as respect for reality (shishi qiushi) and "reliance on the masses" (yikao qunzhong).[86] The historical influence of Mao Zedong Thought, we must note, originated in Chinese communist intellectuals' antielitist

---

[84] Mao Zedong "Zhaojian shoudu hongdaihui fuzeren de tanhua [A Meeting with Beijing's Red Guard Representatives]," in Mao Zedong sixiang wansui [Long Live Mao Zedong Thought] ([1968] 1969), pp. 687–716.

[85] Xu Guansan, Liu Shaoqi yu Liu Shaoqi luxian [Liu Shaoqi and His Line] (Hong Kong: Zhongdao chubanshe, 1980), pp. 303–305.

[86] There are other elements that constitute the Jinggangshan principle as well. Among them, "firm commitment to one's ideal [jianding xinnian] and "fearlessness when facing hardship [jianku fendou]."

attitude – to wit, their intention to shed their pride in their own political knowledge so as to better understand China.[87] Mao, in sum, joined others in creating the tradition of antielitist elitism, indispensable for the legitimacy of the party and the party-state. And it was inside this tradition that he challenged the CCP's intellectual followers to reform themselves and competed with other powerful party leaders. That antielitism continues to shape the Communist leadership today, long after the specific policies of Mao's later years have been set aside.

[87] Knight, *Rethinking Mao*, pp. 197–216.

8 Gendered Mao: Mao, Maoism, and Women

DELIA DAVIN

The young Mao was a champion of women's rights. In early published essays, he attacked the arranged-marriage system and the way women were treated in the family. Later, in his reports on rural areas, he consistently gave attention to women's issues. The revolution that he led accepted the equality of the sexes as a major objective. Although it did not fully succeed in achieving even its own limited vision of equality, it did transform the roles of women in Chinese society. Yet Mao's treatment of the women in his own life did not reflect his ideals. The one thing that his wives had in common was that they suffered through their association with him. In old age, he indulged a lascivious fondness for pretty young nurses and assistants. This chapter explores Mao's attitudes toward gender as manifested in both his writings and his private life and will discuss how these relate to the achievements and deficiencies of Maoist gender policies.

WOMEN IN MAO'S THOUGHT AND WRITING

In his account of his childhood, Mao depicted himself as having been allied with his mother against his father. In hindsight, at least, he saw his father as an authoritarian tyrant and his mother and siblings as "the opposition."[1] When he was 14, Mao, by his own account, rejected the marriage arranged for him, demonstrating his opposition to the traditional marriage system for the first time.[2]

As a radical of the May Fourth Movement, Mao was strongly influenced by the social Darwinism of Chinese nationalism and by the idealization of "modern" love relationships between men and women. For him, as for many educated young Chinese men of his era, a critique of the traditional Chinese family and of the position of women within it

---

[1] Edgar Snow, *Red Star over China* (London: Gollancz,1937), p. 128.
[2] *Ibid.*, pp.144–145.

was fundamental to radical politics. His writings in 1919–20 contain a range of protests against the treatment of women in Chinese society, their sufferings in marriage, their exclusion from work, and the underfunding of women's education in his home province of Hunan. In one striking passage, he takes on the voice of a woman, "We are women.... we are also human beings so why won't they let us take part in politics? ... The shameless men, the villainous men, make us into their playthings, and force us to prostitute ourselves to them indefinitely. The devils, who destroy the freedom to love."[3] Notable also are 10 passionate pieces written in response to the suicide of a young Changsha woman, Miss Zhao, who slit her own throat on her wedding day to escape marriage to the man to whom her parents had betrothed her.[4] In these essays, Mao makes the usual arguments against arranged marriage, but his response to people who asked why Miss Zhao did not simply run away shows more originality. Why, he asks, are all the public toilets in Changsha for men only, why do women not drink in teahouses, why do single women not stay in hotels, why are business and carting done only by men, and why is there a college for men and one for women? His answer is that segregated Chinese society allows women no place. That, he insists, is why Miss Zhao had nowhere to run to.[5] In his next piece, he recognizes the importance of socialization, conceding that women may be psychologically and physiologically weaker than men, but arguing that these defects are not inherent. Rather, they are the result of social customs such as foot binding and a lack of education. To emancipate themselves, women should not marry before they are physically mature, should be equipped with the knowledge and skills to live their own lives before they marry, and should be prepared for living expenses after childbirth.[6]

---

3 "The Great Union of the Popular Masses", Part 2, July 28, 1919; trans. in Stuart Schram, *Mao's Road to Power: Revolutionary Writings 1912–1949*, Vol. 1: *The Pre-Marxist Period, 1912–1920* (Armonk, NY: M. E. Sharpe, 1992), p. 383.

4 "Commentary on the Suicide of Miss Zhao," November 16, 1919; "The Question of Miss Zhao's Personality," November 18; "The Marriage Question – An Admonition to Young Men and Women," November 19; "The Question of Reforming the Marriage System," November 19; 'The Evils of Society' and Miss Zhao," November 21; "Concerning the Incident of Miss Zhao's Suicide," November 21; "Against Suicide," November 23; "The Question of Love – Young People and Old People," November 25; "Smash the Matchmaker System," November 27; "The Problem of Superstition in Marriage," November 28; trans. in Schram, *Road to Power*, Vol. 1, pp. 421–449.

5 'The Evils of Society' and 'Miss Zhao,' November 21, 1919, trans. in Schram, *Road to Power*, Vol. 1, p. 428.

6 "Concerning the Incident of Miss Zhao's Suicide," November 21, 1919, trans. in Schram, *Road to Power*, Vol. 1, pp. 431–433.

Mao also had grasped the importance of economic factors in gender relations. In a critique of Hunan's draft provincial constitution in April 1921, he insisted that women must be given equal rights to inherit because unless women have property, attempts to solve problems such as education, occupation, and participation in politics and marriage were only empty talk.[7] His second suggestion – that there should be a clause on free-choice marriage and the freedom to divorce – reflected what was to be a preoccupation of all communist legislation.

However, at this stage Mao also can be found expressing total opposition to marriage and support for free love. In a letter of November 1920 welcoming the "union based on love" of two friends, he asserted his own resolution not to marry and suggested that those who had marriage contracts should break them and those who did not should not enter into them.[8] (That this letter may have reflected some inner turmoil is reflected by the fact that he himself got married only a few weeks later.)

Mao's early, highly personalized writings on women and the family date from the period when he was not yet a Marxist and when, as a young and as yet unmarried man, he was dealing with his own strong sexual and emotional feelings. His concerns were not unusual. It often has been observed that it was Chinese men who produced many of the critiques of women's position in Chinese society in the May Fourth period. Young radicals followed the ideas of Liang Qichao in arguing that China's weak, uneducated women were enfeebling the Chinese nation. Moreover, this was a generation of young men who through partially Westernized education had become attracted to the idea of romantic love, an ideal that they could pursue only if they were prepared to defy their families and reject the marriages arranged for them. Love and marriage became, as Mao recognized in one of his essays, a battleground between the generations.[9] Love, marriage, and the relationship between the sexes were among the topics often discussed in the New People's Study Society, of which Mao was a founding member in 1918. The society also introduced Mao to the experience of debates in mixed company. By 1920, it had several women members, including an early girlfriend of Mao's, Tao Yi, and Xiang Jingyu and Cai Chang, who later

---

[7] "The Greatest Defects of the Draft Provincial Constitution," April 25–26, 1921, trans. in Schram, *Road to Power*, Vol. 2: *National Revolution and Social Revolution, Dec. 1920–June 1927*, p. 40.

[8] "Letter to Luo Xuezan," trans. in Schram, *Road to Power*, Vol. 1, pp. 607–609.

[9] "The Question of Love – Young People and Old People," November 25, 1919, trans. in Schram, *Road to Power*, Vol. 1, pp. 439–441.

were to become important women members of the Chinese Communist Party (CCP) and to write on the relationship between the CCP and the women's movement.[10]

After Mao became a Marxist and a revolutionary leader, he wrote about women and family questions with less personal passion, but for many years he still gave the gender divide real attention. In his "Report on the Peasant Movement in Hunan" in 1927, he famously remarked that while men were subjected to the domination of three systems of authority – political, clan, and religious – women also were dominated by men in the form of the authority of the husband.[11] He reported with glee the actions of some women in Hengshan County, Hunan, who had ignored a ban on women and forced their way into banquets in the ancestral temple. He also enumerated the (rather small) female membership of peasant associations. His various investigations and reports on rural areas from 1927–34 contained information and comments on the roles played by women in the Revolution, women and land distribution, literacy, education, and mass meetings. These writings also have references to the sale of women and to the problems of introducing freedom of marriage and divorce to peasant society.[12] A report from 1932 provides a particularly useful glimpse of women's lives in the communist area in Jiangxi and the difficulties the party was experiencing in enforcing women's rights, sexual equality, free-choice marriage, and the freedom to divorce.[13] In 1934, commenting on freedom of divorce, Mao says that it is right that if one party firmly requests a divorce, it should be granted, but that for the morale of young men in the Red Army, it was necessary to make an exception in the case of soldiers.[14] The wives of Red Army men should not divorce them without their explicit agreement. This

[10] For information on May Fourth feminism and the various political strands of the women's movement, see Wang Zheng, *Women in the Chinese Enlightenment: Oral and Textual Histories* (Berkeley: University of California Press, 1999); and Christina Gilmartin, *Engendering the Chinese Revolution: Radical Women, Communist Politics, and Mass Movements in the 1920s* (Berkeley: University of California Press, 1995).

[11] "Report on the Peasant Movement in Hunan," February 1927, trans. in Schram, *Road to Power*, Vol. 2, pp. 452–453.

[12] Schram, *Road to Power*, Vol. 3: *From Jinggangshan to the Establishment of the Jiangxi Soviets, July 1927–December 1930*, (Armonk, NY: M. E. Sharpe, 1995), and Vol. 4: *The Rise and Fall of the Chinese Soviet Republic, 1931–1934* (Armonk, NY: M. E. Sharpe, 1997).

[13] "On the Organization and Work of the Committee for Upholding Women's Rights and Improving Women's Lives, Announcement by the Interim Central Government, Directive No. 6 of the Council of People's Commissars," June 30, 1932, trans. in Schram, *Road to Power*, Vol. 4, pp. 225–229.

[14] "Conclusions Regarding the Report of the Central Executive Committee," January 27, 1934, in Schram, *Road to Power*, Vol. 4, pp. 715–716.

echoed provisions already enshrined in law in the communist areas of Jiangxi.[15] Mao also reaffirmed his opposition to early marriage, insisting that minimum ages for marriage of 18 for women and 20 for men were appropriate and should not be lowered as some had suggested.

After 1934, Mao's writings contain fewer mentions of women. There are none in Volume 5 of the Schram collection covering January 1935 to July 1937 and only one glancing reference to women in the War of Resistance in Volume 6 covering August 1937–38.[16] A ritual address delivered by Mao on Women's Day 1939 in Yan'an, "Women Unite," celebrated the achievements of the communist movement for women and urged them on to greater efforts. It set the tone for most subsequent scattered references to women in Mao's works, which usually are brief and celebratory or admonitory. For example, in his 1957 notes on "The Socialist Upsurge in the Chinese Countryside," he both praises women's efforts in production and urges them on to do even more.[17] (In these notes he does at least insist on the importance of equal pay.) The young man's interest in love, sex, and relations between the sexes has disappeared in Mao's later writing. In its place is the preoccupation of the professional revolutionary and party leader with women's potential contribution to the Revolution and production and with the liberating power of these roles.

Mao did, however, show an increasing interest in a subject that was to have a great impact on women, gender, and family relations in China – birth control and birth planning. In an anti-Malthusian stance in the early 1950s, he asserted that China's big population was a source of strength and that even if China's population were to multiply many times, China would be fully capable of finding solutions.[18] This speech was famously used to attack the proponents of birth control in the early

---

[15] See "Regulations on Preferential Treatment for the Chinese Workers' and Peasants' Red Army," November 1931, trans. in Schram, *Road to Power*, Vol. 4, pp. 783–785; and "The 1934 Marriage Law of the Chinese Soviet Republic," in M. J. Meijer, *Marriage Law and Policy in the Chinese People's Republic* (Hong Kong: Hong Kong University Press, 1971).

[16] Schram, *Road to Power*, Vol. 5: *Toward the Second United Front, January 1935– July 1937* (Armonk, NY: M. E. Sharpe, 1999), and Vol. 6: *The New Stage, August 1937–38* (Armonk, NY: M. E. Sharpe, 2004).

[17] *The Socialist Upsurge in China's Countryside* (Beijing: Foreign Languages Press, 1957), is a book of celebratory reports on China's agricultural cooperatives. Some of Mao's comments on them are included in his *Selected Works*, Vol. 5. The two that are concerned with women are "Note to 'Women Are Now on the Labour Front,'" and "Note to 'Labour Shortage Solved by Rallying Women to Production,'" in *Selected Works of Mao Tse-tung*, Vol. 5 (Beijing: Foreign Languages Press, 1977), pp. 263, 269.

[18] "On the Bankruptcy of the Idealist Conception of History," September 16, 1949, in Mao, *Selected Works*, Vol. 4 (Beijing: Foreign Languages Press, 1965), pp. 452–453.

years of the People's Republic.[19] By 1956, however, there is documentary evidence that Mao had accepted the need to propagandize and popularize birth control and to promote planned childbirth.[20] He spoke of the need for birth planning in his February 1957 speech, "On the Correct Handling of Contradictions Among the People," even opining that a planned birth department might be set up.[21] He elaborated the idea in his "Be Activists in Promoting the Revolution" in October.[22] All Mao's pronouncements on birth planning were made in the context of national needs and economic resources rather than gender impact and implications for women. Nonetheless, once translated into policy, they were, of course, to have significant consequences for women.

MAO'S RELATIONSHIPS WITH WOMEN

The woman to whom Mao's parents had arranged his marriage when he was a teenager died of illness a short time after she came to live in his family home. In 1920, he married Yang Kaihui, the 19-year-old daughter of his former tutor. She bore three sons in seven years, staying home with the children while he traveled to different parts of China as a CCP organizer. He left home for the last time in 1927. Letters to Mao that were never sent reflect her love and concern for him together with her inability to tolerate the violence of the revolutionary world to which he belonged.[23] She longs to work or study or go away but must stay and try to conceal her misery in order to care for her children. In January 1930, she wrote of her suspicion that he had abandoned her. In fact, when the CCP retreated to the rural areas, Mao set up a revolutionary base area in Jinggangshan, a remote mountainous region in Jiangxi Province. There, in 1928, he began living with the woman who became his third wife. He Zizhen was a fiery young woman of 18. Two years earlier when the Northern Expeditionary Force had reached her town,

[19] Thomas Scharping, *Birth Control in China 1949–2000: Population and Demographic Development* (London: RoutledgeCurzon, 2003), p. 30.
[20] Tyrene White, *China's Longest Campaign: Birth Planning in the People's Republic 1949–2005* (Ithaca, NY: Cornell University Press, 2006), p. 35.
[21] Mao Zedong, "On the Correct Handling of Contradictions Among the People," in Roderick MacFarquhar, Timothy Cheek, and Eugene Wu, eds., *The Secret Speeches of Chairman Mao: From the Hundred Flowers to the Great Leap Forward* (Cambridge, MA: Council on East Asian Studies, Harvard University, 1989), pp. 160–162.
[22] Mao, *Selected Works*, Vol. 5, p. 488.
[23] The discovery of these writings was reported in an article that appeared in *China Daily* in 1995 about a new film of Yang Kaihui's life (Yu Wentao, "Film Makes Chinese Heroine a Human," *China Daily*, July 10, 1995). The content of Yang's writing is summarized in Jung Chang and Jon Halliday, *Mao: The Unknown Story* (London: Jonathan Cape, 2005), pp. 87–91.

she had joined the CCP and had become head of her county women's department. Subsequently, she helped her brother escape from jail, and she became a guerrilla fighter. She was assigned to work as Mao's secretary in 1928, and they married in the same year. Mao and Yang Kaihui did not meet again. She was executed in Changsha in 1930, refusing to denounce him.

He Zizhen also was to suffer terribly. She gave birth to six children amid extraordinary difficulties. Three were left with others to care for and were lost; two died in infancy. He Zizhen was seriously wounded on the Long March. Arrival in the Northwest brought a brief domestic respite as Mao and He Zizhen lived together with their new baby girl. But Mao's attention to other women provoked quarrels, and in 1937, He Zizhen left to seek medical attention and education in the Soviet Union. Her sixth child, born in Moscow, died before he was a year old. By that time, Mao had already married his fourth wife, the some-time Shanghai actress Lan Ping, who, in Yan'an, changed her name to Jiang Qing. He Zizhen's sole surviving child, Li Min, accompanied her mother to the Soviet Union but later returned to China and was largely brought up by Jiang Qing with her own daughter, Li Na.

He Zizhen had a mental breakdown, and her ill health apparently persisted even after her return to China in 1947. She lived an isolated life, sometimes alone in an apartment, sometimes in hospital. She had contact with her brother and was sometimes visited by her daughter, Li Min, who normally lived in Mao's Beijing household. Mao arranged one surprise reunion with He Zizhen in 1959; otherwise, she never saw him again. She was not allocated an official post despite her veteran revolutionary status. Yet once Mao was dead and Jiang Qing imprisoned, it became politic to acknowledge He Zizhen. She was summoned to Beijing as a member of the Chinese People's Political Consultative Congress in 1979. A book on her life was published in 1983, veteran leaders sent flowers when she died in 1984, and her ashes were interred in the Revolutionary Cemetery in Beijing.[24]

Mao's marriage to Jiang Qing was longer-lived, lasting in name at least until his death in 1976. Their only daughter, Li Na was born in 1940. However, their relations are said to have become difficult even by the establishment of the People's Republic in 1949. They quarreled often, and Jiang Qing, who was in poor health in the 1950s, made long

[24] Details of He Zizhen's life are from Wang Xingjuan, *He Zizhen de lu* [He Zizhen's Road] (Beijing: Zuojia chubanshe, 1985); and *Li Min, He Zizhen yu Mao Zedong* [Li Min, He Zizhen, and Mao Zedong] (Beijing: Zhongguo wenlian chubanshe, 1993). Her story is also told in Lily Hsiao Hong Lee and Sue Wiles, *Women of the Long March* (St. Leonards, Australia: Allen & Unwin, 1999).

visits to the Soviet Union for medical treatment.[25] When she and Mao were no longer personally close, he had a succession of girlfriends.

In his last years, Mao's closest companions were his female nurses and caregivers. Although no rumors of his relations with women had been allowed to leak out, his favorites, Zhang Yufeng (formerly a stewardess on his train) and Meng Jinyun (formerly an actress from an air force entertainment group), became familiar to the public because they were photographed and filmed supporting Mao and helping him walk. After Mao's death, Zhang published a memoir of her time with the Chairman, and various gossipy accounts that became available outside China confirmed the suspicions of the more curious about the nature of Mao's relationships with the young women who had surrounded him.[26]

However, from the early 1960s, as Mao began a new struggle culminating in the Cultural Revolution, against those within the CCP whom he regarded as political enemies, he drew Jiang Qing back into his political inner circle. For the first time, she became a political figure in her own right, shaping, or attempting to shape, the course of the Cultural Revolution. She made frequent public appearances in army clothes to present herself as a militant. Fearing that her past might be used against her in the puritanical climate that now prevailed (and that she exploited in her attacks on others), she used the Cultural Revolution to destroy people in cultural circles who had known her as an actress in Shanghai. She was involved in some of the worst political persecutions of this period. But often, also, she acted for Mao. At her trial, it is said that she claimed, "I was Chairman Mao's dog. I bit anyone he told me to bite."[27]

GENDER UNDER MAOIST RULE[28]

Maoist gender analysis identified the place of women as a key problem in Chinese society. The solution to the "woman problem" was to

---

[25] Sources for Jianq Qing's life are her own account in Roxane Witke, *Comrade Chiang Ch'ing* (Boston: Little, Brown, 1977); Ross Terrill, *The White-Boned Demon: A Biography of Madame Mao Zedong* (New York: William Morrow, 1984); and Ye Yonglie, *Jiang Qing zhuan* [A Biography of Jiang Qing] (Changchun: Shidai wenyi chubanshe, 1993).

[26] Zhang Yufeng, "Wo gei Mao zhuxi dang mishu [I Was Chairman Mao's Secretary]," *Yanhuang chunqiu* 8 (1993); Jing Fuzi, *Mao Zedong yu tade nürenmen* [Mao Zedong and His Women] (Taipei: Lianjing chubanshe, 1991); and Li Zhisui, *The Private Life of Chairman Mao* (London: Chatto & Windus, 1994).

[27] Terrill, *The White-Boned Demon*, p. 15; see also David Bonavia, *Verdict in Peking: The Trial of the Gang of Four* (London: Burnett Books, 1984), pp. 45–46.

[28] For a useful introduction to the English-language literature on women in twentieth-century China, see Gail Hershatter, *Women in China's Long Twentieth Century* (Berkeley: University of California Press, 2007).

redefine gender boundaries by creating a society in which women lived more like men. Discussion of gender policy in the Mao era therefore frequently amounts to discussing policy toward women. What justification is there for attributing this policy to Mao? After the period of the Jiangxi Soviet, judging from the paucity of references in his writing to women, marriage, and the family, he took a less direct interest in CCP work in this area. Both work with women and marriage and family policy were increasingly delegated to female communist leaders and to party-led women's organizations. Nonetheless, CCP policies toward women both in the Jiangxi period and afterwards were largely based on Mao's ideas on social reform and development, and policy changes usually were the result of broader political currents that Mao also inspired or approved.

Before the People's Republic

From the late 1920s onwards, the CCP always controlled and administered small base areas in rural China. It was therefore in a position to translate its ideas on women into law and action. These ideas drew inspiration both from the May Fourth Movement and from Marxist analysis of women's oppression. They included the Marxist propositions that the keys to women's liberation were socialist revolution and participation in productive labor. The right to work was accompanied by some special protections for women under labor law. However, it also was accepted that the state should intervene to enforce the right to free-choice marriage and divorce and to ensure that women had equal rights with men to participate in social and political activity and to receive an education. There was a strong emphasis, especially in the early years, on the mass mobilization of women in support of these ideas. Feminism was condemned routinely as a bourgeois ideology, but the terms *funü jiefang* (women's liberation) and *funü yundong* (women's movement) were taken over and used frequently in communist discourse. Nevertheless, Chinese society under CCP rule was increasingly sexually repressive. May Fourth ideas about free love disappeared. The ideal was premarital chastity for both men and women and sexual fidelity within marriage. The double standard survived in the sense that women were likely to pay much more heavily for any infringement of this code.

Marriage laws were enacted in the Jiangxi Soviet in 1931 and 1934 and in various communist areas in northern China from 1939 onward. These varied in detail, but all were clearly influenced by the May Fourth ideals – in other words, the ideals of an urban intellectual movement.

They stressed free-choice marriage, the principle of monogamy, a high minimum age at marriage, and equality of the sexes. (They also included rules about physical examinations and avoiding marriage with close cousins that are clearly informed by eugenics, popular at that time with progressive thinkers in China, as in the rest of the world.)

Later communist marriage laws were noticeably influenced less by radical idealism and more by experience. The priority for the CCP was to survive and, if possible, expand its power. It was reluctant to do anything that might prove socially divisive and erode its sources of support. When radical policy on marriage and divorce incurred the hostility of male peasants, and indeed of older women, it was modified. Under the Jiangxi marriage laws, divorce was rather freely available even when only one partner wanted it, whereas after the Long March, in the communist areas of the Northwest, if both parties did not agree to divorce, clear grounds had to be cited for it. As in Jiangxi, there were restrictions on divorcing soldiers in the revolutionary army, but the laws in the communist areas of the Northwest and in the People's Republic adopted gender-neutral language for this clause, allowing the possibility that the soldier was female.[29] These later marriage laws also dealt with practical problems that had been neglected in Jiangxi, such as the responsibility for child support after divorce.

Documents from the 1940s tend to downgrade the whole problem of women's oppression within the family, urging women cadres to drop useless slogan campaigns about free-choice marriage and sex equality and to concentrate on building flourishing and harmonious families.[30] In response to difficulties in the economy of the communist areas, from 1942 on, economic work became a more important theme in the communist women's movement. Women leaders such as Cai Chang and Deng Yingchao followed the party line by arguing that the way to liberate women was to involve them in economic work, to teach them agricultural skills, and to mobilize them to spin, weave, and produce uniforms for the army. Communist land reform policies entitled women to a land allocation on equal terms with men. Land reform was suspended during the war against Japan, but when it was undertaken again from 1946 on, cadres were urged to ensure that women's names were included on the land deeds.

[29] For texts of four such laws from the Northwest and the 1950 Marriage Law of the People's Republic of China, see Meijer, *Marriage Law and Policy.*

[30] Delia Davin, *Woman-Work: Women and the Party in Revolutionary China* (Oxford, England: Clarendon Press, 1976).

Women in the communist areas, like women elsewhere, suffered from the double burden of work inside and outside the home. Their difficulties often were blamed on their own backwardness rather than on the way they were oppressed. Mao was personally involved in the silencing of a feminist voice openly critical of the way women were treated. Ding Ling, a famous woman writer and May Fourth feminist, had left Shanghai to live and work in the communist capital of Yan'an. She had been a classmate of Mao's wife, Yang Kaihui, in Changsha and was friendly with Mao when she first reached Yan'an. Although she had joined the CCP in 1932, as a fighter for sexual equality, she was disturbed by the way women were treated in Yan'an. Her story, "When I Was in Xia Village" (1941), concerned Zhenzhen (her name is the character for female chastity reduplicated), a young peasant woman who was first captured by Japanese soldiers and later twice sent back to the occupied areas to collect intelligence for the communists.[31] When she finally comes home, the news that she has been raped many times and has contracted a venereal disease spreads. The villagers are full of spiteful gossip about her. Ding Ling shows that Zhenzhen is judged only in terms of the traditional emphasis on female chastity – her heroism as a spy for the Chinese counts for nothing.

In 1942, Ding Ling published an essay on International Women's Day in the *Liberation Daily* entitled, "Thoughts on March Eighth," which was starkly critical of the treatment of women in Yan'an. If they did not marry, they were gossiped about. When they did marry, they had to give birth to children. Once they had children, if they gave them to others to care for they were condemned for not being good mothers, but if they stayed at home with them they were mocked and accused of backwardness. Backwardness then might be the pretext offered by their husbands for divorce. This essay was doubly dangerous. First, it implied that the patriarchal attitudes toward women still flourished in the communist capital. Second, its attack on men who divorced their "backward" wives as they aged and lost their looks could have been taken as a reference to Mao's treatment of He Zizhen, as well as to several other high cadres. Although there is no evidence that Mao took it personally, it is not impossible that this underlay his angry reaction to the essay. His theoretical response came in his "Yan'an Talks," in which he attacked the petty bourgeois outlook of certain writers and insisted that the task for literature and art must be to serve politics and

---

[31] For a text of this story and a discussion of it, see Tani Barlow, ed., *I Myself Am a Woman: Selected Writings of Ding Ling* (Boston: Beacon Press, 1989).

the broad mass of the people (see chapter 7).[32] Ding Ling lost her post on the *Liberation Daily* and was forced to engage in self-criticism. She accepted charges of irresponsibility and mistaken beliefs but refused to admit to being a "narrow feminist."

The party line continued to be that complete liberation for women could be achieved only through socialist revolution. Women like Ding Ling were criticized when they were considered to have opposed party policy, but CCP policy toward women continued to be based on a program of women's rights. It is true that implementation of the program sometimes was hindered because of the fear of alienating male peasants, the priorities of a predominantly male leadership, and the constant military danger to the communist areas. However, there were certain achievements. The message of sexual equality and the reform of family relationships was heard in the rural areas of northwestern China almost for the first time. Its inclusion in the ideology of national struggle made it more widely acceptable. Tens of thousands of rural women were recruited by women's associations to work for the war effort. Their work brought them into contact with people outside their own families and gave them a new vision of themselves and their potential.

In the PRC: Before the Cultural Revolution

When the communist party came to power nationally in China, it sought to implement measures already tested in its base areas across the whole country. Land reform and collectivization, the implementation of a new marriage law, and the mobilization of women for employment or community activity were all policies expected to contribute to the equality of the sexes.

The All-China Women's Federation was the leading organization pressing for measures that would benefit women. From 1949 to 1957, its most influential years, following what was then the party line, it attempted to draw progressive non-communist figures into its work. Not only was Sun Yat-sen's widow, Song Qingling, its honorary president, the former head of the Guomindang women's organization, He Xiangning and other veterans of earlier women's movements such as Liu-Wang Liming of the Women's Christian Temperance Union and Deng Yuzhi of the YWCA were on its standing committee.

Under the land reform program, men and women counted equally in the per capita calculation of what a household should receive, but

---

[32] "Talks at the Yan'an Forum on Literature and Art," in Mao, *Selected Works*, Vol. 3, pp. 69–102.

women did not hold individual land titles. When collectivization of agriculture ended the private ownership of land and remuneration was made on the basis of the work contributed to the collective, hopes that the new system would improve the position of women were largely disappointed. Rural cadres were predominantly men who valued men's labor higher than women's. The nurseries and canteens that were supposed to relieve women of some of their domestic work proved unpopular and uneconomical, and few survived. Collective farming did increase women's contacts outside their immediate families and ensured that the farm work women did was publicly recognized, but it brought them fewer economic benefits than had been expected. As collectivization brought women in contact with men outside the family, it enabled some at least to achieve the courtship and free-choice marriage that was now being presented as a model.

The Marriage Law of the People's Republic, promulgated on May 1, 1950, was only the second law announced by the new government, reflecting the priority given to family reform in construction of the new society. Drafted by the CCP's Women's Committee led by veterans such as Deng Yingchao and Cai Chang, the law followed familiar lines, with an emphasis on equality, monogamy, and free choice. It was consciously more radical than any laws since Jiangxi, in particular, allowing divorce when one party insisted on it, even if the other was opposed – a point fought for by Deng Yingchao against considerable opposition. All the energies of the All-China Women's Federation (the CCP women's organization) were mobilized for implementation of the new law. Books, comic strips, pamphlets, plays, and films were produced to publicize it and to expose and condemn the "feudal" oppression of women.[33]

There were complaints that the marriage law amounted to a divorce law or that it favored women over men. Opposition was especially strong in the countryside. Women who sought divorce often suffered violence from their husband or in-laws. Tens of thousands of women are reported to have been killed over marriage-related issues in the first years of the People's Republic. The worst effects were when women tried to assert their right both to divorce and to a share of the family land. The backlash was so severe that the campaign to enforce the marriage law was cut back. The new measures contributed to changes in relationships within the Chinese family but suffered from an important defect, especially in relationship to rural families. Neither the new marriage law

[33] Elisabeth Croll, *The Politics of Marriage in Contemporary China* (Cambridge, England: Cambridge University Press, 1981).

nor collectivization challenged the patrilocal marriage system, which put women at a fundamental disadvantage in Chinese society. Women came as outsiders to their new villages, whereas men remained where they were born, and thus it was men who controlled the collective structures. Mao recognized the limitations of the law when he observed in an address to the Youth League in 1953, "[M]any of the articles of the Marriage Law are programmatic and their thorough implementation will take at least a period of three five year plans."[34] Ultimately, the marriage law did bring about considerable change, especially in rural areas.[35]

The view that women's oppression arose from their exclusion from productive labor inspired campaigns to increase women's share in the urban workforce and their role in agriculture. Again, the results were less than had been expected. Rural women usually received fewer work points for a day's work, and in the urban areas, women were disproportionately likely to be allocated work in lower-paid employment such as textiles and light industry or in neighborhood-run workshops that offered fewer benefits than state industry.

It was not only policies specifically designed to change the role of women that transformed the female experience after 1949; indeed, changes in living standards, education, and health arguably were more important. Living standards remained low, food and clothing were rationed, and even running water was a privilege enjoyed only in advanced urban areas, but with the notable and terrible exception of the famine years of 1959–61 when many millions died, improvements in the supply and distribution of food meant that the majority lived better than they had during the long period of war and civil strife. Improved nutrition, together with the introduction of preventive health measures and a focus on maternal and child welfare, brought infant and maternal death rates down dramatically. Life expectancy for women improved further and faster than for men.[36]

From the early 1950s in the urban areas, and very slowly in the rural areas from the 1960s, the availability of contraception and family-planning advice contributed to women's welfare by making it easier for couples to control the number of their children.[37] The 1970s, with

[34] "Take the Characteristics of Youth into Consideration," June 30 1953, in Mao, *Selected Works*, Vol. 5, p. 99.
[35] Neil Diamant, *Revolutionizing the Family: Politics, Love and Divorce in Urban and Rural China 1949–1968* (Berkeley: University of California Press, 2000).
[36] Judith Banister, *China's Changing Population* (Palo Alto, CA: Stanford University Press, 1987).
[37] Scharping, *Birth Control in China 1949–2000*; and White, *China's Longest Campaign*.

the campaign for a two-child family, and the 1980s, with the demand that couples should confine themselves to one child only, saw the introduction of Maoist-style mass campaigns for birth planning. The consequences for women were mixed.[38] On the one hand, the means of contraception became available to all who wanted them, and a woman who wanted a smaller number of children than her husband or his parents thought proper had the state on her side. On the other hand, women did not gain control over their own bodies; rather, their bodies became the site of a battle between the family and the state. All too often it was women who suffered in this situation, especially if they were the mothers of daughters.

The expansion of education was of special benefit to women because they had been overrepresented among those who received inadequate schooling or never attended school. While total enrollment experienced rapid growth, the female share in primary school enrollment rose from 28 percent in 1951 to 43.7 percent in 1974 and in secondary schools from 26.6 percent to 38.1 percent.[39] Education put hundreds of millions of women into a better position to realize their full potential.

Before the Cultural Revolution, the official attitude toward gender difference was somewhat contradictory. On the one hand, there was an insistence on equality and the expectation that women should behave at least in the public sphere much as men did. On the other hand, there was a discourse on gender difference that worked to women's detriment, insisting on women's natural ability to care and nurture, men's natural talent for leadership, and so on. The height of rhetorical insistence on gender equality in China was the period of the Cultural Revolution (1966–76).

The Cultural Revolution
During the Cultural Revolution, Chairman Mao's aphorism, "Times have changed. Men and women are the same. What men can do women can also do,"[40] was quoted constantly to advance individual women. Women played a prominent part in many Red Guard organizations. The freedom from family constraints experienced by young people when

[38] Delia Davin, "Gender and Population in the People's Republic of China," in Haleh Afshar, ed., *Women, State and Ideology: Studies from Africa and Asia* (London: Macmillan, 1987).

[39] All-China Women's Federation, *Zhongguo funü tongji ziliao 1949–1989* [Statistics on Chinese Women 1949–1989] (Beijing: Zhongguo tongji chubanshe, 1991).

[40] "To Fully Bring Out Women's Initiative in Revolutionary Construction," in *Hong Qi* [Red Flag] 10:63 (1971).

they traveled around China "exchanging revolutionary experience" or when families were split up by rural exile changed the nature of gender relations among individuals in this generation and made many young women and men alike stronger and more self-reliant.

"Holding up half the sky" supported women breaking into male-dominated fields of work such as engineering and aviation and even doing underground work in coal mines from which they had been excluded by health and safety legislation. Women were catapulted into leading positions in many institutions. But the effects of the much-vaunted models were limited, and much gender stereotyping survived. Most areas of work remained highly gendered, with, for example, women being preferred for assembly lines and textile manufacture because it was claimed they were more dextrous than men and had a higher tolerance for boredom. It was even still possible to hear cadres explain that it was less of a problem for young women to be "awaiting employment" (unemployed) than for young men because young men were more "lively" and became impatient easily.

Schools were closed in the early years of the Cultural Revolution, and millions of young people, male and female, lost years of education. However, once the schools opened again, the percentage of women in all levels of enrollment rose significantly. Yet despite its insistence on women's equality, the Cultural Revolution did not produce effective attacks on patriarchy or a strengthening of the women's movement. Indeed, for a time, the idea of women's special interests was rejected and the need for women's organizations denied. The Women's Federation came under heavy attack and was closed down temporarily in 1968. Its leading members, such as Cai Chang, Deng Yingchao, and Kang Keqing, had previously steered a difficult path in attempting to reconcile the goals of the women's movement and the CCP. They had trimmed the goals of May Fourth feminism when it was judged necessary in the pragmatic interests of the party, but they also had kept women's issues on the party's agenda and recruited women activists to work for it. Now they were forced to make self-criticisms of their "bourgeois attitudes" and to see their life's work negated. The Women's Federation was accused of opposing gender interests to class interests, of making too much of family problems, and of distracting women from politics. Kang Keqing, wife of Marshal Zhu De, was attacked for being "hostile to Jiang Qing" and was paraded in public in a dunce's cap. Other members of the precommunist women's movement who had become involved in the Women's Federation after 1949 suffered worse fates. Liu-Wang Liming, for example, a Women's Christian Temperance leader, was arrested as a spy and died in prison in 1970.[41] The Women's Federation was revived under leftist leadership in 1973 but did not resume its normal work until after Mao's death.[42]

Many other established institutions of the 1950s came under attack in the Cultural Revolution. However, the Women's Federation may have been particularly vulnerable because at the national level it was still led largely by women against whom Jiang Qing harbored a grudge. This small elite of female Long March veterans, married to male communist leaders, had been important members of the communist establishment since Yan'an days. Jiang Qing, by contrast, had been kept out of the public eye, never holding a major post until the early 1960s. Her comparative obscurity is often said to have been the result of an agreement drawn up by party leaders in Yan'an. Long March veterans, the women in particular, were shocked that Mao wished to divorce a respected revolutionary like He Zizhen to marry a Shanghai actress with an uncertain sexual and political past. The marriage went ahead on the condition that Jiang Qing would play no public role. Whatever the truth of this story, it is clear from various sources that Jiang Qing resented her treatment after her marriage to Mao and was jealous of women who did have leadership roles. She made some forays into cultural politics, denouncing the film *The Story of Wu Xun* in 1951 and attacking the feudal theses of traditional opera in the early 1960s to promote the new revolutionary works. On both occasions, she was roused to fury when she felt ignored and she was able to use Mao's support and her position as his wife to achieve her goals. This pattern was repeated on a far larger scale in 1966. Mao gave her significant power, and she used it to avenge the slights of the past and to make her own bid for the succession.

In the formal political culture, the leaders of the People's Republic did not normally appear publicly with their spouses. All the top party leaders were men; if their wives made public appearances, it was in relation to posts they held in their own right. Jiang Qing would hardly have been recognizable to most Chinese before the 1960s. Exceptions can be made when Chinese state leaders received foreign statesmen or made visits abroad. Thus Deng Yingchao accompanied Zhou Enlai on some occasions, and in 1963, Liu Shaoqi, then China's head of state, took his wife, Wang Guangmei, with him on a tour of Southeast Asia. In Indonesia, the couple was received at a banquet by President Suharto and his wife. Jiang Qing had apparently advised Wang Guangmei to

---

[41] Wang Zheng, *Women in the Chinese Enlightenment.*

[42] Ellen Judd, *The Chinese Women's Movement Between State and Market* (Palo Alto, CA: Stanford University Press, 2002).

dress in black velvet and on no account to wear jewelry. Instead, the unfortunate woman wore a silk dress and a pearl necklace, choices that proved fateful. When she was set before a kangaroo court by Red Guards, Jiang Qing insisted that she be forced to wear a silk dress and a necklace of ping pong balls, a cruel caricature of her appearance on the state visit.

Women's appearance generally was a sensitive issue during the Cultural Revolution.[43] Male and female cadres had dressed very similarly in the Yan'an period, but in the more relaxed atmosphere of the early years of the People's Republic, although dress was still plain and cloth was rationed, styles were less military, and there were clearcut differences between what men and women wore. In summer, urban women even wore skirts or dresses. as photographs of Mao's own family members show. Nonetheless, simplicity in dress was still held to be praiseworthy as a poem by Mao about militia women, written in February 1961 but much in vogue during Cultural Revolution, indicates:

> How bright and brave they look, shouldering five-foot rifles
> On the parade ground lit up by the first gleams of day.
> China's daughters have high-aspiring minds,
> They love their battle array, not silks and satins.[44]

Perhaps inspired by this poem, and also by an understanding of "equal to men" as "the same as men," female Red Guards cut their hair short and wore military-style uniforms with leather belts and army caps.[45] Red Guards also tried to police what everybody, male or female, wore. Women with long hair or perms and those who wore skirts or even flowery blouses often were stopped and humiliated in the street. Superficially, at least, their appearance was condemned in class rather than gender terms. It was not "too feminine"; it was "bourgeois." Men also could get into trouble for a "bourgeois appearance" if their hair was too long, their jackets Western-style, or their trousers too narrow or too wide. However, even during the Cultural Revolution, the clothing of most women did not obscure gender. For men, a Mao jacket and trousers provided an uncontested outfit. For women, the same outfit

---

[43] See Antonia Finnane, "What Should Chinese Women Wear?" in Antonia Finnane and Anne McLaren, eds., *Dress, Sex and Text in Chinese Culture* (Clayton, Australia: Monash Asia Institute, 1999).

[44] Mao Tse-tung, *Poems* (Beijing: Foreign Languages Press, 1976).

[45] For an insightful discussion of Red Guards and gender, see Emily Honig, "Maoist Mapping of Gender: Reassessing the Red Guards," in Susan Brownell and Jeffrey Wasserstrom, eds., *Chinese Femininities and Chinese Masculinities* (Berkeley: University of California Press, 2002).

was acceptable, but they more often wore jackets marked by gender-specific details such as traditional Chinese collars, tailoring at the bust and waist, or the use of patterned cloth.

Jiang Qing's own choice of clothing reflects the contested ideas of how a woman should look. Her public appearances at the height of the Cultural Revolution lent support to the idea that truly revolutionary women should dress like men. Whereas in 1962 she met President and Mrs Marcos wearing a tailored jacket and trousers, from 1966–69, she almost always appeared in an "adult Red Guard uniform" – military clothing with a soldier's cap. By early 1972 when she accompanied President Nixon to the theater, she had reverted to a tailored trouser suit. A few months later when she was interviewed by Roxane Witke, the American scholar who became her biographer, her clothes reflected her personal preferences. Not only did she herself wear silk blouses and slacks, on a whim she decided to kit her whole entourage out in skirts and ordered tailors to stay up that night to make them for the following day.[46] In 1975 she even designed a new national costume for women, a one-piece dress with a pleated skirt for which women cadres were offered extra clothing coupons.[47] The dress was entirely impractical in a country of climatic extremes, where laundry was still laborious, and there was a cloth shortage. It did not catch on. The episode illustrates, however, how highly contested the question of women's public presentation remained in Maoist China.

Ironically, although she had not been involved with the women's movement, in the latter phase of the Cultural Revolution Jiang Qing increasingly associated herself with insistence on the equality of the sexes. In 1974, a new mass campaign to "Criticize Lin Biao and Confucius" was launched. An opaque reflection of a complex power struggle at the top, this campaign attempted to associate the name of Lin Biao, the recently disgraced and deceased minister of defense, with the "reactionary" Confucius. It produced many critical attacks on the Confucian canon, and the *Women's Classic* (*Nü er jing*), a text on proper female comportment used in traditional education for women, also became a target. Early in 1975, all over the country, booklets containing short articles that acclaimed women's abilities and revolutionary potential appeared under titles such as "Criticize the *Women's Classic*."[48] At

---

[46] Witke, *Comrade Chiang Ch'ing*.

[47] Al least this was the case in the Beijing office in which I worked.

[48] For example, in January 1975, the Guangdong People's Publishing House put out "*Criticise the Women's Classic*," and the Hunan People's Publishing House produced "*Criticize the Women's Classic which propagandizes the way of Confucius and Mencius*."

this time, the cult of personality was at its height. The first or second page of every book published was devoted to quotations from Chairman Mao selected to suit the context. The booklets on the *Women's Classic* all opened with, "What men can do, women can do." Articles appeared in the press in praise of famous women in history, in particular, the Empress Lü, wife of the first Han emperor, who had carried on the rule of her husband after his death.

The educated Chinese public had no difficulty in decoding the rather obvious messages of these publications. Now that Lin Biao, Mao's "chosen successor" was dead, Jiang was presenting herself as the "next in line." However, Mao apparently did not agree. Jiang had been useful in his power struggles against his former comrades during the Cultural Revolution, but her clumsy attempts to present herself as his heir seems to have annoyed him. As he grew weaker in his last two years, stories circulated in Beijing that he had warned her that she was too ambitions and had refused to see her any more. Increasingly, he isolated himself in the company of his female nurses/companions.

After Mao's death and Jiang Qing's arrest, she often was caricatured in a way that was both unpleasantly and understandably misogynist. Cartoonists showed her variously as a vamp, a witch, and an ugly old woman. Most significantly, she was portrayed grasping for a crown, wearing a badge engraved with "Party Chairman," or holding a scroll on which was written "A woman can be an empress too." There is an echo in these depictions of the Confucian idea that women cause chaos in politics. By caricaturing her femininity, these depictions attacked Jiang as a woman and in doing so conveyed the message that women should not reach for power.

GENDER POLICY AFTER MAO

The economic reforms and liberalization of the economy that followed have profoundly affected the roles women play and the way they are perceived and depicted. In post-Mao China, the idea that men are more able than women was expressed widely despite the many years of Maoist education to the contrary. Many employers openly discriminated against women in hiring, and women's confinement to the lower-paid sectors of the labor market was hardly even challenged. Cutbacks and closures in the old state-owned industries led to large-scale layoffs in which women usually were the first to go.[49] The media and

---

[49] Liu Jieyu, *Gender and Work in Urban China: Women Workers of the Unlucky Generation* (London: Routledge, 2007).

advertisements commodified women as sex objects or portrayed them in domestic roles.[50] Local governments sponsored beauty competitions. Prostitution became rife. Young women from poor rural regions were trafficked into sex work. Wealthy businessmen and officials set up young women in flats. Hostesses and karaoke bars were used by businessmen and officials as a way of bonding or sealing agreements, creating a male business world from which women were excluded. The one-child family policy, introduced in 1980, resulted in an increasingly unbalanced sex ratio, revealed in the censuses of 1982, 1990, and 2000.[51] It is clear that son preference survived all the years of Maoist propaganda and that for many ordinary Chinese people, men and women are not the same.

From 1978, the Women's Federation, firmly back under the leadership of Deng Yingchao, Cai Chang, and Kang Keqing, tried to restore the old ideas of women's liberation. It lobbied for yet another marriage law to strengthen women's position in the family (which was passed in 1980), campaigned against the violence against women in the family, and opposed the policy urged by some economists to reserve paid work for men and make women return to the home. In the 1980s, as the older leadership withdrew, younger women created new programs to deal with the social problems produced by the economic reforms. In the 1990s, the Women's Federation reinvented itself as a nongovernmental organization (NGO) to facilitate cooperation with international NGOs. It now has a great range of economic and educational programs that target women, including poverty alleviation, assistance to women migrants, and retraining of laid-off women workers.

CONCLUSION

That Mao's vision of gender equality was not well reflected in his personal life is hardly surprising. Few people manage their relationships wholly in accord with their ideals, and it is perhaps particularly difficult for the very powerful to do so. For successful revolutionaries, power tends to be a grievously corrupting influence, as Mao's life illustrates all too clearly. Regardless of gender, Mao could be ruthless toward people to whom he had once been close. Each of his wives suffered great misfortunes because of her relationship with him, but he also bears direct responsibility for the terrible fates of many of the men who once were

---

[50] Emily Honig and Gail Hershatter, *Personal Voices: Chinese Women in the 1980s* (Palo Alto, CA: Stanford University Press, 1988).
[51] White, *China's Longest Campaign*, pp. 201–206.

close to him, whether his secretaries and his chosen successors or his comrades in arms.

In his youth, Mao's private life and his relations with women perhaps influenced his interest in gender policy and his concern for policies that would liberate women. In the Cultural Revolution, the influence of his personal life on gender policy was less benign. When his need for strong allies against other party leaders led him to introduce Jiang Qing into national politics in the 1960s, her desire for revenge on those she believed had opposed her led to the persecution of some women leaders. Her association with violent factionalism and cruel persecutions made her deeply unpopular, and her reputation became even worse after Mao's death when she was a useful scapegoat for all the evils of the Cultural Revolution. Ironically, because Jiang Qing had presented herself as a champion of sexual equality in order to strengthen her hand in the succession struggle, her personal unpopularity helped to discredit the Maoist model of sexual equality and made people more suspicious of powerful women.

Communist policy toward women, based on Mao's interpretations of Marxist theory and May Fourth ideas, offered a form of liberation to women that depended on family reform, equality of the sexes within consensual marriage, women's participation in the workforce, equal rights to education and activity outside the home, and the minimization of gender difference. It allowed little room for diversity and individual choice in the sphere of personal relations or sexual life. Under Maoism, the path to women's liberation was highly prescriptive. Alternative feminist voices and visions that had competed for attention at the time of the May Fourth Movement were suppressed. Despite Mao's early interest in free love, the society that he created was sexually repressive.

Moreover, many of the beliefs and practices that underlie gender inequality in Chinese society survived to reemerge as strong as ever after Mao's death. The belief that women are innately inferior both physically and intellectually is widespread. Chinese society is still characterized by a patrilocal and patrilineal marriage system, son preference, and the sexual double standard. On the other hand, as many Chinese women scholars who grew up in the Mao era have testified, female experience in the Mao era was complex and varied.[52] Maoist gender discourse and policy could have positive effects on women, giving them a certainty that gender discrimination was wrong and allowing them to feel

---

[52] Xueping Zhong, Wang Zheng, and Bai Dai, eds., *Some of Us: Chinese Women Growing Up in the Mao Era* (New Brunswick, NJ: Rutgers University Press, 2001).

a confidence in their gendered identities. Challenges to gender boundaries under Mao were limited but powerful. They restricted the choice of some but brought profound change to others. Life expectancy, health, education, work roles, and opportunities for women all improved. Ideas about the transformation of gender roles reached far beyond the urban educated classes to which they had once been largely confined. Maoism was by no means successful in establishing gender equality, but it did preside over an impressive transformation of existing gender divisions. Perhaps most important, by successfully challenging and moving traditional gender boundaries, Maoism showed that these boundaries are not static and can be contested.

9 Mao the Man and Mao the Icon

DANIEL LEESE

> The politician and the artist each have defects. For the sake of successfully attacking the enemy, uniting with friendly armies and strengthening himself, the politician must be worldly wise, have an excellent command of cunning methods and be good at dealing with both enemies and friends. His defects come from just these merits. When these skills are used in revolutionary tasks, they become the most beautiful and glorious "arts of revolution." But apart from the truly great politician, none can avoid some desire to use these skills for their own reputation, position, and profit and thus to harm the revolution.
>
> Wang Shiwei, "Politicians, Artists" (1942)[1]

The portrait of Mao Zedong prominently on display at the Gate of Heavenly Peace in Beijing ranges among the best-known icons of power around the globe. With the possible exception of Che Guevara, no other communist leader's image has served in similar fashion as a screen for revolutionary projections to both a domestic and international audience. During the late 1960s, Mao portraits and other items of the Chairman's bourgeoning cult, such as the *Little Red Book* and badges, were not only championed by Red Guards in China but became fashionable among Western students as well. Even communal living styles modeled on the canon of texts published under the name of Mao Zedong spread on U.S. and European campuses. Thus the romanticized image of Mao as an austere, down-to-earth philosopher and theoretician of the Chinese Communist Movement, which had first been expounded by journalist Edgar Snow (1905–72) in 1937, was turned into a symbol of world revolution.

In terms of quantity, the dissemination of Mao portraits is also unrivaled by any other modern political leader. According to official

---

[1] Wang Shiwei, "Politicians, Artists," in Dai Qing, *Wang Shiwei and "Wild Lilies": Rectification and Purges in the Chinese Communist Party 1942–1944* (Armonk, NY: M. E. Sharpe, 1994), p. 91.

statistics compiled by the National Printing Management Office, the former Chinese Communist Party (CCP) Chairman's portrait was printed 164.57 million times between the founding of the People's Republic of China (PRC) and the eve of the Cultural Revolution in 1965.[2] With the outbreak of the Cultural Revolution in 1966, basically the whole Chinese publishing industry was geared toward producing the texts and icons of the "great teacher, leader, commander, and helmsman" of the Chinese Revolution. An estimated 4.183 billion Mao portraits were published between 1966 and 1976, and the number does not even include the unofficial reprints of Mao images by various mass organizations. The accumulated total of official Mao texts and images printed between 1949 and 1976 is given as 11.8 billion, making Mao the best-selling author ever.

Four decades have passed since the high tide of the Mao cult during the early days of the Cultural Revolution. Still thousands of Chinese citizens, mainly from the countryside, pay homage to the embalmed relics of the deceased CCP leader on Tiananmen Square every day. His effigy is widely employed as a talisman, merchandise article, or even religious icon worshipped on the family altar. For many observers, however, the Mao portrait on Tiananmen has come to represent the ugly side of the CCP dictatorship rather than nostalgic Mao worship. For them, it is a reminder of the millions of peasants starved to death during the Great Leap Forward or the innumerable victims persecuted during the Maoist mass campaigns. The portrait thus further serves as a symbol of the crimes committed by the CCP dictatorship and has been subjected repeatedly to acts of symbolic violence, for example, during the protests of 1989 and most recently on May 12, 2007, when a migrant worker hurled a burning object at it.

This chapter sets out to provide an overview of the emergence, forms, and relevance of Mao's visual representations and discusses ways in which he instrumentalized his public image. Mao Zedong was well aware of the power of political imagery and its potency in securing symbolic capital. Yet he retained an ambivalent relationship toward his medial and material representations throughout his life. In the following pages, prominent pictures of Mao Zedong, both official and unofficial, are placed in political context, and the idealized image of the "Great Helmsman" is juxtaposed with reminiscences of the historical Mao

---

[2] Fang Houshu, "'Wenge' shi nian Mao Zedong zhuzuo, Mao Zedong xiang chuban jishi [Records About the Publication of Mao Zedong's Works and Images During the Decade of the 'Cultural Revolution']," in Song Yuanfang, ed., *Zhongguo chuban shiliao: Xiandai bufen* [Historical Materials on Chinese Publishing: Modern Part] (Ji'nan: Shandong jiaoyu chubanshe/Hubei jiaoyu chubanshe, 2000), p. 216.

traced from his own records and the remembrances of foreign visitors, colleagues, and foes. The chapter is divided into two parts: First, the evolution of Mao imagery in the early stages of the Chinese Revolution is traced. It looks at the artistic forms and political instrumentality of employing a personalized icon in innerparty and national struggles. The second part focuses on the developments in the PRC period, when Mao's stance toward his medial representations underwent significant changes, as did the imagery itself. By looking at both artistic representations and glimpses of the historical Mao, this chapter provides an introduction to the complex relationship between Mao the man and Mao the icon.

"SAVIOR OF THE CHINESE PEOPLE": THE CREATION OF A COMMON MYTH

The image that first comes to mind when thinking about portraits of Mao Zedong is probably a photograph taken by Edgar Snow in 1936 in Bao'an, northern Shaanxi Province. It shows Mao wearing a faded, padded wool suit, warily looking at the photographer. The photograph very well conforms to Snow's written assessment of Mao, whom he described as "a gaunt, rather Lincolnesque figure, above average height for a Chinese, somewhat stooped, with a head of thick black hair grown very long, and with large, searching eyes, a high-bridged nose and prominent cheek-bones. My fleeting impression was of an intellectual face of great shrewdness."[3] Snow had been the first foreign journalist to gain access to Mao and the communist leadership after the Long March. With his book, *Red Star over China* (1937), which had only been published after numerous revisions by, among others, Mao Zedong himself, Snow was to play an important role in fashioning Mao's image as the natural leader of the Chinese Revolution. The account incited worldwide influence and through its Chinese-language edition inspired large numbers of young Chinese to join the movement. The famous Mao portrait, however, was not published as part of Snow's account, and although Edgar Snow described Mao's pervasive influence within the CCP, he explicitly commented on the lack of a leader cult fostered around "the Chairman":

> He is a member of nearly everything.... His real influence is asserted through his domination of the political bureau.... Yet, while everyone knows and respects him, there is – as yet, at

[3] Edgar Snow, *Red Star over China* (London: Victor Gollancz, 1937), pp. 79–80.

least – no ritual of hero-worship built up around him. I never met a Chinese Red who drivelled "our-great-leader" phrases, I did not hear Mao's name used as a synonym for the Chinese people, but still I never met one who did not like "the Chairman" – as everyone called him – and admire him. The role of his personality in the movement was clearly immense.[4]

It was the song and dance epic "The East Is Red" (*Dongfang hong*), supervised by Premier Zhou Enlai and first staged in 1964, that gave the picture its supreme importance. Edgar Snow himself witnessed a performance in 1965 and observed: "As a climax of that performance ... I saw a portrait copied from a photograph taken by myself in 1936, blown up to about thirty feet high."[5] The original photograph had been colorized and now showed a close-up of Mao's face, rather like a painting, set off against a bright background. It perfectly matched Mao's cult image as brilliant military strategist and theoretician.

Adaptations of Snow's photograph with similar intent had already appeared in Yan'an days. On June 22, 1937, the Communist newspaper *Jiefang zhoukan* (*Liberation Weekly*, shortly thereafter called *Liberation*) had published one of its first illustrations, a 11 × 12 cm Mao woodcut (see Fig. 9) in the tradition of the New Woodcut Movement inspired by famous writer Lu Xun (1881–1936). The woodcut bears a striking resemblance to Snow's portrait, and yet it is the carefully crafted background that deserves attention. Instead of standing before his loess cave, Mao is portrayed in front of heavily armed columns of soldiers marching toward the East, guided by sun rays that form a slight halo around Mao's head. The image has been called the first visual trace of the emerging Mao cult.[6] A comparable portrait of Red Army Commander Zhu De published two weeks later did not show similar attributes of hero worship. Although the print run of *Liberation Weekly* in the early stages ranged between 3,000 and 5,000 copies only,[7] it nevertheless had a tremendous impact within the party, and the picture's symbolic content was not lost among Mao's colleagues and competitors.

Snow's observations were based on a highly contingent historical situation. By mid-1936, Mao did not occupy the supreme leadership

---

[4]   Snow, *Red Star*, pp. 82–83.

[5]   Edgar Snow, *The Long Revolution* (New York: Random House, 1972), pp. 68–69.

[6]   Raymond F. Wylie, *The Emergence of Maoism: Mao Tse-tung, Ch'en Po-ta and the Search for Chinese Theory 1935–1945* (Palo Alto, CA: Stanford University Press, 1980), p. 41.

[7]   Zhang Yanping, ed., *Yan'an zhongyang yinshuachang biannian jishi* [Chronicle of the Yan'an Central Printing Plant] (Xi'an: Shaanxi renmin chubanshe, 1989), p. 10.

position within the party. Forged in a period of turmoil and character-ized by competing layers of command, the CCP in the two decades after its founding congress in Shanghai (1921) had been disrupted by frequent changes in political line and leading personnel (see details in Chapter 3). Mao had not held any important posts within the party hierarchy prior to assuming the chairmanship in the Central Soviet in Jiangxi Province in 1931 and was rotated out of power several times during the follow-ing years. At the Zunyi conference in 1935, Mao was promoted to CCP Secretariat membership, but his influence was by and large confined to military affairs. When Snow arrived in Bao'an, most of Mao's leader-ship comrades were absent. Had Snow arrived a year later instead, when Communist International (Comintern) Presidium member Wang Ming (1904–74)[8] returned from Moscow in November 1937 or even in late 1936 with the return of Mao's rival Zhang Guotao (1897–1979), the impression conveyed most certainly would have been less focused on Mao's person-ality. Yet Mao grasped the chance he had been offered and readily agreed to deliver his first autobiographic reminiscences.

The importance Mao Zedong attached to the role of the media and arts for both securing new followers and elevating his own profile had during earlier occasions already distinguished him from among his fellow CCP leaders.[9] An early example is a collection of 50 postcard-size images that was published by the Red China Publishing House on October 5, 1933 to commemorate the second anniversary of the found-ing of the Jiangxi Soviet. The collection included portraits of Marx, Engels, and Lenin, as well as the current CCP leadership. Despite Mao's official ranking below provisional party leader Qin Bangxian (1907–46) and Zhou Enlai (1898–1976), his image – a woodcut showing Mao with solemn expression and his characteristically backward-combed hair – was arranged immediately behind the gallery of the Marxist-Leninist founding fathers. It is the earliest existing artistic representation of Mao as party leader. Besides the symbolic rearrangement of the actual

---

[8]   Wang Ming also recognized the importance of an elevated media profile and estab-lished his credentials as a CCP theoretician when Mao had published only a scarce number of articles. See, for example, *Chen Shaoyu* [Wang Ming] *jiuguo yanlun xuanji* [Selected Speeches of Chen Shaoyu on How to Save the Nation] (Hankou: Zhongguo chubanshe, 1938).

[9]   The sending of press clippings about his successful capture of Zhangzhou in May 1932 to the Jiangxi Soviet Central Office and provisional government has been pointed out by Jung Chang and Jon Halliday, *Mao: The Unknown Story* (New York: Alfred Knopf, 2005), p. 117. For the original reference, see Pang Xianzhi, ed., *Mao Zedong nianpu* [Chronology of Mao Zedong], Vol.1 (Beijing: Zhongyang wenxian chubanshe, 1993), p. 374.

ranking order, it is the discussion of the relationship between art and politics in the short Preface that merits attention. The Preface starts out by emphasizing that art should be regarded as a product created by the masses for the masses. Given the high rate of illiteracy among China's peasants, the author attached greatest importance to employing visual representations as an effective way of communicating party policies. Not only should art serve the masses, but it also should rely on resonant forms in order to liberate them from feudal and capitalist oppression. Thus finally the masses were to be given means to create their own forms of expression:

> Art does not only serve the masses but it should also derive from the masses.... Among the arts, painting is the most figurative. If we can make use of lines and colors to convey our strength and our work, well, then this is our most valuable weapon of propaganda and agitation, because painting is the easiest to the comprehended, and therefore it is also closest to the masses.[10]

Although the text does not give away the author's identity, the lines bear a striking resemblance to what Mao 10 years later elaborated on in his famous May 1942 "Talks at the Yan'an Forum on Literature and Art" when he defined a clearly subservient role for the arts as an important battlefront to secure communist political victory. The message of the Communist Movement was to be conveyed both via text and image and was to unify the "hearts and minds" of cadres and populace alike.

The aim of providing the party with a unified perception of China's history and the present political situation stood at the center of the Rectification Movement in 1942–43 that witnessed Mao Zedong's formal accession to party leadership. Quintessentially, the campaign consisted of a reinterpretation of recent CCP history into correct and incorrect "lines," the former being represented by Mao Zedong and the latter by his erstwhile opponents (see Chapter 4). The study of Mao texts constituted the main part of the study program, and the campaign thus resulted in the firm rooting of Mao's texts and images as core symbols of the CCP.[11] There are a number of contemporary photographs that show

---

[10] "Daixu [Foreword]," in *Geming huaji* [Collection of Revolutionary Paintings] (Bao'an(?): Hongse Zhonghua chubanshe, 1933), quoted in Yang Haocheng, *Mao Zedong tuxiang yanjiu* [Research on Mao Zedong Images], Ph. D. dissertation, Nanjing shifan daxue, 2005, p. 8.

[11] David Apter and Tony Saich refer to this process as "exegetical bonding"; see David Apter and Tony Saich, *Revolutionary Discourse in Mao's Republic* (Cambridge, MA: Harvard University Press, 1994), pp. 263–293. For an English introduction to the canonization of Mao's works during this period, see Helmut Martin, *Cult &*

Mao delivering speeches during the campaign (see Figure 1). They offer the impression of his natural authority within the CCP movement – of his effortless philosophical and strategic mastery that accorded him his elevated place as the one to have adapted Marxism-Leninism to Chinese circumstances. Numerous recollections of the Yan'an era tend to confirm this impression of an approachable leader who would join the common people in attending local theater performances while at night working on new strategies on how to cope with the external threats.[12]

The building of a leader cult around Mao Zedong, as well as praise of his theoretical contributions, dubbed "Mao Zedong Thought," accelerated soon after the beginning of the Rectification Movement in September 1941 and gained force during the following two years. A first reference to Mao's writings in systematic fashion as the "Thought of Comrade Mao Zedong" (*Mao Zedong tongzhi de sixiang*) was made in an article by Zhang Ruxin (1908–76) in February 1941. A few months later he would rise to become one of Mao's secretaries and play an important role in propagating the crucial importance of Mao Zedong within the CCP. According to Gao Hua, for example, "Zedong Day" was celebrated on February 8, 1942, and Zhang Ruxin contributed to the event with a report on "How to Study Mao Zedong."[13] This was a mere week after the official start of the Rectification Movement, indicating that the decision to focus on Mao and his thought had already been accepted by party leaders. The Yan'an Central Party School in 1942 was the first official building to be adorned with a Mao emblem, created by two young sculptors, Wang Chaowen (1909–2004) and Qi Jun (born 1912), from the Lu Xun Academy of Fine Arts. In the same year, the first series of official Mao portraits was published, and Mao buttons were handed out to participants of study classes. Activists or model workers would receive Mao paraphernalia as rewards for their efforts, and the symbolic value attached to these items can be imagined by the local attempts to recreate the icons of power by way of simple sketches and images of Mao Zedong that emerged in the communist areas of northern China in the

Canon: The Origins and Development of State Maoism, 1935–78 (Armonk, NY: M. E. Sharpe, 1982).

[12] See, for example, Zhang Kunsheng, "Yong bu wanghuai de shenke yinxiang [A Deep Impression Never to Be Forgotten]," in Yan'an zhongyang dangxiao zhengfeng yundong bianxiezu, ed., *Yan'an zhongyang dangxiao de zhengfeng xuexi* [The Rectification Studies of the Yan'an Central Party School], Vol.2 (Beijing: Zhonggong zhongyang dangxiao chubanshe, 1989), p. 147.

[13] Gao Hua, *Hong taiyang shi zenyang shengqi de: Yan'an zhengfeng yundong de lailong qumai* [How the Red Sun Rose: The Origins and Development of the Yan'an Rectification Movement] (Hong Kong: Zhongwen daxue chubanshe, 2000), pp. 606–607. See further Wylie, *Emergence of Maoism*, pp. 154–157.

early 1940s. The Rectification Movement resulted in a domination of public space by the icons of the Mao cult while his writings became the ultimate arbiter of party discourse. It resulted in a thorough association of Mao's image with the CCP as institution and thus might be called an effective "branding" strategy.[14]

The sole focus on the developments in the remote Yan'an region, however, distorts the fact that in most parts of China, at least those which had not been occupied by Japanese forces already, it was the Guomindang (GMD) leadership headed by "director general" Chiang Kai-shek (Jiang Jieshi) that was perceived as legitimate heir to rule China. With the publication of Chiang's book *China's Destiny* in March 1943, GMD claims to rule China were renewed, and the leader cult around Chiang Kai-shek was pushed to new heights:

> The independence of our nation hinges upon the success of the Kuomintang [i.e., Guomindang] Revolution. Without the Kuomintang, there would be no China. In a word, China's destiny is entrusted to the Kuomintang.[15]

The CCP closely monitored Chiang's publicity campaign. During a highly important Politburo meeting in mid-March 1943, Mao Zedong immediately commented on the present situation:

> The recent struggle points to a decline in the standing of the Kuomintang and a rise in that of the Communist Party.... All this has compelled Chiang Kai-shek to reconsider his own position and attitude.... he is posing as a "national leader" who is above domestic contradictions and feigning impartiality to class and Party.... But this attempt of his will certainly prove futile.[16]

The fostering of the Chiang cult was an important factor in propelling the CCP leadership to adopt a similar approach. Mao was formally elected chairman of the CCP Politburo on March 20, 1943, and over the summer, the whole civilian and military leadership joined in praise of his achievements and unique contributions for the consolidation of the party and the fate of the Revolution.[17] While praise of individual leaders had been an exception in CCP politics until the 1940s, now at

---

[14] Daniel Leese, "The Mao Cult as Communicative Space," *Totalitarian Movements and Political Religions* 8:3–4 (2007), pp. 623–639.

[15] Chiang Kai-shek, *China's Destiny* (New York: Macmillan, 1947), p. 220.

[16] "The Situation after the Repulse of the Second Anti-Communist Onslaught," March 18, 1941, in *Selected Works of Mao Tse-tung*, Vol. 2 (Beijing: Foreign Languages Press, 1967), p. 460.

[17] Compare Gao Hua, *Hong taiyang*, pp. 608–614.

basically every occasion the correct leadership and strategic brilliance of Mao Zedong was emphasized to display party unity. Especially outspoken in this regard was Liu Shaoqi (1898–1969). Liu understood the function of Mao's image as a powerful brand symbol representing the CCP to increase domestic appeal and to strengthen innerparty unity. His active contribution was instrumental in establishing an element of charismatic leadership within the supposedly rational and "scientific" workings at the CCP Center, but Liu was to experience the consequences of elevating Mao above party constraints brutally during the Cultural Revolution when he became the movement's most prominent victim.

The Rectification Movement not only resulted in cult building but also in growing pressure that Mao exerted on his perceived opponents or competitors. Between late 1943 and 1945, the former party leadership, including Qin Bangxian, Zhou Enlai, and Wang Ming, was severely criticized for its mistaken policies. While none of the accused faced the fate of Stalin's victims during the Great Terror five years earlier, the campaign revealed the dark side of Mao's ascent to power. Humiliation and public confessions certified that his former colleagues and superiors would not pose a future threat to his rule. Against the background of criticisms and persecutions in the wake of Mao's consolidation of power, praises of Mao Zedong became ever more outspoken. While the elevation of Mao Zedong as symbol of the CCP primarily had been due to political reasons, popular rhetoric from the beginning was infused with religious metaphors and eased Mao's later incorporation into the local syncretistic pantheon. At Chinese New Year 1943, a local peasant tune was appropriated, complete with new lyrics, now entitled, "The East is Red." It was later turned into the unofficial hymn of the CCP:

> *The East is red, the sun is rising,*
> *China has brought forth a Mao Zedong.*
> *He is devoted to the people's welfare.*
> *Hu-er-hai-yo, he is the people's great savior.*

At the Seventh Party Congress in April 1945, Mao Zedong's supremacy had become pervasive. His image assumed center stage in the decoration of the meeting hall, and Mao personally saw to it that his former competitors such as Wang Ming, who owing to illness was carried on a stretcher to the assembly, delivered public self-criticisms and demonstrated their unconditional subordination to Mao's leadership. The congress served its aim of demonstrating the ultimate success of the Rectification Movement in merging Mao's personal image with the fate of the CCP and the Chinese nation and populace. Former party chairman Zhang Wentian emphasized this intimate relationship in clear terms:

> His thoughts and feelings are the thoughts and feelings of the people. His pain, joy, and sorrow are the people's pain, joy, and sorrow.... This is how [close] his connection with the people is. Therefore, in the end it is impossible to draw a line of separation regarding whether he is the people or the people are him.[18]

No other event was to lend Mao's carefully crafted prestige more credence than the successful reunification of China after the Civil War of 1945–49. Against all odds, the CCP had suppressed internal factionalism and defeated the superior GMD troops. With the proclamation of the PRC by Mao Zedong on October 1, 1949, the rhetoric about the national savior seemed to have found its factual proof, and the historical figure of Mao Zedong increasingly receded behind the mythical "savior of the people."

FROM CCP CHAIRMAN TO "REDDEST RED SUN"

Many CCP members still regard the early 1950s as a kind of golden age, as a time during which the party was held in high esteem by the populace and was not yet corrupted by the later disasters of the Great Leap Forward and the Cultural Revolution. Mao Zedong's superiority within the Politburo was beyond question, but collective leadership was not yet merely a facade (see Chapter 6). The massive leader cult that had been fostered around Mao Zedong in the mid-1940s in order to prevent factionalism within the CCP and to compete with the publicity campaigns of Chiang Kai-shek as "national leader" did not find expression in Mao statues or other monuments at this point. At the Second Plenum of the Seventh Party Congress in March 1949, the CCP leadership explicitly forbade the naming of cities, streets, and factories after living political leaders or the celebration of leaders' birthdays. On several occasions during the 1950s, Mao personally intervened against establishing the outer forms of a leader cult or against euphuistic titles in official documents.[19] Mao's seemingly contradictory behavior, from fostering a leader cult in Yan'an to interdicting cult symbols in the early

---

[18] Quoted from Gao Hua, *Hong taiyang*, p. 638.
[19] See, for example, *Jianguo yilai Mao Zedong wengao* [Manuscripts of Mao Zedong Since the Founding of the State], Vol. 1: *1949.9–1950.12* (Beijing: Zhongyang wenxian chubanshe, 1987), p. 362.

PRC and then again allowing for a most exuberant leader cult during the Cultural Revolution, has long puzzled party historians. Yet Mao's attitude toward the leader cult remained consistent throughout his life. He clearly understood the instrumental value of a personality cult to fend off competitors and to establish a noninstitutional link with the masses. As long as Mao's position and political aims remained uncontested, he expressed contempt for the outer forms of worship that he later linked to "feudal remnants"[20] in the superstructure. In times of crisis, however, this criticism did not prevent Mao from relying on his public prestige and supposed proximity to the masses to circumvent the institutional restrictions posed by his office, even at the cost of destroying the party itself.

During the celebrations of communist "liberation" (*jiefang*) on October 1, 1949 Mao's portrait adorned the Gate of Heavenly Peace, where just two years earlier the image of Chiang Kai-shek still had been on display. The Ministry of Culture had commissioned an official Mao portrait from the Beiping State Academy of Arts, and the task had been assigned to artist Zhou Lingzhao (born 1919). His adaptation of a Yan'an-era Mao photograph to a huge oil painting on canvas, however, did not receive universal approval. Even before the founding ceremony, Commander Nie Rongzhen (1899–1992) in his capacity as vice chairman of the organization committee ordered a repainting of Mao's open collar to make the image look more formal.[21] The following year, Mao's portrait was replaced with a new image painted by Zhang Zhenshi (1914–92), which after a number of revisions showed Mao in the nowadays-accustomed frontal fashion looking benevolently above the heads of the crowd.[22]

In the early years of the PRC, Mao's portrait was on public display at Tiananmen only twice a year, during the celebrations of National Day and Workers' Day. It was part of an increasingly elaborate arrangement of leadership images administered by the Ministry of Culture for the respective occasions. With the exception of Chinese National Day, Stalin as the leader of the International Communist Movement enjoyed

[20] Daniel Leese, *Performative Politics and Petrified Image: The Mao Cult During China's Cultural Revolution*, Ph. D. dissertation, University of Bremen, 2006, p. 44; available at www.jacobs-university.de/phd/files/1187983533.pdf.

[21] Yang, *Mao Zedong tuxiang yanjiu*, p. 36.

[22] Zhang continued the task of producing the official Mao portrait until 1963, when, owing to age, Wang Guodong (王国栋) replaced him. Following Wang Guodong's retirement in 1992, Ge Xiaoguang (葛小光, born 1974) took over charge of delivering the annual Mao portrait. For a fictional account of the highly obscure world of the Maoist court painters, see the book by German Sinologist Tilman Spengler, *Die Stirn, die Augen, der Mund* [The Forehead, the Eyes, the Mouth] (Reinbek b. Hamburg: Rowohlt Verlag, 1999).

the most prominent position. Yet, unlike Mao's later impression, the reprints of Stalin's picture and his own picture in the Chinese state media were equal in size (see Fig. 10). Furthermore, Soviet influence was noteworthy with regard to style. Chinese propaganda posters in the 1950s followed the tradition of Socialist Realism and showed Mao with children, together with "the masses," or during historical events in CCP history. A well-known example is Dong Xiwen's (1914–73) painting, *The Founding of the Nation*, in October 1949 (see Fig. 11), which depict the event in a highly symbolic arrangement. Mao is positioned at the center of the painting, accompanied by a half circle of high-ranking party members. Owing to changes in CCP leadership, the original work had to be repainted several times to remove Communist personae non gratae such as Lisu Shaoqi during the Cultural Revolution. Censorship and the technical alterations of photographs or even works of art played an important role in making the depicted reality conform to political circumstances.

The crude nature of most leader portraits had been accepted by the party leadership during the years of warfare, but now the artistic quality and standardization of the images became increasingly important. In Yan'an, the CCP had explicitly encouraged the use of traditional art forms, for example, Chinese New Year posters, operas, or paper cuts, to convey the messages of communism.[23] Tapping into the local traditions had enhanced the Communist appeal and supplanted traditional connotations with new content. But it also had created a large specter of image production outside the boundaries of party control. In a series of directives, the CCP Center interdicted, among others, the use of "floral designs" as background, the reprint of unedited snapshots of party leaders (see Fig. 15), or the sale of portraits with the sole aim of pecuniary profits. By 1954, the manufacturing and printing of all leader portraits was assigned to the Xinhua bookstores in order to guarantee quality and correct designation.[24]

While the symbolic display of power became increasingly standardized and spread from public places to private homes, actual encounters

[23] On Chinese New Year prints, see James Flath, *The Cult of Happiness: Nianhua, Art, and History in Rural North China* (Vancouver, BC, Canada: University of British Columbia Press, 2004). For a selection of propaganda images and New Year prints during the first PRC decades, see Stefan Landsberger's Chinese Propaganda Posters at www.iisg.nl/~landsberger/.

[24] See, for example, *Zhongyang guanyu xuangua lingxiu xiang de tongzhi* [Circular of the CCP Center Concerning the Placement of Leader Portraits], December 23, 1954, Hebei Provincial Archives 855-17-215. In times of upheaval, however, the guidelines were frequently violated and had to be renewed.

between the populace and the party leadership decreased markedly with the move of the CCP Center to Zhongnanhai, the "New Forbidden City" in the heart of Beijing. Here, the top leadership with their families, bodyguards, and servants lived in a separate, closed-off quarter that developed into a distinct microcosm. Mao had chosen the Fengzeyuan compound as his new domicile, into which he moved with his third wife, Jiang Qing, and their daughter, Li Na, as well as temporarily with the three surviving children from his earlier marriages and other relatives (see Fig. 7). At least until the Cultural Revolution, when his nephew, Mao Yuanxin (born 1941), rose through the ranks, Mao's children enjoyed only limited privileges and rarely came to see their father owing to his habit of working at night and sleeping until noon. Even today, Mao is widely admired in China for his lack of nepotism that is favorably compared with the self-enriching mentality of the CCP offspring in the early reform era. The death of Mao's eldest son, Mao Anying (1922–50), during the Korean War is often cited as proof of Mao's consistent attitude toward equality in serving the cause of socialism.

Generally speaking, Mao's relationship with his family remained far from intimate. Instead, the role played by his personal entourage of bodyguards, nurses, and doctors came to assume increasing importance. This innermost circle, at the time referred to as "Group One," was hierarchically structured and solely directed at caring for Mao's physical well-being and comfort. The memoirs of one of Mao's former personal physicians, Li Zhisui (1919–95),[25] despite numerous factual errors and exaggerations,[26] provide ample material about the inner workings at "Mao's court."[27] They reveal a system founded on personal loyalty and institutionalized rivalries that allowed Mao to play off different factions or individuals against each other and to assume the role of ultimate arbiter of power. Li's revelations accord with a number of common *topoi* in the constantly growing Chinese memoir literature on the private Mao. First and foremost are the numerous references detailing Mao's negligence regarding common working or living conventions. Based on

[25] Li Zhisui with Anne F. Thurston, *The Private Life of Chairman Mao: The Memoirs of Mao's Personal Physician* (New York: Random House, 1994).

[26] For a Western scholarly critique of the memoirs, see Frederick C. Teiwes, "Review: Seeking the Historical Mao," *China Quarterly* 145 (March 1996), pp. 176–188. For criticisms by other members of Mao's medical staff, see Lin Ke, Xu Tao, and Wu Xujun, *Lishi de zhenshi – Mao Zedong shenbian gongzuo renyuan de zhengyan* [Historical Truth – Evidence Recounted by Mao Zedong's Personal Staff] (Beijing: Zhongyang wenxian chubanshe, 2003 [1998]).

[27] This is a phrase Frederick C. Teiwes uses in *Politics at Mao's Court: Gao Gang and Party Factionalism in the Early 1950s* (Armonk, NY: M. E. Sharpe, 1990).

the presumption that Mao was not an ordinary man and neither were his habits, much of the literature has catered toward a hagiographic portrayal of Mao's supposed austerity and thriftiness in personal affairs. He would not touch money himself, stuck to oily peasant food ("four dishes and a soup"), and preferred comfortable, worn-out clothes (even pyjamas) to the high-quality suits specifically tailored for him by Paris-educated Wang Ziqing on Wangfujing Street.[28] When dealing with matters of great importance, Mao simply would stop eating or sleeping for several days in a row. Since he preferred to work in utmost silence, his surroundings had to be arranged accordingly. He worked mainly at night and would not hesitate to order his Politburo colleagues to impromptu meetings at 3 a.m. At times, he would not even deem it necessary to change his sleeping gown, even with the Soviet ambassador in attendance.

Unlike Mao's laxity in personal matters and hygiene, he conducted his daily perusal of intelligence reports and the drafting of documents with utmost precision. The 13-volume edition of *Mao Manuscripts*,[29] covering the period from 1949 to 1976, reveals the meticulous attention he paid to the correct phrasing of articles down to the level of single characters. Mao maintained interest in every piece of potentially useful information but remained skeptical about the reliability of his sources.[30] He therefore tried to multiply his access to local information, for example, by way of deploying his personal staff on investigative tours. He kept a huge personal library and devoured books of every kind. Mao would make use of his classical knowledge to overcome his nervousness on meeting with new persons by discussing content and previous meanings of the characters constituting the person's name. In similar fashion, he would impress his CCP comrades with classical allusions, whereas on other occasions he would lapse into vulgar expressions to emphasize his proximity to the masses.[31]

Contact with the masses, however, remained scarce. Shielded from the public in one of his numerous villas, Mao led an increasingly isolated

---

[28] Li Yinqiao and Han Guixin, *Zai Mao Zedong shenbian shiwu nian* [15 Years at Mao Zedong's Side] (Shijiazhuang: Hebei renmin chubanshe, 2006), pp. 227–229.

[29] *Jianguo yilai Mao Zedong wengao* [Manuscripts of Mao Zedong Since the Founding of the State] (Beijing: Zhongyang wenxian chubanshe, 1987–1998).

[30] See Michael Schoenhals, "The Central Case Examination Group, 1966–79," *China Quarterly* 145 (March 1996), pp. 87–111.

[31] At the Seven Thousand Cadres Conference in January 1962, Mao characterized his Politburo critics in this way: "They complain all day long and get to watch plays at night. They eat three full meals a day – and fart. That's what Marxism-Leninism means to them." Quoted from Roderick MacFarquhar, *The Origins of the Cultural Revolution*, 3: *The Coming of the Cataclysm, 1961–1966* (Oxford, England: Oxford University Press, 1997), p. 169.

life. Owing to the alienation from his wife and fellow CCP leaders, Mao's daily interactions were by and large defined through work meetings and the interaction with his staff. There is no mention of personal friends with whom Mao would have enjoyed a casual chat. From the late 1950s onward, this gap was filled by politically reliable young women, chosen for their looks, who would accommodate "the Chairman," although references to Mao's ferocious sexual appetite are not made in Chinese accounts. This obvious taboo seems all the more conspicuous because the CCP's approach to demystifying Mao even allows for publishing detailed descriptions about the use of enemas to solve his constant problem of constipation.[32]

The impression of Mao's personality that emerges from the literature is disturbing. It reveals a certain temporal development from a down-to-earth leader, who was amicable when uncontested and occasionally reflected on the limits of his power, to an increasingly ruthless and self-indulging dictator. Mao's preparedness to accept criticism decreased continuously, paralleled by a trend of "working towards the Chairman"[33] among his fellow leaders and subordinates. A strong charismatic element of leadership had pervaded CCP politics ever since Mao Zedong's elevation as a symbol of party unity in the 1940s, when Mao's ability to form "charismatic relationships"[34] by way of winning over important allies from the ranks of his competitors had become an important pillar in his ascent to power. He appears as a highly capable strategist and politician who, in the words of Wang Shiwei (1906–47) quoted at the beginning of this chapter, increasingly came to concentrate his skills on securing his own reputation, which for him was synonymous with securing the success of the Chinese Revolution.

This trend grew more pronounced during the 1950s, when in the wake of Khrushchev's Secret Speech and the following Sino-Soviet split, Mao set out to define China's own path to socialism. With the failure of both the Hundred Flowers Movement and the disastrous Great Leap Forward, Mao objected to being held solely responsible for the outcome. Mao's unwillingness to be restrained by conventions of working time

---

[32] Li Jiaji and Yang Qingwang, *Lingxiu shenbian shisan nian: Mao Zedong weishi Li Jiaji* [13 Years at the Side of the Leader: Mao Zedong and Li Jiaji], Vol. 2 (Beijing: Zhongyang wenxian chubanshe, 2007), p. 557.

[33] Roderick MacFarquhar and Michael Schoenhals, *Mao's Last Revolution* (Cambridge, MA: Belknap Press, of Harvard University Press, 2006), p. 47. The concept has been borrowed from Ian Kershaw, "'Working Towards the Führer': Reflections on the Nature of the Hitler Dictatorship," *Contemporary European History* 2 (1993), pp. 103–118.

[34] M. Rainer Lepsius, "The Model of Charismatic Leadership and Its Applicability to the Rule of Adolf Hitler," *Totalitarian Movements and Political Religions* 7:2 (2006), pp. 175–190.

or space now came to apply to formal aspects of rule as well. He came to rely on extraconstitutional bodies such as the later Central Cultural Revolution Group to advance his aims and spent increasingly longer periods outside the capital to strengthen his bonds with local party and army leaders while the possibilities of access for his fellow CCP leaders dwindled (see Chapter 6).

Against this background, Mao reversed his objections against the outer forms of the leader cult that he had voiced during the early days of the PRC and openly relied on its symbolic power to mobilize the masses. This tendency is clearly revealed in the propaganda images that in the early 1960s accompanied the People's Liberation Army (PLA) campaigns to celebrate the victories of Mao Zedong Thought. Countless model heroes such as Lei Feng (1940–62) were displayed as championing the works of Mao Zedong. In these images, Mao assumed iconic presence as a portrait in the study chamber of the model heroes or on the cover of the study books. The trend of glorifying Mao Zedong reached its heyday in the first years of the Cultural Revolution and witnessed both the unparalleled upsurge of Mao icons and the partial loss of party control over the images of power. Pictures of the "Great Teacher," "Great Leader," "Great Supreme Commander," and "Great Helmsman" contributed to spreading the seeds of the Cultural Revolution nationwide. Ever since the Yan'an days, Mao had been referred to occasionally as the "savior of the Chinese people" or had been linked with the sun. At the outset of the Cultural Revolution, these attributes became the rule, and the CCP Chairman was commonly referred to as the "reddest red sun in our hearts" by the youthful Red Guards (see Fig. 14)

In scientific works and memoir literature alike, the Cultural Revolution Mao cult is often treated as a kind of inexplicable and irrational "craze" resembling a primitive religion with its icons and rituals. While belief in the Maoist doctrines played a role in sustaining the leader cult – and especially in rural areas, the cult clearly assumed religious functions – it is important to take the temporal changes and the political context into account as well. In the early stages of the Cultural Revolution, collections of Mao's writings, such as the famous *Quotations from Chairman Mao Tse-tung*,[35] posters, and buttons became the most prominent icons of power. The cult was instrumental in Mao outmaneuvering the party bureaucracy, but the steering of the movement by way of his iconic presence turned out to be hampered by various restraints. Given the lack of clear guidelines or party organs to

---

[35] On the unusual history of the *Little Red Book* and rival editions, see Leese, *Performative Politics*, pp. 122–133.

implement Mao's directives, factions all over the country claimed to represent the will of the Chairman best and engaged in symbolic and physical struggles against competitors for power. A prominent example is the establishment of the first Cultural Revolutionary Mao statue, which was unveiled at Qinghua University on May 4, 1967, to demonstrate the revolutionary conviction of the local Jinggangshan faction.[36]

While these early expressions of loyalty to Chairman Mao still developed from local competition, it was the period of reestablishing political order between late 1967 and the Ninth Party Congress in April 1969 that witnessed the massive rise of cult commodities, ranging from porcelain ware to enamel mugs to little red plastic hearts imprinted with the character "*zhong*" (loyalty). By way of deploying PLA soldiers nationwide to conduct "study classes" in the tradition of the Yan'an Rectification Movement, the need to express loyalty in every word and deed in order to distinguish the real from the bogus revolutionaries eased the rise of ritual forms of worship, such as the daily "asking for instructions in the morning and reporting back in the evening" (*zao qingshi, wan huibao*). Other types of worship that developed without official approval included the "loyalty dance" (*zhongziwu*) and "quotations gymnastics" (*yulucao*).[37] Although these rituals in part resembled religious worship, their primary function was of a disciplinary nature, and the CCP Center tolerated them only until the PLA had enforced a ritualized acceptance of Mao's supreme authority. Mao Zedong himself started to curb the outer phenomena of the cult once revolutionary committees had been established. In June 1969, all expressions of the cultlike worship were forbidden,[38] and by 1970, Mao confided to Edgar Snow that it had been necessary to allow for a certain degree of worship to strike down the supposed enemy of the people, Liu Shaoqi. By now, however, Mao declared that the worship had become excessive:

> At that time I said I did not care about personality cults, yet there even was a necessity for a bit of personality cult. The situation now is not the same anymore; the worship has become excessive, resulting in much formalism. Like those "four greats," "Great Teacher, Great Leader, Great Supreme [*sic*] Commander, Great

---

[36] *Ibid.*, pp. 196–203. On developments at Qinghua University during the Cultural Revolution, see Tang Shaojie, *Yi ye zhi qiu: Qinghua daxue 1968 nian "bai ri da wudou"* [One Leaf Heralds the Autumn: The "Hundred Day Armed Struggle" at Qinghua University in 1968] (Hong Kong: Chinese University Press, 2005).

[37] On the development and forms of these rituals, see Leese, *Performative Politics*, Chapters 7 and 8.

[38] See *Mao Zedong wengao*, Vol. 13, p. 50.

Helmsman" [English in original], annoying! One day these will all be deleted, only keeping the "teacher" [English in original].[39]

Within the multiple official and nonofficial items of the Cultural Revolution Mao cult, there are only a small number of works that gained nationwide importance. Probably the most famous image of Mao during the Cultural Revolution was the oil painting entitled *Chairman Mao Going to Anyuan* (1967) by Liu Chunhua (born 1944) that was published with huge media attention on July 1, 1968 (see Fig. 16).[40] It is an ideal-type example of Revolutionary Romanticism showing a youthful Mao clad in long, traditional Chinese attire with an umbrella under his arm striding along mountaintops toward the coal mines of Anyuan to organize a worker uprising against the capitalist oppressors. The confident young Mao in the painting is positioned at the center; he is moving toward the observer and shown in bright colors. The image is "red, bright, and vivid" (*hong, guang, liang*) and in this respect a typical example of Cultural Revolution art. There are two aspects of the painting that merit historical attention: (1) the gap between the depicted youthful image and the increasingly geriatric leader troubled by various illnesses and (2) the subversion of historical facts. In 1960, a similar romanticized image of the young Liu Shaoqi had been painted by Hou Yimin (born 1930) that showed Liu in his accustomed role as organizer of the 1923 Anyuan coal miners' strikes. At the high tide of the anti-Liu propaganda in 1967–68, *Chairman Mao Going to Anyuan* not only served the aim of elevating the status of Mao Zedong even further but also negated Liu Shaoqi's merits as organizer of the workers' movement. The image is a telling example of the "utilization of art to re-create history"[41] and reveals that the cult to a certain extent functioned as a "countercult" to discredit opponents.

In late 1975, the ailing Mao Zedong one last time tried to reshape his public image, this time for posterity. Mao was to peruse a number of photographs for a collection chronicling his life. According to former staff members, none of the heroic images of the Cultural Revolution caught Mao's attention, but the images of the Yan'an era did. Mao is said

---

[39] Mao Zedong, "Huijian Sinuo de tanhua jiyao" [Notes of the Conversation with Snow]," December 18, 1970, in Song Yongyi, ed., *Chinese Cultural Revolution Database* (Hong Kong: Chinese University Press, 2002), CD-ROM.

[40] For information on the background of the painting and Cultural Revolution art in general, see Wang Mingxian and Yan Shanchun, *Xin Zhongguo meishu tushi, 1966–1976* [Art History of the People's Republic of China, 1966–1976] (Beijing: Zhongguo qingnian chubanshe, 2000), pp. 54–69.

[41] Maria Galikowski, *Art and Politics in China, 1949–84* (Hong Kong: Chinese University Press, 1998), p. 149.

to have specifically singled out a photograph taken in 1942 that shows him lecturing cadres in front of his loess cave during the Rectification Movement (see Fig. 1).[42] It seems to have best captured his perceived self-image as teacher of the masses in liberating China from the shackles of feudalism and imperialism and of merging Chinese reality with the abstract truths of Marxism-Leninism. Mao's repeated policy changes and persecutions against former CCP leaders, however, incited quite the opposite result of his aim to secure the eternal victory of communism. His policies left a disillusioned populace, a factionalized party membership, and suspicious power groups at the apex of power vying for his succession. Mao Zedong died on September 9, 1976, presided over by members of the competing factions who oversaw that no one tampered with the instruments preserving the late Chairman's life.

CONCLUSION

The question of how to deal with the legacy of Mao Zedong, how to separate man from myth, ranged among the most difficult tasks faced by the new CCP leadership. The close interrelation of Mao as symbol of the Chinese Revolution with CCP politics demanded a cautious treatment in order not to tarnish the party's claim to legitimate rule. Deng Xiaoping (1904–97), who emerged as the "architect" of the process of gradual reform after December 1978, had been actively involved in repudiating the impact of Khrushchev's de-Stalinization policies in 1956 and thus was highly aware of the potentially disastrous consequences of debunking the CCP's most prominent symbol. Mao Zedong's elevated status was to be reduced. He was to become "man, not God," as a popular Chinese biography was to put it later,[43] but his achievements were not to be discredited by way of a thorough de-Maoization process. The most illuminating account on how to evaluate Mao's historical role and on how to deal with the icons of the former CCP Chairman was offered by Deng in an interview with Italian journalist Oriana Fallaci in August 1980:

> *Oriana Fallaci*: Is the portrait of Chairman Mao at the Gate of Heavenly Peace to be preserved forever?
>
> *Deng Xiaoping*: It is to be preserved forever. In the past there were too many portraits of Chairman Mao; they were hung everywhere.

[42] Yang, *Mao Zedong tuxiang yanjiu*, p. 19.
[43] Quan Yanchi, *Mao Zedong: Man, Not God* (Beijing: Foreign Languages Press, 1992).

This had not at all been a solemn occasion and did not solely express respect toward Chairman Mao. Although Chairman Mao has committed a number of errors in the past, he ultimately remains the principal founder of the CCP and the People's Republic of China (PRC). When looking at his achievements and excesses, the errors definitely rank second. The things he has done for the Chinese people cannot simply be eradicated. If we approach the question from the emotional perspective of the Chinese people, we will always cherish him as the founder of our party and state.[44]

In 1981, these views were enshrined as official party ideology in the "Resolution on Certain Questions in the History of Our Party Since the Founding of the Nation," although without giving a clear percentage regarding the relation of achievements versus errors. The infamous 70/30 formula, which Mao himself had applied to Stalin in 1956, is not to be found in official documents, although it is often quoted without citation. A closer analysis of Mao's faults would have required probing deeply into the dark sides of CCP rule and thus was beyond question. While Deng decided to curb the manifestations of Cultural Revolution Mao worship, now termed "modern superstition" or "God-building activities" with as little public attention as possible, crucial icons of power such as Mao's image on Tiananmen Square remained in place in order not to give rise to rumors. Yet rumors about Mao's life could not be contained despite the CCP's ban on critical research. Thus, during the following years and especially in the wake of Mao's 100th birthday in 1993, a large number of official and unofficial histories about various facets of Mao's personality were published,[45] a trend that continues unabated until the present day.

The early 1990s also witnessed a renewed interest in Mao's writings that spread among university students and especially those who had become increasingly disenchanted with Deng's reform policies in the wake of the Tiananmen Square Incident in 1989. Yet it was the nonofficial production of Mao icons that gained international interest in the "Mao Fever" or "Mao Craze," the "posthumous cult of the Great Leader."[46] Taxi drivers championed small Mao talismans to fend off evil,

---

[44] "Da Yidali jizhe Aolinyina Falaqi wen [Answers to the Questions of Italian Journalist Oriana Fallaci]," in *Deng Xiaoping wenxuan* [Selected Works of Deng Xiaoping], Vol. 2, 2nd ed. (Beijing: Renmin chubanshe 1994), p. 344.

[45] See Thomas Scharping, "Review Essay: The Man, the Myth, the Message: New Trends in Mao-Literature from China," *China Quarterly* 137 (March 1994), pp. 168–179.

[46] Geremie R. Barmé, *Shades of Mao: The Posthumous Cult of the Great Leader* (Armonk, NY: M. E. Sharpe, 1996).

vendors sold karaoke editions of Cultural Revolution songs extolling the "reddest red sun," and in Mao's home province of Hunan, even temple statues were erected in his name. Similar incidents of commodification or sacralization had been noted during the high tide of the Cultural Revolution Mao cult as well, when according to internal documents Mao quotations had come to adorn even towels, toys, and candy paper.[47] The political context between both periods, however, varied considerably. By 1993, the production and consumption of Mao memorabilia were no longer an attempt to demonstrate revolutionary conviction or loyalty but in many cases owed to a blend of nostalgia and folk religious sentiments. The perceived loss of moral order and growing social disparities fueled nostalgic remembrances of the Maoist era during which, despite its violence, egalitarian values had been championed. In many cases, however, commercial interests stood at the fore of employing Mao's image. "The Chairman" as a brand symbol made for profitable business and thus all types of Mao paraphernalia, ranging from caps to musical lighters, continued to be sold even as the fad ebbed away in the mid-1990s.

The greatest difference between both periods rests with the degree to which the party effectively tried to control Mao's public image. While in the late 1960s people were sentenced to death for having desecrated the words or image of the CCP Chairman, for example, by misspelling a character in a Mao quote or unintentionally dropping a porcelain statue, by the 1990s, the artistic subversion of Mao's public image had developed into a profitable genre. Mao thus finally had become a pop-art icon open for all types of utilization and interpretation, and this fact is owed to a large extent to the party's failure to allow for an open and critical assessment of his historical role. Today, crude fakes and reprints of Mao's books and images dominate China's souvenir markets (see cover photo of Mao tapestries in a street market), and despite the CCP's attempts to preserve Mao Zedong as symbol and founding stone of legitimacy to rule China, the image of Mao both in China and abroad has become increasingly pluralized, contested, and commodified. Mao's self-chosen image as simple teacher therefore is bound to be complemented and possibly superseded by the image of the ruthless dictator, willing to employ the "arts of revolution" to secure his own power and to sacrifice innumerable people as *Menschenmaterial* along the way to attain his communist utopia.

[47] See, for example, Tianjin shi geming weiyuanhui, Jin'ge [69] 082, "Guanyu dangqian xuanchuan gongzuo zhong cunzai de jige wenti he jinhou yijian [Questions and Future Suggestions Regarding a Number of Problems in Our Present Propaganda Work]," May 9, 1969.

Part II

Mao's Legacy

10 For Truly Great Men, Look to This Age Alone: Was Mao Zedong a New Emperor?

GEREMIE R. BARMÉ

In 1980, the political scientist Yan Jiaqi offered a critique of what he called the "disguised monarchism" of twentieth-century China. He was writing during a unique period of reevaluation following the death of Mao Zedong in September 1976 and the formal end of the Cultural Revolution era (1964–78).[1]

What Yan meant by "disguised monarchism" was the persistence in twentieth-century China of a politics that saw "the concentration of supreme power in the hands of one person and his secretive courtiers, for life." Yan argued that despite the notional end of two millennia of dynastic rule when the last emperor abdicated the throne in 1911, monarchism survived as a style of rule. In practice, it included such features as "the deification of the ruler; the periodic slaughter of meritorious ministers below the ruler, whose jealousy of such ministers was preordained; incessant struggles among court factions; and the occasional usurpations of power by eunuchs or by the ruler's relatives, including relatives of his mother or wives."[2] For Yan, among many others in the

My thanks to Sang Ye, Gloria Davies, Duncan Campbell, Hal Kahn, John Minford, Richard Rigby, and Mark Selden for their comments on various drafts of this chapter. I am particularly grateful to Timothy Cheek for inviting me to revisit the history and cult of Mao Zedong.

[1] The Communist Party, its historians, and subsequently, majority opinion frame the Cultural Revolution as "ten years of chaos." In terms of the policies that were pursued, however, the era can well be dated from the Socialist Education Campaign launched in 1964 up to the time of the Third Plenum of the party's Eleventh Congress in late 1978.

[2] Yan Jiaqi, "Wangguo xunhuan yuanyin lun [On the Reasons for the Cycle of Monarchic Rule]," in his *Quanli yu zhenli* [Power and Truth] (Beijing: Guangming ribao chubanshe, 1987), pp. 89–90. I base the second paragraph of this chapter on Alexander Woodside, "Emperors and the Chinese Political System," in Kenneth Lieberthal, Joyce Kallgren, Roderick MacFarquhar, Frederic Wakeman Jr., eds., *Perspectives on Modern China: Four Anniversaries* (Armonk, NY: M. E. Sharpe, 1991), pp. 5–30 at p. 5.

late 1970s and early 1980s, these were all characteristics of Mao Zedong's last two decades in power.

In an important study of the lingering traditions of, and hankerings for, the imperial in China, the historian Alexander Woodside pointed out that apart from "change-resistant links to the old emperorship" (i.e., real "remnants of feudalism"), there have been "other phenomena related to the inability of post-1911 Chinese governments to create widespread respect for new institutions quickly enough; their need to legitimize themselves at various levels of the popular consciousness; and their consequent deliberate tactical exploitation of what they imagine to be traditional values."[3]

THE AIR OF A KING, THE WILES OF A MONKEY[4]

The late 1970s and early 1980s constituted a period during which the Chinese Communist Party (CCP) was struggling with the legacy of its recently deceased leader, Mao Zedong. In 1981, it would approve an official evaluation of the Chairman and his controversial role in the first decades of the People's Republic. It also was a time when public opinion found expression in *samizdat* publications, wall posters, art, and various forms of literature. Academics employing a veiled language spoke of "feudal despotism" and persistent historical traits.[5] Although many of the countervailing views of Mao eventually would be outlawed, or at least fall into abeyance, the career, impact, and heritage of the Chairman continue to be debated. Over the years, a sanitized corpus of "Mao Zedong Thought," now interpreted as the crystallization of the party's collective wisdom, would be used by both the CCP itself and various of its opponents as a source of self-justification and for the purposes of self-preservation.[6]

Mao Zedong – political leader, strategist, thinker, "demagogue-oracle," writer, poet, and symbol of national revival, rebellion, and revolution – retains an appeal for many, just as his leadership during the

---

[3]   Woodside, "Emperors and the Chinese Political System," p. 7.

[4]   See Mao's self-description in his putative July 8, 1966 letter to Jiang Qing. Liu Changqing, ed., *Mao Zedong jiashu pindu* [Reading Mao Zedong's Letters to Family Members] (Beijing: Hongqi chubanshe, 2004), pp. 247–248.

[5]   See, for example, Lawrence R. Sullivan, "The Controversy over 'Feudal Despotism': Politics and Historiography in China, 1978–82," in Jonathan Unger, ed., *Using the Past to Serve the Present: Historiography and Politics in Contemporary China* (Armonk, NY: M. E. Sharpe, 1993), pp. 174–204.

[6]   For details of the new cult, see my *Shades of Mao: The Posthumous Career of the Great Leader* (Armonk, NY: M. E. Sharpe, 1996).

first decades of the People's Republic continues to elicit heated discussion. This chapter revisits some well-known material. It also attempts to offer its own perspective on some issues related to Mao's contested legacy. To do so, I address the question of whether Mao Zedong was a new emperor. In many writings about Mao and his era – in Chinese as well as in English – it is assumed that the answer is in the affirmative.

In a review essay of the best-selling 2005 biography, *Mao: The Untold Story*, by Jung Chang and Jon Halliday, I remarked

> Not only do Chang-Halliday bruise the protocols of serious history writing and reinforce, albeit unintentionally, a callousness in regard to the nature and ongoing problems of China's situation, but they also employ a language that all too readily evokes the image of oriental obliquity. Mao's colleagues are spoken of as a court, the Chinese people are his subjects (pp. 337, 500);[7] the mayor of Shanghai, Ke Qingshi, is "a favourite retainer" (p. 515); PLA Unit 8341 charged with the security of Zhongnan Hai is dubbed "the Praetorian Guard" (pp. 274ff). Wang Dongxing is the leader's "trusted chamberlain" (p. 532), and Zhou Enlai his "slave" (pp. 271–272). Even when Mao employs the pronoun of *faux* Party collectivity, the authors claim that, as usual, he is using the "royal we" (p. 589).[8]

In China itself, casting the party leader as a new emperor is nothing new. As we will see, it was a common political tactic employed both by Mao and by his opponents from the 1940s. To define him, or indeed his successors, as "new emperors," however, is not simply, or merely, an act of careless essentialism that promotes a belief in an unchanging Chinese essence that predetermines political or cultural behavior. As I observed in my review of *Mao: The Untold Story*, in the case of the Chairman, it also generates "a metaphorical schema that places Mao firmly at some quaint, incomprehensible oriental remove, reducing a complex history to one of personal fiat and imperial hauteur." This, in turn, aids and abets a distorting cultural determinism, be it in the context of Sinophone discourse or, more broadly, in the international realm. Similarly, we are ill-served by attempts to ignore or exaggerate the persistent elements of dynastic heritage when considering Mao. It is important to consider the extent to which framing Mao and his achievement predominantly in terms of imperial politics and history – as did

---

[7] These page references are to the UK and Commonwealth edition of the book.
[8] See my "I'm So Ronree," *China Journal* 55 (January 2006), pp. 128–139.

Yan Jiaqi in 1980 – obscures the complex relationship between tradition and modernity. Just as crucially, we should ask whether limiting Mao to the role of a nondynastic founding emperor undermines our ability to appreciate his abiding attraction as a thinker and political leader.

Simon Leys, a prescient commentator on the Cultural Revolution era, remarked on Mao and his cult that

> More than two thousand years of imperial tradition have created in the collective consciousness the constant need for a unique, supreme, quasi-mystical head; the shaky and brief republican interlude did not succeed in providing any convincing substitute for this, and Mao knew shrewdly how to manipulate this traditional legacy to his own advantage.[9]

In considering this paradox, we enter into the very quandary faced at every turn by thinking Chinese people and by students of the Sinophone world: Where does the dynastic/imperial/imperious end and the modern/civil and individual begin? Indeed, how do they overlap and relate to one another? As I have remarked elsewhere, "As much as Mao and his fellow revolutionaries might rail against the habits of the feudal past, their language, literary references and political infighting were carried out in its shadow.... Throughout their rule, Mao and his supporters would use the symbols and language of the dynastic past and convert them into elements of their own political performances and vocabulary. They employed tradition when it suited them and repudiated it when the need arose."[10]

The heritage of the dynastic past is never simple or unproblematic. It enthralls and constrains just as it enlivens. This chapter offers a review of the ways in which Mao invoked the image of the emperor or dynastic politics in his writings, as well as for specific political purposes in speeches, asides, and comments. It also touches on the fact that Mao's colleagues, as well as his opponents (sometimes they were one and the same), drew on the tradition in their engagement with as well as in their resistance to the Chairman. It considers, too, the elements of the imperial tradition that we can identify as being particular to an emperor and how their evocation also enmeshes those who employ them. In the context of history and its tensions, I will attempt to delineate those

---

[9] Simon Leys, "Aspects of Mao Tse-tung (1893–1976)," in *Broken Images: Essays on Chinese Culture and Politics*, trans. Steve Cox (New York: St. Martin's Press, 1979), p. 64.

[10] Barmé, *The Forbidden City* (London: Profile Books, 2008), pp. xiv–xv.

things that are "imperial," that belong to the heritage of autocracy, and those that militate against it. In this I will touch on some of the ambiguities that lie at the heart of modern Chinese history, ambiguities that concern the relationships between dynastic rule and modern political behavior, as well as between the imperial cultural order and the symbolism of the evolving modern state.

Mao's repeated use of historical allusions makes it easy to frame many of his views and actions in the context of the imperial tradition or in terms of a "persistent monarchism."[11] The CCP itself, in its evolution both in opposition and as a ruling power, also reinforced elements of traditional statecraft. However, it should be evident that by laying too much emphasis on the weight of tradition and presumed cultural inertia, the revolutionary character of much that Mao and his cohort pursued is too easily overlooked or discounted.[12] As a result, both the history of his times and the behavior of his successors become perhaps harder, not easier, to understand.

This discussion presupposes another fundamental question: What was an emperor as understood in the context of Chinese dynastic practice? Like the subject at hand, this, too, is a complex topic and one that can only be covered in the most cursory fashion here. An emperor was the head of a lineage to which the Mandate of Heaven (*tianming* 天命) passed in what was thought of as a numinous or predestined fashion. The Mandate sanctioned the rule of an imperial house whose head, the emperor (referred to as the Son of Heaven, or *tianzi* 天子), would act as the intermediary between Heaven and Earth, a semidivine yet human instrument for the terrestrial realization of the moral order of heaven. He would rule over All Under Heaven (*tianxia* 天下), the geocultural realm in which he and his ministers held sway and one that over time could transform the uncivilized or barbaric peoples beyond it. Through ritual observance, he, or those acting on his behalf, would modulate the ways in which the *dao* (道), or Way of Heaven, would find expression via virtuous government. Through the observance of *li* (礼), the codes of ritual behavior, the emperor also was at the pinnacle of social relationships, an encompassing framework of formal behavior and etiquette that ordered all social strata.

---

[11] A relevant study in this context is Zhengyuan Fu's *Autocratic Tradition and Chinese Politics* (Cambridge, England: Cambridge University Press, 1993), esp. pp. 187ff.

[12] In this context, see Benjamin I. Schwartz, "The Reign of Virtue: Some Broad Perspectives on Leader and Party in the Cultural Revolution," *China Quarterly* 35 (July-September 1968), p. 17.

As a cultivated individual (*junzi* 君子), and as well as being a moral and a cultural exemplar, an emperor theoretically would hold sway over the civilizing aspects of the society. He would be succeeded by a son or, in some cases, a brother. A crown prince – a chosen successor, often but not always the eldest son – might be named while the emperor was still alive. An emperor's formal injunctions were treated as "sacred edicts" (*shengzhi* 圣旨) and were regarded as inviolable. Imperial instructions and decisions often invoked historical precedent, and the study of the past provided a guide or at least a cloak for present political action.

The founding emperor of a new dynasty – a particular type of ruler, as understood both historically and in popular culture – often would exhibit a number of other traits. Such a founder in particular tended to act as an absolute monarch who would brook little interference. With the general run of emperors, however, a camarilla of advisers, courtiers, empresses, concubines, and eunuchs, who were not constrained by formal dynastic statecraft, could exercise considerable influence. Thus members of the imperial seraglio or harem could and did become involved in politics, and there are notorious cases of their unbridled exercise of power or intimate involvement in court politics. The Mandate of Heaven was made manifest when the emperor or his court ruled well and the empire flourished. Natural disasters, uprisings, and unusual astronomical phenomena, however, would be interpreted as signs of Heaven's displeasure or of a decline in the Way. This would open up the possibility that the Mandate justifiably should pass into the capable hands of one who, through his personal virtue (and, by extension, righteous might), was deemed more fit to hold sway over All Under Heaven. More often than not, a victorious ruler would justify his rise to power by divining post facto signs that the Mandate had passed to him.

POETIC FANCY

Speculation about Mao Zedong's imperial ambitions found public expression as early as 1945, during a crucial turning point in the unsteady history of the Republic of China. As the country faced the prospect of peace after the long years of war with Japan, there were renewed attempts to form a coalition government between the antagonistic forces of the Communists, led by Mao, and Chiang Kai-shek's (Jiang Jieshi) Nationalists, whose wartime government was based in the Sichuan city of Chongqing. To this end, in August 1945, Mao traveled from his wartime base at Yan'an in the loess hills of Shaanxi Province in the country's Northwest to meet with Chiang.

Shortly after that trip and its fruitless negotiations, a *ci*-lyric poem from Mao's hand was published in the Chongqing press. The poem, "Snow, to the Tune of 'Spring in Qinyuan'," was dated February 1936. This was shortly after the Red Army had reached Yan'an following the Long March that had seen the Communists break through the deadly encirclement campaigns launched by Chiang in an attempt to obliterate the bumpkin rebels under their "peasant king" (*tu huangdi* 土皇帝).

The second stanza of the poem reads:

This land so rich in beauty
Has made countless heroes bow in homage.
But alas! Qin Shihuang and Han Wudi
Lacked literary grace;
The founding emperors of the Tang and Song
Had little poetry in their souls;
And Genghis Khan,
Proud Son of Heaven for a day,
Could only shoot eagles, bow outstretched.
All are past and gone!
For truly great men
Look to this age alone.[13]

江山如此多娇, 引无数英雄竞折腰。
惜秦皇汉武, 略输文采;
唐宗宋祖, 稍逊风骚。
一代天骄, 成吉思汗, 只识弯弓射大雕。
俱往矣, 数风流人物, 还看今朝。

In the poem, Mao ostensibly rejected the emperors of tradition and extolled in their place the "true heroes" of history, the people of modern China, or at least their progressive vanguard, the CCP and its military arm.[14] Following its appearance, the poem sparked spirited debate in Chongqing, and a number of writers, including those of a

[13] For an illuminating discussion of this poem in the context of the Chinese literary tradition, see C. N. Tay, "From *Snow* to *Plum Blossoms*: A Commentary on Some Poems by Mao Tse-Tung," *Journal of Asian Studies* 25:2 (February 1966), pp. 287–303.

[14] The poem was published under Mao's original name, Mao Runzhi. In October 1945, Mao had a copy of the poem sent to his old acquaintance in Chongqing, Liu Yazi. It was published on November 4, 1945, in the evening supplement of the left-leaning newspaper *Xinmin Bao* [New Citizen]. It was immediately widely reprinted. The handwritten version of the poem eventually appeared in the Shanghai *Wenhui Bao* [Wenhui Daily] on January 8, 1951. A formal version of the text was carried in the January 1957 issue of *Shi Kan* [Poetry].

more progressive, or pro-communist bent, detected in it an unsettling message. The publisher, Wang Yunsheng, for example, sent a handwritten copy of "Snow" to the noted historian Fu Sinian, who had himself only recently returned from a meeting with Mao in Yan'an (more of this below). "I've specifically made a copy of it, ... " Wang wrote, adding, "so that you can see what kind of ideas fill this man's head."[15] Indeed, Wang was so unsettled by the poem that he published a critique and declared himself fearful that history might repeat itself. He hinted that perhaps another autocrat like Yuan Shikai (the early republican president who declared himself emperor) might now attempt to found a new dynasty and mount the dragon throne. Wang exhorted the Chinese people: "Stand up for yourselves, work hard for the present, be not mired in outmoded thinking. May the little people of China advance towards democracy!"[16]

The novelist and literary historian Wu Zuxiang had only recently noted in a diary entry that the Chongqing press had published Mao's 1942 "Talks at the Yan'an Forum on Literature and Art." which emphasized the needs of the masses and the importance of collective creativity. In this poem, however, Wu divined a message that was completely at variance with this avowed policy. "When he says, 'For truly great men / Look to this age alone,'" Wu remarked, "it appears that he regards himself as being in personal competition with hegemons like Qin Shihuang and Emperor Wu of the Han, as well as with the great rulers of the Tang and Song dynasties. In his titanic struggle with Mr. Chiang [Kai-shek] he has revealed himself to be a person of inordinate pride. He declares that the 'rich beauty of the land' is the reason why heroes both of today and the past struggle for domination. By so doing he claims to be one of these heroes. There's a malodour about it all that makes me extremely uncomfortable."[17] Not surprisingly, Chiang Kai-shek, a man hardly lacking in political afflatus himself, also was perturbed by the poem.

[15] This quotation can be found in Wang Fansen and Du Zhengsheng, eds., *Fu Sinian wenwu ziliao xuanji* [Selected Cultural Materials of Fu Sinian] (Taipei: Fu Sinan xiansheng bailing jinian choubeihui/Zhongyang yanjiu yuan Jindaishi Yanjiu Suo, 1995), p. 216; also quoted in Xie Yong, "Guanyu *Qinyuan chun, Xue* de liangze shiliao [Two Documents Related to 'Snow']," *Nanfang Zhoumo* [Southern Weekend], May 7, 2008.

[16] Wang Yunsheng, "Wo dui Zhongguo lishide yizhong kanfa [My View of Chinese History]," *Dagong Bao* [L'Impartial], December 8, 1945; quoted in Du Zhongming, "*Qinyuan chun, Xue* chuanqi [The Legend of "Snow"] (Beijing: Zhongyang wenxian chubanshe, 2007), p. 137.

[17] Shangfang Xide on Wu Zuxiang, in *Xin wenxue shiliao* [New Historical Materials on Literature] (2008), pp. 1, 34; quoted in Xie Yong, "Guanyu *Qinyuan chun, Xue* de liangze shiliao," *Nanfang Zhoumo*, May 7, 2008.

It confirmed his view that Mao had gone to Chongqing not to engage in substantive peace negotiations but in effect to "declare himself emperor" (*cheng di* 称帝).[18]

Mao's initial intentions in composing and eventually publishing the poem remain unknown. After 1949, he would assert that he only meant to praise the proletariat, the true heroes of the day.[19] But evidence involving another poem that Mao used in 1945 would suggest a somewhat more complex motivation behind the writing and publication of "Snow." The August 1945 Chongqing meetings followed from protracted negotiations with Yan'an, and only the previous month a delegation of six republican government counselors had visited the CCP base.[20] The delegation included Fu Sinian, a noted May Fourth-era activist and a leading historian who, among other things, had been writing *A Revolutionary History of the Chinese Nation*.[21]

Fu was a student leader during the May 4, 1919 demonstrations[22] and was already an established cultural figure when he first encountered Mao, who was a lowly library assistant at Peking University. The Communist leader recalled with chagrin that famous men like Fu had no time for a country bumpkin like himself. When they met again in Yan'an in 1945, however, Mao did not mention this long-harbored grievance. Instead, during the course of a private conversation on July 4, Mao praised Fu for his intellectual contributions to the antifeudal push of the May Fourth era, which itself helped engender the creation of the CCP. With suitable modesty, Fu responded that his generation of agitators was

[18] See Zhang Yunxin, "Mao Zedong *Qinyuan chun, Xue* 'fabiao qianhou' [Events Surrounding the Publication of Mao Zedong's 'Snow']," *Dang'an daguan* [Archival Overview] 380 (September 12, 2008), p. 3. Much would be made of Chiang's own imperial behavior, pointedly denounced by Chen Boda in the 1940s as representing "the Chiang family dynasty [*Chiang jia wangchao*]."

[19] On December 21, 1958, Mao finally published a note aimed at the conflicting interpretations. He wrote that "Snow" was "anti-feudal, a critique of one reactionary aspect of two millennia of feudalism.... Other interpretations are incorrect. As for the last three lines ... they refer to the proletariat." See "Dui Mao zhuxi shici shijiu shoude pizhu [Notes on Nineteen Poems by Chairman Mao]," in Mao Zedong, *Mao Zedong wenji* [Writings of Mao Zedong], Vol. 7 (Beijing: Renmin chubanshe, 1999), pp. 430–431.

[20] The delegation consisted of Chu Fucheng, Huang Yanpei, Leng Yu, Fu Sinian, Zuo Shunsheng, and Zhang Bojun.

[21] Although never completed, the manuscript contains ideas that have over time become part of China's national discourse. See Q. Edward Wang, *Inventing China Through History: The May Fourth Approach to Historiography* (Albany, NY: State University of New York Press, 2001), pp. 173–175.

[22] See Xu Jilin, "Historical Memories of May Fourth: Patriotism, But of What Kind?" trans. by Duncan Campbell, in *China Heritage Quarterly* 17 (March 2009); available at www.chinaheritagequarterly.org.

like the upstarts Chen Sheng and Wu Guang who had rebelled against the tyranny of the Qin Dynasty (second-century BCE); it was Mao and his colleagues who were the real heroes, like Liu Bang and Xiang Yu. After all, Liu Bang went on to become the founding emperor of the Han, one of the greatest dynasties in Chinese history. It was a tactful response, one that flattered the Communist leader while preserving Fu's own sense of dignity. It was an exchange also well suited to Yan'an, which was in the heartland of the area that formed the core of the Qin empire over two millennia earlier.

As was common practice among men of letters at the time, Fu asked Mao for a piece of calligraphy as a memento of their encounter. The following day he received a handwritten copy of "The Pit of Burned Books" (*Fen shu keng* 焚书坑) by the late-Tang poet Zhang Jie (章碣) (eighth century). In the accompanying note Mao remarked, "I fear you were being too self-effacing when you spoke of Chen Sheng and Wu Guang.... I've copied out a poem by a Tang writer to expand [on our discussion]."[23] The poem spoke of the vain attempt by Qin Shihuang (the First Emperor of the Qin, hereafter referred to as the First Emperor) to quell opposition to his draconian rule by burning books and burying scholars. The last lines read, "The ashes in the pit not yet cold, rebellion rose in the east, / Liu Bang and Xiang Yu were hardly men of letters" (*keng hui wei leng shan dong luan, Liu Xiang yuanlai bu du shu* 坑灰未冷山东乱， 刘项原来不读书). (In full, the poem reads: 竹帛烟销帝业虚， 关河空锁祖龙居。坑灰未冷山东乱， 刘项原来不读书。).

It was Mao's way of chiding a man who had been at the intellectual forefront for many years. In effect, he was saying that Fu Sinian's rebellion against the feudal traditions of China was indeed vainglorious, more so than the failed uprising of the peasant rebels Chen Sheng and Wu Guang against the Qin. And besides, real heroes like Liu Bang and Xiang Yu were men of action and had no care for book learning – to Mao the fatal flaw of so many May Fourth-era intellectual activists. Mao's false modesty in claiming that he and his cohort were, like Liu and Xiang, unlettered rebels also betrayed a confidence that he would lead the Communist army to victory over the existing political order. It was a theme to which he would return many times.[24] Nearly 30 years

[23] "Mao Zedong song Fu xiansheng ziji xinfeng [Envelope Bearing Mao Zedong's Handwriting Sent to Mr. Fu]," Fu Sinian Dang'an, I-38 [Fu Sinian Archive, I-38], at the Fu Sinian Library, Zhongyang Yanjiuyuan Lishi Yuyan Suo, Taipei. See also Yue Nan, *Chen Yinque yu Fu Sinian* [Chen Yinque and Fu Sinian] (Xi'an: Shaanxi shifan daxue chubanshe, 2008), Chapter 10, pp. 225–232.

[24] See, for example, Chen Jin, ed., *Mao Zedong dushu biji jiexi* [Exegesis on Mao Zedong's Reading Notes], Vol. 2 (Guangzhou: Guangdong renmin chubanshe, 1996), pp. 926–931.

later, for example, during a conversation with the prominent Cultural Revolution–era party activists and Politburo members Zhang Chunqiao and Wang Hongwen in July 1973, Mao once more mocked the bookishness of would-be rebels and praised the guile of leaders like Liu Bang.[25]

In the exchange with Fu Sinian, coupled with the publication of Mao's famous poem "Snow" later that same year, we see both the self-regard of the Communist leader and his ambivalence in regard to traditional rulership. He evokes that tradition both through historical reference and in actual practice. By placing his cause, and that of the Chinese people, in the context of dynastic-era peasant uprisings, Mao Zedong expressly, and repeatedly, identified with a history of rebellion. He declared that this latest uprising, led by a proletarian vanguard and directed by visionary revolutionary leaders with a modern antifeudal political philosophy, would break the dynastic cycle forever (the persistent dangers of the "cyclical law" of autocracy were famously discussed by educationalist Huang Yanpei during his own meeting with Mao in Yan'an) and found a new government that would outshine in achievement all the greatness of the past. It was this same ambivalence – a claim both for legitimacy in traditional terms and a self-identification with the role of rebel outsider at war with the past – that would be evident a few years later when the Communist forces marched on the old imperial capital of Beiping.

A METAPHORICAL EMPEROR

In 1948, as the Civil War between the Communists and Nationalists that broke out following withdrawal of the defeated Japanese neared a dramatic conclusion, Mao and his colleagues prepared to set up their capital in the former majestic imperial city of Beijing, which had reverted to its early Ming name of Beiping in 1928. The Communist leader famously admonished his followers not to repeat the mistakes of Li Zicheng and his peasant army – dismissed as "wandering bandits" (*liukou* 流寇), as were Mao's own forces some 300 years later. Li had entered Beijing victoriously in 1644 after defeating the Ming army but following a period of disastrous misrule soon was forced to flee. At the same time, Mao employed another kind of historical analogy to alert his comrades to the mammoth task that, despite their hard-won victory resulting from an extraordinary era of guerrilla warfare, now confronted them.

[25] See, "Qin Shihuang zuowei, yuansheng shusheng yiqi [The Actions of the First Emperor Were Far Superior to the Willfulness of the Bookish]," in Chen Jin, ed., *Mao Zedong dushu biji jiexi*, Vol. 2, pp. 1271–1272.

Referring to the long-defunct triennial imperial examinations that had been used to select the most capable men to rule the empire, on the eve of victory Mao said, "Today we're heading into the capital to take the big test [*gan kao* 赶考], no wonder everyone is nervous." He added, "If anyone has to retreat it means we've all failed. Under no circumstances can we be like Li Zicheng. All of us have to make the grade."[26] Here Mao used two mutually conflicting tropes to discuss the party and its army: On the one hand, they were candidates taking part in an orderly examination to prove their fitness to rule the empire within the context of the traditional world order. On the other hand, Mao encouraged his colleagues to identify with a peasant-led rebellion that overturned the last Han Chinese imperial dynasty, the Ming. The tensions of this double-edged schema would be a feature (although hardly the only one) of Mao's direction of the party in the first decades of the People's Republic.

Years later, when evaluating his achievement, Mao would reiterate that he had accomplished two things in his political career. One was to have forced Chiang Kai-shek and the Nationalists to retreat to Taiwan and to have "fought our way to Beijing, at last entering the Forbidden City" (although it is noteworthy that despite taking up residence in the Lake Palaces, Zhongnan Hai (中南海), after 1949, Mao never entered the Forbidden City proper). The other, far less acclaimed achievement was to have launched the Cultural Revolution.[27] Although the Nationalists would continue to claim legitimacy as the rulers of China and inheritors of a national enterprise that recalled the Ming Dynasty, in other respects harking back to the Ming and a revival of the fortunes of the Han Chinese also would be a prominent feature of the early years of the People's Republic. During that time, it also was easy to detect in Mao's political persona and even some of his less-than-revolutionary actions the shadow of the first Ming ruler, Zhu Yuanzhang. As Simon Leys remarks:

> The fact is, the founder of the Ming dynasty, Zhu Yuanzhang, shared a remarkable number of significant features with the founder of the People's Republic. Zhu was an adventurer, from peasant stock, poorly educated, a man of action, a bold and shrewd

---

[26] The material in these paragraphs is based on my *The Forbidden City*, pp. 143–144. See also the online notes for that book at www.chinahertiageproject.org/theforbiddencity/notes.php?chapter=chapter7.

[27] Quoted in Frederick C. Teiwes and Warren Sun, *The End of the Maoist Era: Chinese Politics During the Twilight of the Cultural Revolution, 1972–1976* (Armonk, NY: M. E. Sharpe, 2007), p. 595. Interestingly, Mao did not mention the War of Resistance Against Japan, although the defeat of the Nationalists might include this.

tactician, a visionary mind, in many respects a creative genius; naturally coarse, cynical, and ruthless, he eventually showed symptoms of paranoia bordering on psychopathy.[28]

It was not long after "entering the Forbidden City" that Mao visited Ming Xiao Ling, the tomb of the first Ming ruler outside Nanjing. It was here in 1912 that Sun Yat-sen, the founding father of the Republic of China, had read a eulogy reporting to the long-dead imperial ruler that China had rid itself of the foreign yoke of the Manchu-Qing oppressors and that the country was ruled again by Han Chinese. Visiting the tomb after a trip to the Zijinshan Observatory in February 1953, Mao remarked that although Zhu Yuanzhang started out life as a cowherd, he was "by no means a fool and had a very insightful strategist" to advise him. He went on to say that Zhu had developed effective policies against the foreign Yuan Dynasty led by the Mongols. It was a strategy summed up in the words "store up grain reserves, build city walls and, in due season, claim the throne" (*guang ji liang, gao zhu qiang, huan cheng wang* 广积粮，高筑墙，缓称王). The policy gained Zhu wide-based popular support among the disaffected masses, and, Mao claimed, it was this that "eventually allowed him to win All Under Heaven." Some two decades later, during the Cultural Revolution, Mao would recast Zhu's winning strategy as part of his own "Three Worlds" international policy; in their opposition to the two superpowers, the United States and the Soviet Union, he called on the people of China to "dig deep [air raid] shelters, store up grain reserves, and not to claim [global] hegemony" (*shen wa dong, guang ji liang, bu cheng ba* 深挖洞，广积粮，不称霸).[29]

More immediately, although the new state made the old Ming and Qing imperial city of Beijing its capital, in other ways the legacy of the past came under attack. Plans soon were advanced for demolition of the Ming-era walls of a city that was the center of imperial power in China from the time of the third Ming ruler, Yongle (r. 1403–25), until the end of the Qing Dynasty some five centuries later. The remaking of Beijing was a central feature of the physical realignment of the former center of dynastic power, and it was a process that reflected both imperial-scale symbolism and radical iconoclasm.[30] Simon Leys would later remark

---

[28] Simon Leys, "Ravished by Oranges," a review of Jonathan D. Spence's *Return to Dragon Mountain: Memories of a Late Ming Man*, in *New York Review of Books* 54:20 (December 20, 2007).

[29] Wu Jiangxiong et al., eds., *Mao Zedong tan gu lun jin* [Mao Zedong on the Past and Present], Vol. 2 (Hefei: Anhui renmin chubanshe, 1998), pp. 601–607.

[30] For details, see Wu Hung, *The Remaking of Beijing: Tiananmen Square and the Creation of a Political Space* (Chicago: University of Chicago Press, 2005), pp. 15ff; and Barmé, *The Forbidden City*, pp. 1–25.

on the destruction of imperial Beijing and other vainglorious assaults on what was blithely dubbed "feudalism" during the first decades of the new nation. His observations bear some relevance to the present discussion:

> The extent of their depredations gives Maoists the cheap illusion that they have done a great deal; they persuade themselves that they can rid themselves of the past by attacking its material manifestations; but in fact they remain its slaves, bound the more tightly because they refuse to realise the effect of the old traditions within their revolution.[31]

It was in the more ineffable area of behavior and rulership that both the iconoclasm of revolution and the lure of the old came into play. Mao's (and indeed the CCP's) own ambivalent relationship with tradition (be it real, imagined, or invented) increasingly played itself out in pronouncements and decisions made within the context of the changing terrain of state socialism. The one-party state was, however, caught on the horns of a dilemma. Its avowedly radical revolutionary enterprise was carried out under the tutelage of the late-Stalinist Soviet Union while at the same time attempting to give form to China's national aspirations. One noted critic would sum up the confluence of these forces in a powerful and succinct expression.

Chu Anping (d. 1966) was a liberal journalist and editor pressed into the service of the party. Encouraged to participate in the Hundred Flowers campaign of 1956, ostensibly launched to elicit the help of outsiders to help the party to improve its rule, after much prodding, Chu reluctantly wrote a speech addressed to both Mao and the premier, Zhou Enlai. In it he spoke about what he dubbed the "Party Empire" (*dang tianxia* 党天下).[32] Chu coined this neologism to denote the powerful commingling of China's imperial tradition and its notion that the whole nation was the property of the court, with the ethos of a modern totalitarian political party that had insinuated itself into every corner of what was a modernizing and aspirational society. The result was not just that Mao behaved like a would-be emperor; the CCP itself became the mechanism for an imperial-scale domination of China's present, as well as of its past. Chu warned that this state of affairs would have dire consequences for the well-being and development of the nation.

---

[31] Simon Leys, *Chinese Shadows* (New York: Viking, 1977), p. 58.
[32] See Chu Anping, "The Party Empire: Some Advice to Chairman Mao and Premier Zhou Enlai," in Geremie Barmé and Linda Jaivin, eds., *New Ghosts, Old Dreams: Chinese Rebel Voices* (New York: Times Books, 1992), pp. 360–361.

Mao's abrupt volte-face during the Hundred Flowers period and the purge of critics during the subsequent Anti-Rightist Movement in 1957 mark for many the Chairman's own autocratic transformation. Mao and his cohort had long employed aspects of the imperial tradition in their creation of a new state and in the careful management of the Chairman's public image. But Mao's ultimate ascent to "imperial hauteur" was to follow soon thereafter. In 1958, the party launched the Great Leap Forward, a mass movement aimed at hastening the country's realization of socialism and its advance toward an ideal communist society. One could argue that this was a period in which, more than before, Mao Zedong became a "metaphorical emperor." Ironically, this happened during a period when party policy itself declared that "man could conquer nature" (*ren ding sheng tian* 人定胜天), a voluntarist proposition that was in stark contrast to the imperial ethos, according to which human activity must accord with the ways of nature.

Much has been written about Mao's own realization that the precipitous Great Leap push toward utopia was faltering and causing great suffering. Some believe that he was considering curtailing the excesses of the movement when he was petitioned by an old comrade, Minister of Defense Peng Dehuai, at the July 1959 Lushan Conference. Peng's formal submission to Mao called for a rethinking of the Great Leap in light of the devastation the policies had already visited on the nation. This document is usually spoken of as being a "petition to the throne" (*shangshu* 上书). In the event, Mao was outraged by Peng's temerity and deeply suspicious that it was a ruse that disguised an insidious plot against him and party policy. He turned on Peng and his associates. Resorting once more to words that recalled the language of peasant rebellion, the Chairman declared that if the clash at Lushan led to nationwide divisions, he "would go to the countryside to lead the peasants to overthrow the government."[33] In couching his response to Peng in such terms, Mao expressed a view that despite his paramount position, he felt himself somehow to be still an outsider, a rebel set against the status quo. The subsequent purge of what was dubbed "rightist deviation" is regarded as a turning point in the party's generally collective-style leadership that had featured since the Yan'an days of the 1930s and 1940s (see Chapter 6).

Despite what would be seen as increasingly erratic behavior and the imminent danger for those who dared disagree, Mao still encouraged colleagues to speak out and criticize errors in the party's work. In

---

[33] Quoted in Frederick C. Teiwes, *Politics and Purges in China: Rectification and the Decline of Party Norms, 1950–1965* (Armonk, NY: M. E. Sharpe, 1979), p. 414.

other speeches during the Great Leap period, for example, the Chairman availed himself of traditional literature and dynastic history when making his point. Quoting the scheming Wang Xifeng from the famous eighteenth-century novel, *The Dream of the Red Chamber* [*Honglou Meng*], he would repeatedly use the line "dare to drag the emperor off his horse even if it means you'll suffer a death of a thousand cuts" (*shede yishen gua, gan ba huangdi laxia ma* 舍得一身剐，敢把皇帝拉下马) to extol what he called "the dauntless spirit needed in our struggle to build socialism and communism."[34] His other historical exemplar was an outspoken critic of the Ming Dynasty Jiajing Emperor (r. 1522–66), an official by the name of Hai Rui.

AN APOTHEOSIS

During this time, Deng Tuo (1912–66), a leading party intellectual, was exemplary of the relationship between the loyal party man and the increasingly quixotic leader. Just as Mao employed historical anecdote and oblique literary allusions to communicate many of his opinions, a small coterie of well-connected writers such as Deng began to express their frustrations and sense of duty as engaged loyal party men of letters by using the cloaked language of tradition. In the ideological and policy struggles of the late 1950s, Deng soon found himself sidelined.

In a poem published in 1960, Deng Tuo praised the Donglin Academy, a center of learning in Wuxi, the site of which he had once visited. During the early seventeenth century, scholars at the Donglin Academy openly expressed their opposition to the corrupt rule of the court in Beijing, reserving their particular ire for the notorious "eunuch dictator" Wei Zhongxian who held sway during the Tianqi reign (1621–27). Deng's poem recalled those scholars and invoked the tradition of loyal opposition:

> *Donglin's teachings inherit those of Guishan*
> *Forever concerned with human affairs.*
> *Think not that men of letters are vacuous*
> *The blood stains mark where their heads fall.*[35]

---

[34] Mao, "Speech at the Communist Party's National Conference on Propaganda Work," March 12, 1957 and again in March 1958, when he also attacked Chu Anping by name. See Mao, "Talks at the Chengdu Conference (Talk of March 22)," in Stuart Schram, ed., *Mao Tse-tung Unrehearsed: Talks and Letters: 1956–71*, trans by John Chinnery and Tieyun (Harmondsworth, Middlesex, England: Penguin Books, 1974), p. 122.

[35] Zuo Hai (Deng Tuo), "Gechang Taihu – 'Jiangnan yincao' zhi san [Praise for Taihu Lake]," *Guangming Ribao* [Guangming Daily], September 7, 1960; later collected in

东林讲学继龟山，事事关心天地间。
莫谓书生空议论，头颅掷处血斑斑。

In the cultural topography of that period, historical incident and precedent provided crucial *lieux de memoire* for engaged activists, writers, and thinkers, as well as revolutionary leaders. Recalling or writing about the Ming Dynasty had been a feature of Han Chinese oppositionist culture during the Qing era (1644–1911), as well as in the revolutionary culture of the republican era. The use of "the past to satirise the present" (*jie gu feng jin* 借古讽今) that unfolded in the early 1960s has been depicted as a "turn inward," one that also opened up a narrow avenue for possible critique to writers such as Deng Tuo.[36] At the time, the party intelligentsia might have wished to castigate "the emperor," but they stopped short of calling the system itself into question. Just as the post–Cultural Revolution evaluation of the Chairman critiqued Mao's autocratic behavior and partially absolved the party of responsibility, in the early 1960s, critics of the leader's increasingly tyrannical actions would shy away from drawing out the implications for one-party rule.

Mao Zedong's own shifting attitude toward history during these years was evident in his initial praise for the daring critical spirit of the Ming minister Hai Rui mentioned earlier. Only a few years later it was followed by his rejection of that same minister for his having upbraided the emperor of the day, Jiajing. One of Deng Tuo's colleagues, Wu Han, a Ming historian and vice mayor of Beijing, had been encouraged initially by Mao to write about the daring of the "Hai Rui spirit." He did so in essays and in two plays, one of which, "Hai Rui Is Dismissed from Office," was denounced eventually, as were the poems and essays of Deng Tuo, as part of the pretext for launching the Cultural Revolution. Just as Mao's evaluation of the First Emperor varied depending on the exigencies of the moment (see below), so too did the reputation of Hai Rui fluctuate.

In 1965, Mao was behind the claims that Wu Han was part of a covert antiparty clique within the central leadership, supporting accusations that Wu's praise for Hai Rui was a coded appeal for the rehabilitation of

---

Deng Tuo shici xuan [Selected Poems of Deng Tuo] (Beijing: Renmin wenxue chubanshe, 1979), p. 79, my translation. Referred to in Timothy Cheek, *Propaganda and Culture in Mao's China: Deng Tuo and the Intelligentsia* (Oxford, England: Clarendon Press, 1997), p. 201.

[36] See Merle Goldman, "The Unique 'Blooming and Contending' of 1961–62," *China Quarterly* 37 (January-March 1969), p. 63; and Stephen Uhalley Jr., "The Cultural Revolution and the Attack on the 'Three Family Village,'" *China Quarterly* 27 (July-September 1966), pp. 149–161.

the ousted Defense Minister Peng Dehuai and a rejection of the Great Leap Forward and, more generally, of the socialist line. By means of this political sleight of hand, Mao declared that if Peng Dehuai was Hai Rui, then the man who had denounced him – Mao himself – was none other than the capricious Jiajing emperor.[37] As the political struggle of 1965–66 unfolded through this series of historical feints, one prescient, young nonparty writer by the name of Yu Luoke was quick to describe the Cultural Revolution as neither cultural nor revolutionary in nature. He rejected the party media's version of events, one that spoke of intense class struggle, a titanic battle between two opposing political lines, and the supposedly frenzied attempts by the long-defeated bourgeoisie to regain lost power through dupes in the party bureaucracy. In a diary entry written on July 29, 1966, Yu described the purge involving Deng Tuo, Wu Han, and the Beijing Municipal Committee as being nothing less than a "palace revolt" (*gongting zhengbian* 宫廷政变).[38]

As the Cultural Revolution unfolded, Mao's status as the "savior of the Chinese people" and the omniscient guide of world revolution was further enhanced. The irony is that this final transformation occurred in the midst of the collapse of party rule and the reimposition of the very kinds of controls that had made Mao rebel against the status quo. Regardless, in the years 1964–71, Mao would achieve something akin to an apotheosis, a status of sanctity and omnipotence with which few, if any, imperial-era rulers could have competed. The one historical ruler who did offer a measure of comparison, however, was the First Emperor.

Early in his political career, Mao had spoken approvingly of the First Emperor, Qin Shihuang. He might have chided the Qin emperor for "lacking literary grace" (*lüe shu wencai* 略输文采) when listing the great rulers of China's past in his 1936 poem "Snow," but overall he approved of the draconian nature of "Qin rule" (*Qin zheng* 秦政).[39] He would return to the theme of the Qin era and his own relationship with the tradition in the early months of 1966. In a rescript dated April 14, 1966, written on a document related to students at arts colleges in Beijing who were combining study with labor in factories or the communes,

---

[37] For studies of this incident, see James Pusey, *Wu Han: Attacking the Present Through the Past* (Cambridge, MA: East Asian Research Center, Harvard University, 1969); Rudolf Wagner, *The Contemporary Chinese Historical Drama: Four Studies* (Berkeley: University of California Press, 1990); and Cheek, *Propaganda and Culture in Mao's China*.

[38] Yu Luoke, *Riji* [Diary], July 29, 1966; available at www.tianyabook.com/renwu2005/js/x/xuxiao/ylk/011.htm.

[39] See Jia Yi's famous second-century BCE essay "Guo Qin [The Faults of Qin]."

Mao once more quoted the poem of the Tang Dynasty writer Zhang Jie mentioned earlier. He remarked, "Some comrades [that is, himself] are of the opinion that 'Those with little learning overthrow the learned; the young overthrow the old.' This is an age-old principle."[40]

Mao was not the only one to invoke the First Emperor when referring to his domination of the CCP in those years. As the Cultural Revolution progressed, some of his colleagues also would remark on the unsettling similarities between their own Great Leader and the founder of the Qin.

In "Notes on 'Project 571'," the alleged plans for an armed insurrection against the Chairman attributed to Lin Biao's sou, Lin Liguo, in 1971, the rationale for a coup was expressed in the following way:

> Of course, we don't deny the historical role he [Mao] played in uniting China. It is for this very reason that historically our revolutionaries gave him a well-deserved place and their support. But now he is abusing the trust and position bestowed on him by the Chinese people, and he is heading in the wrong historical direction. In reality, he has already become a modern-day First Emperor. Our sense of responsibility to the Chinese people and China's history will not allow us to stand by patiently! He is not a true Marxist-Leninist. Rather he is the greatest feudal tyrant in Chinese history who is pursuing the path of Confucius and Mencius while wrapping himself in the guise of a Marxist-Leninist and behaving like the First Emperor.[41]

After the failure of the plot against Mao and the death of those involved in it (including the Chairman's handpicked successor, Lin Biao), the unflattering comparison did not force Mao to abandon his penchant for referring to the Qin ruler. Indeed, not long after the Lin Biao debacle, the Chairman wrote a poem to the party hack scholar Guo Moruo referring to the abiding relevance of Qin and the reactionary nature of the

[40] Mao Zedong, "Dui 'Zai Jing yishu yuanxiao shixing bangong (nong) bandu' yiwende piyu (1966 nian 4 yue 14 ri) [Rescript on the Document 'Implementing Study and Manual Labor at the Tertiary Arts Schools of the Capital, (14 April 1966)]," in Zhonggong zhongyang wenxian yanjiushi, ed., *Jianguo yilai Mao Zedong wengao* [Mao Zedong's Manuscripts Since the Establishment of the People's Republic of China], Vol. 12 (Beijing: Zhongyang wenxian chubanshe, 1998), p. 35.

[41] Lin Liguo et al., "'571 gongcheng' jiyao [Notes on 'Project 571']," in "Fan geming zhengbian gangling ('571 gongcheng' jiyao) (shougao yingyinjian) [Program for a Counterrevolutionary Coup (Notes on 'Project 571') (Photocopies of Handwritten Materials)]," material appended to "Zhongfa 1972 di 4 hao [Central Party Document 1972 No. 4]," Beijing, 1972.

Confucian tradition (with which Lin Biao was now, absurdly, associated). In it he made oblique reference to the poem by Zhang Jie that he had given to Fu Sinian in the mid-1940s:

> *I advise you not to criticize the Emperor of Qin,*
> *The last word remains to be said about burning the books and*
>   *burying the scholars.*
> *The ancestral dragon may be dead but Qin lives on,*
> *While Confucian scholarship despite its reputation is but chaff.*
> *A hundred generations have pursued the rule of Qin....* [42]

> 劝君少骂秦始皇, 焚坑事业要商量。
> 祖龙魂死秦犹在, 孔学名高实秕糠。
> 百代都行秦政法.…

It also was in these last years that Mao returned to the theme of power and cooptation. As was the case of his 1945 exchange with Fu Sinian in Yan'an, Mao in his decline continued to make frequent reference to historical upstarts and peasant rebellions. He would be regarded as behaving like an isolated emperor in his dotage, but after a life-long political career in which he supported turning historical verdicts on their head, the Chairman continued to side with outsider rebels. In August 1975, just over a year before he died, he made a series of comments on the band of sworn brothers and rebels that feature in Shi Nai'an's fourteenth-century novel, *Water Margin* [*Shuihu Zhuan*]. He criticized the ultimate message of the book for being one that extolled slavish compliance to the power holders. "[The novel] only opposes corrupt officials, not the emperor himself," he remarked. [43]

Isolated by physical infirmity as well as by the increasingly idiosyncratic nature of his rule, Mao featured in the international media as a lone figure surrounded by political schemers. The Chinese press in Hong Kong and Taiwan frequently used imperial metaphors to describe the twilight of this "red court." In 1970, in remarks made to a sympathetic American journalist Edgar Snow (to whom, some three decades

---

[42] Mao Zedong, "Du *Fengjian lun* cheng Guo lao [Presented to Guo Moruo after Reading 'On the Feudal']," August 5, 1973, from Zhonggong zhongyang wenxian yanjiushi, ed., *Jianguo yilai Mao Zedong wengao*, Vol. 13, p. 361.

[43] Chen Jin, ed., *Mao Zedong dushu biji jiexi*, Vol. 2, pp. 1374–1375. Mao chose not to mention that the literary paragon, Lu Xun, whose reputation survived the Cultural Revolution, offered the same insight some 50 years earlier. This observation, which appears in several of Lu Xun's essays, is a particular feature of his 1929 reflections on "the evolution of hooligans." See his "Liumangde bianqian [Evolution of the Louts]," in *Lu Xun quanji* [The Complete Works of Lu Xun], Vol. 4 (Beijing: Renmin wenxue chubanshe, 1981), pp. 155–158.

earlier, Mao had criticized self-important May Fourth academics such as Fu Sinian) during the National Day parade in Beijing, the Chairman supposedly lamented that he was like "a lone monk walking the world with a leaky umbrella."[44] Snow's understanding of the comment was the result of a delicious combination of undertranslation and misperception. Mao had, in fact, used a common kind of allegorical humor, a *xiehou yu* (歇后语), in which the second punning part of the saying is left unstated. He was "a monk carrying an umbrella" (*heshang da san* 和尚打伞). What he left unsaid (and his interpreter therefore did not communicate to Snow) was that like a monk he was "hairless" (*wu fa* 无法: a pun for lawless) and that since he was carrying an umbrella, there was no sky above him (*wu tian* 无天: a pun for following no preordained principle). Mao was in effect saying that he, or rather the revolutionary enterprise he led, was beyond restraint. It was a remarkable, and given Mao's usual linguistic acrobatics, hubristic admission. It also was a statement that, while perhaps imperial in portent, had little to do with the Chinese tradition of kingship. If there was much in Mao's life, persona, and behavior that reflected the imperial, one also could argue that his belief in the manifestation of history in his actions related more to European traditions of divine rulership and revolutionary sagehood than it did to Chinese notions of imperial authority. One could argue that he saw himself as a Napoleon-like *homme providentiel*.

UNQUIET GRAVE

The advantage of democratic systems is that they allow men of destiny to be dumped as soon as the storm blows over (cf. Churchill, de Gaulle, etc.); in fact, in a normal everyday situation where "his giant's wings prevent him from walking," any Great Leader worth his salt has a strong tendency to stir up artificial gales in order to get some wind back under his pinions. At that point he can become a nuisance, and nations which do not have the opportunity of getting rid of their geniuses are sometimes liable to pay very dearly for the privilege of being led by them.[45]

A popular saying dating back to the Jin Dynasty (fourth century CE) holds that only after the coffin of the deceased has been sealed can a final judgment on an individual's life be advanced (*gai guan lun ding* 盖棺论定). Mao himself observed that the verdict on a person could only

[44] *Life* Magazine, April 30, 1971.
[45] Simon Leys, "Mao Tse-tung and Chinese History," in his *Broken Images*, pp. 54–55.

be determined posthumously.[46] Various official and popular verdicts have been passed on the achievements and legacies of the Chairman. Historians and political scientists have pronounced, as have the mass media and the regnant Chinese propaganda authorities. But, as I have argued elsewhere, Mao's remains an unquiet grave. His death marked but the beginning of what has already been an eventful posthumous career.[47]

Mao might have spoken often to visitors and colleagues of the inevitability of "going to meet Marx" (*qu jian Makesi* 去见马克思), yet few practical steps were taken to provide for his actual demise. Many years earlier, the Chairman had proposed that his mortal remains, along with those of other party leaders, should be cremated. But following his death in the Lake Palaces in the early hours of September 9, 1976, it was quickly decided to preserve his body so that it could be put on public display, ostensibly to inspire ongoing revolutionary fervor. Even before a final resting place had been decided, the party's Politburo removed the body for safekeeping to the underground bunker and medical center at Maojia Wan, coincidentally Marshal Lin Biao's former residence. This temporary home for the corpse had been built as a subterranean hospital for the emergency use of Mao's handpicked successor. As part of the Chairman's legacy, it was decided also to proceed with the editing and publication of a written monument to the dead leader: the fifth volume of *Mao Zedong's Selected Works*. The editorial work on this crucial political corpus was similarly carried out at Maojia Wan. Thus the living word of the late Mao was prepared for publication in offices above what was in effect a mininecropolis.

To ensure the reliability and appropriateness of the medical procedures undertaken to maintain Mao's body in a presentable form (How much water should be retained in the corpse? At what levels should the cocktail of preservatives be kept? And so on), it was deemed necessary to find a "standard body" (*biaozhun ti* 标准体) on which to experiment. The task to enlist the unwitting services of a suitably proportioned corpse fell to Xu Jingxian, the pro-Maoist party leader of Shanghai, a city that was ideologically proximate to the wishes of the leadership even though

---

[46] He first quoted the third in a series of five poems by Bo Juyi entitled, "Fang yan wu shou" to this effect in a 1939 speech entitled, "Yongyuan fendou [Struggle Forever]." He returned to the theme and quoted the last lines of the poem again in 1972 when discussing the fall of Lin Biao. See Chen Jin, ed., *Mao Zedong dushu biji jiexi*, Vol. 2, pp. 1295–1296.

[47] See "The Irresistible Fall and Rise of Chairman Mao," in Barmé, *Shades of Mao*, pp. 3–73, esp. pp. 53–54.

physically at an appropriate remove from the political center. In his memoirs, Xu recalls that it was necessary to bring forward the execution of a criminal on death row so that such a "standard body" could be procured at short notice. While today actors specializing in playing Mao on stage and screen might come and go,[48] in death, the corpse of that nameless double still shadows the Chairman so that, to distort the Bard, "age cannot wither him, nor custom stale."[49]

In late-dynastic tradition, emperors would devote considerable thought to the selection of a geomantically suitable tomb site (a *wannian jidi* 万年吉地, literally, "a propitious location for eternity"). When it came to finding a permanent home for the embalmed corpse of Mao, a different set of problems and possibilities presented itself to party leaders. The devotion of time, energy, and resources to the preservation and eventual final resting place of Mao's body was, nonetheless, regal in scale. If Mao had employed imperial tropes to considerable effect during his life, in death his successors would be equally drawn to, entrapped by, and wary of traditional precedent and practice.

The most recent entombment of a national leader prior to that of Mao Zedong was itself indirectly imperial, and in 1976, party leaders drew inspiration from the Zhongshan Mausoleum built for the founding father of the Republic of China, Sun Yat-sen (d. 1925 and formally entombed in 1929), located in the hills outside Nanjing. Sun's mausoleum (*ling* 陵 – the term itself has imperial overtones) was in a tradition that consciously invoked imperial funerary custom.[50] Mao's own corpse eventually found a final resting place in the southern precinct of Tiananmen Square, but this was by no means the only choice considered for a grand monument to the dead leader. For a short time in September-October 1976, a number of alternate locations were under discussion.[51]

---

48 See "In a Glass Darkly: An Interview with Gu Yue," in Barmé *Shades of Mao*, pp. 177–182; and David Moser, "Red Stars over China: The Mao Impersonators," October 7, 2004; available at danwei.org: www.danwei.org/tv/david_moser_on_mao_impersonato.php.

49 Xu Jingxian, *Shi nian yi meng* [A Decade in a Dream] (Hong Kong: Shidai guoji chuban gongsi, 2005), pp. 410–413.

50 For more on the funeral of Sun Yat-sen in Beijing in 1925 and his eventual entombment in the Purple Mountains outside Nanjing in 1929, both events that were echoed in the mourning for and burial of Mao, see Henrietta Harrison, *The Making of the Republican Citizen: Political Ceremonies and Symbols in China, 1911–1929* (Oxford, England: Oxford University Press, 2000), pp. 133–144, 207–235.

51 For more on the sites for Mao's final resting place, see Sang Ye and Geremie R. Barmé, "A Beijing that Isn't (Part I)," *China Heritage Quarterly* 14 (June 2008); available at www.chinaheritagequarterly.org/features.php?searchterm=014_BeijingThatWasnt.inc&issue=014.

Most of these sites were ruled out owing to the odium of imperial associations. The final choice in favor of Tiananmen placed Mao in the heart of what had been designed as a majestic imperial capital in a square that had been built to lay claim to the grand sweep and vision of the city's dynastic rulers. Inside the actual Mao Memorial Hall – an unprepossessing marble box – a statue of a seated Mao was positioned to greet mourners in obvious emulation of the Lincoln Memorial in Washington. The wall behind the statue featured a landscape mural bearing the words, "This land so rich in beauty" (*jiangshan ruci duo jiao* 江山如此多娇) in Mao's calligraphy: a line from that famous 1936 poem "Snow" discussed at the beginning of this chapter.

During his life, Mao had been obsessed with the ever-present danger of counterrevolution, which included not only presumed threats against party rule from the defeated bourgeoisie but also the menace of the hierarchical order of old China. It is of some ironic interest to note that on the night of Mao's state funeral held in Tiananmen Square on September 18, 1976, a peasant by the name of Li Pirui in Liling County, Hunan Province, declared that he would be the prime minister to a new emperor who would soon establish his own dynasty, the Great China Buddhist Kingdom (*Dazhonghua foguo* 大中华佛国). Working with followers attracted by the moral rightness of his cause, Li declared the following year that he had discovered the new True Dragon Emperor (*zhenlong tianzi* 真龙天子) in the person of an illiterate peasant by the name of Shi Jinxin. Together they amassed a court of over 100 civilian and martial officials in Hunan and Jiangxi provinces. Shi Jinxin "mounted the throne" (*deng ji* 登极) in October 1983, whereupon a new dynasty was formally inaugurated. Its mission was "to overthrow the Communist Party, establish the Great China Buddha Kingdom in China, and to extend its rule over the whole planet." The presumptive dynasty was short-lived. In December 1983, Shi and his court were arrested. Li Pirui was sentenced to death in May 1985, and Shi, along with 17 courtiers, was given a lengthy prison sentence.[52]

Others saw no need to support the establishment of a new dynasty; they argued that Mao had anointed a successor of his own. Although the Chairman's son, Mao Anying, a man thought of as a potential political heir, had died in the Korean War, people would claim that Hua Guofeng

[52] See Mo Xin, ed., *Dimeng jing Hua* [Imperial Dreams Shock China] (Guangzhou: Guangzhou chubanshe, 1998), pp. 1–35. For another instance of imperial presumption dating from early 1980s Hunan, see Ann S. Anagnost, "The Beginning and End of an Emperor: A Counterrepresentation of the State," *Modern China* 11:2 (April 1985), pp. 147–176.

(d. 2008) was in fact Mao's offspring and that he had created a dynastic handover by selecting him as the new party chairman in 1976. Although Hua's tenure was brief – and despite rumors that he was Mao's illegitimate child – continuity has worked in other ways. With each subsequent leader – Hu Yaobang, Zhao Ziyang, Jiang Zemin, Hu Jintao – there have been favorites, and the veiled politics of the CCP has seen their rise and, in some cases, fall. Mao immersed himself in Chinese history and literature, but for all his familiarity with the pitfalls of rulership, he failed to establish an orderly transfer of power. Deng Xiaoping, a man far less interested in the past (one recalls here the line from Zhang Jie's poem: "Liu Bang and Xiang Yu were hardly men of letters"), in contrast, proved his talent at "ruling behind the screen" (*chuilian tingzheng* 垂 帘听政 – a reference to the Empress Dowager's rule during the late-Qing Dynasty and one used to criticize Deng from the time of the 1989 Protest Movement). If one is to talk of the maintenance of "dynastic stability" and "imperial succession," Deng was far more adept in his management of affairs than his predecessor. Indeed, during the Deng era and ever since, the language of court politics has continued to influence both formal and informal discussions of China's power holders.

The post–Cultural Revolution era also has witnessed the precipitous rise of what is called the "Princelings' Faction" (*taizi dang* 太子党), the term *taizi* enjoying a dynastic provenance and meaning "crown prince." At the writing of this chapter, Xi Jinping, the son of the late military leader and former member of the Politburo Xi Zhongxun, is rumored to be a possible successor to the present incumbent. Thus, while not dynastic, the CCP continues to follow "ways that are dark" – those influenced by premodern politics and traditions, be it in overt actions or through immanent behavior.[53]

SHADES OF MAO

Given the history of twentieth-century China, the rise of modern Han Chinese nationalism, the significance that the Ming Dynasty had in both the founding of the Republic of China in 1912 and in the

---

[53] As noted earlier, the Hong Kong and Taiwan media have used dynastic language to describe mainland politics for decades. English-language accounts also have frequently used imperial metaphors to discuss the communist era, something evident even in the titles of works such as George Paloczi-Horvath's *Mao Tse-Tung, Emperor of the Blue Ants* (London: Secker & Warburg, 1962); Dick Wilson's *Mao: The People's Emperor* (London: Hutchinson, 1979); and Harrison Salisbury's *The New Emperors: China in the Era of Mao and Deng* (Boston: Little, Brown, 1992).

establishment of the capital of the People's Republic in the ancient Ming capital of Beijing in 1949, it is perhaps not surprising that some of the first posthumous criticisms of Mao Zedong were articulated in reappraisals of Zhu Yuanzhang, the Ming founding Emperor Taizu.[54]

Many writers found in Mao's persona and actions in the first decades of the People's Republic resonances of a "founding emperor complex." Like rulers of the past, they identified him as being a canny local rebel who led a mass army to seize power. Once in control of a new political regime, he grew accustomed to the authority and charisma associated with leadership. In ways that are reminiscent of the behavior of other founders of new states, to maintain stability in the crucial first years of power, he introduced harsh measures to ensure unity, order, and stability regardless of the individual or, indeed, social cost. The great paradox is that the series of political ructions that saw Mao Zedong's apotheosis in pursuit of his political ideals and authority during the Cultural Revolution also fatally undermined the very ideology and unity that had turned him into a revolutionary leader and demigod in the first place. Despite this shorter-term failure, however, Mao and his cohort were successful in melding powerful symbolism from the past with the requirements of a developing nation-state. In the rituals, symbols, and behavior of the new nation, tradition has been repeatedly reinvented and refined to provide continuities that are today more evident than at any other period in the history of the People's Republic.

The contradictory evaluations of Mao that range from acknowledging him primarily as a patriot or revolutionary leader to being a later-day imperial autocrat or even a monster were encouraged by party-state-ordained denunciations of his last circle of followers, the "Gang of Four" from 1976.[55] Attacks on Jiang Qing, Mao's widow, as the "Empress of the Red Capital" (*Hongdu nühuang* 红都女皇 – the title of the Chinese translation of Roxane Witke's 1977 *Comrade Chiang Ch'ing*) reflected back on Mao himself. While the dead Chairman could not be denounced directly, in works of art and literature throughout the late 1970s and

---

[54] See Sullivan, "The Controversy over 'Feudal Despotism,'" in Unger, *Using the Past to Serve the Present*, p. 193, note 48.

[55] For example, shortly after their detention in early October 1976, Guo Moruo, "the most notorious intellectual prostitute in China," wrote a poem denouncing the "Gang of Four" and Jiang Qing in particular:

> … The white skeleton ghost
> Who likened herself to Empress Wu
> Is gone in one sweep of the broom….

See Leys, "Comrade Chiang Ch'ing," *Broken Images*, p. 83.

early 1980s, frequent, often oblique references were made to his imperial style. It would take the party some five years to evaluate Mao and his later career in terms that would retain the rationale of the Chinese Revolution while erasing the politics of the left from his legacy.

Was Mao the last Chinese autocrat? Certainly, he was self-educated in the tradition of autocratic rule, or *diwang shu* 帝王术, just as he was an avid student of modern ideologies. Like many politically active members of his generation, he too deployed the tradition as he understood it, with devastating effect. While it is meaningful to investigate issues related to Mao's personal psychology, his arrant and idiosyncratic behavior, I would argue that to concentrate on these aspects of his life and thought distracts too readily from or dominates discussions of other historical dimensions and abiding elements of the Mao era (see Chapter 1).

As we have seen, Mao made numerous contradictory and complex references to rulership and to traditional modes of imperial power. In his last years he appeared to be surrounded by a court, his associates, sychophants, and his long-term colleagues engaged in a constant struggle to gain access to him. His gnomic utterances were used to direct the party and the nation. Even in his waning years, he had a voracious appetite for classical histories and literature. Given his career and his later years, it is then hardly surprising that commentators have repeatedly availed themselves of the imperial metaphor. Moreover, one can argue that the CCP itself has allowed metaphors of the imperial to occlude the revolutionary message of Mao Zedong Thought and to mask its legacy of ideas relating to equality, class differences, bureaucracy, and power and their continuing relevance to contemporary Chinese politics, the economy, and society.

Obversely, to leave unmentioned the imperial and dynastic in discussions of the Maoist era and contemporary China is to blind ourselves to the persistence, reinvention, manipulation, and limitations of tradition. Mao used history – he claimed that he obsessively read the Song Dynasty work, *The Mirror of Government* [*Zizhi tongjian* 资治通鉴], among other classical histories – in his political life—but also by so doing he undermined the revolutionary reordering of society that he oversaw. His obsession with tradition and dynastic history was a central feature of high Maoism. To ignore this reality in favor of some facile and acceptable Maoism, one evacuated of live content and reconstituted for the benefit of contemporary left-leaning political causes (and academic careers), is to limit our understanding of Mao, just as an excessive emphasis on his "imperial pretensions" locates him within narratives of industrial-scale autocracy but beyond the pale of revolutionary modernity. It is the enlivening and entrapping heritage of the past, as relived in the present, that lies at the core of an understanding of modernity in the Chinese context.[56]

The incidents and historic moments discussed in this short chapter offer some indication of how the language of China's classical past, in particular the rhetoric of dynastic rule and Confucian statecraft, was married to political thought and action in the revolutionary heyday of twentieth-century China. Needless to say, this same language has been put to quite different, though perhaps even more potent, uses in the post-Maoist era. The longevity of this kind of rhetoric must be understood in the context of its ever-changing connotations. This differs fundamentally from any Orientalist assumption about "dynastic China." The idea of "Mao the emperor" has the same essentializing effect. Cleaving to it holds history captive to an imagined "eternal" pattern.[57]

It is in this broader historical perspective that we can hope to understand the abiding fascination with, if not the cult of, Chairman Mao. His memory lives both within the history of which he was a part and which, as one of the "truly great men," he helped forge. The continuous evocations of that past allow for the constant reinvention of Mao himself. New leftist thinkers and essayists ransack the Maoist-era heritage in search of renewal; the CCP itself inherits a complex legacy, one that it can use for its present ideological needs (after all, the "harmonious society" that is presently in vogue can be traced back to Confucian thought but equally to Mao's own use of the expression *li zhi yong, he wei gui* (礼之用, 和为贵). In terms of popular culture, Mao and his era continue to provide rich material for films, TV shows, and popular literature. However, as I argue in *Shades of Mao*, the Chairman is also within and above contemporary history. He is part of a narrative continuity, one that offers a populist and popular story about the historical record. As the founding figure of a new state, he will continue to share fame with such rulers as the First Emperor, Liu Bang of the Han, Taizong of the Tang, and so on, all of whom he lists in his poem "Snow."

Mao's hubristic belief that the "truly great men" would be able to change objective reality through sheer will and human effort goes, as

---

[56] For an engaging overview of evaluations of Mao in the English-language and Chinese media over recent years, see Mobo Gao, *The Battle for China's Past: Mao and the Cultural Revolution* (London: Pluto Press, 2008).

[57] In this context, see Daniel Frederick Vukovich, "Sinological-Orientalism: The Production of the West's Post-Mao China," Ph. D. thesis, University of Illinois, Urbana-Champaign, 2005; cited in Gao, *The Battle for China's Past*, p. 38.

has been noted, against the very nature of traditional Chinese imperial thinking. It also was the failure of "imagined reality" to create a realignment of the stars and to change practical realities that marked his years as the demiurge of high socialism. It is his heroic voluntarism, as well as his ideological and nationalist conceit, however, that still generates a charismatic aura for Mao personally and, for some, a sense of abiding possibility within the Maoist legacy. Or, as it is expressed in the concluding lines of *Morning Sun*, the 2003 film on the Cultural Revolution:

> For many the revolution is dead. Utopian promise now appears in different guises.
>
> But the specter of Mao is never far away. When people feel oppressed and powerless, when a system permits no legitimate protest or dissent, Mao emerges as a possibility, a champion of the right to rebel.[58]

Anecdotal evidence may, however, suggest a more ironic reality. A writer and long-time China specialist with a background in journalism reported that during her travels in China in late 2008 she frequently encountered young people who, when they spoke about the "old society" or the "feudal past," were invariably referring not to pre-1949 "Old China" and the founding of the People's Republic but to the dark days of their parents' lives. These were then the oppressive years during which their parents had been sent off to the countryside or attacked and abused by quixotic party policy. This "old society," this "feudal past," was for them none other than the era of Chairman Mao.[59]

In 1976, Simon Leys noted that although Mao did not pass away until September 9 of that year, Maoism itself had died on April 5, 1976, the day of the Qingming Festival, when masses of people gathered in Tiananmen Square to commemorate the recently deceased Premier Zhou Enlai and to attack the "modern-day First Emperor," Mao Zedong. Exactly 20 years earlier, the *People's Daily* had published an editorial denouncing Nikita Khrushchev's secret attack on Stalin at the Twentieth Congress of the Soviet Communist Party. At the time, an enlarged meeting of the Politburo of the CCP had discussed the issue of Khrushchev at length and formulated the editorial that marked a parting of the ways with the Soviets. At the meeting, Mao recited a famous poem by the Tang

---

[58] Carma Hinton, Geremie R. Barmé, and Richard Gordon, *Morning Sun* (Boston: Long Bow Group, 2003); see www.morningsun.org.

[59] These observations were made to the author by novelist and writer Linda Jaivin.

writer Du Fu.[60] The last lines contain sentiments that perhaps best sum up his own posthumous career, one that, as I have argued elsewhere, has only just begun:

Wang, Yang, Lu, and Luo are the writers of the day
You may mock them now, but
While you and your fame will fade
The rivers flow on eternally.
王杨卢骆当时体，
轻薄为文哂未休，
尔曹身与名俱灭，
不废江河万古流。

---

[60] Based on a memoir written by Huang Kecheng; see "Ercao shen yu ming ju mie, bu fei jianghe wangu liu, [While you and your fame will fade, The rivers flow on eternally]" in Wu Jiangxiong, *Mao Zedong tan gu lun jin*, Vol. 2, pp. 674–681.

11 Recent Mao Zedong Scholarship in China

XIAO YANZHONG

This chapter is a critical review of recent Mao Zedong scholarship in China based on a reading of relevant literature of nearly 3 million Chinese words. It aims to acquaint Western readers with the various points of view, assumptions, and controversies in Mao scholarship in the People's Republic of China (PRC). In consideration of the limited space, this chapter will give only a general account of the positions taken by Chinese scholars, with quotations only from original literature.

This chapter is divided into four parts: (1) the subtle changes of official ideology, (2) the criticisms of the Liberal school, (3) the arguments of the New Left scholars, and (4) the narratives of the Historical school. I will recapitulate the main points and themes of these schools in succession and then offer a brief conclusion.

THE SUBTLE CHANGES IN OFFICIAL IDEOLOGY

Official ideology refers to the interpretation of Mao and his thought by the ruling party [the Chinese Communist Party (CCP)], which controls the power of political discourse in Chinese Mao scholarship in order to reinforce its own political legitimacy. From this perspective, the primary task of Mao studies is to strengthen the influence of the official political discourse. It is worth noting that there exists an approach of subofficial ideology that reinterprets the official points of view on Mao by decorating them with academic language without deviating from the orthodox teaching. Researchers following this approach are usually from universities and the academies of social science at the central and provincial levels, whose essays dominate official academic journals.[1]

Translated by Huo Weian (霍伟岸), graduate student at Peking University, and Wang Ying (王英), graduate student at Renmin University of China. Final revisions and corrections by Timothy Cheek.

[1]   These official journals include *Zhonggong dang shi yanjiu* [CCP History Research] and *Dangde wenxian* [*CCP Literature*] both by the Party History Research Office of

While appreciating the advantages of other perspectives, this research group does not want to play a role in political and social criticism.

Since the "Resolution on Certain Questions in the History of Our Party Since the Founding of the Nation" (1981),[2] the official ideology has witnessed remarkable changes concerning the problematique of Mao, albeit in an implicit form. An obvious illustration can be cited from the Political Report presented by CCP General Secretary Hu Jintao to the Seventeenth National Congress of the party in 2007:

> The theory of socialism with Chinese characteristics constitutes a system of scientific theories including Deng Xiaoping Theory, the important thought of the Three Represents, and the Scientific Outlook on Development and other major strategic thought. This system represents the party's adherence to and development of Marxism-Leninism and Mao Zedong Thought and embodies the wisdom and hard work of several generations of Chinese Communists leading the people in carrying out tireless exploration and practice. It is the latest achievement in adapting Marxism to Chinese conditions, the party's invaluable political and intellectual asset, and the common ideological foundation for the concerted endeavor of the people of all ethnic groups.[3]

This official statement indicates that "Mao Zedong Thought" – in the form in which it exists in Mao's writings – is no longer part of the Theory of Socialism with Chinese Characteristics. Mao's ideas have been "enriched," that is, supplanted, by more recent ideological developments. In other words, the CCP no longer follows the guidance of Mao Zedong Thought, which has turned into an historical object on which the Theory of Socialism with Chinese Characteristics has been built.

To this important change in the political ideology, the authority of the CCP did not render any further explanation. However, Shi Zhongquan,

---

the Central Committee of the CCP, *Dangdai Zhongguo shi yanjiu* [Contemporary China History Studies] by the Contemporary China Research Institute and *Mao Zedong sixiang yu Deng Xiaoping lilun yanjiu* [Studies on MaoZedong and DengXiaoping Theories] by the Shanghai Academy of Social Sciences.

2   The English version can be found in *Beijing Review* 27 (July 6, 1981), pp. 10–39.

3   Hu Jintao, "Gaoju Zhongguo tese shehuizhuyi weida qizhi; Wei duoqu quanguo jianshe xiaokang shehui xinshengli er fendou [Hold High the Great Banner of Socialism with Chinese Characteristics and Strive for New Victories in Building a Moderately Prosperous Society Nationwide]," in *Shiqida baogao fudao duben* [A Guidebook for the Report to the Seventeenth National Congress of the Communist Party of China] (Beijing: People's Publishing House, 2007), p. 11.

the retired deputy director of the Party History Research Center of the CCP Central Committee, published two articles in *Wenhui Bao* and *Henan Daily* on November 7 and 13, 2007, respectively, explaining the ideological changes made by the central leaders of the CCP. The title of the second article is "Why Is Mao Zedong Thought Excluded from the Theory of Socialism with Chinese Characteristics?" According to Shi, history from 1949 to 1978 is called "modern" (*xiandai*), whereas from 1978 until now is called "contemporary" (*dangdai*). The various later contributions to the Theory of Socialism with Chinese Characteristics are concerned with contemporary China. In addition, Marxism as adapted to Chinese conditions can be divided into two parts: the foundation and the innovation. Mao Zedong Thought belongs to the former. Therefore, if the Theory of Socialism with Chinese Characteristics belongs to the part of innovation, "it is hard to say that the system contains Mao Zedong Thought."[4]

Although Shi's explanation did not receive much response from academic circles partly owing to its tortuous language, it has received much attention by the top leaders of the CCP. Xi Jinping, member of the Standing Committee of the CCP's Politburo, made a contribution to a core theoretical journal of the party recently, claiming that "Deng Xiaoping Theory, the important thought of the Three Represents, and the Scientific Outlook on Development and other major strategic thought inherit the great ideological heritage left by Comrade Mao in exploring the laws of socialist construction, while at the same time developing these important ideological fruits based on the new practice of reform and opening up." Finally, he asserts that Hu Jintao's judgment that "the Theory of Socialism with Chinese Characteristics represents the party's adherence to and development of the important ideological achievements made by Comrade Mao Zedong in exploring the law of socialist construction, and has clarified the internal link between this system and Mao Zedong Thought."[5]

For me, Xi's article is meant to clarify the intention of the CCP leadership both theoretically and in practice. It shows that in the

4   Shi Zhongquan, "Zhongguo tese shehuizhuyi lilun tixi wei shenmo bu baokuo Mao Zedong sixiang? [Why Is Mao Zedong Thought Excluded from the Theory of Socialism with Chinese Characteristics?]," *Henan ribao*, November 13, 2007; "Zhongguo tese shehuizhuyi lilun tixi: Dangdai Zhongguo chuanxin lilun de kexue tixi [The Theory of Socialism with Chinese Characteristics: A Scientific System of Innovative Theory in Contemporary China]," *Wenhui bao*, November 7, 2007.

5   Xi Jinping, "Guanyu Zhongguo tese shehuizhuyi lilun tixi de jidian xuexi tihui he renshi [Some Lessons and Understandings Concerning the Theory of Socialism with Chinese Characteristics]," *Qiushi* [Seeking Truth] 7 (2008).

official ideological system, Mao's thought and image are still a sensitive political problem. In the framework of the official ideology, however, Mao Zedong Thought seems merely to be a symbol for political legitimacy.

In terms of academic value, the most important research achievement from the perspective of the official ideology is doubtlessly the *Biography of Mao Zedong, 1949–1976*, published in two volumes by the Central Literature Publishing House in 1996 and 2003.[6] On the value of the book's historical materials, Pang Xianzhi, former director of the Party Literature Research Center of the CCP Central Committee as well as editor-in-chief of the *Biography*, made the following comment: The book "makes use of and discloses a large amount of first-hand archive materials" to tell a good story of the first 27 years of the People's Republic of China from 1949 to 1976: "[I]t has put much ink to these major events, giving detailed accounts of their causes, background, course, historical effects, Mao's decision-making concerning them, and the interaction between Mao and other leaders in the process of decision-making, etc.... The biggest feature of the *Biography* is to tell the truth with facts."[7] It is understandable that the writing of the *Biography* cannot go against the principle of avoiding things that might hurt the reputation of notable people, a tradition in orthodox Chinese historiography. But as Li Jie, deputy director of the Party Literature Research Center, as well as one of the major contributors to the *Biography*, put it: "To be honest, we cannot write everything in the book because of the limited space and various contingent limitations. We found some things difficult to incorporate into the book. The main reason is not because if this were done, it would hurt Mao's reputation, but that someone else who is still alive might suffer. So there are still some forbidden zones in the book. But we assure the reader that all the things we have written are true."[8] In sum, from the perspective of historiography, the book is one of the most important contributions to recent Chinese Mao scholarship.

---

[6] Pang Xianzhi and Jiu Chongqui, eds., *Mao Zedong zhuan* (Beijing: Zhongyang wenxian chubanshe, 1996, Vol. 1; 2003, Vol. 2).

[7] Pang Xianzhi, "*Mao Zedong zhuan* dui jianguo hou zhongda lishi wenti de yanjiu [Research on the Great Historical Questions Since the Founding of the People's Republic of China in the *Biography of Mao Zedong*]," in *Dangde wenxian* [*Party Literature*] 2 (2006).

[8] Li Jie: "*Dui Mao Zedong xin Zhonguo tansuo de zai sikao* [A Reconsideration of Mao's New China Exploration]," *Hunan keji daxue xuebao: Shehui kexue ban* [Journal of Hunan University of Science and Technology: Social Science Edition] 2 (2006).

THE CRITICISMS OF THE LIBERAL SCHOOL

In general, Chinese scholars doing research from the perspective of liberalism hold a strongly critical attitude toward Mao. If a certain degree of reductionism is allowed, we can identify five critical elements from their research as a whole. They are the utopianism in Mao's belief system, his personal despotism in politics, his political scheming, a narcissistic tendency in his psychology, and his political cognitive structure integrating the above-mentioned four elements. Liberal scholars argue that all these elements led Mao in his later years to a political track that imposed great adverse influence on China's normal development.

The Liberal school can be divided into the radical wing and the moderate wing. Basically, the radical wing rejects Mao's political thought and behavior in his later years. The view of Li Rui, a famous Mao scholar in China, is typical of this school. He made a general assessment of Mao in three sentences: "He contributed to China's Revolution, made mistakes in his reign, and committed a crime in launching the Cultural Revolution."[9] Li argues

He [Mao] hoped to be both a king and a mentor, both the First Emperor of China and Confucius.... With the rulership of China in his hands and the overturning of the Three Big Mountains of imperialism, feudalism, and bureaucracy, Mao attempted to rule the country by carrying out Mao Zedong Thought. It was Mao himself who added "Long Live Chairman Mao" to the May Day slogan released in 1950. In this way Mao made the whole country come over and pledge allegiance to him, who, as both the emperor and the mentor, was extremely conceited and could decide everything. Especially after the disclosure of the Stalin issue, Mao increasingly persisted in his old ways and could not tolerate any challenge to him. While knowing the mistakes he had made in the "Great Leap Forward," the "emperor" could never blame himself, and even proposed formally in a meeting that "some degree of personality cult is necessary." Therefore, without democracy, the rule of law, and restraints on power, Mao, whose literary talent and

---

[9] Li Rui, "Ruhe kandai Mao Zedong: Hafo daxue Fei Zhengqing dongya yanjiu zhongxin juban de Mao Zedong danchen de 100 zhounian xueshu taolunhui de fayan gao [How to Look at Mao Zedong: A Speech Delivered at the Symposium in Commemoration of the 110th Anniversary of Mao's Birthday Held by Fairbank Center for East Asian Research, Harvard University]," in *Li Rui tan Mao Zedong* [Li Rui Talking About Mao Zedong] (Hong Kong: Shidai guoji chuban youxian gongsi, 2005), p. 2.

military achievement is not inferior to that of any sage emperor in imperial China, went so far in taking his own course willfully.[10]

The monographs by Shan Shaojie and Xin Ziling express a similar attitude.[11]

The moderate wing of the Liberal school pays more attention to the nature and internal logic of the Mao problematique while at the same time avoiding making emotional reviews. As a participant in these historical events, Wang Ruoshui's remarks can be said to be to the point. Wang's general assessment of Mao was: "First, loneliness, fear, alienation. Second, no personal relationships; comrades and friends were tools for Mao to achieve his own political aims. Third, the greatest feature of Mao's character was taking on challenges, flaunting his superiority, and enjoying victory. Fourth, the books Mao read frequently were 'string-bound books' (i.e., traditional Chinese texts), he read *The Mirror of Government* from the Song Dynasty seventeen times, but rarely read any Western works, even a single classic of Marxism. Fifth, anything that Mao had decided he did not want others to oppose; he never corrected his mistakes or repented."[12]

From a more academic perspective, a scholar noted that for Mao, "coming to power was just the beginning, what he really wanted was an unprecedented revolution to reconstruct society radically."[13] As a man who disliked talking about theories in the abstract, Mao tended, in his political practice, to define the thought of the proletariat as "common" or "public" (*gong* 公), the thought of the bourgeoisie as "private" (*si* 私). By infusing the concept of common good into and driving that of private interest out from the mind of the people, Mao was prepared to attack human nature. In this way emerged the concept of "the class struggle in the ideological field." Thus it is less exact to say that despotism characterizes Mao's reign than that deep inside Mao's thought lay a paradoxical structure:

> On one hand, although Mao was proud of his persistent position against feudalism, his despotism was worse than that of most

[10] *Ibid.*, p. 3.

[11] Shan Shaojie, *Mao Zedong zhizheng chunqiu* [Mao Zedong in Power (1949–1976)] (Hong Kong: Mingjing chubanshe, 2000); Xin Ziling: *Hong taiyang de yunluo* [The Red Sun Falling from the Sky] (Hong Kong: Shuzuo fang, 2008).

[12] Wang Ruoshui, *Xin faxian de Mao Zedong: Puren yanzhong de weiren* [A Newly Discovered Mao Zedong: The Great Man in the Eyes of His Servant] (Hong Kong: Mingbao chubanshe, 2002), esp. pp. 2–3.

[13] Wang Lixiong, "Mao Zedongzhuyi yu renjian tiantang [Maoism and the Earthly Paradise]," in Song Yongyi, ed., *Wenhua da geming: Lishi zhenxiang he jiti jilü* [Cultural Revolution: Historical Truth and Collective Memory], Vol. 1 (Hong Kong: Maitian shuwu, 2007), p. 205.

emperors of China. On the other hand, he tried to endow the masses at the grassroots level with a rather high political position and rights, continuously practicing his ideal of people's sovereignty. It is true that politicians always pay lip service to the people, but Mao was the only one who motivated and mobilized the masses to overturn the political and party systems under his rulership.[14]

It is the coexistence of and balance between this "serious despotism" and "people's sovereignty" in Mao's thought that constitutes the focus of research. Behind the seeming contradiction lies a strong motivation to change the political order by transforming people's souls.

One scholar describes the distinguishing feature of Mao's thought as a "papacy complex," that is, a desire to nurture and cultivate the secular society in the name of an agent of some sovereign spiritual authority. This self-appointed role has

> ... as a necessary logical result the belief in the power of moral force and mass movements. The main responsibility of the papacy is to preach rather than to order. To some extent, it is the papacy complex that distinguishes Mao from other dictators in the world. To force a change in the mind and to order the "voluntary" confession of the "crime committed" is one of the political arts of theocracy. But the force of morality Mao believed in was mainly that of his own; in truth his belief in the masses was that he only believed in those masses who blindly followed him, and he valued the passion instead of the sense of the masses.... Mao never regarded "the masses" as a group of individuals equal to himself. The value of the existence of "the masses" was to legitimize his control of sovereign power; the masses only had instrumental value. The point of the slogan "Serve the People" was not "the people" but "the serving." "The people" were there to offer rather than to receive service. Actually, "the people" referred to a group that could only be served but could not do service themselves.... Due to the ignorance of the masses, China could only follow the road of despotism. Given this, all the political struggles were necessarily those about who would be the dictator. This was the core of Mao Zedong Thought.[15]

[14] *Ibid.*, pp. 225–226.
[15] Ren Bumei, "Xueshu shiye zhongde Mao Zedong sixiang [Mao Zedong's Thought from an Academic Perspective]"; available at http://bmzy.126.com.

Obviously, the radical wing of the Liberal school continued the critical trend of social thought of the 1980s with its methodological basis in empirical and intuitive judgments. Their remarks are, to a large extent, the result of reflecting on the painful history of such political movements as the Anti-Rightist Movement, the Great Leap Forward, and the Cultural Revolution. On the one hand, they stick to the tradition of Chinese historiography, including Confucius' techniques of moral evaluation in *The Spring and Autumn Annals* [*Chunqiu*] writing and Sima Qian's principle of history writing in *Historical Records* [*Shiji*] that a clear judgment must be made on historical events with moral implications even under great political pressures.[16] On the other hand, however, these critical statements leave the reader with a strong impression that the history of China from 1949 to 1976 seems to be only a record of Mao's follies. Indeed, we admire these authors' conscientious responsibility and moral strength toward history, but academically, they fail to give satisfactory answers to such complicated questions as "How can one man control history so completely?" In contrast, the arguments of the moderate wing contain a clear, logical structure. Following their approach, the social phenomena that resulted from the spirit of Maoism, such as the personality cult, anti-intellectualism, and populism, can be explained and understood in a theoretical rather than intuitive way.

THE ARGUMENTS OF THE NEW LEFT SCHOLARS

In line with the overall transformation of Chinese academic circles, one of the most important changes in Mao scholarship in China since 1990 is the rise of the trend of New Left [*xin zuoyi*] thought.

According to Xiao Gongqin, the New Left school also can be divided into the moderate wing (postmodernism) and the radical wing (populism).[17] I will focus my remarks on the former. These scholars often

---

[16] Confucius' approach to historical writing in the *Chunqiu* entailed facing a crumbling era that was past all redemption, so he wrote the history of Lü Kingdom in the *Chunqiu* by making implicit moral judgments on the merits and faults of historical personalities. Some scholars argue that China's cultural tradition did not contain religion in the Western sense, but its rich historical literature actually played a similar role in formulating value standards and in making social criticism. For English readers, see Hsiao Kung-ch'uan (Xiao Gongquan), *A History of Chinese Political Thought*, trans. by Frederick W. Mote (Princeton, NJ: Princeton University Press, 1979).

[17] Xiao Gongqin, "Xin zuopai yu dangdai Zhongguo zhishifenzide sixiang fenhua Sichao: Zhongguo [The New Left and the Ideological Split Among Contemporary Chinese Intellectuals]," in Gong Yang, ed., "*Sichao: Zhongguo "xin zuopai" jiqi yingxiang* [Tides of Thought: China's New Left and their Influence] (Beijing: China Social Science Publishing House, 2003), pp. 406–414.

have a background in Western education or are quite familiar with modern Western social and political theories. Their theoretical assumptions often come from neo-Marxism or postmodern theories. Their theories are characterized by a high level of awareness and alertness toward the globalization of the international market economy and the damage that the trend of boundless consumption may do to human nature. They are also deeply concerned about the evils of modernity in postcapitalist society, in particular its adverse effects on contemporary Chinese society, such as the distortion of value and morality as well as the huge inequality of economic status. As a result, they hope to build a new society different from the Western mode.[18] These New Left scholars are critical of the mainstream ideology of Western liberalism. They do not totally deny China's reform and opening-up policy but argue that the evils caused by the new policy need to be remedied by "the real spirit of Mao."

The remedies proposed by the New Left scholars can be summed up in two essential thoughts: One is the "rigid triangle" theory based on egalitarianism, moralism, and nationalism; the other is a theory of Mao's advanced thought, which can be seen as a result of that triangle.

From the first perspective, New Left scholars argue that the reason Mao launched the Cultural Revolution was to defeat his political opponents as well as to resolve the international difficulty of preventing the bureaucratization necessarily caused by the process of rationality in the Weberian sense. Thus the "Great Democracy" advocated by Mao in his late years was "to endow the people with full freedom of assembly, association, press, and speech," and the radical revolutionary ideology of the Left became the weapon of the people, instead of the empty creed or tool of bureaucrats. This was without a doubt an unprecedented "large-scale experiment in political reform."[19] Mao in his later years referred to

---

[18] The theoretical sources of the Chinese New Left are, on the one hand, Antonio Gramsci's theory of cultural hegemony and Louis Althusser's overdetermination theory, and, on the other, Fredric Jameson and Arif Dirlik's postmodernism or the cultural logic of late capitalism. See Tong Xiaoxi, "The Dialectic of Elites and the Masses: Mao Zedong's Political Sociology," *Hunan keji daxue xuebao: Shehui kexue ban* [Journal of Hunan University of Science and Technology: Social Science Edition] 2 (2008); Guo Jian, "Dangdai zuopai wenhua lilun zhongde wenge youling [The Specter of the Cultural Revolution Looming in Contemporary Left-Wing Cultural Theory]," in *Ershiyi shiji* [21st Century] (Hong Kong) 2 (2006). A good set of translations from these Chinese New Left writers, including Cui Zhiyuan and Wang Hui, appears in Xudong Zhang, ed., *Whither China? Intellectual Politics in Contemporary China* (Durham, NC: Duke University Press, 2001).

[19] Xiao Xidong, "'Liangge wenge,' huo yige wenge? ['Two Cultural Revolutions,' or One?]," in Luo Jinyi and Zheng Wenlong, eds., *Haojie yiwai: Zailun wenhua da*

"the group of bureaucrats within the party" as "the bourgeoisie within the party." It is true that Rosa Luxemburg, Leon Trotsky, and Milovan Djilas had proposed the concepts of a new bureaucracy and new class of communism before Mao, "but what distinguishes Mao from others is that he, in the capacity of a political leader, had the courage to propose a theory for preventing the emergence of a new class in socialist society and for realizing extensive democracy, and even to put it into practice."[20] Thus, if it is possible to reinterpret the "extensive democracy" of the Cultural Revolution in a new historical context, at least the An Gang Constitution[21] is "the part that deserves most of our attention." "It is a necessary condition for building China's highly democratic political system in the 21st century to dialectically develop the useful and discard the useless parts of Mao's Cultural Revolution theory."[22]

Wang Hui, a famous New Left scholar, pointed out recently that depoliticization as an important feature of modernity tries to use neutral discourse such as market economy and globalization to disguise and replace the realities of political subjection in party politics, theoretical debates, and class problems. For Wang, this wave of "depoliticized politics" has spread across the world and has posed a "global problem" over the last few decades. In China's case, the Cultural Revolution is paradigmatic of "politicization" owing to its "efforts to carry out a social remobilization and to stimulate political spheres and political values outside the party-state context in order to create a mass participatory democracy." "Mao reaffirmed the political values of the revolutionary

geming [Beyond the Great Disaster: Cultural Revolution Revisited] (Taipei: Feng Yun Forum, 1997), pp. 136–172.

[20] Cui Zhiyuan, "Mao Zedong 'wenge' lilunde deshi yu 'xiandaixing'de chongjian [The Success and Failure of Mao Zedong's Cultural Revolution Theory, and the Reconstruction of Modernity]," in Xianggang shehui kexue xuebao [Hong Kong Social Sciences] 7 (Spring 1996), pp. 49–74. Extensive democracy (da minzhu) was promoted in the Cultural Revolution as allowing the masses freely to put up big-character posters, hold great debates, and carry out exchanges of revolutionary experience (by traveling around the country); see Lin Biao's call to Red Guards to carry out "extensive democracy" in Renmin ribao [People's Daily], November 4, 1966.

[21] The An Gang Constitution refers to the comments Mao wrote on "The Report on the Development of the Movement of Technical Innovation and Revolution on the Industrial Battlefront by the An Shan Municipal Party Committee," approved and transmitted by the CCP Central Committee in March 1960. The core content of Mao's comments is "Cadres should participate in labor, and workers should participate in management. Unreasonable rules and systems should be reformed. Technicians, managers, and workers should cooperate in production practice and technical innovation."

[22] Cui Zhiyuan, "An Gang xianfa yu hou-Futezhuyi [The An Gang Constitution and Post-Fordism]," Dushu [Reading] (March 1996).

party and attempted to smash the absolute authority of the party and the state through political debate and social activism. His purpose was to establish a social mechanism with the impulse of self-critique and self-negation, which would not be a state in the conventional sense but one capable of self-critique and self-negation."[23] However, with the disappearance of the 1960s came the sweeping wave of depoliticization. Disillusioned with revolution in general, people turned to economic life and began to venerate pragmatism. Through new political arrangements that were accomplished under the rubric of depoliticization, new social inequalities were naturalized. In conclusion, Wang claims that the political essence of criticizing modernity in Mao's Cultural Revolution will be revealed naturally with the disappearance of the guise of depoliticized politics.

From the second perspective, some New Left scholars believe that Mao's thought in his later years has been seriously misunderstood because the problems highlighted by Mao at that time were far beyond the understanding of the general public or even top party leaders. According to He Xin, in the era when all communists in the world regarded the works of Marx and Lenin as the "political Bible," Mao "encouraged the people to take care of state affairs with the spirit of independent thinking, urged rebellion against authority and the courage to go against the stream, and advocated extensive democracy. In this way he replaced the collective rationality of party organizations and society with personal rationality as the standard of authority. This just characterized the spirit of enlightenment." Since Mao's thought was far more advanced, it was hard to understand for the common people. Therefore, the Cultural Revolution should be seen as "Mao's Religious Reformation Movement in Contemporary China."[24] Some even claim that "Mao played a role in communism similar to F. W. Nietzsche in Christianity!"[25] Mao is doubtless subject to controversy, but it is his advanced creative criticism that stimulates endless debates. One netizen goes so far as to compare the Cultural Revolution to Mao's cross: "Christ was betrayed by Judas and had to die. He chose to die and carried the cross on which he was

---

[23] Wang Hui, *Quzhengzhihuade zhengzhi: Duan 20 shijide zongjie yu 90 niandai* [Depoliticized Politics: The End of the Short Twentieth Century and the 1990s] (Beijing: Sanlian shudian, 2008), pp. 14–15.

[24] He Xin, "Lun wenhua da geming yu Mao Zedong wanqi sixiang [On the Cultural Revolution and Mao Zedong's Thought in His Late Years]"; available at www.hexinchina.com, 2004-4-8.

[25] Wu Zhenrong, "Lun 'shinian wenge' zhongde Mao Zedong [On Mao Zedong of the Cultural Revolution Decade]"; available at www.newcenturynews.com, 2006-11-15.

going to die to the execution ground. Mao also had to carry such a cross to die, which was the Cultural Revolution. Different from Christ, Mao was willing and careful to build the cross and to die on it.... Mao 'killed himself' on the 'cross' but liberated the people. Those saved by Mao released him from the cross, and thus he was resurrected and will never die any more, becoming the refuge of the heart and soul of every weak person."[26]

In my view, the reinterpretation of Mao's thought in his later years by the New Left and their reflection on the problems of modernity are doubtless profound and provocative. But it is worth noting that through their reinterpretation, the rich and complicated history of Mao's thinking becomes a coherent theory, and Mao as both a statesman and political thinker is taken out of historical context, with his personal impulses and strong desires being abstracted as an idealized picture with universal implications. As a result, what the New Left scholars have constructed is actually a "should be" Mao by inevitably projecting their own vision of a hero into a charismatic personality.

THE NARRATIVES OF THE HISTORICAL SCHOOL

In striking contrast to the approach of the New Left that focuses on theoretical analysis is the Historical school. These well-trained historians firmly believe that historical interpretation has to be based on historical facts, including archives, documents, and oral materials. For them, theoretical overinterpretation, though popular for a while, will not last long. For these scholars, when an interpreter takes historical personalities, in particular, their fragmented words, out of their context, many conclusions go against common sense and fail to give a real picture of Mao.

Gao Hua's *How the Red Sun Rose: A History of the Yan'an Rectification Movement* (2000) tells a detailed story of "how Mao came to be widely recognized as the top leader of the party and how Mao Zedong Thought came to be the guiding ideology of the party," by patiently collecting, selecting, investigating, and comparing various historical materials (given the unavailability of essential archives). The book gives a thick description with many details of the story, combining organizational mechanisms, ideological infusion, emotional communication, and political integration. Talking about his motivation to

---

[26] Anonymous, "Gudude Mao Zedong [A Lonely Mao Zedong]"; available at www.wyzxsx.com/Article/Class14/200709/23852.html; accessed July 22, 2009.

write the book, Gao said: "From the perspective of the CCP overturning the Guomindang's rule through revolution, the Yan'an Rectification Movement contributed greatly to the success of the CCP's revolution. On the other hand, however, some concepts and paradigms from the movement exerted an adverse influence on the development and progress of China in that the ultra-leftist thought and political schemes converged to point the ideological field to a series of ultra-leftist movements after 1949 and eventually to the disaster of the Cultural Revolution." Gao added that his own concern was to "judge the things hidden under the publicly expressed discourse."[27] History circles praised Gao's book as "the fullest and the most accurate research on the Yan'an Rectification Movement," a masterpiece showing how the CCP "radically changed its Russian characteristics and rebuilt the superstructure with Mao as the sovereign authority, from which it generated a series of concepts and paradigms that changed the life and fate of millions of Chinese people after 1949."[28] In my opinion, the value of Gao's contribution lies not only in its excellent arrangement of historical materials but also in its correction of, departure from, and even subversion of the official interpretative structure established by Chen Boda and Hu Qiaomu since the 1940s. With a brand-new mode of historical narrative, Gao's monograph has become paradigmatic of the new historiography in the CCP.

As famous researchers on contemporary Chinese history, Shen Zhihua and Yang Kuisong have published several influential books and numerous papers on cold war history, the CCP, and Mao.[29] Their contributions can be seen in two respects. On the one hand, they have corrected long-established misconceptions of historical facts and revealed the historical process unknown before. For example, when the Polish crisis broke out in 1956, Khrushchev arrived in Warsaw to meet with Gomulka on October 19 in an attempt to force the Polish people to submit. But Khrushchev chose to go back to the Soviet Union only on the second day while at the same time the Russian Army stopped military

---

[27] Gao Hua, "Wo weishenme yanjiu Yan'an zhengfeng [Why I Research the Yan'an Rectification Movement]," in *Hong taiyang shi zenyang shengqi de: Yan'an zhengfeng yundong de lailong qumai* [How the Red Sun Rose: The Origins and Development of the Yan'an Rectification Movement] (Hong Kong: Zhongwen daxue chubanshe, 2000) pp. 655, 653.

[28] Han Gang, "Zhonggong lishi yanjiude ruogan redian nandian wenti [Some Topical and Difficult Problems in CCP History Research]"; available at www.xschina.org, 2008–6–24.

[29] See their personal Web pages: www.yangkuisong.net and www.shenzhihua.net. A representative book is Yang Kuisong, *Kaijuan youyi* [Reading Books Causes Doubts] (Nanchang: Jiangxi renmin chubanshe, 2007).

action. However, according to the memory of Wu Lengxi, who attended
the meeting of the CCP politburo as a nonvoting delegate, the reason
was that when Mao received the notice from the Communist Party
of the Soviet Union (CPSU) that it would take military action against
Poland, he urgently summoned the Soviet ambassador and expressed
China's strong opposition to it. But the declassified minutes of the
Presidium of the Central Committee of the CPSU and the telegraphs
sent to the Soviet embassy in China show that at that time the CPSU
did not intend to disclose to the CCP anything about its planned military action against Poland, and Mao did not know about it until the
crisis was put to an end. Thus the mistaken memory of an important
participant of the historical event was corrected.[30] On the other hand,
the two authors try to reveal the causes and effects of a seemingly isolated incident by linking it to multiple relevant elements in the original
context. For instance, how does one explain why Mao, who used to be
perspicacious, got carried away by the Great Leap Forward that practiced fraud, even to the point that he radically changed his state of mind
and never repented his erroneous decisions that led to a series of serious
political events? Yang's research approach is, first of all, to restore the
rather complicated historical situation with which Mao was confronted
in 1958: (1) At the end of 1957, the United States unilaterally downgraded
its negotiator with the People's Republic of China (PRC) from ambassador to chargé d'affaires, (2) in late July of the same year, the Soviet Union
proposed to establish a long-wave radio station and a joint submarine
fleet with China under unequal terms, and (3) given prosperous economic prospects in 1957, the editorial of the *People's Daily* on January
1, 1958, declared that China would spend about 15 years catching up
with Great Britain economically and another 20 to 30 years to catch
up with the United States. Thereafter began the vigorous Great Leap
Forward. When we put Mao's way of decision making into the context of
the triangular relations among China, the United States, and the Soviet
Union as well as the Great Leap Forward, it can be seen that "since
Mao had long had a feeling of oppression and humiliation in handling
relations with the two great powers of the United States and the Soviet
Union, the conspicuous achievements of the Great Leap Forward gave
him unprecedented spiritual relief and made him feel proud and elated.
Therefore, he would be sensitive and react drastically to the contempt
with which the United States and the Soviet Union dealt with China.

---

[30] Shen Zhihua, "Archives: Restoring Historical Truth," *Beijing Daily*, November 28,
2005.

That's why afterwards even when acknowledging that the claims of the Great Leap Forward could largely be ascribed to pompous statistics, he was always hostile to any negative remarks about it." Researchers should not "overlook the psychological effect that the extremely special situation had imposed on Mao, and the influence of the Great Leap Forward that trapped him into a state of ecstasy." Hence we can see it is rather superficial to explain Mao's launch and defense of the Great Leap Forward merely in terms of his personality characteristics, such as his craving for greatness and success or his psychology of jealousy.[31]

In this way, the Historical school shows its strength by "telling the truth with facts." But the event-centered research approach might ignore the perspective of long-term historical observation and sacrifice the transgenerational and transindividual vantage point particular to historiography. Additionally, since these historians do not take kindly to the crude intrusions of ideological power into their historical narratives, they almost unconsciously exclude any research associated with official historiography. However, this emotional preference unfairly smears those portions of official history writing that do have value with one broad brush.

CONCLUSION

The controversies in Mao scholarship in China have a double meaning: On the one hand, Mao studies in China from various perspectives and at different levels form a diversified system of scholarship that is the presupposition of academic discussion. In this sense, fierce contention marks the real beginnings of Mao scholarship. On the other hand, the continual interest in Mao indicates that to a certain degree Mao has become a symbol. On the surface, scholars are discussing an irreplaceable statesman and political thinker, but their real concern is the political development of contemporary China. Hence we have good reason to believe that Mao will long be an important topic in China's academic circles. There seems no sign of compromise among the above-mentioned approaches to Mao, and violent controversy will continue. For me, Mao scholarship is always a bellwether that can indicate changes in China's politics, economy, and society, as well as the state of mind of the Chinese people.

[31] Yang Kuisong, *Mao Zedong yu Mosikede enenyuanyuan* [Gratitude and Resentment Between Mao Zedong and Moscow] (Nanchang: Jiangxi People's Publishing House, 2005), pp. 10–11.

12 Third World Maoism

ALEXANDER C. COOK

The idea of the third world developed in the wake of World War II to describe the nations of Asia, Africa, and Latin America. While the first world of capitalism led by the United States and the second world of socialism led by the Soviet Union fought for global domination in the cold war, the third world often was the battleground and theater of operations. This supposedly underdeveloped third world served simultaneously as the cannon fodder, barometer, and spoils of a war over the fate of global modernity – as that two-thirds of the world with "its futures mortgaged to either capitalism or socialism."[1] Obviously, this cold war model discounts the third world, seeing it as the passive object of a contested but nevertheless teleological history. The people of the third world did not necessarily share this view, instead seeing the postwar period as a global moment of anticolonial, anti-imperialist movements. Revolutionaries seized on their designation as third world subjects to push for solidarity in what they perceived as a shared struggle for national liberation. For many, Maoism provided the ideological underpinnings and a practical blueprint for the struggle.

THIRD WORLD TO THREE WORLDS

Maoism and the Emergence of the Third World

Mao's China took an interest in third world politics from the beginning, dispatching senior statesman Zhou Enlai to attend its seminal organizing moment, the 29-nation Afro-Asian Conference held in Bandung, Indonesia, in April 1955. The third world movement taking shape at the Bandung conference was essentially a nonaligned movement, seeking a "third way" beyond the development models of the two cold war superpowers. Accordingly, Zhou Enlai there promoted the

---

[1] Arif Dirlik, "Spectres of the Third World: Global Modernity and the End of the Three Worlds," *Third World Quarterly* 25:1 (2004), p. 131.

so-called Five Principles of Peaceful Coexistence recently negotiated between China and India – a stance of ideological neutrality that still informs Chinese foreign policy today.[2] Despite this official doctrine of noninterference, the founding of the People's Republic of China (PRC) in 1949 had provided third world revolutionaries with a concrete historical example of winning national liberation through a strategy of "people's war."

Mao's revolutionary strategy embraced the peasantry as "the biggest motive force of the ... revolution, the natural and most reliable ally of the proletariat, and the main contingent of [the] revolutionary forces."[3] The doctrine of people's war empowered the world's peasants – the third world – to rise up just as Mao once had predicted China's peasants would:

> They will rise up like a mighty storm, like a hurricane, a force
> so swift and violent that no power, however great, will be able to
> hold it back. They will smash all the trammels that bind them
> and rush forward along the road to liberation. They will sweep all
> the imperialists, warlords, corrupt officials, local tyrants and evil
> gentry into their graves.[4]

Just as prerevolutionary China consisted of a vast semifeudal countryside surrounding a few semicolonial cities, so too was the third world an impoverished hinterland to the developed world: "Taking the entire globe, if North America and Western Europe can be called 'the cities of the world,' then Asia, Africa and Latin America constitute 'the rural areas of the world.'"[5] The metaphorical implication was clear. Peasant insurgencies in their particular national contexts were part and parcel of the world revolution; soon the global countryside would overwhelm the global cities. By the mid-1960s, Maoist insights into peasant insurgency

---

[2] The Five Principles of Peaceful Coexistence are mutual respect for territorial integrity and sovereignty, mutual nonaggression, noninterference in each other's internal affairs, equality and mutual benefit, and peaceful coexistence. See "Premier Chou En-lai's Main Speech at the Plenary Session of the Asian-African Conference," April 19, 1955, in *China Supports the Arab People's Struggle for National Independence: A Selection of Important Documents*, compiled by Chinese People's Institute of Foreign Affairs (Peking: Foreign Languages Press, 1958), pp. 9–19.

[3] Mao Zedong, "The Chinese Revolution and the Chinese Communist Party" (December 1939), *Marxists Internet Archive (MIA)*; available at www.marxists.org/reference/archive/mao/selected-works/volume-2/mswv2_23.htm.

[4] Mao Zedong, "Report on an Investigation of the Peasant Movement in Hunan," March 1927, *MIA*; available at www.marxists.org/reference/archive/mao/selected-works/volume-1/mswv1_2.htm#s5.

[5] Lin Biao, "Long Live the Victory of People's War!" September 1965, *MIA*; available at www.marxists.org/reference/archive/lin-biao/1965/09/peoples_war/ch07.htm.

had exerted influence among revolutionaries both near and far, from Korea and Vietnam to Cuba and the Congo. Thus could Mao's closest comrade-in-arms Lin Biao brag in "Long Live the People's War" (1965):

> Comrade Mao Zedong's theory of people's war has been proved by the long practice of the Chinese revolution to be in accord with the objective laws of such wars and to be invincible. It has not only been valid for China, it is a great contribution to the revolutionary struggles of the oppressed nations and peoples throughout the world.[6]

Maoism initially appealed as a military doctrine, as a way to mobilize peasant society for the goal of national liberation.

It was really only after the emergence of the Sino-Soviet split in the 1960s – and especially after the onset of the Cultural Revolution (CR) in 1966 – that Maoism was appreciated in the third world as a complete military, political, cultural, and economic ideology distinct from Soviet communism. The deepening rift between the world's two largest socialist nations had many causes. The Soviets were alarmed by China's increasingly reckless policies, both domestic and foreign. The Chinese Communist Party (CCP), in turn, accused the Soviets of capitulationism (proposing peaceful coexistence between irreconcilable capitalism and socialism), revisionism (advocating the peaceful transition to socialism), and social imperialism (heavy-handed interference in foreign communist movements). Within the global communist camp, the Maoist position was a minority view: The mainstream parties siding with China came from smaller nations such as Albania, Burma, Thailand, and Indonesia. Nevertheless, nearly every national communist organization also produced a breakaway Maoist faction. This chapter focuses on some of those parties that advocated Maoism as a dynamic and uncompromising ideology of revolution.

As the other chapters in this book attest, Maoism is a complex and sometimes contradictory set of ideas and practices that have developed over time. These ideas and practices have continued to develop in different ways in the varied historical contexts of the third world. Nevertheless, certain aspects have been emphasized with more or less consistency as Maoism has traveled around the globe. The following section takes up the example of Maoism in India to introduce and explain the common features of what we might generally call "third world Maoism."

---

[6]   Lin, "Long Live the Victory."

China's Path Is Our Path: The Case of the
Communist Party of India (Marxist-Leninist)

The most important attempt to emulate an explicitly Maoist revolution in Mao's lifetime occurred in India, which had achieved independence from the British Empire and established a parliamentary
democracy in 1947. A peasant insurrection, beginning in May 1967
in the village of Naxalbari in the Darjeeling District of West Bengal,
soon spread across India and over the borders into neighboring Nepal
and Bengal (then called East Pakistan, now Bangladesh). This so-called
Naxalite movement, under the guidance of the Maoist Communist
Party of India (Marxist-Leninist) (CPI-ML), was primarily a rural insurgency but also drew support from urban intellectuals and even inspired
students to launch a small-scale "cultural revolution" on the streets
of Calcutta in 1970. However, Indian security forces had effectively
repressed the Naxalites by the end of 1970 and in 1972 killed their top
leader, Charu Mazumdar. The movement in India soon died down into
a smoldering, low-level insurgency, although in the long term it influenced the successful Maoist revolution that erupted in Nepal in the
1990s. More important for our purposes here, the Naxalite case illustrates the three most salient features of third world Maoism: (1) analysis
of society as semifeudal and semicolonial, (2) adoption of the strategy
and tactics of people's war to seize state power, and (3) mirroring the
domestic Chinese agenda of the CR, continuation of the revolution to
combat revisionism and establish socialism.

The decisive influence of the CR is reflected in the texts most widely
cited by the Naxalites, which included two small CR-era distillations of
Mao Zedong's works, both compiled by Lin Biao: "the Little Red Book"
(*Quotations from Chairman Mao*, in both English and Bengali) and
"The Three Old Essays.[7] Also well known were Mao Zedong's incendiary "Report on an Investigation of the Peasant Movement in Hunan"
(1927), his military treatises "On Guerrilla Warfare" (1937) and "On
Protracted War" (1938), and Lin Biao's paean to Mao, "Long Live the
Victory of People's War!" (1965). The Naxalites also were avid readers of
China's English-language periodical *Peking Review*, which ran frequent
reports on the Indian insurgency in the late 1960s. This same corpus
of texts would inspire later third world Maoist movements. Thus the
version of Maoism emulated in the third world was, and continues to

---

[7] Sreemati Chakrabarti, *China and the Naxalites* (New Delhi: Radiant, 1990),
pp. 60–62. The "Three Old Essays" are "Serve the People" (1944), "Remembering
Norman Bethune" (1939), and "The Foolish Old Man Who Moved the Mountains"
(1945).

be, the relatively late and retrospective ideology of China's CR period. Here, all the experiences of a half-century of Chinese Revolution are condensed into digest form, and the most recent development, the rejection of Soviet revisionism, is given utmost prominence.

In the third world, under the influence of the CR, party splits and purges preceded even the initiation of people's war. The Naxalites' CPI-ML (formally organized on April 22, 1969, the one-hundredth anniversary of Lenin's birth) emerged from two major party splits, first along the international lines of the Sino-Soviet conflict and again in opposition to perceived revisionism at the national party level.[8] The original Communist Party of India (CPI), founded overseas in 1920 and established in India in 1925, maintained close ties with the Communist Party of the Soviet Union (CPSU) and its Communist International (Comintern). By contrast, CPI relations with the CCP were severely strained by the Chinese invasion of buffer state Tibet in the 1950s, the Sino-Indian border clash of 1962, and China's steadfast support of rival Pakistan. Despite the depth of Sino-Indian tensions, in 1964, the larger Sino-Soviet split inspired a broad antirevisionist group to break away from the CPI, rejecting parliamentary democracy in favor of violent revolution. This antirevisionist group divided yet again in 1967, at the height of China's CR, when radical Maoists led by Charu Mazumdar called for an immediate start to the revolution. The split solidified when the less radical CPI factions, which had fared well in recent elections, helped the government to quash the Maoists' peasant insurrection at Naxalbari. Even within the Maoist camp, defending the correct ideology ("the line struggle") took precedence over Leninist party discipline, resulting in multiple purges and organizational chaos similar to the CR.[9] For better or worse, the CPI-ML adopted as its slogan, "China's chairman is our chairman; China's path is our path."[10]

The first step along China's path is Mao's analysis of society as "semi-feudal, semi-colonial." Marxism posits that any effort to change society must begin with an objective assessment of its material and economic conditions. Marx argued that the European revolutions represented a fundamental historical advancement from feudalism (an agricultural economic system, whose typical political form is monarchy) to

---

8   "The Communist Party of India (Marxist-Leninist) Founded," *Peking Review* 28 (July 11, 1969); reprinted in *Spring Thunder over India: Anthology of Articles on Naxalbari* (Calcutta: Radical Impression, 1985), p. 18.

9   "The Naxalite Movement Is Characterized by Its Disorganized Organization," in Chakrabarti, *China and the Naxalites*, p. 80.

10   Charu Mazumdar, "China's Chairman Is Our Chairman; China's Path Is Our Path," *Liberation (Calcutta)* 3:1 (November 1969), pp. 6–13.

capitalism (an industrial economic system, whose typical political form is the bourgeois democratic nation-state). Moreover, he said, another round of revolutions would transform capitalism into socialism. China in the first half of the twentieth century did not fit Marx's description of the type of society – modern, industrial, capitalist – ripe for socialist revolution. However, Lenin updated Marx's theory with the observation that global imperialism had exported capitalism around the globe and, with it, the possibility of world socialist revolution. Perhaps even more important, Lenin proved that a dedicated Communist Party could seize control of a feudal, agrarian monarchy, namely, czarist Russia. Mao, in turn, argued for the creative application of Marxism-Leninism to describe the prerevolutionary Chinese situation as collaboration between feudal elements in the vast countryside and capitalist elements in the colonized coastal cities. Mao's formulation had great appeal in the third world because it could be easily adapted to nearly any poor country. In the case of India, which had already expelled the British and instituted land reforms, the term indicated a transitional (rather than partial) stage of development from feudal and colonial to capitalist and postcolonial.[11] The main concern of Mazumdar's peasant movement was the semifeudal rural economy; only later did the urban student movement draw attention to India's semicolonial culture.[12] For both, the real significance of Mao's analysis lay in its revolutionary imperatives: For Mazumdar, it required a "people's war," and for the students, a continuing cultural revolution.

According to Mao, the revolutionary path for a semifeudal, semicolonial society is to launch a "people's war." A people's war is a life-and-death struggle against reactionaries and imperialists: There is no possibility for parliamentary negotiation with the enemy or a peaceful transition to socialism. It is this all-or-nothing stance that distinguishes revolutionary socialism from social democratic reformism or revisionist appeasement. That violence alone can effect social transformation is summarized by Lin Biao:

> In the last analysis, the Marxist-Leninist theory of proletarian revolution is the theory of the seizure of state power by

[11] "While completely wrong in their sociological orientation, choice of words and understanding of the Indian economy, the Naxalites intended by their use of the term 'semifeudal, semicolonial' to draw attention to the twin concerns of rural poverty and exploitation and the relative weakness of Indian voices on the international stage." Rabindra Ray, *The Naxalites and Their Ideology* (New Delhi: Oxford University Press, 1988), p. 197.

[12] Ray, *Naxalites*, p. 196.

revolutionary violence, the theory of countering war against the people by people's war. As Marx so aptly put it, "Force is the midwife of every old society pregnant with a new one." ... It was on the basis of the lessons derived from the people's wars in China that Comrade Mao Zedong, using the simplest and the most vivid language, advanced the famous thesis that "political power grows out of the barrel of a gun."[13]

However, recognizing the need for violence is not enough: Only the correct strategy and tactics will guarantee victory. Lin Biao summarized the connection between strategy and tactics: "Comrade Mao Zedong points out that we must despise the enemy strategically and take full account of him tactically."[14] To "despise the enemy strategically" means that the practitioners of people's war must develop sufficient hatred of the enemy to commit to protracted struggle; to "take full account of him tactically" means to give play to the full range of guerrilla methods. A Naxalite leader in West Bengal explained the relevance of Mao's people's war doctrine: "Ours is a protracted people's war and the enemy is now much stronger than us. Our weapon is Mao Zedong Thought and our method guerrilla struggle."[15]

The strategy of protracted war is based on the realization that the people's war begins as an asymmetrical conflict, where the enemy is stronger and better equipped. Defeating such a superior foe takes patience. The enemy has short-term advantages, but if he can be drawn out and stretched thin over time, the tide will turn, and he will be exposed as a "paper tiger." The people, on the other hand, have long-term advantages: strong motivation and superior numbers. The balance of power will shift gradually, from defense to equilibrium to offense. History is on the side of the people, and victory is inevitable: They need only overcome their fears and "dare to win." The power of the people has great appeal in the third world, where people are a ready resource. Thus the outgunned Naxalite leader Mazumdar frequently quoted Mao's pronouncement: "Weapons are an important factor in war, but not the decisive factor; it is people, not things, who are decisive."[16]

[13] Lin, "Long Live the Victory."
[14] *Ibid.*
[15] "Report on the Armed Struggle by the Debra Thana Organizing Committee of the CPI-ML," *Peking Review* 5 (January 30, 1970); reprinted in *Spring Thunder*, pp. 42–45.
[16] Chakrabarti, *China and the Naxalites*, p. 91, quoting Mao Zedong, "On Protracted War" (May 1938), *MIA*; available at www.marxists.org/reference/archive/mao/selected-works/volume-2/mswv2_09.htm.

Mao espoused familiar guerrilla tactics, inflected with equal parts Marxist dialectics and Sun Zi's *Art of War*:

> In guerrilla warfare, select the tactic of seeming to come from the east and attacking from the west; avoid the solid, attack the hollow; attack, withdraw; deliver a lightning blow, seek a lightning decision. When guerrillas engage a stronger enemy, they withdraw when he advances, harass him when he stops, strike him when he is weary, pursue him when he withdraws.[17]

As the people's war reaches a state of equilibrium, Mao said, the people's army should emphasize a new tactic: "the establishment of rural revolutionary base areas and the encirclement of the cities from the countryside." These bases provide safe havens, economic resources, and opportunities to implement progressive policies. The Naxalites set up bases covering some 300 villages by the end of 1969, following the example set by earlier Indian communists in the 1940s.[18]

After waging people's war and establishing a dictatorship of the proletariat, the final part of the Maoist path is continuing the revolution – though it is not clear when, if ever, the path ends: Mao went to his deathbed still advocating cultural revolution in China. Because third world Maoist movements arose during or after the CR, the chronology of the Chinese model often was compacted or muddled. For example, though the Naxalites never seized state power in India, they still had their own cultural revolution. Beginning in mid-April 1970 and persisting for several months, students in Calcutta vandalized images of Indian and Bengali heroes, assaulted heads of educational institutions, and boycotted school exams.[19] Mazumdar, who theretofore had focused on rural mobilization, called on the urban youth to form Red Guard organizations, to "bombard the party headquarters" (as Mao had said to his Red Guards), to go down to the villages (with Mao's *Quotations* in hand), and to experience first hand the hardships of peasant life.[20] At the same time that students were encouraged to root out traditional and bourgeois cultural elements, the peasants were encouraged to annihilate

[17] Mao Zedong, "On Guerrilla Warfare" (1937), *MIA*; available at www.marxists.org/reference/archive/mao/works/1937/guerrilla-warfare/index.htm.
[18] "A Single Spark Can Start a Prairie Fire," *Peking Review* 7 (February 13, 1970); reprinted in *Spring Thunder*, p. 46.
[19] Sanjay Seth, "Indian Maoism: The Significance of Naxalbari," in Arif Dirlik, Paul Healy, and Nick Knight, eds., *Critical Perspectives on Mao Zedong's Thought* (Atlantic Highlands, NJ: Humanities Press International, 1997), pp. 289–312.
[20] Charu Mazumdar, "A Few Words to the Revolutionary Students and Youths," *Liberation* 3:5 (March 1970), pp. 13–14, 84–91.

their remaining class enemies. During this period, the "Notes" section of Naxalite newsletter *Liberation* frequently celebrated class hatred, gleefully recounting gratuitous decapitations of landlords, heads stuck on bamboo poles, and slogans painted in blood. However, the excess of violence was not uncontroversial: It led to defections from the party during Mazumdar's lifetime and denunciations of his leadership after his death.[21] Later, Zhou Enlai lamented the lack of previous coordination between the CCP and the CPI-ML, saying that they could have corrected the Naxalites' rigid mechanical application of the Chinese experience, unqualified adoration of Chairman Mao, and propensity to unnecessary killing.[22] Zhou's critique reiterated the point that Maoism demanded a creative and flexible application of Marxism-Leninism to local circumstances. Zhou's critique also reflected the broader, more pragmatic, and arguably less radical attitude that Mao took toward the world in the 1970s.

China's Realignment and Mao's Theory of the Three Worlds

The PRC drastically reoriented its foreign policy in the early 1970s, pursuing detente with the United States and assuming China's seat in the United Nations (previously held by the Republic of China on Taiwan). The mysterious death of Lin Biao in an apparent coup attempt brought an end to China's overtly belligerent tone and struck a blow to the credibility of Chinese radicalism. Mao still decried American imperialism, but the USSR had recently brought Eastern Europe to heel, and now Mao saw Soviet social imperialism as the greatest threat to world peace. Meanwhile, China built relationships throughout the third world with aid and trade, offering favorable loans and technical expertise for massive capital-intensive projects such as a railway connecting Tanzania and Zambia. It was in a meeting with Zambian President Kaunda that Mao first presented his reorientation of the third world concept, an idea that would become known as the "three worlds theory."[23]

Deng Xiaoping presented Mao's three worlds theory in an April 1974 speech to the UN General Assembly:

> [T]he world today actually consists of three parts, or three worlds, that are both interconnected and in contradiction to one another.

---

[21] Chakrabarti, *China and the Naxalites*, pp. 56–57; Seth, "Indian Maoism," p. 298.

[22] Chakrabarti, *China and the Naxalites*, pp. 150–175.

[23] "On the Question of the Differentiation of the Three Worlds," February 22, 1974, in *Mao Zedong on Diplomacy*, compiled by the Ministry of Foreign Affairs of the People's Republic of China and the Party Literature Research Center under the Central Committee of the Communist Party of China (Beijing: Foreign Languages Press, 1998), p. 454.

The United States and the Soviet Union make up the First World. The developing countries in Asia, Africa, Latin America and other regions make up the Third World. The developed countries between the two make up the Second World.[24]

The third world was geographically the same under the three worlds theory, but the first and second worlds were no longer organized according to cold war alignment. The primary contradiction was no longer the struggle between capitalism and socialism but the threat of global imperialism. The first world superpowers were locked in a struggle for global hegemony, threatening to conquer the world with U.S. imperialism or Soviet social imperialism or else to destroy it in a nuclear holocaust.

The three worlds theory opened the possibility of strategic alliance between the third world and the second world, which increasingly suffered from "superpower control, interference, intimidation, exploitation, and the shifting of economic crises."[25] The idea was not entirely new: Mao had toyed with the thought of global realignment when the PRC established diplomatic relations with France in 1964,[26] and in 1969, Lin Biao had called for it explicitly: "All countries and people subjected to aggression, control, intervention or bullying by U.S. imperialism and Soviet revisionism, let us unite and form the broadest possible united front and overthrow our common enemies!"[27]

However, with Lin Biao gone and the height of the CR over, China's foreign policy stressed practical engagement over radical principles. In the 1970s, China established cordial relations with a diverse array of third world monarchs and reactionaries, from the Shah of Iran to Chile's right-wing dictator Augusto Pinochet. Ironically, even as the three worlds theory allowed Maoism to spread its influence ever wider, it became divested of its particular ideological character. Sometimes the influence of Maoism meant little more than a pose, an imitative adoption of Mao's personal authoritarian style. To give just two examples, Zaire's Mobutu Sese Seko imposed on his cadres the Mao jacket following his

---

[24] Deng Xiaoping, "Speech by Chairman of the Delegation of the People's Republic of China Deng Xiaoping at the Special Session of the UN General Assembly," April 10, 1974, *MIA*; available at www.marxists.org/reference/archive/deng-xiaoping/1974/04/10.htm.

[25] Deng, "Speech by Chairman of the Delegation."

[26] "Talk with Edgar Snow on International Issues," January 9, 1965, in *Mao Zedong on Diplomacy*, pp. 416–428. By 1963, Mao was already discussing Europe, Japan, and Canada as "intermediate zones" in the cold war.

[27] Lin Biao, "Report to the Ninth National Congress of the Communist Party of China," April 1, 1969, *MIA*; available at www.marxists.org/reference/archive/lin-biao/1969/04/01.htm.

first visit to Beijing in 1973, and Libya's Colonel Qaddafi issued his political treatises in a set of three slim volumes known collectively as the "Green Book," a nod to Mao's ubiquitous "Little Red Book." Mobutu and Qaddafi were political opportunists of the first stripe; there was nothing specifically Maoist about their ruling ideologies. Still, Zhou Enlai pushed for diplomatic relations with countries across the ideological spectrum: "We should ally ourselves with all the forces in the world that can be allied with to combat colonialism, imperialism and above all superpower hegemonism. We are ready to establish or develop relations with all countries on the basis of the Five Principles of Peaceful Coexistence."[28]

The death of Mao Zedong in 1976 marked the end of an era in China. The CR came to a close, and the most radical faction of the CCP, deprived of Mao's personal patronage, was purged. By the end of 1978, Deng Xiaoping's reformist faction had taken the reins of Chinese domestic policy from Mao's loyal successor Hua Guofeng.[29] Despite the domestic transition, however, China sustained a foreign policy based on the three worlds theory. That same year, Albania, erstwhile ally in the Sino-Soviet split, denounced China's slide toward revisionism. Albanian Labor Party leader Enver Hoxha's *Imperialism and the Revolution* (1978) explained that the main reason for the Sino-Albanian split was China's stubborn adherence to the "false, counterrevolutionary, and chauvinist" three worlds theory. Hoxha argued that the three worlds theory was "based on a racist and metaphysical world outlook," a static and stereotyped vision of the world that ignored the diversity among developing nations and the contradictions internal to societies at all levels of development:

> The Chinese leadership takes no account of the fact that in the "third world" there are oppressed and oppressors, the proletariat and the enslaved, poverty-stricken and destitute peasantry, on the one hand, and the capitalists and landowners, who exploit and fleece the people, on the other.[30]

[28] Zhou Enlai, "Report on the Work of the Government," January 13, 1975, in *Documents of the First Session of the Fourth National People's Congress of the People's Republic of China*, *MIA*; available at www.marxists.org/reference/archive/zhou-enlai/1975/01/13.htm.

[29] Hua Guofeng, *Continue the Revolution under the Dictatorship of the Proletariat to the End: A Study of Volume V of the Selected Works of Mao Tsetung* (Beijing: Foreign Languages Press, 1977), *MIA*; available at www.marxists.org/reference/archive/hua-guofeng/1977/x01/x01.htm.

[30] Enver Hoxha, *Imperialism and the Revolution* (Chicago: World View, 1979). Hoxha saw no difference in principle between the two sides of the power struggle, the

Instead, Hoxha repeated Lenin's view that "there are now two worlds: the old world of capitalism, that is in a state of confusion but which will never surrender voluntarily, and the rising new world, which is still very weak but which will grow, for it is invincible." In other words, there are just the two worlds of capitalism and socialism, and within each is being waged a dynamic, historical struggle between the exploiters and the exploited, between the bourgeoisie and the proletariat. Hoxha argued that U.S. imperialism must be fought just as fiercely as Soviet social imperialism, but so too must reactionary and revisionist views in the so-called second and third worlds.

The Sino-Albanian split dealt a major blow to the international Maoist movement because many revolutionary parties – including nearly all the leading anti-Soviet parties in Latin America – sided with Hoxha. The International Conference of Marxist-Leninist Parties and Organizations (ICMLPO) divided into Maoist and Hoxhaist factions, with the Maoist camp centered on the Communist Party of the Philippines. In 1984, the Maoist faction spawned the Revolutionary Internationalist Movement (RIM), led by the Communist Party of Peru (Shining Path). Curiously, the founding manifesto of the RIM contested the attribution of the three worlds theory to Mao Zedong, linking it instead to the Chinese revisionists in charge of diplomacy (presumably Zhou Enlai, Hua Guofeng, and Deng Xiaoping), who had "turned their backs on the revolutionary struggles of the proletariat and the oppressed peoples or tried to subordinate these struggles to the state interests of China."[31] Thus the RIM rejected both Hoxha and the post-Mao Chinese leadership in favor of the radical line espoused by Mao at the height of the CR.

Maoism as a radical ideology had been severely weakened in China by the end of the 1970s. Even so, the collapse of radicalism in China did not attenuate the growth of Maoism overseas. A selective examination of three Maoist worlds will illuminate the common themes and diverse experiences of third world Maoism from the mid-1970s to the present. The following section explores the history of three important Maoist organizations: the Khmer Rouge in Cambodia, the Shining Path in Peru, and the reemergence of South Asia's Naxalite movement in Nepal.

"bankrupt Maoism" of Hua Guofeng and the "Rightist-revisionist fascism" of Deng Xiaoping.

[31] "Declaration of the Revolutionary Internationalist Movement," March 1984; available at www.csrp.org/rim/rimdec.htm.

THREE MAOIST WORLDS: CAMBODIA, PERU, NEPAL

Exceeding Mao: The Communist Party of Kampuchea ("Khmer Rouge")

Cambodia (called Kampuchea in the Khmer language), along with Vietnam and Laos, was part of French colonial Indo-China from the late nineteenth century until the Vietnamese Vietminh, using Maoist military doctrines, expelled French forces from Southeast Asia in 1954.[32] In a display of third world postcolonial solidarity, the restored Cambodian monarch Prince Norodom Sihanouk met with Zhou Enlai at the Bandung conference in 1955 and with Mao Zedong in Beijing the following year. By the early 1960s, however, the radical Communist Party of Kampuchea (CPK, known to its opponents as the "Khmer Rouge"), was advocating a people's war against the "feudal" monarchy. The CPK took advantage of a civil war in the 1970s to seize state power, founding Democratic Kampuchea in 1975. In the scant four years that followed, the CPK under its leader Pol Pot distinguished itself as one of the most absurdly brutal regimes of the twentieth century. At the height of their power, the Khmer Rouge pressed Maoism to its most horrible extremes.

The CPK rose to power amid superpower conflict in Indo-China and later benefited from Sino-Soviet rivalry in the region. The Vietnam War spilled into Cambodia in 1970 as the United States first stepped up its secret bombing of communist hideouts across the border and then backed a military coup against Sihanouk, who took refuge in China. A united front of Cambodian royalists, nationalists, and communists immediately responded, launching a civil war against the American-installed government. In 1973, as U.S. bombing reached its peak, Sihanouk and Princess Monique made a much publicized pilgrimage to visit the guerrilla headquarters, lending international credibility and prestige to the ragtag fighters. The guerrillas advanced steadily, filling the voids left by U.S. bombing. Finally, the U.S. withdrawal from Vietnam in 1975 left its Cambodian puppet government defenseless, and neither food shortages nor lack of popular support could prevent the guerrillas from taking power. The guerrillas dumped Sihanouk (declaring, "the king's shit smells like everyone else's"), set up a dictatorship, and drove all city dwellers out to the countryside.[33] With the common enemy of U.S.

---

[32] William J. Duiker, "Seeds of the Dragon: The Influence of the Maoist Model in Vietnam," in Dirlik et al., ed., *Critical Perspectives*, pp. 313–341.

[33] Henri Locard, *Pol Pot's Little Red Book: The Sayings of Angkar* (Chiang Mai: Silkworm Books, 2004), p. 301.

imperialism gone, and Vietnamese communists warming to the Soviet Union, Sino-Soviet rivalry took center stage. Mao had provided logistical, material, and financial support during the civil war, and despite the obvious incompetence and brutality of the CPK rulers, aid continued to flow from Hua Guofeng and Deng Xiaoping, who feared Soviet domination in Southeast Asia. Sino-Vietnamese relations quickly worsened through the late 1970s, eventually erupting into war. Under the three worlds theory, it did not matter whether Khmer Rouge ideology was strictly Maoist; it was enough to be anti-imperialist (meaning both anti-American and anti-Soviet).

Strangely, although CPK policies and rhetoric owed an obvious debt to Mao, the Cambodians themselves made no overt claim to being Maoists. They were known outside the party ranks only as Angkar – "the Organization." Indeed, it was not until September 27, 1977, nearly two and a half years after the fall of Phnom Penh, that Pol Pot revealed the truth: Angkar was none other than the CPK.[34] Even then, Angkar remained a nameless and faceless terror – a cult of *impersonality*. "Big Brother No. 1" continued to sign his correspondence and issue all directives under the name of an anonymous party center. The terrifying, mysterious, and ubiquitous Angkar demanded complete loyalty and compliance: The Organization was both omniscient ("Angkar has the many eyes of the pineapple," it was said) and omnipotent ("Angkar is the master of the waters, master of the earth").[35] Those suspected of deviance simply disappeared. The CPK also adopted from Mao's China techniques of control and discipline, including self-criticism, study sessions, and reform through labor. Yet the importance of Maoism relative to other factors is not always clear. For example, while the CPK conducted their guerrilla war by expanding rural base areas to surround the cities, the decisive factor in their victory was probably foreign aid. We also must question their supposed reliance on the peasantry as the main force of revolution because landless farmers comprised just 20 percent of Cambodia's population by 1970.[36] Most confusing of all, the ideological underpinnings of their highly secretive organization remain murky: Until 1977, the CPK systematically concealed its communist

---

[34] "Speech by Comrade Pol Pot, Secretary of the Central Committee of the CPK," Phnom Penh, September 27, 1977, in *Third World Peoples in Struggle* 2 (Montreal, Canada: Red Flag Publications, 1978).

[35] Locard, *Pol Pot's*, pp. 53, 112.

[36] Kate G. Frieson, "Revolution and Rural Response in Cambodia: 1970–1975," in Ben Kiernan, ed., *Genocide and Democracy in Cambodia: The Khmer Rouge, the United Nations, and the International Community*, Monograph Series 41 (New Haven, CT: Yale University Southeast Asia Studies, 1993), pp. 33–50.

orientation; like the clandestine Vietminh, the CPK espoused the more popular cause of national liberation. When Pol Pot finally did discuss the party's path to power, he did so using the most superficial of Maoist terminology ("applying Marxism-Leninism to the concrete realities of Kampuchea," waging a "new democratic revolution" to be followed by "building socialism," and so on) but without acknowledging Mao. Instead, the CPK stubbornly insisted its "unprecedented" revolution was exceeding, outstripping, and surpassing all others. CPK doctrines of absolute iconoclasm and self-reliance demanded that their cult of impersonality be depersonalized with respect to Mao as well.

Nevertheless, the CPK imitated and exceeded two of Mao's most distinctive and disastrous campaigns: outdoing the Great Leap Forward with a "*Super* Great Leap" and surpassing the CR with "Year Zero," a program of total cultural *annihilation*. The CPK marked the capture of Phnom Penh on April 17, 1975, as a new beginning. Loudspeakers incessantly repeated the surreal injunction, "Brothers! Leave Phnom Penh for three hours ... " (so we can root out hidden enemies) or "for three days ... " (for fear of U.S. bombing).[37] A chaotic exodus began, emptying the city completely. From that day forward, society was divided into two basic groups: the "old people" who had remained in the countryside to support the advancing rebels and the "new people" who had lived in the cities or even merely fled there. These "new people" were ideologically suspect for their wealth and education (although many were in fact displaced peasant refugees). The evacuation of the cities inaugurated a cultural revolution *par excellence*, "a clean sweep," premised on the complete erasure of history. A common CPK slogan advised, "When pulling out weeds, remove them roots and all."[38] Complete eradication was no mere metaphor: In their brief tenure, the CPK killed perhaps one-fifth of Cambodia's 8 million people.

Many of the dead were "new people" relocated to the countryside to carry out the CPK's "Super Great Leap." It is not clear whether the Khmer Rouge did not know or simply did not care that China's Great Leap Forward had been a debacle of famine and waste, a disaster for which Mao himself was forced to make a self-criticism. "The Party's Four-Year Plan to Build Socialism in All Fields, 1977–1980" (adopted in 1976) called for the closure of markets, the elimination of money, the collectivization of meals, and most important, a tripling of agricultural

---

[37] See, for example, Haing Ngor with Roger Warner, *Survival in the Killing Fields* (New York: Carroll & Graf, 2003), pp. 87–108.

[38] Locard, *Pol Pot's*, pp. 38, 77.

yields to be fueled by the ideological zeal of the "old people" and the forced labor of the "new people."[39] The resulting surpluses would be applied toward socialist industry, culture, and defense. In reality, the "new people" (and increasingly, the "old people") faced 16-hour work days, starvation, endemic disease, and authoritarian rule. The "Super Great Leap" stumbled mightily, even precipitating an attempted coup within the CPK leadership. Nevertheless, Pol Pot reported in 1978 with characteristic mendacity and hubris that "the present situation of our revolution is excellent in all fields."[40] As the CPK flared out in a genocidal fury, Chinese advisors withdrew and the Vietnamese army invaded.

Vietnam set up a client state called the People's Republic of Kampuchea and eagerly exposed the genocidal abuses of the Khmer Rouge, concluding that the Pol Pot regime "in essence, was the combination of a blood-thirsty dictatorship and medieval feudal tyranny disguised as socialism."[41] Meanwhile, the CPK retreated deep into the forests of Cambodia and Thailand, renewing their awkward civil war coalition with the royalists and nationalists. Incredibly, this coalition government in exile enjoyed continuing UN recognition and massive foreign aid until the withdrawal of Vietnam in 1989 and the conclusion of the Paris Agreement in 1991. The United Nations oversaw a comprehensive peace settlement in the 1990s, prompting several Khmer Rouge leaders to defect from the party in support of peace. Pol Pot died under house arrest in 1998, convicted by his own men of assassinating a top defector. The CPK was done for, and in 2006, the UN began preparations to try surviving Khmer Rouge leaders for crimes against humanity.

The CPK had pushed forward its version of extreme Maoist dictatorship, with Chinese help, even as China was undergoing de-Maoification in the late 1970s. When Vietnam and its client states in Cambodia and Laos then decried "Chinese expansionism and hegemonism" in Indo-China, they were calling out Deng Xiaoping on his own corollary to the three worlds theory:

> If one day China should change her color and turn into a
> superpower, if she too should play the tyrant in the world,

---

[39] "The Party's Four-Year Plan to Build Socialism in All Fields, 1977–1980," July-August 1976, in David P. Chandler, Ben Kiernan, and Chanthou Boua, trans. and eds., *Pol Pot Plans the Future: Confidential Leadership Documents from Democratic Kampuchea, 1976–1977*, Monograph Series 33 (New Haven, CT: Yale University Southeast Asia Studies, 1988), pp. 36–118.

[40] "Speech by Comrade Pol Pot," p. 36.

[41] Truong Chinh, *On Kampuchea* (Hanoi: Foreign Languages Publishing House, 1980), p. 8.

and everywhere subject others to her bullying, aggression and exploitation, the people of the world should identify her as social-imperialism, expose it, oppose it, and work together with the Chinese people to overthrow it.[42]

Perhaps the Vietnamese critique of post-Mao China could be dismissed as more Sino-Soviet posturing, but what are we to make of the dead dogs found hanging from lampposts in the streets of Lima, Peru, in 1980, with hand-scrawled signs reading, "Deng Xiaoping, son of a bitch!"[43] If Maoism were to survive, it would need to find a home elsewhere in the third world, outside China.

Acclimatization: The Communist Party of Peru (Shining Path)

The people's war in Peru began almost unnoticed in May 1980 with a few burned ballot boxes, small dynamite blasts, and some scattered attacks on policemen. By the time hostilities slowed in the mid-1990s, however, the conflict between Maoist guerrillas and government forces had claimed at least 50,000 lives – most of them rural, uneducated, and poor.[44] For more than a decade, the Communist Party of Peru (Shining Path) (CPP-SP) carefully prosecuted a violent and uncompromising insurgency along orthodox Maoist lines, demonstrating the resilience of Maoism after Mao and in a context far removed from the cultural and political orbit of China.

The CPP-SP emerged from factional politics within the Peruvian Communist Movement. Peruvian Maoists first split from the main Communist Party in 1964, rejecting Soviet and Cuban influences. Then, in 1970, a former philosophy professor and communist organizer who had trained at a Chinese cadre school during the CR led Maoist militants to form the CPP-SP. Abimael Guzmán Reynoso had attracted supporters among his students and local peasants in the poor and mountainous South-Central Andes – the locals called him the "Red Sun" in their indigenous language, whereas his critics called him "Shampoo" for his brainwashing abilities. Guzmán called himself by the nom de guerre Presidente Gonzalo and described himself as "the greatest living

---

[42] Deng, "Speech by Chairman of the Delegation."

[43] Gustavo Gorriti, "The War of the Philosopher-King," *New Republic* (June 18, 1990), p. 15.

[44] UK Parliamentary Delegation to Peru, June 12–25, 2004, *Truth and Reconciliation: An Agenda for the Future* (London: Peru Support Group, 2004), p. 5. The report attributes somewhat more than half of all casualties to the CPP-SP.

Marxist-Leninist." As the intellectual successor to Marx, Lenin, and Mao, his "Gonzalo Thought" became the "Fourth Sword of Marxism." A Mao-like personality cult developed around Guzmán very early in the movement, and the CPP-SP would later make use of such CR agitprop staples as incendiary wall posters and dunce caps for enemies, even to the point of reciting Mao songs in Mandarin.[45] Unlike the rusticated style of Mao, however, party propaganda always depicted Guzmán in the glasses and dark blazer of an erudite professor.

Guzmán preached a return to a genuinely Peruvian Marxism, heeding Mao's call to adapt universal theory to local conditions. This meant a return to and adaptation of the teachings of CPP founder José Carlos Mariátegui, who in the 1920s had first pointed out the "shining path of revolution" in Peru. As Guzmán explained in a 1988 interview, "[T]he more I understood Mao Zedong, the more I began to appreciate and value Mariátegui. Since Mao urged us to apply Marxism-Leninism creatively, I went back and studied Mariátegui again, and saw that we had in him a first rate Marxist-Leninist who had thoroughly analyzed our society."[46] Mao's malleable concept of "semifeudal, semicolonial" society proved highly compatible with Mariátegui's description of Peru in the first half of the twentieth century, with multiple coexisting worlds: indigenous peasant communities practicing primitive agrarian communism, colonial-era haciendas maintaining a feudal economy in the highlands, semifeudal coastal estates producing crops for export, and bourgeois urbanites with ties to international capitalism.[47] Though much had changed in the intervening half-century, Guzmán summarized the Peruvian situation with an appropriately Andean metaphor of three mountains to climb: the imperialism of the international superpowers, the semifeudalism of the Peruvian nation, and the bureaucratic capitalism of the regime in Lima. Mariátegui provided the analysis of Peruvian society; Mao provided the strategy to change it.

For Guzmán, the "shining path to revolution" in Peru had to follow the course of a protracted people's war, demanding a dynamic balance between patience and violence. Maoism taught Guzmán that "the need

---

[45] Orin Starn, "Maoism in the Andes: The Communist Party of Peru–Shining Path and the Refusal of History," in Dirlik et al., eds., *Critical Perspectives*, p. 276.

[46] "Interview with Chairman Gonzalo," in *El Diario*, trans. by the Peru People's Movement (Red Banner Publishing House, 1988); reproduced by *Red Sun*; available at www.redsun.org/pcp_doc/pcp_0788.htm.

[47] Lewis Taylor, *Shining Path: Guerrilla War in Peru's Northern Highlands, 1980–1997*, Liverpool Latin American Studies, New Series 6 (Liverpool, England: Liverpool University Press, 2006), pp. 10–11.

for violence is a universal law without exception," yet the conditions for armed struggle were less than ideal when the CPP-SP launched its people's war in 1980.[48] Not only was the CPP-SP small and poorly armed, but various reform movements had drained the urgency of the radicals' agenda. Peru's military government had instituted a number of far-reaching reforms, including land reform, in the early 1970s. Furthermore, a wave of popular movements and general strikes in the late 1970s had addressed the shortcomings of government reforms and brought a return to civilian government. Still, the guerrillas cultivated support among the rural poor and disaffected youth by targeting the common scourges of village life, from cattle thieves and petty extortionists to adulterers and corrupt officials. Much less popular were the rebels' dogmatic study sessions, draconian social programs, and terroristic attacks on well-intentioned grass-roots organizations.[49] Moreover, the ready recourse to violence of Marxism's "fourth sword" was double-edged: Violent acts could challenge state authority and catalyze revolution, but they also could alienate the people in counterproductive ways. Guzmán's statement that "the masses have to be taught through overwhelming acts so that ideas can be pounded into them" betrays an ambivalent and elitist attitude toward the common people.[50]

Despite lukewarm popular support, the CPP-SP benefited from authoritarian discipline and ideological purity to become, in Degregori's memorable phrase, a "dwarf star" – a concentrated power whose immense mass is disproportionate to its small size.[51] Shining Path built a clandestine party organization that was "strategically centralized and tactically decentralized," a "pearl necklace" of vertically linked but autonomous cells, affording timely initiative to local fighters.[52] Moreover, the party approached protracted war with patience and planning, adapting to what Michael L. Smith has called the "ecopolitics" of Peru's diverse and fragmented terrain to wage a "War of Little Wars."[53] The guerrillas also were resilient, weathering the state's "dirty war" (1983–1985), in which government troops indiscriminately destroyed

---

[48] "Interview with Chairman Gonzalo."
[49] Taylor, *Shining Path*, pp. 22–35.
[50] Quoted in Carlos Iván Degregori, "Return to the Past," in David Scott Palmer, ed., *The Shining Path of Peru* (New York: St. Martin's Press, 1992), p. 40.
[51] Degregori, "Return," p. 35.
[52] Michael L. Smith, "Taking High Ground: Shining Path and the Andes," in Palmer, ed., *Shining Path of Peru*, p. 26; Gabriela Tarazona-Sevillano, "The Organization of Shining Path," in Palmer, ed., *Shining Path of Peru*, p. 173.
[53] Smith, "Taking High Ground," pp. 19, 29.

villages in rebel-controlled regions. A massive prison riot in 1986, leading to the death of hundreds of CPP-SP partisans, was glorified by the party as a "Golden Seal on the Great Leap of Maoism" in Peru: "Blood does not drown the revolution but irrigates it!"[54] The people's war continued to expand, and by 1989, the guerrillas were preparing to bring their people's war to the capital, largely funded by the cocaine trade. Working from footholds in shantytowns, Shining Path orchestrated an urban strategy of violence, blackouts, and industrial sabotage throughout the Lima-Callao metropolitan region. That same year, however, the government finally devised a comprehensive and coordinated response to the insurgency that focused on winning back the support of Peru's rural poor. In 1992, forces from Alberto Fujimori's liberal government captured Guzmán, along with half of the CPP-SP Central Committee. Guzmán issued a statement from prison in 1994 advocating peace; since then, Shining Path has been on the decline.

The collapse of the CPP-SP at the height of its people's war illustrates the difficulty of repeating Mao's success in China. The CPP-SP expertly extended its strategy of protracted warfare but could not finish the job. In the end, they discovered for themselves the mortal weakness of the Maoist personality cult: Just as Mao's death brought a sudden end to the CR in China, the capture of the great teacher Guzmán all but doomed the Maoist movement in Peru. The Peruvian adaptation of Maoism was supposed to work, as one scholar has said, "from the top down geographically, but from the bottom up in political, social, and economic terms."[55] Instead, the CPP-SP built a top-down organization with its Spanish-speaking, educated vanguard of intellectuals out ahead of the indigenous masses.[56] What was supposed to be a creative acclimatization of Marxism to the Andean highlands instead assimilated many of the same feudal and colonial social divides it had intended to destroy. The doctrines of Maoist people's war had spread far beyond China in the 1980s, but nowhere had a Maoist revolution again succeeded in seizing control of a state. Yet, despite the fall of international Maoism's leading light, Shining Path (to say nothing of the global decline of Soviet-style communism), third world Maoism proved its resilience once again when a people's war erupted in Nepal in the mid-1990s. This time, remarkably, the Maoists would win.

---

[54] Quoted in Cynthia McClintock, "Theories of Revolution and the Case of Peru," in Palmer, ed., *Shining Path of Peru*, p. 230.

[55] Smith, "Taking High Ground," p. 17.

[56] Starn, "Maoism in the Andes," pp. 277–282.

Globalization: The Communist Party of Nepal (Maoist)

From 1996 to 2006, Maoist guerrillas waged a successful civil war against Nepal's parliamentary monarchy. The Maoists' victory, at a cost of at least 10,000 to 15,000 Nepalese lives (about two-thirds killed by government forces, one-third by rebels), resulted in elimination of the monarchy and founding of the Federal Democratic Republic of Nepal. Their victory had another, most unexpected result: The Communist Party of Nepal (Maoist) (CPN-M) did not set up a "New Democratic" dictatorship of the proletariat on the Maoist model; instead, the party has become a peaceful participant in a representative democracy.

Nepal is a small, poor, landlocked nation bounded by the Chinese-controlled Tibetan Himalayas to the north and by India to the south, east, and west. Because of its geographic isolation and economic dependence on India, Nepal's fate traditionally has been determined by its giant South Asian neighbor. Today, however, the CPN-M has responded creatively to global and regional challenges, demonstrating the capacity of third world Maoism to take on new political forms at the turn of the twenty-first century.

Nepalese Maoism has its roots in the broader South Asian Maoism of the Naxalites.[57] The original Communist Party of Nepal began as a mirror of the parliamentary CPI, but in the early 1960s, the monarchal ban on political parties in Nepal, the Sino-Indian War, and the revelation of the Sino-Soviet split all splintered the Nepalese Communist Movement into numerous underground factions.[58] India's Naxalite movement spilled into Nepal in the late 1960s and in the early 1970s inspired rebels to launch a short-lived guerrilla war in the remote Jhapa District bordering West Bengal. These Jhapa rebels and other Maoist groups eventually reunited with other communists, and this united front was well positioned for the first parliamentary elections to be held after reinstatement of political parties in 1990. However, a group of militant Maoists led by Comrade Prachanda (nom de guerre Pushpa Kamal Dahal) refused to accept the persistence of the monarchy or to participate in its pliant parliament; in 1994, the newly formed CPN-M vowed to wage a people's war.

---

[57] Rabindra Mishra, "India's Role in Nepal's Maoist Insurgency," *Asian Survey* 44:5 (September-October 2004), pp. 627–646.

[58] The CPN has spawned at least 20 notable factions since its founding in 1949, pulled apart by the regional and global ambitions of India, China, the Soviet Union, and the United States – especially by Nepal's desire to break free from Indian interference. Narayan Khadka, "Factionalism in the Communist Movement in Nepal," *Pacific Affairs* 68:1 (Spring 1995), pp. 55–76.

In orthodox Maoist fashion, Prachanda called for a protracted people's war based on the strategy of surrounding the city from the countryside in order to revolutionize a "semifeudal, semicolonial" society dominated by "foreign [especially Indian] imperialism and its running dog, the domestic reactionary ruling class."[59] The armed struggle started modestly in 1996, but within two years Prachanda announced that the CPN-M was establishing Maoist New Democracy and carrying out cultural revolutions in rural base areas.[60] Then, in the latter half of 2001, a rapid succession of events escalated the conflict and thrust Nepal onto the international scene. In June, the crown prince massacred the reigning king and most of the royal family in the Royal Palace and later died from his wounds. In August, in the midst of a ceasefire, the CPN-M joined forces with Maoist groups from India, Bangladesh, Sri Lanka, and Bhutan to form the Coordinating Committee of Maoist Parties of South Asia (CCOMPOSA). Just as the rebels were expanding their vision to a regional scale, the attacks of 9/11 reframed the insurgency on a global scale. Over the next year, while the Maoists stepped up their attacks, the convulsed and panicked monarchy declared a state of emergency, dissolved parliament, canceled elections, and mobilized the Royal Nepalese Army against the rebels. Meanwhile, the United States, Great Britain, the European Union, and India all provided military and economic support to fight the CPN-M as part of the "global war on terror." The civil war continued to escalate, and in 2004, the CPN-M boasted that the conflict had reached the stage of strategic offensive.[61] Already in control of most of rural Nepal, the Maoists engineered a blockade of the capital Kathmandu. In 2005 the Maoists formed a united front with the main political parties against the monarchy. In April of the following year, a general strike paralyzed the nation and forced a negotiated settlement: The Maoists accepted peace in exchange for participation in an elected constituent assembly (CA).

From a comparative and historical perspective, formation of the CA appears to be an unlikely resolution to the civil war in Nepal. We have seen that Maoism as a matter of principle generally is antireformist and

---

[59] Prachanda, "Strategy and Tactics of Armed Struggle in Nepal," March 1995, *A World to Win* 23 (1998); available at www.aworldtowin.org/back_issues/1998–23/nepStrategyTactics_23Eng.htm.

[60] Prachanda, "Two Momentous Years of Revolutionary Transformation," *A World to Win* 24 (1998); available at www.aworldtowin.org/back_issues/1998–24/nepal_Prachanda24Eng.htm.

[61] FO (pseudonym), "The People's War in Nepal: Taking the Strategic Offensive," *A World to Win* 31 (2005); available at www.aworldtowin.org/back_issues/2005–31/nepal.htm.

antiparliamentary, and the CPN-M from its inception criticized the Nepalese parliament for acting as a mouthpiece of the monarchy and the bourgeoisie. Why, then, did the CPN-M not press its advantage to insist on a Maoist dictatorship? The Maoists explained their advocacy of the CA as a "minimum, forward-looking solution" based on a sober and objective assessment of the situation. Internationally, the CPN-M had no allies to counterbalance the global spread of capitalism and the global war on terror. Regionally, India had shown its willingness to intervene by force. Nationally, escalating violence had generated popular support for a negotiated resolution but not sufficient momentum to topple the entire system through insurrection. Whatever advances the CPN-M had made in Nepal, larger forces militated against an outright Maoist victory. The Maoists concluded that "to continue analyzing strategic offensive even after the revolution in the world and the country itself has faced a serious defeat can only be termed a mockery."[62] The CA offered a tactical solution by which the Maoists could force out the monarchy and take control of the military. The CPN-M chose to consolidate its gains and maintain the protracted struggle in a position of strategic equilibrium – in effect, making Nepal a tiny base area to hold the fort until the global prospects for international revolution turned favorable again.

In 2008, the CPN-M won a plurality of seats in free and open elections to the new CA, and although the non-Maoist parties built a majority and selected a moderate president, Prachanda became prime minister.[63] The CPN-M dutifully took up the role of loyal minority, and in its first months the CA fulfilled the primary goal of the people's war through peaceful vote, declaring the abolition of the monarchy and the establishment of a new republic. Prachanda assured his political opponents that while "our ideologies, political tendencies, norms and values collide against each other," the CA could unify Nepal and solve problems as a pluralistic "garden of many flowers."[64] Before the conclusion of the civil war, the CPN-M had explained that the CA was a transitional form of government, a necessary intermediate step along the way to the

---

[62] FO, "People's War."

[63] Under the complex election formula, the CPN-M won 229 of 601 available seats, about twice as many as either the Social Democratic Nepali Congress Party or the Moderate-Leftist CPN (United Marxist-Leninist). These latter two parties formed a coalition with the Federalist MJF Party, electing Nepali Congress Member Ram Baran Yadav as the first president of the republic.

[64] Prachanda, "The Real Garden of Many Flowers"; available at www.krishnasenon-line.org/theredstar/issues/issue12/prachanda.htm.

eventual withering away of the state under communism.[65] Prachanda explained that this "development of democracy in the twenty-first century" would guarantee that "the new state will be under the observation, control and hegemony of the general masses. There will be free competition among political parties, [provided they] oppose feudalism and imperialism and work for the service of the masses."[66] Perhaps this "observation, control and hegemony of the general masses" is just a euphemistic reworking of the "dictatorship of the proletariat" because Prachanda significantly reserved the right to repress those who fail to "oppose feudalism and imperialism." It remains to be seen how the CPN-M will react if the new government fails to implement policy initiatives such as land reform, declines to repudiate Indian influence, or otherwise neglects the transition to socialism. Under what conditions would the Maoists revert to an armed strategic offensive?

For now, at least, the institution of true multiparty democracy in Nepal is a real innovation in Maoist practice. The CPN-M has argued that genuine competition between parties can serve the same political function as Mao's continuous cultural revolutions, combating bureaucratic ossification and unprincipled revisionism while simultaneously staving off the corrupt abuses inherent to single-party rule: The CA directly empowers the people to install an alternative revolutionary party "if the Party fails to continuously revolutionize itself."[67] As the civil war ended, Prachanda summarized history's lessons for the international Maoist movement:

> We had a very serious discussion in the party about the Khmer Rouge, and also about the Peruvian Maoists, and we think that we are completely different from them. We are not dogmatists; we are not sectarians; we are not traditionalists. We want to be ever more dynamic, adapting to our environment, understanding modernity.[68]

---

[65] "Building Red Power in Nepal," *A World to Win* 30 (2004); available at www.aworldtowin.org/back_issues/2004–30/building_Red_Power_in_Nepal.htm.

[66] Prachanda and Alex Perry, "Our People's War Is a Totally New 21st Century War," April 23, 2005, Time.com; available at www.countercurrents.org/nepal-perry230405.htm.

[67] Quoted in Baburam Bhattarai, "The Question of Building a New Type of State," *The Worker: Organ of the Communist Party of Nepal (Maoist)* 9 (2004); available at http://cpnm.org/new/English/worker/9issue/article_baburam.htm.

[68] Prachanda, "Our Revolution Won," interview with Alessandro Gilioli, November 9, 2006, *L'espresso*; available at http://espresso.repubblica.it/dettaglio/Prachanda:-Our-Revolution-Won/1431107//1.

In the third world as in China, Maoism has proved a highly effective military doctrine but a much less effective ruling ideology. The Cambodians showed the disastrous consequences of pushing dogmatic Maoism too far, and the Peruvians showed that even a patient expansion of the people's war could be fraught with danger. The Nepalese hope to alter that reality with a form of Maoism at long last flexible and resilient enough to survive in a globalized world.

13   Mao's Journeys to the West: Meanings Made of Mao

CHARLES W. HAYFORD

In the West, Mao has been cast in many roles, sometimes as the Mao people needed and sometimes as the one they feared. Depending on whether their story was that of liberating revolution and historical progress or one of communist expansion and destructive violence, and depending on whether China was an ally of the West – first against Japan, later against the USSR – Mao has appeared in the role of nationalist unifier, peasant rebel, Red Emperor, knockoff Stalin, humane modernizer, model of third world revolution, or leading political murderer of the twentieth century.[1]

Mao collaborated with his audiences to produce a range of conflicting stories that cannot be reconciled because they reflect differences in politics and philosophy that cannot be corrected by reference to facts. Yet Mao is not some gigantic historical Rorschach test, an inkblot in which to see what we will. My purpose here is neither to chronicle confusion nor correct misperceptions. In this chapter I rehearse the stories told in the West, mainly those based on some direct knowledge of China, to see where the honestly competing meanings made of Mao will lead us and what they tell us of twentieth-century world history.

I would like to thank Delia Davin, Richard Edmonds, Joseph Esherick, Bernard Mosher, Gwendolyn Stewart, and Ross Terrill.

[1]   Charles W. Hayford, "The Storm over the Peasant: Orientalism, Rhetoric and Representation in Modern China," in Shelton Stromquist and Jeffrey Cox, eds., *Contesting the Master Narrative: Essays in Social History* (Iowa City: University of Iowa Press, 1998), pp. 150–172; Lee Feigon, *Mao: A Reinterpretation* (Chicago, IL: Ivan Dee, 2002), pp. 3–12; Anita M. Andrew and John A. Rapp, *Autocracy and China's Rebel Founding Emperors: Comparing Chairman Mao and Ming Taizu* (Lanham, MD: Rowman & Littlefield, 2000); Michael H. Hunt, *The Genesis of Chinese Communist Foreign Policy* (New York: Columbia University Press, 1996), pp. 148–158; He Di, "The Most Respected Enemy: Mao Zedong's Perception of the United States," *China Quarterly* 137 (1994), p. 144.

1789–1920: THE STAGE IS SET, THE COLD WAR BEGINS

The first Western Maos were framed in a nineteenth-century "Grand Story" that grew out of the French Revolution of 1789: Progress, in the view of revolutionaries, came from destroying the ancient regime and leaping from feudalism of the Dark Ages to the sunlight of liberty, equality, and fraternity. Romantic heroes – Napoleon, George Washington, Mazzini – created nation-states and rational control of society. Critics distrusted this story. British conservatives and liberals both held that revolutionary destruction led to anarchy, not liberty, and to mob rule, not equality. In England, they felt, a middle class had gradually and peacefully replaced the inbred feudal aristocrats and bumbled into a modern market and democratic government by means of common sense, common law, and the common man. In the United States, the Anglo-Saxon Protestants who dominated foreign relations added the codicil that their own happy revolution was an exception; the New World was a land of yeoman farmers and creative entrepreneurs, with no aristocrats or peasants in sight. There was no need for violence or state power to overthrow feudalism. These pleasant myths painted over considerable violence and oppression, but then, comforting self-delusion is a prime function of national storytelling.

This nineteenth-century pageant of history cast China as a bystander, immobile and isolated from history. Europeans, even Karl Marx and Adam Smith, were oblivious to basic changes in early modern China. The Western powers used force and diplomacy on the assumption that Old Asian society had to be destroyed to clear the way for modern – that is, Western – civilization. After the intervention to put down the Boxers in 1900, Americans assumed that a commercial Open Door and removal of the obstructive Manchus would lead to an "orderly revolution" as naturally the removal of a logjam allows water to flow downstream.[2]

After the Great War of 1914–18, two leaders from the periphery called for a world of democratic independent nations and, among other things, for a new China. The first, Woodrow Wilson, linked human progress to individualism, market capitalism, and a world community of middle classes. China was to become a middle-class democracy, preferably Christian. The other revolutionary, Vladimir Lenin, mounted a parallel challenge in the name of justice, equality, collective production,

[2]   Charles W. Hayford, "The Open Door Raj: Chinese-American Cultural Relations, 1900–1945," in Warren Cohen, ed., *Pacific Passages* (New York: Columbia University Press, 1996), pp. 139–162.

national planning, and a world community of working classes. Wilson had freely deployed the U.S. Marines in Central and Latin America, but his rhetoric invoked moral example and free trade – what is now called "soft power." Lenin proclaimed that only an armed proletarian dictatorship could protect the Soviet Union from revanchist attacks and only a global uprising against imperialism would allow world revolution to succeed. China welcomed and tested each of these universalist ideologies.[3]

The clash between these two approaches led to telling Mao's story in different ways.

THE HEROIC AGE, 1921–49

... several hundred million peasants will rise like a mighty storm, like a hurricane.... They will sweep all the imperialists, warlords, corrupt officials, local tyrants, and evil gentry into their graves.

Mao Zedong, "Report on the Peasant Movement in Hunan" (1927)[4]

Open Door Americans and British in the treaty ports feared that the popular nationalism of the 1925–27 Northern Expedition was the return of Boxer violence and xenophobia. But Mao, along with many young Chinese, saw Leninist revolution as a tool to build a rich and independent nation. Marxism labeled China as "feudal" when in fact late imperial China had a centralized civilian government and an economy organized around petty capitalist farmers and national markets, that is, not feudal in any technical sense. Yet the label "feudal" reframed China from being backward and exotic, as it was in the nineteenth-century grand story, to being at a stage in universal world history that came before revolution. "Revolution" meant strong government to make China rich and powerful.

Westerners took years to understand. Pearl Buck, even before she wrote *The Good Earth*, sympathized with Chinese nationalism but doubted that revolution would suit China. The "young Chinese rants a little and philosophizes a great deal," she wrote in 1924, but his age-old "foundation of commonsense" will make him see that Bolshevism

---

3   Odd Arne Westad, *The Global Cold War: Third World Interventions and the Making of Our Times* (Cambridge; New York: Cambridge University Press, 2005), pp. 8–16, 39–57; Erez Manela, *The Wilsonian Moment: Self-Determination and the International Origins of Anticolonial Nationalism* (Oxford; New York: Oxford University Press, 2007).

4   Stuart R. Schram, *Mao's Road to Power: Revolutionary Writings, 1912–1949* (Armonk, NY: M. E. Sharpe, 1994), Vol. 2, p. 430.

is "barren of fruit" and "cling to a saner, slower order of progress." The treaty port journalist Rodney Gilbert spoke for Shanghailand. His *What's Wrong with China* (1926) agreed with Buck that China was eternal and unchanging but scorned her respect for Chinese abilities: Their minds were childlike and incapable of rational thought, their "standards of manhood" were greatly lacking, and turning China over to these people would produce chaos in which Bolshevism would thrive. Some Shanghailanders even felt that Japan should be allowed to discipline China in the way that the United States disciplined Latin America. The British Foreign Office was more realistic. In their fear that this "Shanghai Mind" would endanger trade, they calmly negotiated with Chiang Kai-shek (Jiang Jieshi).[5]

In these years, Mao was a bit player. A 1931 account mentioned Zhu De and his "equally well known ... cooperating military officer," Mao Zedong. In 1934, Peter Fleming, the intrepid British travel writer, yearned to tour the Red Areas but had to content himself with noting that "Mao Dsu Tung," as he spelled it, was "a gifted and fanatical young man of thirty-five suffering from an incurable disease." *Time* magazine mentioned Mao first in 1935 as "the Chinese Lenin," reporting that he had "no fixed headquarters or abode but moves with his Chinese Soviet Government in nomadic fashion from province to province," so "ill that he has to be carried on a stretcher."[6]

The two most influential Western books on China in the 1930s told stories that were different and perhaps even opposite. Pearl Buck was careful to call Wang Lung, the protagonist of her *The Good Earth* (1931), a "farmer," not a feudal "peasant," and shows him as a petty capitalist no more in need of revolution or scientific farming than he was of foreign missions; Edgar Snow's *Red Star over China* (1937), on the other hand, presented a "dark living peasantry" in need of revolution to bring enlightenment and modern values. (Neither Snow nor Buck would have said so, but Wang Lung was much like Mao's father, an upwardly mobile village entrepreneur.) In July of 1936, Snow, by then an experienced China journalist with an international reputation, was conducted by his party

[5] Robert Bickers, *Britain in China: Community, Culture, and Colonialism, 1900–1949* (Manchester; New York: Manchester University Press, 1999), pp. 27–31; Pearl Buck, "China the Eternal," *International Review of Missions* (October 1924); Rodney Gilbert, *What's Wrong with China* (New York: Fleming Revell, 1926), pp. 166–200.

[6] Harley Farnsworth MacNair, *China in Revolution* (Chicago: University of Chicago Press, 1931), p. 213; Peter Fleming, *One's Company* (London: 1934), p. 185; "Young Marshal's Escape," *Time* (April 29, 1935). The first mention of Zhu and Mao in the *New York Times* was in 1930. Reports of Mao's death appeared regularly until 1976, at which time they were no longer exaggerated. Feigon, *Mao*, p. 4.

contacts through the Nationalist blockade and soon found what he was looking for: Mao Zedong, a "gaunt, rather Lincolnesque figure, above average height for a Chinese," with an "intellectual face of great shrewdness" and the "simplicity and naturalness of the Chinese peasant." With Snow seated on a backless stool, Mao lounged on the stone bed and spoke over the course of several nights, once turning down his trousers to look for insect "guests," completely indifferent to personal appearance.[7]

Snow's scoop was that Mao was alive and leading an anti-Japanese social revolution, but Mao had further goals in talking to Snow. Stalin, concerned to form a buffer against Japan, had recently jolted Mao with an order to join a United Front with Chiang Kai-shek. Mao acquiesced but used the United Front to his own ends. A multiclass coalition suited his need for the support of all classes to fight Japan, aligned him with the global struggle against fascism, and appealed to urban intellectuals and Western progressives. As the only independent communist with a territorial base, he also could not afford to be associated with Leon Trotsky's apostate attack on Stalin. Through Snow, Mao told the world that the Chinese Revolution was Marxist, loyal to the Soviet cause, but unique and nationalist.[8]

As an optimistic American progressive, Snow reported that Mao's aim was

> ... to awaken China's millions to belief in human rights, to combat the timidity, passiveness, and static faiths of Taoism and Confucianism, to educate, to persuade, and no doubt at times to beleaguer and coerce them to fight for a life of justice, equality, freedom, and human dignity, ... a new conception of the state, society, and the individual.

Snow's book links this domestic revolution with the international system. Tinged with a hostility toward British imperialism reflecting both his Asian experience and his Irish forebears, Snow declared that liberation of Asia from imperial control depended both on Russia and on the success of the Chinese Revolution.[9]

In October 1937, just as Japanese armies were advancing on Nanjing, *Red Star* was published in London by the Left Book Club, which

[7] Edgar Snow, *Red Star over China* (New York: Random House, 1938), pp. 66–74.
[8] Anne-Marie Brady, *Making the Foreign Serve China: Managing Foreigners in the People's Republic* (Lanham, MD: Rowman & Littlefield Publishers, 2003), pp. 46–48; Hunt, *Genesis*, pp. 236–237; David Apter and Tony Saich, *Revolutionary Discourse in Mao's Republic* (Cambridge, MA: Harvard University Press, 1994).
[9] Snow, *Red Star*, pp. 106–107; 449.

specialized in defending the Soviet Union, followed the next spring by publication in New York by Random House, which did not. Reviewers of the London edition welcomed news of Chinese resistance to Japan, but the Communist Party of the United States of America detected the spoor of Trotskyism in Mao's critique of Stalin. Snow softened but did not remove the offending views for the American edition.[10]

After 1941, Chiang Kai-shek closed Western access to Red zones in northern China but in the summer of 1944 reluctantly allowed the "Dixie Mission" to establish a military liaison in Yan'an in preparation for the invasion of Japan. Foreign Service Officer John Service was greeted by a grumpy Chen Yi, who had studied English with Service's father, a YMCA missionary in Sichuan. *Time* magazine correspondent Theodore White arrived later in the summer, followed by a string of reporters who again and again contrasted sunny, democratic, modern-minded Yan'an with rainy, feudal Chongqing.[11]

"All of our party have had the same feeling," reported Service, "that we have come into a different country and are meeting different people." Another said, "I find myself continually trying to find out just how Chinese these people are." With the exception of Mao, who lived outside of town, access to top leaders was easy because they "prided themselves on their democracy." Mao grew tobacco to support his habit, with enough left over to supply party headquarters. Zhu De grew cabbages and was loved, observed the long-time leftist journalist Agnes Smedley, but Mao was only respected. Mao practiced his English with Smedley, who recalled his "high-pitched voice" and hands as "long and sensitive as a woman's." Mao asked about romantic love and if Smedley had ever loved any man and why. On Saturday nights there was a veritable hoe-down with music supplied by a "sad collection of horns, paper-covered combs, and native stringed instruments." Mao's pride prevented him from trying to dance: "He had no rhythm in his being." Service, whose standards in dance may have been less demanding than Smedley's, reported that Mao danced in a manner that, remembering his normally quiet and reserved bearing, "can only be called gay."[12]

[10] Part Three, "Red Star Over China, and Elsewhere," in S. Bernard Thomas, *Season of High Adventure: Edgar Snow in China* (Berkeley: University of California Press, 1996), pp. 151–189; Harvey Klehr, John Earl Haynes, and K. M. Anderson, *The Soviet World of American Communism* (New Haven, CT: Yale University Press, 1998), pp. 336–341 lists the changes Snow made.

[11] Kenneth E. Shewmaker, *Americans and Chinese Communists, 1927–1945: A Persuading Encounter* (Ithaca, NY: Cornell University Press, 1971), pp. 110–124.

[12] *Foreign Relations of the United States* (FRUS), Vol. 6 (China, 1944) (Washington, D.C.: Government Printing Office, 1967), pp. 518, 637; Agnes Smedley, *Battle Hymn of China* (New York: Knopf, 1943), pp. 168–170.

In August of 1944, Mao summoned Service for a private session of several hours to lobby for American support. He assured Service that the communists "will not be afraid of democratic America influence" and concluded that "we must have American help.... we cannot risk crossing you." Democracy was more important than socialism, Mao said, and after all, Chiang had been elected by fewer voters than Hitler. They both assumed that the war would last perhaps another two years.[13]

These "China hands" – reporters, soldiers, foreign service officers, and even missionaries who visited Mao – assumed that the United States and the Soviet Union would continue to cooperate and support the Nationalists, who had preponderant power, and that the invasion of Japan would require communist support. There is no sign, however, that policymakers in Washington read the dispatches that looked at Mao as a possible strategic partner.

The China hands also heard the thunder produced by Mao's hurricane. Theodore White, although later criticized, in fact, described the authoritarian side of Mao's regime in some detail. He concluded that communists were "masters of brutality," but they realized that "if you take a peasant and treat him like a man," he will fight for you. The peasantry were "putty in the hands of their communist mentors."[14] But this violence fit into a new grand story, no longer that of the collision of (Western) civilization with a stagnant and unique China, but the *Götterdämmerung* of feudalism and birth of New China. One American who traveled in China during the war remarked that since the New World had never needed a "real revolution," Americans therefore found it hard to understand that "in a society like China's, revolution can be a fundamental and entirely natural fact of life, as hard to slow up as a pregnancy." In *Thunder Out of China* (1946), Theodore White and Annalee Jacoby wrote that less than a thousand years ago "Europe lived this way; then Europe revolted.... The people of Asia are going through the same process."[15] Whatever his faults, Mao was riding a wave of history.

After the unexpectedly early end of the war in August 1945, Stalin and the Americans pressured Mao to join a coalition government and brought him to Chongqing, his first airplane ride. At the farewell banquet to celebrate the tenuous accord (Zhou Enlai tested the dishes for

---

[13] "Subject: Interview with Mao Tse-tung (August 27, 1944)," *ibid.*, pp. 604–614, quote at p. 614.

[14] Theodore White and Annalee Jacoby, *Thunder Out of China* (New York: Sloane, 1946), p. 202.

[15] Graham Peck, *Two Kinds of Time* (Boston, MA: Houghton Mifflin, 1950), pp. 20, 189; White and Jacoby, *Thunder Out of China*, p. xix.

poison), Mao was seated on the dais near Henry Luce, founder and publisher of *Time* magazine. Luce's diary entry remarks on Mao's "sloppy blue-denim garment" and on his "intense but not unfriendly curiosity." The two exchanged "polite grunts."[16]

The United States and the USSR were swept into cold war, but both continued to support Chiang Kai-shek. Mao was not a headline figure outside China; few of his works were translated and those only by publishers on the sectarian left. The American foreign policy public saw Mao as a Soviet puppet and revolution in China as Soviet global expansion. The arguments of the wartime China hands were published widely at home but in the end had little traction. John K. Fairbank, who returned from wartime service in Chongqing to write in relative safety from Harvard University, put the China hands' argument into his *The United States and China* (1948). The Communists were in fact home grown but had to demonstrate their independence of Russia. Mao, he noted, "like Marx has had a bad Western press and is consequently little studied."[17]

The last of the major reporters' books, Jack Belden's *China Shakes the World* (1949), presciently portrayed village revolution, not cold war ideological competition, with little mention of Mao. On his return to China in 1946, Belden had avoided Yan'an: "that cave village had become a tourist center" and might be "very hard for me to get in close contact with the people, the war or their revolution." *Their* revolution, Belden says – not Mao's or the party's. Belden told the stories of practical village people pursuing practical goals; for him, Mao represented the party apparatchik or the intellectual. The Communists took power by meeting the needs of the Chinese people, which were not being met by the "feudal minded" Nationalists, but in doing so, they built a "wholly new power apparatus" that "confused the power of the people with the liberty of the people." If pure intellectuals gain the upper hand, Belden warned, then in another 25 years there might arise a "set of managers standing above the Chinese masses" who would not be subject to democratic checks and may "force their dreams on others, blunder into grave political mistakes and finally plunge into outright tyranny." Belden was mistaken: It did not take 25 years.[18]

[16] Robert Herzstein, *Henry R. Luce, Time, and the American Crusade in Asia* (Cambridge; New York: Cambridge University Press, 2005), p. 10.

[17] Hunt, *Genesis*, pp. 160ff; Simei Qing, *From Allies to Enemies: Visions of Modernity, Identity, and U.S.-China Diplomacy, 1945–1960* (Cambridge, MA: Harvard University Press, 2007), pp. 58–59; *Time*, November 13, 1944; White and Jacoby, *Thunder Out of China*, p. 202; John K. Fairbank, *The United States and China* (Cambridge, MA: Harvard University Press, 1948), pp. 263–267, 364.

[18] Jack Belden, *China Shakes the World* (Boston: Houghton Mifflin, 1949), pp. 14, 88, 242, 463, 504, 472–473.

The People's Liberation Army (PLA) took city after city with little or no contact with Americans, who did not ask "who failed to win Mao?" They asked "who lost China?" Republicans, truculent after five consecutive presidential defeats, charged that the United States had saved China from Japan only to lose it to the Soviets. Henry Luce set his magazines, *Time*, *Life*, and *Fortune*, on a campaign against the China hands. Since his father had been a Presbyterian missionary in a village in Shandong, Luce felt qualified to assert that the Chinese people were democratic by nature and that only active betrayal could explain the spread of communism. Even though the weekly circulation of *Time* was several times the total number of copies ever sold of *Red Star* and *Thunder Out of China* combined, he blamed the lies and misrepresentations of his former correspondent White for the loss. Mao's portrait on the cover of *Time* on February 7, 1949, was labeled, "The Communist Boss Learned Tyranny as a Boy."[19]

In the late summer of 1949, the State Department issued a white paper to explain the deep causes of revolution in China. Like *Time*, the white paper did not accept (or even seriously consider) the view of the China hands that revolution was the culmination of a long struggle to create a strong and independent nation. Instead, the causes were "unbearable pressure upon the land" and the impact of the West. The "tragedy" of the years of war, it continued, was that "physical and human devastation to a large extent destroyed the emerging middle class which historically has been the backbone and heart of liberalism and democracy." The white paper charged that the Communists had "foresworn their Chinese heritage" and "publicly announced their subservience" to Russia, an accusation partly intended to shame Mao into defying Stalin as Tito had done in Yugoslavia. The names of Nationalist officials appear on almost every page, Mao's only in passing.[20]

RED BOSS, BLUE ANTS, AND THE YELLOW PERIL, 1949–66

Mao Zedong entered Beijing guarded by an American-made tank and wearing a Russian-style parka and fur hat. He announced that China

---

[19] David D. Perlmutter, *Picturing China in the American Press: The Visual Portrayal of Sino-American Relations in Time Magazine, 1949–1973* (Lanham, MD: Lexington Books, 2007), pp. 34–35.

[20] United States Department of State, *United States Relations with China, with Special Reference to the Period 1944–1949* (Washington, D.C.: Government Printing Office, 1949; reprinted: Stanford University Press, 2 vols., 1967), pp. iv-vi, xvi; Qing, *From Allies to Enemies*, pp. 68–73, 84–88.

had "stood up" but would "lean to one side," the Soviet side. Ironically, Americans now viewed Japan as an ally, although it had recently killed thousands of Americans, but China, with which it had no material quarrel, became an enemy. The cold war cast Mao in the role of a Hitler, not to be appeased, and the Korean War made the reversal of China's and Japan's roles seem inevitable.

American diplomatic policy was "nonrecognition," and "nonrecognition" described its cultural stance as well. American ideological descendants of Woodrow Wilson and the Chinese disciples of Lenin shared a common vocabulary of progress, democracy, liberation, and independence, but neither could comprehend the other's incomprehension. They used the same words to tell conflicting, incomplete stories to each other and to themselves. The China hands explained the historically progressive and nationalistic sources of Mao's power but had difficulty seeing the revolution's demonic Leninism. The broader American public did not understand why so many Chinese welcomed strong government and saw Chinese anti-Americanism as being pro-Soviet. Calmer heads pointed out that Americans could not "lose" a country that had never been theirs, but in fact, Americans had lost a China, the Open Door China of their imaginations.

As Mao disappeared behind the Bamboo Curtain, cold war America invented "contemporary China studies," the study of China from a distance. Scholars (initially housed in Russian research institutes) agreed that China was a model totalitarian system and debated whether the People's Republic of China (PRC) was now more Marxist or more nationalist.[21] John K. Fairbank, a historian of Qing foreign relations, and his student, Benjamin I. Schwartz, perhaps the first Mao-ologist, undercut the view of Mao as a Soviet puppet by proposing that "Maoism," a word they pioneered, represented the "Sinification of Marxism." Fairbank asked "Is Mao Merely the Latest 'Emperor' in China's Age-Old Cycle of Dynasties?" The answer was a balanced "Maybe, maybe not."[22]

Karl August Wittfogel, a Sinologist who had been a communist at the time he fled Nazi Germany in the 1930s, disputed the politics behind

[21] Pt One, "La Chine Contemporaine, un invention Américaine," in Yves Viltard, *La Chine Américaine: Il faut étudier la Chine contemporaine* (Paris: Belin, 2003).

[22] Conrad Brandt, Benjamin I. Schwartz, and John King Fairbank, eds., *A Documentary History of Chinese Communism* (Cambridge, MA: Harvard University Press, 1952; Russian Research Center Studies 6); Benjamin I. Schwartz, *Chinese Communism and the Rise of Mao* (Cambridge, MA: Harvard University Press; 1951; Russian Research Center Studies 4), pp. 189–190; John King Fairbank, "Past and Present: Is Mao Merely the Latest 'Emperor' in China's Age-Old Cycle of Dynasties?" *New Republic* 136:19 (May 1958).

the study of Maoism. He testified to the American Congress in 1951 that Fairbank and the China hands were complicit in the fall of China. Wittfogel denied Fairbank's contention that "Chinese Communism has been a peasant, not a proletarian, movement" and that "in this respect it follows the Chinese tradition of revolution more than the Marxist." Wittfogel denied the very idea of "Maoism," much less that Mao was original or independent. In his magisterial *Oriental Despotism*, Wittfogel asserted that "a Mao Tse-tung who viewed entrenchment in the countryside as a permanent principle and not as a temporary strategic device, would be no deviant Communist, but merely a fool."[23] Schwartz and Wittfogel agreed, however, in seeing Mao at the center of revolution.

While the scholars debated, a charmingly preposterous piece of urban folklore reflected popular American fears: Mao would command all Chinese to climb on stools and at his command jump off simultaneously, knocking the earth from its orbit – "China shakes the world." But because the State Department refused passports for travel to China, Americans had to rely on foreign writers for first-hand accounts such as those of Simone de Beauvoir. Based on a 1955 visit (and on reading Pearl Buck), she challenged the accounts of hostile journalists. Where they saw "blue ants" and slavery in the emerging communes, de Beauvoir saw "freedom," though in a particular sense: "to be free to eat meat is to have the money to buy some." But since she saw the communes as the "only possible way out for China," there was no need to have a genius in order to invent them. Mao's name dots her text, but his role is functional, not charismatic.[24]

Edgar Snow, now living in Switzerland, visited China in 1960 to extol Mao's communes and report that famine was a thing of the past – at a time when millions were starving. Snow visited again in 1965, a time when the first steps of the Cultural Revolution must have been on Mao's mind, but reported that Mao was "reflecting on man's rendezvous with death and ready to leave the assessment of his political legacy to future generations." His inheritors could either continue development of the revolution toward communism or "negate the revolution, make peace with imperialism, bring the remnants of Chiang Kai-shek, he couldn't judge."[25]

[23] Karl A. Wittfogel, "The Legend of 'Maoism'," *China Quarterly* 1 (January-March 1960), pp. 73–75, quoting from Fairbank, *The United States and China*, pp. 260 ff; *Oriental Despotism* (New Haven: Yale University Press, 1957), p. 442.

[24] Simone de Beauvoir, *The Long March*, (trans. by Austryn Wainhouse Cleveland, OH: World, 1958; Paris: Gallimard, 1957), pp. 490, 496, 501.

[25] Edgar Snow, *The Other Side of the River: Red China Today* (New York: Random House, 1962); "Interview with Mao," *New Republic* 152:9 (February 27 1965), p. 23.

CULTURAL REVOLUTIONARY, DIPLOMATIC PARTNER

The Mao of the 1950s had little relevance in the developed world except as "red menace." In the 1960s, though, "Chinese modernization" ceased to seem a contradiction in terms, and Maoism came to challenge both Western and Soviet models and to animate third world anti-American guerrilla wars from Vietnam to Mozambique. For those who doubted capitalism, the Cultural Revolution became a liberating attack on bureaucratic idiocy and bourgeois consumerism in the name of equality, frugal lifestyles, and lack of selfishness. American cold war policymakers and counterculture activists agreed on few things, but both groups saw Mao as the enemy of American consumer capitalism and imperialism.

In France, the students who filled the streets with protests in 1968 cast Mao in the role of a revolutionary philosopher king. Jean-Luc Godard's 1967 film, *Les Chinoises*, shows a cell of radical students who fill the room with ceiling-high stacks of Mao's "Little Red Book" as they talk exquisitely about how to act. President Charles de Gaulle cast Mao as counterweight to American hegemony. His Minister of Culture was André Malraux, whose riveting 1933 novel, *La Condition Humaine*, dramatized the Chinese revolution (although he had spent only a few days in China). Malraux had a taste for philosophical heroes and apparently created one to fit the bill. Although his *Anti-mémoires* includes a lengthy dialogue with Mao, a skeptical critic calculated that on his 1965 visit there had barely been time for an official photo, much less a philosophical exchange.[26]

In these years, Mao's Little Red Book was even more widely translated than the Bible, which had the advantage of a head start. The Beatles, perhaps jealous of a rival pop star, proclaimed in their 1968 song "Revolution" that "if you go around carrying pictures of Chairman Mao, nobody's going to want to make it with you anyhow." Andy Warhol, the pop artist, turned Mao into a literal icon in a 1972 silk screen that repeated image after garish image of the Chairman following the technique he also used for Campbell's soup cans and Marilyn Monroe.[27]

Edgar Snow visited China for the last time in 1970 and reported or, more likely, misreported a different Mao. He and Mao chatted at a several-hour-long breakfast, and then Mao saw Snow to his car. Mao

---

[26] André Malraux *Anti-Mémoirs*, trans. by Terence Kilmartin (New York: Holt Rinehart and Winston, 1968), pp. 356–377; Feigon, *Mao*, p. 7, citing Simon Leys, *New York Review of Books* (May 29, 1997).

[27] Jeremi Suri, *Power and Protest: Global Revolution and the Rise of Detente* (Cambridge, MA: Harvard University Press, 2003), pp. 73–87.

was contemplative, remarking that he was "not a complicated man, but really very simple." He was "only a lone monk walking in the world with a leaky umbrella." Yet Mao undoubtedly meant something quite different: "I am like a monk holding up an umbrella" (heshang da san), a phrase that demands the second half of the couplet, wufa wutian. This is a punning phrase that can be read as either "having neither hair nor [because of the umbrella, a view of] heaven" or, as Mao meant, "having [regard for] neither law nor heaven." That is, he was taking proud credit for the Cultural Revolution and chaos under heaven.[28]

America began to follow the French model in which counterculture activists and establishment strategists both cast Mao as a hero. When President Richard Nixon and Henry Kissinger, his national security adviser, went to Beijing in February of 1972, they needed to see the Chairman as, for all his frailty, a diplomatic master capable of balancing the Soviet Union, easing the American exit from Vietnam, and preparing for the 1972 elections, in view of which Nixon's appearances in China were scheduled at peak television hours at home. Opera was an apt genre for "Nixon in Beijing," by the American composer John Adams, since all the players struck poses and acted heroic roles.

Nixon wrote in his memoirs that Mao had a mind that moved "like lightning." Kissinger, as Jonathan Spence points out, portrayed Mao in the "grand exotic tradition of the Chinese emperor," ascribing "enormous calculation and cunning." Kissinger wrote that he had "met no one, with the possible exception of Charles deGaulle, who so distilled raw, concentrated willpower," and when he died, that "great, demonic, prescient overwhelming personality disappeared like the great Emperor Ch'in Shih Huang-ti, with whom he often compared himself while dreading the oblivion which was his fate." Mao was again a Napoleonic romantic hero.[29]

Nixon and Kissinger promoted American power; captains of industry sought markets to preserve capitalism; activists looked for alternatives to both. In fact, activist groups had beaten Nixon to Beijing. Delegations included doctors, lawyers, entomologists, city planners, and historians

[28] "Inside China," Life Magazine (April 4, 1971); John S. Rohsenow, A Chinese-English Dictionary of Enigmatic Folk Similes (Xiehouyu) (Tucson: University of Arizona Press, 1991), p. ix.

[29] Richard Nixon, RN: The Memoirs of Richard Nixon (New York: Grosset & Dunlop, 1978), p. 562; Jonathan D. Spence, "Mystiques of Power," in The Chan's Great Continent: China in Western Minds (New York; London: Norton, 1998), pp. 218–225; Henry Kissinger, The White House Years (Boston: Little, Brown, 1979), pp. 1065–1066; Margaret MacMillan, Nixon and Mao: The Week That Changed the World (New York: Random House, 2007).

of late imperial China. The loosely organized Committee of Concerned Asian Scholars, for instance, which had come together first in opposition to the American war in Vietnam, in 1971 sent a delegation that was received by Zhou Enlai. Medical reformers rejected Western health care based on technology, hospitals, and doctors who cured rather than prevented disease but turned instead to Mao's "Barefoot Doctors," acupuncture, and traditional Chinese medicine. Perhaps the unconscious reasoning was that China, as always, was upside down and opposite, and therefore, Chinese medicine was more natural and effective than what now came to be called "Western medicine." There also was something practical involved. One professional delegation, Science for the People, wrote that on their 1972 China trip they got reports of "a functioning society where food was adequate, disease limited, health care available, crime at a minimum, the children in school; a society that was making great strides in industry, agriculture, science, and military strength." The Chinese model now could appear not as resisting modernity but as a new form of it – "China's special modernity."[30]

These alienated Western intellectuals who visited the lands of Ho Chi Minh, Fidel Castro, and Mao were "political pilgrims," charged the sociologist Paul Hollander, and were sitting ducks for revolutionary hospitality, ego massage, and selective exposure. Yet Orientalism and liberal guilt do not explain the serious curiosity about the Maoist experiment. By the 1970s, the Western experience of modernity could no longer be unquestionably seen as unique, definitive, and self-contained. The values of liberal developmentalism had been tainted in justifying the American war in Vietnam, where democracy was the goal and technology was the means. But many came to see America as stifling democracy and using technology as the means for efficient murder. Mao's promise of participatory and responsive state developmentalism seemed a "ray of hope" inspiring a way out of the modernizers' dead end.[31]

[30] Committee of Concerned Asian Scholars, *China! Inside the People's Republic* (New York: Bantam, 1972); *A Barefoot Doctor's Manual: The American Translation of the Official Chinese Paramedical Manual* (Philadelphia, PA: Running Press, 1977); Science for the People, *China: Science Walks on Two Legs* (New York: Avon, 1974), pp. 1, 303–304; Jon Saari, "China's Special Modernity," in Bruce Douglass and Ross Terrill, eds., *China and Ourselves: Explorations and Revisions by a New Generation* (Boston, MA: Beacon Press, 1970).

[31] Paul Hollander, "The Pilgrimage to China: Old Dreams in a New Setting," in *Political Pilgrims: Travels of Western Intellectuals to the Soviet Union, China, and Cuba 1928–1978* (New York; Oxford: Oxford University Press, 1981), ch. 7, pp. 278–346; Michael E. Latham, *Modernization as Ideology: American Social Science and "Nation Building" in the Kennedy Era* (Chapel Hill: University of North Carolina Press, 2000); Richard Madsen, *China and the American Dream: A Moral Inquiry* (Berkeley: University of California Press, 1995), pp. 92–94.

China scholars agreed to evaluate these delegation reports on Chinese developmental experience. One group concluded that Mao's insistence that human initiative could solve social problems did indeed challenge widely held assumptions about the nature of state and society, but the "differences between Chinese and American societies are too great to permit simple cultural transfers."[32] Soon after Mao's death, *The China Quarterly* gathered scholars more to praise than to bury him. In effect, they found him to be both precapitalist and postmodern. Though he ruled a quarter of mankind for a quarter of a century, in the Cultural Revolution Mao's power was "limited and discontinuous," he felt "let down" when the masses failed him, and he was surprised at the "unbridled power struggles" that he had unleashed. In the end, however, Mao was "surely the first non-white, non-Western person" to subvert the "myths" of "the West's monopoly on moral and intellectual leadership" and of the "supremacy of the industrial nation-state as the ultimate frame for our activities." Mao had launched the "de-bureaucratization of the Party" and showed the world that the "glittering prizes of socialism are not won only by the white or Western world but can be enjoyed by others even *before* capitalism."[33]

LEGACIES: MAO THE MONSTER AND THE COMMODIFICATION OF CHARISMA

Almost as soon as American reporters and scholars were allowed to live in China, they found a different picture and produced a different Mao. They reported Mao's China to be authoritarian, bureaucratic, insular, and backward. One political pilgrim quoted the Chinese guide who a few years earlier had shown him "Potemkin villages": "We wanted to deceive you," he said, but "you wanted to be deceived."[34]

Since Chinese citizens now could leave China, a new genre was born – or at least a new publishing niche – the "expatriate memoir," written by recent émigrés, usually from urban intellectual backgrounds, published in Western languages, and aimed at Western audiences. Here we find a Western Mao told in Chinese voices that took for granted

---

[32] Michel Oksenberg, *China's Developmental Experience* (Boulder, CO: Praeger, 1972).

[33] Dick Wilson, ed., *Mao Tse-tung in the Scales of History: A Preliminary Assessment* (Cambridge; New York: Cambridge University Press, 1977), pp. 1–5, 115.

[34] Harry Harding, "From China with Disdain: New Trends in the Study of China," *Asian Survey* 22:10 (1991), pp. 934–958; Jonathan Mirsky, "Message from Mao," *New York Review of Books* (February 16, 1985), p. 17.

what the earlier generation had fought for, that is, the unity and autonomy of China, and told personal stories of family life and urban society.
Their stories began not in humiliated pre-1949 China but in the 1950s,
a golden age that served to make the Cultural Revolution even more
starkly bleak. Mao, said one, "presided over us like a benevolent god, and
I believed the apples, grapes, everything good had been given us because
he loved us." Jung Chang's *Wild Swans* explained that Mao motivated
the Red Guards by cleverly occupying the moral high ground – harshness to class enemies was loyalty to the people; total submission to Mao
was selfishness. But Nien Cheng, who came of age before 1949, doubted
in her *Life and Death in Shanghai* whether one person, even Mao, could
have been responsible for all the grief; there "must be something lacking in our own character ... that made it possible for his evil genius to
dominate."[35]

These émigré memoirs appeared at a time when Ronald Reagan's and
Margaret Thatcher's conservative revolutions repudiated liberal big government and reasserted values of individual initiative, even selfishness,
and profit, even greed. The China watchers' reference point for political folly was no longer the American war in Vietnam but the Cultural
Revolution. Historian Peter Zarrow suggests that émigré memoirs confirmed the "ideological dichotomies of the Cold War – Western freedom, rationalism, individualism, and order versus Chinese despotism,
irrationality, group-think, and chaos" and in contrast to the reports of
activist delegations did not give "full consideration of such things as
Red Guard freedom or Maoist rationalism."[36] Later, younger Chinese
scholars who had trained in the West added revisionist memoirs that
related their own stories of a "youth without regrets." Some wrote that
they never had been more thrilled to be women than when they were
Red Guards and never so free. For them, the atrocities and the exhila-
ration were undeniable but part of a picture that also included family
life and careers that would not have been possible before Mao. In these
revisionist memoirs, Mao was fallible but not a madman.[37]

[35] Liang Heng and Judith Shapiro, *Son of the Revolution* (New York: Knopf; Distributed
by Random House, 1983); Jung Chang, *Wild Swans: Three Daughters of China* (New
York: Simon & Schuster, 1991), p. 261; Nien Cheng, *Life and Death in Shanghai* (New
York: Grove Press, 1987), p. 259.

[36] Peter Zarrow, "Meanings of China's Cultural Revolution: Memoirs of Exile," *positions* 7:1 (1999), pp. 165–191, quote at p. 172.

[37] Weili Ye and Xiaodong Ma, *Growing Up in the People's Republic: Conversations
between Two Daughters of China's Revolution* (New York: Palgrave Macmillan,
2005); Xueping Zhong, Zheng Wang, and Bai Di, eds., *Some of Us: Chinese Women
Growing Up in the Mao Era* (New Brunswick, NJ: Rutgers University Press, 2001);
Mobo Gao, "Maoist Discourse and a Critique of the Present Assessments of the

Foreign researchers combed new archives and experienced everyday life as Deng Xiaoping's reforms, the experiments in Eastern Europe, and most of all, the crackdown of 1989 changed their views of Mao. The situation was the reverse of the 1950s, when government officials condemned Chinese tyranny and liberal academics called for realistic dealings with China. Andrew Walder described "actually existing Maoism" as a paranoid political world view whose notion of freedom actually enforced conformity and whose notion of democracy meant total unanimity under the will of the Great Leader. Joseph Esherick's 10 "theses" on the Chinese Revolution did not view the 1949 revolution as liberation or even a rupture, but rather the substitution of one form of domination for another. He lists the causes of the revolution not as Western imperialism and Chinese feudal class relations, but the depression, the Japanese invasion, and the dedication of the revolutionary party. Strikingly, the 10 theses did not include Mao's ideology or leadership.[38]

Biographies of Mao reflected these controversies and also the differences between academic and popular styles. Academics expect complicated interactions of contingency and structure, whereas popular audiences want straightforward sequences, direct relations of cause and effect, and heroes who bestride the age.[39] The public chokes on theory; academics feed on it. Ross Terrill was the first biographer to use new documents and memoirs to trace Mao's seamy personal life and psychological pathology. He still concluded that as an "actor-thinker" Mao showed that a "new deal for the backward peoples required not only cursing the West, but a total by-the-bootstraps transformation at home." Philip Short, former correspondent for the BBC, relied on English-language scholarship to write a lucid life and times. On the question of Mao's crimes, he observed that Western law distinguishes first- and second-degree murder, manslaughter, and death caused by negligence. The overwhelming majority of those killed by Mao's policies were unintended casualties of famine – not murder but manslaughter.[40] The

Cultural Revolution," *Bulletin of Concerned Asian Scholars* 26:3 (July-September 1994), pp. 13–31.

[38] Andrew Walder, "Actually Existing Maoism," *Australian Journal of Chinese Affairs* 18 (July 1987), pp. 155–166; Joseph Esherick, "Ten Theses on the Chinese Revolution," *Modern China* 21:1 (January 1995), pp. 45–76, reprinted in Jeffrey N. Wasserstrom, ed., *Twentieth-century China: New Approaches* (London; New York: Routledge, 2003), pp. 39–65.

[39] David S. G. Goodman, "Mao and the Da Vinci Code: Conspiracy, Narrative, and History," *The Pacific Review* 19:3 (September 2006), pp. 359–384, reprinted in Gregor Benton and Chun Lin, eds., *Was Mao Really a Monster? The Academic Response to Chang and Halliday's "Mao: The Unknown Story"* (New York: Routledge, 2010).

[40] Ross Terrill, *Mao: A Biography* (New York: Harper & Row, 1980; rev. and expanded: Palo Alto, CA: Stanford University Press, 2000), p. 464; Philip Short, *Mao: A Life* (New

last great émigré memoir came from one of Mao's private physicians, Li Zhisui. Random House, which some 60 years earlier had published *Red Star over China*, commissioned specialists to rewrite Li's drafts and supplement them with Western scholarship. The public was titillated by Mao's predatory sexual habits, his refusal to bathe or brush his teeth, and his extended bouts of sleeplessness and neurasthenia and shocked by his charismatic tyranny over his "court." The scholar Lucian Pye found confirmation that Mao was a "borderline personality" who periodically went over the edge into paranoia.[41]

More damning was *Mao: The Unknown Story*, by Jung Chang, author of *Wild Swans*, and her husband, Jon Halliday. One is a Chinese native speaker, and the other is a trained historian, but neither is both. President George Bush recommended their portrait of Mao because it "really shows how brutal a tyrant he was." This Mao was a monster: he was motivated from youth solely by lust for power; despised and murdered his comrades; ignored his family, whom he coldly watched being killed; and gained power only with help from Stalin, moles within the Nationalist government, and the incompetence of Chiang Kai-shek. The book opens with the widely quoted declaration: "Mao Tse-tung, who for decades held absolute power over the lives of one-quarter of the world's population, was responsible for well over 70 million deaths in peacetime, more than any other twentieth-century leader." There is no source or explanation of how the number of deaths was calculated, nor an explanation of how someone with "absolute power" suffered such loss of control during the Cultural Revolution.[42]

Snow's *Red Star* was an act of faith in the possibilities of human initiative; *Mao: The Unknown Story* was a cry of rage, even blood revenge

York: Holt, 2000). The earliest book-length biography in English was *Mao Tsê-Tung: Ruler of Red China* (New York: Schuman, 1950) by the British man of letters Robert Payne, and in French by Claude Roy, *Premières clefs pour la Chine; Une vie de Mao Tse Toung* (Paris: Éditeurs français réunis, 1950). Other strong biographies include: Stuart R. Schram, *Mao Tse-Tung* (Baltimore, MD: Penguin Books, 1967); Jerome Ch'en, *Mao and the Chinese Revolution* (London: Oxford University Press, 1965); Jonathan Spence, *Mao Zedong* (New York: Viking, 1999); Michael J. Lynch, *Mao* (London; New York: Routledge, 2004).

[41] Dr. Li Zhisui, with Anne Thurston, *The Private Life of Chairman Mao* (New York: Random House, 1994). Thurston describes the editing process in "The Politics of Survival: Li Zhisui and the Inner Court," *China Journal* 35 (January 1996), pp. 97–105; Lucian W. Pye, "Rethinking the Man in the Leader," *China Journal* 35 (January 1996), pp. 107–112.

[42] Jung Chang and Jon Halliday, *Mao: The Unknown Story* (New York: Knopf, 2005); "White House Letter," Elisabeth Bumiller, *New York Times*, January 23, 2006; Gregor Benton and Chun Lin, eds., *Was Mao Really a Monster?* reprints, with an analytical introduction, reviews of the book.

against history and perhaps against China. Chang and Halliday's story is mythic rather than literal, daring readers to expose their own moral shortcomings by measuring Mao's infinite crimes with specified numbers. Its explanations are psychological, not historical – would history have been changed if Mao's disposition had been sunnier? They do not address the question so often put in first-year history courses: Do the times make the man or the man make the times?

CONCLUSION

Mao's huge portrait presides over Tiananmen Square, and his mausoleum is placed centrally in the square, but they no longer bring to mind Mao's "hurricane" slogans of the 1920s – "A single spark can start a prairie fire," "To rebel is justified," "Never forget class struggle" – much less the millennial hopes and chaos of the 1960s. In the West, Mao has become a pop icon, and in China, as the party's claim to legitimacy shifted from Marxism and revolution to economic development and nationalism, a defanged Mao is teamed with Confucius, Buddha, and Yao Ming, the basketball star, to show the nation's historic greatness.[43]

Yet Mao remains a figure as compelling and enigmatic as the twentieth century itself. The modern nation-state is a jealous beast and demands blood sacrifice. "It is sweet and fitting to die for one's fatherland," said the noble Roman, but the modern patriot whispers that it is even sweeter and more fitting to kill for it. The stability, unity, and international dignity of Mao's New China were paid for by brutality whose scale was unmatched but whose nature is found in all our nation-states. Did Mao derail the promise of the nation-state, indeed modernity itself, or did he fulfill its dark fatefulness?

The radicals of the French Revolutions could not, any more than could their liberal and conservative critics, produce the terms in which to convey this story. The individual accounts of Mao have not conveyed this complexity; perhaps only a Shakespeare could. Mao was a Caesar who survived the attempts of any Brutus to limit his power, an Othello who needed no emulous Iago to goad his jealousy, an overreaching and sleepless Macbeth who murdered reason, and a Lear who turned himself into an heirless and crazed old man. Yet our Western stories of Mao gain power when we read them together. They are battlefield reports, a genre that Leo Tolstoy in *War and Peace* calls "necessary lies."

[43] Michael Dutton, "The Mao® Industry," *Current History* 103:674 (September 2004), pp. 268–72; Geremie R. Barmé, *Shades of Mao: The Posthumous Cult of the Great Leader* (Armonk, NY: M.E. Sharpe, 1996).

14   Two Perspectives on Mao Zedong

JIANG YIHUA AND RODERICK MACFARQUHAR

We close this critical introduction with two reflections on the entirety of Mao's life – one from a senior Chinese scholar and one from a senior Western scholar. Professor Jiang Yihua is a distinguished scholar of modern Chinese history at Fudan University, Shanghai. His research on Mao is extensive, as is his broader historical work. In addition, he lived through much of Mao's rule and now works and writes under the rule of Mao's successors in China. Professor Roderick MacFarquhar has resolutely made history part of the study of Chinese politics, from his work as founding editor of The China Quarterly, *to his monumental trilogy,* The Origins of the Cultural Revolution. *As Professor in the Department of Government and leading force in the Fairbank Center for East Asian Research at Harvard University, MacFarquhar has shaped our views of Chinese politics under Mao.*

Perspective 1: On Mao Zedong

JIANG YIHUA

I

There is an ancient Chinese saying that runs "Seal the coffin, offer a verdict," meaning "final judgment" or to draw a final conclusion. But this sentence cannot be used to describe Mao Zedong, even though he is dead and buried. In fact, I fear we will not be able to draw any final conclusions on him for a long time.

Drawing final conclusions on Mao Zedong will be a long, involved historical process because distinguishing between the imagined Mao and the real Mao is something that cannot be achieved in a day. In his

Translated by Nick Simon, a Ph.D. student in Chinese history at the University of British Columbia, and Tang Xiaobing (唐小兵), a Ph.D. student in history at East China Normal University, Shanghai. Final revisions and corrections by Timothy Cheek. All footnotes in this chapter are by Professor Jiang Yihua, with the exception of citations to published English translations provided within brackets.

lifetime, Mao was respected and admired by the people, and in most cases, his image was almost completely deified. Since his death, Mao's image has begun to be taken down from the sacred alter. However, if he is removed completely from the sacred alter, this will involve too many practical interests. The ruling party needs Mao in order to guarantee a legitimate base for itself to hold power. The army, the state, and other fundamental institutions, in order to guarantee their authority and continuation, also require Mao. The old sacred image of Mao wavers, whereas at the same time a new sacred image is being produced. With the great changes in China after Mao's death, both the current and former beneficiaries use Mao's image either to support or to challenge today's reforms. Within these images, Mao is either deified or demonized, but these only reflect different uses of Mao. None of these is the real Mao. If the world continues to require such demands, the imagined Mao inevitably will continue to coexist with the real Mao to the point that once again the real Mao will be overwhelmed.

Coming to a conclusion on Mao is also a historical process because the publishing and use of various archives, documents, and materials related to Mao, as well as the true facts concerning the various people and events related to Mao, all involve too many feelings of right or wrong, gratitude and enmity, and love and hate. To date, people can read only certain historical documents selected and published by the government. They are unable to use the original archives related to Mao. What we have been able to read of Mao Zedong are abridged and edited versions that have been reworked on the basis of certain basic principles. These are not the original texts. Only a small portion of Mao's speeches at meetings and on other occasions have been collected and published. The materials on many important incidents have genuine and false documents mixed together, and most of the great narratives currently available evade concrete processes and details. To solve these problems certainly requires ample time.

Despite these difficulties, it should be possible to accomplish a pertinent, if preliminary, critique of Mao's life.

2

Looking over the course of Mao Zedong's life, we find that his successes and defeats are all closely bound up with solving the problem of China's peasantry. In the first half of his life, Mao devoted himself to liberating the Chinese peasants, who were 80 percent of the population, from the oppression of the "three big mountains" of imperialism, feudalism, and bureaucratic capitalism. In the later half of his life, he devoted himself to liberating the peasants from the social division of labor under the private ownership of the means of production, which included the division of labor between workers and peasants, between city and countryside, between physical and mental labor, and between state officials and lesser officials or the leadership and the masses.

Among the founders of the Chinese Communist Party (CCP), indeed among all of China's twentieth-century revolutionaries, Mao Zedong attached the most importance to the peasant problem and believed most firmly that peasants were China's main revolutionary force. Zhang Guotao's *Memoirs* record that on June 6, 1923, at the Third CCP Congress, Mao Zedong, who was from a peasant background, pointed out to the congress that "in any revolution the problem of the peasants is the most important," "in all previous Chinese dynasties, rebellion and revolution depended on the peasant insurrection as its main force."[1] Mao enthusiastically threw himself into the practice of the peasant movement. In the "Report on an Investigation of the Peasant Movement in Hunan" (1927), Mao pointed out that the peasants wanted to throw off the four great fetters of state power, clan authority, religious authority, and patriarchy. Furthermore, Mao claimed that "without the poor peasants there would be no revolution. To deny their role is to deny the revolution. To attack them is to attack the revolution. They have never been wrong on the general direction of the revolution."[2]

Mao successfully launched the Autumn Harvest Uprising, marched to the Jinggang Mountains, established a rural revolutionary base area, put into practice "the independent regime of armed workers and peasants," and initiated the revolutionary path to surround the cities from the countryside. The victory of the Chinese Revolution proved the success of Mao Zedong's rural and peasant-based revolutionary military tactics, strategies, and road in the construction of the army, the party, and the establishment of political power. The position of leader and commander of the CCP, the People's Liberation Army (PLA), and the People's Republic of China (PRC) naturally and irrefutably belongs to Mao Zedong.

---

[1]   Zhang Guotao, *Wode huiyi* [My Memoirs], Vol. 1 (Shanghai: Dongfang chubanshe, 1998), p. 294.

[2]   In *Mao Zedong xuanji* [Selected Works of Mao Zedong], rev. ed. (Beijing: Renmin chubanshe, 1967), p. 21. English from *Selected Works of Mao Tse-tung*, Vol. 1 (Peking: Foreign Languages Press, 1967), p. 33.

Throughout, Mao gave a very high assessment of peasant wars of the past.[3] The peasant complex, or rather the aspiration of primitive socialism of the poorest peasants, had already taken root deeply within Mao Zedong's soul.[4] It became part of his subconsciousness or unconsciousness; that is to say, it became a starting point for his spiritual life, one of his primary motive forces. Because of this, he not only strove to carry on the various peasant wars of China's history but moreover struggled to surpass them. In the end, these historical peasant wars never really delivered to the peasants equality and freedom but rather handed them losses and were merely the tools for dynastic change and the replacement of a ruler. In "The Chinese Revolution and the Chinese Communist Party" (1939), Mao attributed these failures to a lack of new social productive forces and the advanced leadership of the proletariat. To surpass these historical peasant wars, the first and fundamental step is the development of the productive forces and the establishment of a proletarian leadership to overcome these earlier systemic impediments. The revolution thus produced a fundamental transformation: Previously it was a revolution of the peasants themselves; now it was a revolution to change the peasants. Although the starting point in both is the peasants, formerly the peasants were the motive force of the revolution, but now they have become the object of the revolution.

Mao Zedong, then, was firstly most deeply influenced by Lenin's argument that small producing peasants are a breeding ground for spontaneous, large-scale, and pervasive capitalism and a restoration of the bourgeoisie.[5] So that most peasants would not again follow this historical road to disaster, Mao adhered to an anxious and serious

[3]   See Mao Zedong, "Zhongguo geming he Zhongguo gongchandang [The Chinese Revolution and the Chinese Communist Party]," in *Mao Zedong xuanji* [Mao's Selected Works], Vol. 1, p. 625. This is a checklist of the most famous peasant rebels in Chinese history, well known to any educated Chinese in the PRC, most notably the Yuan rebel Zhu Yuanzhang, who became Ming Taizu, founder of the Ming Dynasty.

[4]   See "Comment Written for the Reproduction of 'Biography of Zhang Lu'" (December 7 and 10, 1958), in Mao Zedong, *Jianguo yilai Mao Zedong wengao* [Mao Zedong Manuscripts since the Founding of the Nation], Vol. 7 (Beijing: Zhongyang wenxian chubanshe, 1992), pp. 627–628.

[5]   See Lenin, "Gongchanzhuyi yundong zhong de 'zuopai' youzhibing [The Infantile Disorder of 'Left' Communism]," in Zhonggong Zhongyang Ma, En, Lie, Si Zhuzuo Bianyizhu, eds., *Liening xuanji* [Selected Works of Lenin], Vol. 4 (Beijing: Renmin chubanshe, 1972), p. 181. Mao Zedong read this article at least six times. In December 1975, Mao once again emphasized, "Lenin said, small producers regularly, daily, always spontaneously and on a large-scale produce capitalism and the bourgeoisie. A part of the working class and some among party members are also in this sort of circumstance." (See *Jianguo yilai Mao Zedong wengao*, Vol. 13, pp. 413–414).

idealism that, compared with Lenin's and Stalin's, was much more rapid in its elimination of the divisions between workers and peasants, town and country, and physical and mental labor. In April 1948, Mao had attacked the tendency of agricultural socialism, calling it a backward, even reactionary position.[6] However, since the 1950s, these criticisms of populism and agricultural socialism have been dismissed, kept secret, and made taboo. "Millenniums are far away. The moment is all!" Mao wrote in 1963.[7] Mao Zedong was determined to achieve this great goal within his own lifetime. Popular ideas from the May Fourth period, such as total labor-ism (*fan laodongzhuyi*), work-study-ism (*gongduzhuyi*), and new village-ism (*xinnongzhuyi*), caused Mao to believe unreservedly that the individual could work, farm, and study at the same time. People's communes had workers, peasants, merchants, students, and soldiers and engaged simultaneously in the work of farming, forestry, animal husbandry, handicrafts, and fishing based on the assessment that this "Golden Road" would promptly abolish the three great divisions.

The promise of a future socialism genuinely inspired and attracted a number of peasants, but the speed with which the agricultural cooperative movement and the people's communes were brought about was chiefly dependent on the state, from the top down to the countryside, for their overall budget and mobilization. This process depended on a state monopoly for purchasing and marketing and on a system of residence registration (*hukou*) that cleaved the free connection between the peasants, the market, and the city. Peasants who were mainly engaged in manual labor lost the ownership of their land, lost decision-making power regarding the production process and the final products, and

---

[6]   In April 1948, in the "Jin-Sui ganbu huiyi shangde jianghua [Speech at a Conference of Cadres in the Shansi-Suiyuan Liberated Area]," Mao Zedong pointed out that "in the villages which are now smashing industry there is the ideology of advocating absolute egalitarianism in land reform, which is a form of agrarian socialism. This ideology in its essence is reactionary, backward, regressive, and we must criticize it." (See "Muqian xingshi he womende renwu [The Current Situation and the Party's Tasks for 1949]," standard version, pp. 88–89.) This part of the speech was deleted in the official *Mao Zedong xuanji* [Selected Works of Mao Zedong].

[7]   See Mao Zedong's poem, "Manjianghong, he Guo Morou tongzhi [Reply to Comrade Guo Morou]", written on January 9, 1963. This quote falls in the following verse: "So much to do, Always in urgency! Heaven and earth revolve, Night and day press on. Millenniums are far away. The moment is all!" Mao Zedong's "time waits for no one" mood became even more apparent from this time forward. Quoted in Zhonggong Zhongyang wenxian yanjiushi, ed., *Mao Zedong shici ji* [Mao Zedong Collected Poems] (Beijing: Zhongyang wenxian chubanshe, 1996), p. 135. [English taken from: *Reverberations: A New Translation of Complete Poems of Mao Tse-tung*, trans. by Nancy T. Lin (Hong Kong: Joint Publishing Co., 1980), p. 77.]

lost control of other things, such as the right to choose an alternative occupation, the freedom to migrate, and other privileges, leading to a generalized impoverishment. Mao's goal and ideal for a grand and thorough liberation of the peasants in practice produced the exact opposite. Mao's relationship with the party, the state, and the majority of cadres went from harmonious to strained. In Mao's eyes, the party and the army were no longer reliable. State politics, it seemed, was no longer in his hands. In his declining years, Mao repeatedly pondered, "Since ancient times everyone must die; none can avoid imbibing sorrow and choking back tears."[8] This is a vivid portrayal of a man who persisted in his own opinions and ambitions without having the ability to carry them out.

3

Mao characterized himself as "having some of the spirit of the lion which is dominant, but also some of the spirit of the monkey, which is secondary."[9] If the lion refers to a spirit of struggle, the monkey refers to a spirit of accommodation; if the lion refers to a sense of principle, the monkey refers to flexibility; if the lion refers to staunchness, the monkey refers to compromise; if the lion refers to claiming self-power, the monkey refers to the decentralization of power; if the lion refers to centralization and unity, the monkey refers to duality; if the lion refers to permanent revolution, the monkey refers to temporary reprieve. The lion appeared suddenly in Mao Zedong as the grand and magnificent strategist; the monkey indicated Mao's mastery of military tactics and political resourcefulness. The lion was strong in Mao Zedong. He belonged to the generation of people influenced by Yan Fu's translation of T. H. Huxley's *Evolution and Ethics*. The struggle for survival, the law of natural selection, and the survival of the fittest subverted the Chinese traditions of goodness, respect, and frugality in the Confucian classic, *Doctrine of the Mean*. Mao's maxim from 1916 held true for all his life: "To struggle with Heaven, the joy is boundless! To struggle with Earth, the joy is boundless! To struggle with people, the joy is boundless!"[10]

---

[8] Jiang Yan, "Henfu [A Sorrowful Stanza]." According to Mao Zedong's annotations from May 10, 1974, see Wang Shoujia et al., *Mao Zedong wannian guoyan shiwen lu* [Mao Zedong's Comments on Literary Works in His Later Years], Vol. 2, Shijiazhuang: Huashan wenyi chubanshe, 1993), p. 802.

[9] "Gei Jiang Qing de xin [A Letter to Jiang Qing]," in *Jianguo yilai Mao Zedong wengao*, Vol. 12, p. 72.

[10] From Mao Zedong's "Diary as a Teacher in Hunan in 1916." See Zhonggong zhongyang wenxian yanjiushi, ed., *Mao Zedong nianpu (1893–1949)* [Chronicle of Mao

The combination of lion and monkey in Mao Zedong was given most vivid expression in mass political movements, such as the land revolution, the Rectification Movement, and the Production Movement, among many others. These political movements for the most part possessed widespread mass support. At times, they were mixed with serious mistakes, but at that time and under those circumstances, allowances and understanding were given by the masses. These movements extended the participation of the masses in political movements, they attracted the masses to the side of the revolution, and they gave the development and establishment of the revolution its base in the masses. Beginning in the 1950s until the end of the Cultural Revolution, political movements developed in rapid succession and grew in intensity. Instead of focusing on economic development by means of marketization, industrialization, urbanization, internationalization, and the promotion of Chinese civilization from traditional agrarian to modern industrial form, Mao sought to change the course of history itself. These political campaigns were personally directed and begun by Mao, and they were directed for the sake of eliminating private ownership from the bourgeoisie and small farmers, or for removing the "three great divisions," or for removing resistance and conflicting opinions from inside and outside the party, or simply used to prevent possible challenges to his leadership.[11] These political campaigns were only nominally mass movements; in fact, they were movements using the masses. In a majority of circumstances, most were directed and mobilized at every level from the top to the bottom and accompanied by powerful political pressure. Too frequently this resulted in tragedy and farce, and a great man such as Mao Zedong, as he faced the melancholy prospect of his own departure, could not help but commenting with a deep sigh that "only heaven knows" the future outcome.[12]

4

Mao has been designated the supreme representative of "Mao Zedong Thought." Without hesitation, he laid its foundations by

Zedong's Life (1893–1949)], Vol. 1 (Beijing: Renmin chubanshe, Zhongyang wenxian chubanshe, 1993), p. 25.

[11] See, for example, Mao Zedong, "Gongzuo fangfa liushi tiao (cao'an) [Sixty Articles on Work Methods (draft)]," number 22, in *Jianguo yilai Mao Zedong wengao* [Mao Zedong Manuscripts Since the Founding of the Nation], Vol. 7 (Beijing: Zhongyang wenxian chubanshe, 1997), p. 53.

[12] On June 15, 1976, Mao summoned Hua Guofeng and Wang Hongwen, among others, for a talk. See Jiang Yihua, ed., *Zhongguo jindai mingjia zhuzuo xuancai: Mao Zedong juan* [Selections of Modern Chinese Academic Writers: Mao Zedong] (Hong Kong: Shangwu yinshu guan, 1994), p. 653.

combining the universal truths of Marxism-Leninism with the particular circumstances of the Chinese Revolution. The creation of Mao Zedong Thought and its leading role in the CCP and national politics have confirmed Mao as the leading revolutionary thinker and theorist of the twentieth century. Mao Zedong ascended the historical stage by smashing traditional thinking, concepts, morals, and institutional bonds. Yet, to evaluate Mao as a complete antitraditionalist is a serious misjudgment. The most notable characteristic of Mao Zedong Thought and theory is its deep-rooted connection to Mao's local conditions. He smashed traditional political power, clan authority, religious authority, and patriarchal bondage and to a large degree used both Western and Soviet neologisms as personal weapons, but decisiveness has to be given to the large part he took from Chinese tradition.[13]

On July 8, 1966, in a letter to Jiang Qing, Mao wrote, "I am both self-confident and a little unconfident. When I was young I once heard: a confident man lives two hundred years, looking very dignified. But for those not so quite self-confident, they reckon when the mountain is without tigers then the monkey can be king. I became such a monkey king."[14] Figuring out which questions Mao Zedong was confident about and the ones about which he was not will make it possible to give an accurate understanding of Mao's approach to smashing traditional bonds and the limitations of his efforts.

It was in the backward countryside, not in the advanced cities, that Mao established revolutionary base areas and revolutionary control. It was peasant small producers and small property owners that made up the Revolution's base, not the representatives of large-scale socialized production, the proletariat. It was not the city that would bring along the countryside, but the countryside that would surround the cities. In this, then, it was not only Marx's but also Lenin's points of view and theories that Mao subverted. Mao therefore had to remain confident in the face of the Communist International (Comintern), the Communist Party of the Soviet Union (CPSU, Bolsheviks), and their representatives who

---

[13] Mao's comments on classical themes are legion. On the notorious first emperor, Qin Shihuangdi, see Mao Zedong's interview and talk with foreign guests on June 24, 1964; Chen Jin, *Mao Zedong zhi hun* [The Spirit of Mao Zedong] (Changchun: Jilin renmin chubanshe, 1993), pp. 273, 282; Mao Zedong, "Qilu: Du (fengjianlun) cheng Guo lao." See *Jianguo yilai Mao Zedong wengao*, Vol. 13, p. 361. On Mozi, a competitor to Confucius, see Mao Zedong: "Guanyu 'Mozi zhexue sixiang' yi wen gei Chen Boda de xin [Regarding 'Mozi's Thought and Philosophy, A Letter to Chen Boda]," in *Mao Zedong wenji* [Collected Works of Mao Zedong], Vol. 2 (Beijing: Renmin chubanshe, 1993), p. 156.

[14] "Gei Jiang Qing de xin," p. 72.

returned to China from Moscow as "higher-ups" to lead the Revolution. And this self-confidence came from Mao's affirmation of China's conditions and its revolutionary reality, the preponderance of the peasantry as the most crucial part in the worker-peasant alliance, the Red Army, and the PLA.

Mao's understanding of modern industrial civilization was not as deep as his understanding of agricultural civilization. During his life, Mao read the *The Mirror of Government* [*Zizhi tongjian*] (from the Song Dynasty) at least seven times, the *Dream of the Red Chamber* at least eight times, "The Twenty-Four Dynastic Histories," at least once through and several volumes of it repeatedly, as well committing to memory many ancient poems and stories, but of Marx's *Das Capital*, he only read a few sections and chapters, and of Marx's voluminous work on political economy, Mao never touched one. Unlike Deng Xiaoping, who had direct experience and involvement with Western capitalism and socialist production, Mao had no part in the political or economic fight of the Western proletariat. Mao's understanding of Marxism was received from Stalin's, *History of the Communist Party of the Soviet Union (Bolsheviks), Short Course*, which had a profound impact on him. He read it at least 10 times and assessed it as an encyclopedia of Marxism: "It is the best synthesis and summing-up of the world communist movement of the past hundred years"[15] and should be read a hundred times. In understanding capitalism, Stalin was Mao's principal source, likewise for his understanding of socialism. Mao's one major creative contribution from the Eastern world to Marxism was the theory and practice of New Democracy (1940). However, after the Revolution gained national success, the realization of socialism became the party's mission, and Mao quickly abandoned New Democracy and unhesitatingly opted for the Soviet model, initiating the "all round study of the Soviet Union."

From 1949, Mao stressed the results achieved through the socialist transformation of agriculture and class struggle. This enhanced his personal self-confidence in the control of economic construction and propelled his belief in the effectiveness of wartime communism toward the ends of egalitarianism and the use of vigorous mass movements for the purpose of modernizing the economy and cultural and educational

---

[15] See Mao Zedong, "Gaizao women de xuexi [Reforming Our Studies]," in *Mao Zedong xuanji* [Mao's Selected Works] (in one volume), pp. 760–761 [Translation from *Selected Works of Mao Zedong*, Vol. 3 (Peking: Foreign Languages Press, 1967), p. 24].

construction. In August 1958 at the Beidaihe conference, Mao, in an even more intense criticism, said, "Since entering the cities, some have commented that we have a 'rural way' or a 'guerrilla attitude.' This [criticism] is bourgeois ideology corroding us. We have cast aside some of our good things; the rural work style has become unpopular; cities demand regularization [of procedures].... In my view, the rural work style and guerrilla practices are, after all, better. In twenty-two years of war we were victorious: Why is it that building communism doesn't work?"[16] To this end, he concluded that "the 'rural way' and the 'guerrilla attitude' are the Marxist way."[17] Consequently, the whole nation set about to construct "backyard furnaces," the whole people began to produce steel, and so on. This resort to coercion and commandism resulted in the waste of natural resources and a critical waste of environmental, agricultural, and industrial production. The entire nation's producers simultaneously fell into hunger, and 23 million people met their "unnatural death."

In the 1930s and 1940s, Mao Zedong was brimming with confidence. This is so because what he advocated then fit with Chinese realities. From the 1950s, Mao's "lack of confidence" accompanied this earlier "self-confidence." The reality then was that China's development was deviating from what Mao wanted. In the latter part of his life, Mao turned his back on materialism and toward voluntarism, from the historical materialist view and toward political determinism. All this had a direct connection to the increasingly fervent personality cult around him. In his youth, Mao had been directly influenced by Song and Ming Confucian thought: Those who wish to move the world "must move the world's hearts and minds."[18] He regarded the institutions of industry and commerce, the constitution, the parliament, and so on as secondary things. After 1958, it gradually became clear that Mao had returned to his vision of the people's ideas, the people's thought, and the people's spirit to resolve everything. His political determinism was embodied in the proposal "politics in command" and in the slogan "Give priority to

---

[16] Li Rui, *Dayuejin qinli ji* [The Great Leap Forward: A Personal Record], Vol. 2 (Beijing: Nanfang chubanshe, 1999), p. 105 [English taken from Roderick MacFarquhar, Timothy Cheek, and Eugene Wu, eds., *The Secret Speeches of Chairman Mao* (Cambridge, MA: Council on East Asian Studies, Harvard University, 1989), pp 416–417].

[17] Li Rui., *Dayuejin qinli ji*, Vol. 2, p. 123.

[18] August 23, 1917, "Letter to Li Jinxi," Zhonggong Zhongyang wenxian yanjiushi, Zhonggong Hunan shengwei, *Mao Zedong zaoqi wengao* [Writings from the Early Mao Zedong], 2nd ed. (Changsha: Hunan chubanshe, 1995), pp. 85–86 [English available in Stuart R. Schram. *Mao's Road to Power: Revolutionary Writings, 1912–1949*, Vol. 1 (Armonk, NY: M. E. Sharpe, 1992), pp. 131–132].

politics."[19] Giving priority to politics and prominence to class struggle solved problems for Mao in the political struggle. At this time, social class was defined by political and ideological disposition – any ideologically or politically dissenting views, and all dissident social classes, were indicative of a different point of view from Mao's and thus proof of an enemy class. All this displays a lack of "self-confidence," an overabundance of stubbornness, and the forceful implementation of a personal intention and superficial philosophy.

"Many, many were those / Who laid down their lives in noble resolve, / Who dared to move Sun and Moon / To lay out a New Sky!"[20] Mao Zedong's life was one of devotion and huge sacrifice. On June 15, 1976, Mao summarized his life: "I've done but two things in my life: one was to struggle with Jiang Jieshi for some decades and send him off to some island and fight the war of resistance for eight years when we sent the Japanese back home. On these there's little disagreement.... The other thing you all know, it is my promoting of the 'Great Cultural Revolution.' Not many support this thing and more than a few oppose it. These two things are not finished but are something to hand over to the next generation."[21] In summarizing Mao's 83 years, we must note: First, is the defeat of 2,000 years of oppression and especially the oppression of the peasants by the traditional empire. Second, is the tenacious attempt to establish and realize a thorough egalitarianism and new egalitarian utopia. With regard to the first point, Mao achieved eternal success. With regard to the second, Mao's bold vision and unparalleled efforts can only be regarded as a failure. This pained Mao until his end; he could not understand why so few opposed the first thing but "very few supported, and very many opposed" the second. At first, Mao admitted that at most he was one-tenth personally at fault; afterwards, he conceded that 70 percent was achievement and 30 percent a mistake. However, he never conceded that his utopian vision itself was a mistake.

---

[19] "Guanyu gongye bumen xue jiefangjun de xin [Letter Regarding Industrial Departments Studying the PLA]," December 16, 1963, in *Jianguo yilai Mao Zedong wengao*, Vol. 10, p. 455. In 1964, at a meeting of the Military Commission of the CCP Central Committee, Mao once again praised "the four firsts"; see Wu Faxian, *Suiyue jiannan* [The Difficult Years], Vol. 2, 2nd ed. (Hong Kong: Beixing chubanshe, July 2007), p. 543.

[20] Mao Zedong, "Dao Shaoshan [At Shaoshan"; see *Mao Zedong shici ji*, p. 110 English taken from *Reverberations: A New Translation of Complete Poems of Mao Tse-tung*, trans. by Nancy T. Lin, p. 61].

[21] On June 15, 1976, Mao summoned Hua Guofeng and Wang Hongwen, among others, for a talk. See Jiang Yihua, ed., *Zhongguo jindai mingjia zhuzuo xuancai*, pp. 652–653.

Regardless of what appraisal one gives of Mao, his legacy is reserved for later generations. Both the positive and negative aspects of his legacy are extraordinarily valuable because, when all is said and done, millions of people both passively and actively and over several decades were on the march together in this costly historic experiment. It also can be said that without this great experiment there never would have arisen "an order out of chaos" or the grand new development of socialism with Chinese characteristics in the post-Mao era.

Perspective 2: Mao Zedong Lun

RODERICK MACFARQUHAR

During a long life, Mao Zedong displayed many personae. Ultimately, though, his self-definition was as a revolutionary. In the last months of his life, he told his radical supporters that he had two accomplishments to his name, the Chinese Revolution and the Cultural Revolution. He acknowledged that while few would dispute the first, the second was more in doubt.[22] Deng Xiaoping and other survivors of the Cultural Revolution attempted to leave no doubt that it had been an unmitigated disaster, "the most severe setback and the heaviest losses suffered by the Party, the state and the people since the founding of the People's Republic."[23] Responsibility for the idea of the Cultural Revolution was attributed to Mao, although blame for the mayhem was assigned to the Lin Biao and Jiang Qing "cliques." While there are dissenters – the "New Left" within China and some Chinese academics abroad[24] – this

[22] Mao referred to the Chinese Revolution as sending Chiang Kai-shek (Jiang Jieshi) off to Taiwan. Mao's remarks are quoted in Wang Nianyi, *Da dongluande niandai* [A Decade of Great Upheaval] (Zhengzhou: Henan renmin chubanshe, 1988), pp. 600–601. According to Wang, there is some uncertainty as to whether the talk took place on January 13 or June 15, 1976; the remarks are not to be found on either date in the relevant volume of *Jianguo yilai Mao Zedong wengao* [Mao Zedong's Manuscripts Since the Founding of the State] (Beijing: Zhongyang wenxian chubanshe, 13 vols. between 1987 and 1998), Vol. 13.

[23] *Decision of the Central Committee of the Chinese Communist Party Concerning the Great Proletarian Cultural Revolution*, hereafter *Decision* (Beijing: Foreign Languages Press, 1981), p. 32.

[24] For the New Left in China, see the story by Ariana Eunjung Cha, "For China's New Left, Old Values," *Washington Post* Foreign Service, April 19, 2009; Cha identifies academics Wang Hui, Cui Zhiyuan, and Zuo Dapei as among its leaders. For overseas supporters, see, for instance, Mobo Gao, *The Battle for China's Past: Mao and the Cultural Revolution* (London: Pluto Press, 2008), and Mobo Gao, *Gao Village* (Honolulu: University of Hawaii Press, 2007), pp. 142–170.

negative appraisal of the Cultural Revolution and of Mao's culpability is widely accepted in the West and probably in China, too. In official Chinese eyes, this leaves the Chairman with the conquest of China as his major accomplishment, which is probably about right and still constitutes an enormously impressive record: 28 years of revolution finally ending in victory, from his joining the Chinese Communist Party (CCP) in 1921 to the founding of the People's Republic of China (PRC) under his leadership in 1949.[25]

Much of Mao's life and times, his words and actions, are covered in the chapters in this book. Other important Western sources are biographies by Short, Terrill, Pye, and Schram and the latter's introductions to the seven volumes of *Mao's Road to Power*.[26] In Chinese, the sources are, of course, enormously more numerous, the most important being the three massive volumes of the "official" life, *Mao Zedong zhuan*, by Jin Chongji (covering 1893–1949) and Pang Xianzhi and Jin Chongji (1949–76 in two volumes).[27] In a category of its own is Dr. Li Zhisui's *The Private Life of Chairman Mao*.[28]

It is not the purpose of this section to distill the wisdom of these and other sources, although it will find succor in them. Rather, this section seeks to plumb the significance of Mao's deathbed celebration of the two revolutions. Why did Mao feel that his seasoned colleagues who had fought alongside him in the first revolution and thereafter worked with him to construct a new nation were insufficiently revolutionary to join him in the Cultural Revolution? Or to put it in another way, what were the differences between the two revolutions that made the great helmsman feel that he would have to go it virtually alone on the second one, with Lin Biao as his first mate and with Zhou Enlai as the helmsman to keep the country from foundering? The short answer is that the first revolution was a patriotic one; its ultimate aim was nation

---

[25] For the written record of how Mao succeeded, see his revolutionary writings translated in Stuart Schram, ed., *Mao's Road to Power* (Armonk, NY: M. E. Sharpe, seven volumes covering 1912–1941 published 1992 to 2010).

[26] Philip Short, *Mao: A Life* (New York: Owl Books, 1999); Ross Terrill, *Mao: A Biography* (Palo Alto, CA: Stanford University Press, revised and expanded edition, 1999); Lucian Pye, *Mao Tse-tung: The Man in the Leader* (New York: Basic Books, 1976); Stuart Schram, *Mao Tse-tung* (Harmondsworth, Middlesex, England: Pelican Books, 1966); *Mao's Road to Power* is introduced in note 25. The most recent life, Jung Chang and Jon Halliday, *Mao: The Unknown Story* (London: Jonathan Cape, 2005) is more polemic than biography.

[27] Both books were published in Beijing by Zhongyang wenxian chubanshe in 1996 and 2003, respectively.

[28] New York: Random House, 1994.

building. The second was an ideological one; its aim was purification of the people, whatever the cost to nation building.

It is a commonplace that, like many educated Chinese youths born around the end of the nineteenth century, Mao was deeply unhappy about the state of his country and determined to do something about it. One of the most famous quotations from his autobiographical account to Edgar Snow tells of his political awakening at about age 13:

> I began to have a certain amount of political consciousness, especially after I read a pamphlet telling of the dismemberment of China. I remember even now that this pamphlet opened with the sentence: "Alas, China will be subjugated!" It told of Japan's occupation of Korea and Taiwan, of the loss of suzerainty in Indo-China, Burma and elsewhere. After I read this I felt depressed about the future of my country and began to realise that it was the duty of the people to help save it.[29]

But Mao was above all a revolutionary optimist, and his fears about the future changed. In 1919, on the verge of formally committing himself to Marxism, he wrote:

> I venture to make a singular assertion: one day, the reform of the Chinese people will be more profound than that of any other people, and the society of the Chinese people will be more radiant that that of any other people. The great union of the Chinese people will be achieved earlier than that of any other people. Gentlemen! Gentlemen! We must all exert ourselves! We must all advance with the utmost strength! Our golden age, our age of glory and splendor, lies before us![30]

The following year he wrote to close friends in France indicating that he had abandoned his predilection for anarchism and was committing himself to a "Russian-style revolution."[31] The patriot would become a revolutionary.

But all Mao's senior colleagues would have justifiably considered themselves patriotic revolutionaries. Zhou Enlai, who emerged as one of

---

[29] Edgar Snow, *Red Star over China* (Harmondsworth, Middlesex, England: Penguin Books, 1st revised and enlarged edition, 1972), p. 159.

[30] "The Great Union of the Popular Masses," trans. in Schram, ed., *Mao's Road to Power*, Vol. 1: *The Pre-Marxist Period, 1912–1920*, p. 389.

[31] "Letter to Xiao Xudong, Cai Linbin, and the Other Members in France," trans. in *ibid.*, Vol. 2: *National Revolution and Social Revolution, December 1920–June 1927*, pp. 5–15.

the leaders among those patriotic young Chinese who went to France as worker-students around the end of World War I, wrote a poem to encourage his peers:

> Go abroad
>> Cross the East Sea, South China Sea, Red Sea and Mediterranean Sea,
> With surging waves
>> rolling on in the vast oceans,
>> You are bound for the coast of France, the hometown of freedom.
> On that land
>> Take up the tools,
>> be wet with sweat in labor
>> make your brilliant achievements.
> Develop your ability and maintain your innocence.
> When you are back someday,
>> Unfold the banner of freedom
>> and sing the song of independence.... [32]

Deng Xiaoping, who was among those peers, aged 16 when he landed in 1920, later recalled the reality of the Chinese experience in the "hometown of freedom":

> Upon arrival in France, I learned from those students studying on a work-study program who had come to France earlier that two years after World War I, labor was no longer as badly needed as in the wartime ... and it was hard to find jobs. Since wages were low, it was impossible to support study through work. Our later experiences proved that one could hardly live on the wages, let alone go to school for study. Thus, all those dreams of "saving the country by industrial development," "learning some skills," etc., came to nothing.[33]

The experiences of Deng in France – "[t]he sufferings of life and the humiliations brought upon by the foremen, the running dogs of capitalists"[34] – had a great effect on him and doubtless on his colleagues, who, like him, joined the Chinese Socialist Youth League, of which Zhou was a leader, and the CCP as a result. The young Liu Shaoqi, whose patriotism had been aroused by Japan's 21 Demands,[35] was unable

---

[32] Quoted in Deng Maomao, *Deng Xiaoping, My Father* (New York: Basic Books, 1995), p. 47.

[33] *Ibid.*, p. 61.

[34] *Ibid.*, p. 81.

[35] *Liu Shaoqi zhuan* (Biography of Liu Shaoqi) (Beijing: Zhonggong wenxian chubanshe, 1998), Vol. 1, p. 11.

to raise the funds to go to France and less keen to go after hearing of the tribulations of those who were there; instead, he joined the Socialist Youth League and went to the Soviet Union.[36]

The objective of all these patriotic revolutionaries, whether they went to France or the Soviet Union or simply stayed in China, was to develop their abilities, as Zhou put it, and to devote their talents to restoring their country's greatness. A good few, Zhou in particular, rose rapidly in the CCP, outranking and even displacing Mao on occasion. But it was Mao who early on grasped the revolutionary potentialities of rural China and the importance of developing armed forces in soviet areas as bases for launching guerrilla offensives against the Guomindang (GMD).[37] And it was Mao who outlasted and outmaneuvered his Communist International (Comintern)–blessed colleagues, beginning his rise to supreme power at the Zunyi conference in January 1935 during the Long March, later thrusting aside challenges from Zhang Guotao and Wang Ming, and finally obtaining the title of Chairman of the CCP in 1943 with the right to override his peers if and when necessary.

During his rise to power, Mao did not shrink from terror or bloodshed – "[A] revolution is not like inviting people to dinner," he famously wrote[38] – even among the ranks of revolutionaries. In the 10 years starting with the Futian "incident," the worst example of bloodshed,[39] there were about 100,000 executions of party members, including 15,000 during the Yan'an Rectification Campaign under Kang Sheng's aegis.[40] After the Seventh Party Congress in 1945, though, when Mao's chairmanship was confirmed and his primacy seemed no longer at risk, he put together a senior leadership team – Liu Shaoqi, Zhou Enlai, Zhu De, Ren Bishi, and Chen Yun[41] – that remained unchanged for over 20 years until he launched the Cultural Revolution in 1966.

---

[36] *Liu Shaoqi nianpu* (A Chronology of Liu Shaoqi) (Beijing: Zhongyang wenxian chubanshe, 1996), Vol. 1, pp. 18–21. Liu was in Moscow for less than a year. Others spent longer: Zhang Wentian, Wang Jiaxiang, Kang Sheng, Yang Shangkun, and, of course, Wang Ming.

[37] The classic account of Mao's strategy is Benjamin I. Schwartz, *Chinese Communism and the Rise of Mao* (Cambridge, MA: Harvard University Press, 1951). For Mao's early base area activities, see Stephen C. Averill, *Revolution in the Highlands: China's Jinggangshan Base Area* (Lanham, MD: Rowman & Littlefield, 2006).

[38] Schram, *Mao's Road to Power*, Vol. 2, p. 434.

[39] See, for instance, Short, *Mao*, pp. 265–281.

[40] *Ibid.*, pp. 383–389. The death toll figures are attested to by Li Rui in Zhang Bozhu, ed., *Hu Yaobang yu Zhongguo zhengzhi gaige* [Hu Yaobang and China's Political Reform] (Hong Kong: Chen zhong shu ju, 2009), p. 27.

[41] Chen Yun replaced Ren Bishi after the latter's death in 1950.

One major reason for this longevity almost certainly was the formidable array of organizational talents that these men represented, complementing the visionary outlook and strategic mastery of the Chairman. Liu Shaoqi played the major role of ensuring that an expanding CCP was tightly organized, well disciplined, and ideologically Maoist as it quickly extended its control throughout the country and that it responded faithfully to Mao's directives. Premier Zhou Enlai, with Chen Yun as his chief economic czar in the government, speedily ended one of the worst inflations in modern world history and initiated the nation's 5-year plan system. Zhu De's principal deputy in the military, Peng Dehuai, fought the American-led UN forces to a draw in the Korean War.

But despite this array of talent, and unlike in later years, Mao was very much a hands-on leader during the early PRC. Having achieved power, he threw himself into bringing about socialist transformation. A study of Mao's writings during the period 1950–55 reveals him taking a keen interest and issuing instructions in the various campaigns that characterized the early years of the PRC: land reform; the two campaigns against counterrevolutionaries, *zhenfan* and *sufan*; the three anti, five anti campaigns; the thought reform of the intellectuals; and rural collectivization followed by the transfer of private commerce to state or joint state-private ownership.[42] What Mao accomplished between 1949 and 1956 was in fact the fastest, most extensive, and least damaging socialist revolution carried out in any communist state. In his most signal triumph, Mao pushed collectivization far faster than Liu Shaoqi and others believed prudent, and when the success of Mao's policy became evident, Liu self-criticized himself at a CCP plenum for believing that after land reform some time should elapse before collectivization was broached.[43] Liu, it would seem, still harbored the "new democratic" ideas that Mao had preached in 1940 when he was groping for allies against the GMD ideas under which a rich peasant economy would be permitted to flourish after land reform.[44]

Those seven years of establishing a socialist system from 1949 to 1956 surely should figure as part of Mao's revolutionary triumphs. Approaching his end, Mao was understandably concerned with the biggest of big pictures. Victories along the way may have faded in significance.

[42] See the first five volumes of *Jianguo yilai Mao Zedong wengao*.

[43] *Liu Shaoqi nianpu*, Vol. 2, p. 345.

[44] Schram, *Mao's Road to Power*, Vol. 7: *New Democracy 1939–41*, p. 343. See the discussion of the fate of "New Democracy" after 1949 in Yu Guangyuan (with notes by Han Gang), *"Xin minzhuzhuyi shehui lun" de lishi mingyun* [The Historical Fate of "On New Democratic Society"] (Wuhan: Changjiang chubanshe, 2005), especially pp. 115–117.

Or possibly for Mao, a true revolution had to involve some form of war-fare. Possibly, too, he did not want to concede the contributions of Liu, Zhou, and others to those early victories and so confined himself just to the revolutions in which he was effectively sole commander. For in his eyes, none of those men were his true comrades-in-arms.

According to Li Rui in a recent volume, Mao tended to promote favorites. He had three: Gao Gang, Lin Biao, and Deng Xiaoping. Li, who was Gao's political secretary, asserts that his one-time boss was Mao's choice as his successor. The Chairman admired his swashbuckling air (*lulin haojie*).[45] When regional leaders were summoned to join the center, Gao was given the plum job of head of the Planning Commission. After Gao Gang fell, having failed to topple Liu Shaoqi,[46] both Lin Biao and Deng Xiaoping were brought quickly into the Politburo and subsequently elevated above their seniors.

In the discussions of the reorganization of the central leadership prior to the CCP's Eighth Congress in 1956, Mao proposed Deng for party general secretary on the grounds of his talents and character and that he was effectively doing the job already; disingenuously, he pointed out that in translation, Deng's title (*mishuzhang*) would be the same as his new one! But there was a real difference in the two roles, and Mao's aim was clearly to ensure that Deng would not just be a senior official carrying out Politburo Standing Committee (PSC) orders (*mishuzhang* is normally rendered "secretary general") but would himself be a member of the PSC and, as *Zong shuji*, part of the top leadership. Rightfully, the job should have gone to Peng Zhen, 10 years senior to Deng in the Politburo, but Peng ended up as Deng's deputy in the Secretariat and excluded from the PSC. And in a move seemingly designed to ensure that Liu Shaoqi, though retaining his number two ranking under Mao, should not necessarily be considered the Chairman's designated successor, Mao proposed that all his senior colleagues – Liu, Zhou, Zhu, and Chen Yun – should be ranked as vice chairmen under him.[47] When

---

[45] Zhang, ed., *Hu Yaobang yu Zhongguo zhengzhi gaige*, pp. 27–28. Li Rui attributes the assessment of Mao's personnel decisions to General Huang Kecheng, former PLA chief of staff.

[46] The most complete account of the Gao Gang affair is Frederick C. Teiwes, *Politics at Mao's Court: Gao Gang and Party Factionalism in the Early 1950s* (Armonk, NY: M. E. Sharpe, 1990). Teiwes concludes that Gao Gang's attempt to replace Liu Shaoqi was based on a misreading of Mao's grumblings about his second in command. For an alternative view, see Roderick MacFarquhar, *The Origins of the Cultural Revolution: 3, The Coming of the Cataclysm, 1961–1966* (New York: Oxford and Columbia University Presses, 1997), p. 639, note 8.

[47] Shi Zhongquan, Sheng Zhengle, Yang Xiancai, and Han Gang, eds., *Zhonggong bada shi* [A History of the CCP's Eighth Congress] (Beijing: Renmin chubanshe, 1998),

Lin Biao was promoted to the PSC in 1958, thereby outranking Defense Minister Peng Dehuai, and despite being conspicuous more by his absence than by his involvement in political and military affairs, he, too, automatically became a vice chairman.

In all political systems, leaders attempt to promote their "best pupils" in order to preserve their prestige and their legacy. But succession is particularly important in a dictatorship, where the leader is likely to have broken many heads during his period in power, and there will be no independent historians to set the record straight. The Cultural Revolution was about succession in general:

> In the final analysis, the question of training successors for the revolutionary cause of the proletariat is one of whether or not there will be people who can carry on the Marxist-Leninist revolutionary cause started by the older generation of proletarian revolutionaries ... whether or not we can successfully prevent the emergence of Khrushchev's revisionism in China. In short it is an extremely important question, a matter of life or death for our Party and our country.[48]

Hence the mobilization of the youth into the Red Guards to train as revolutionaries by bombarding various headquarters. But the Cultural Revolution also was about individual successors, and the question is not why Lin Biao was promoted to replace Liu Shaoqi as heir, but rather why was Mao's other favorite, Deng Xiaoping, cast out? And if he was to be dismissed like Liu, why did Deng not suffer the same fate? In particular, why did Mao insist, against the urgent and repeated desires of his radical supporters (later known as the "Gang of Four") that Deng retain his party membership?

The possible difference between Lin and Deng is that the former stuck far more loyally by Mao during the dark days of the great famine. In particular, Deng, like Liu and others, believed in rolling back collectivization in the countryside to aid recovery. They had jumped on the bandwagon of the Great Leap Forward, but when disaster loomed, they

pp. 115–138. The one time Mao was forced to say that, in effect, if not in title, Liu was first vice chairman was in response to a direct question from the British Field Marshal, Viscount Montgomery, who visited China in autumn 1961; see *Liu Shaoqi nianpu*, Vol. 2, pp. 540–541. When Montgomery's Chinese escort had warned that he would ask Mao who his successor was, Mao seemed put out, asserting that the party did not think like that.

[48] Quoted from the ninth polemic against the Soviet communists and their allies, issued in July 1964, in Roderick MacFarquhar and Michael Schoenhals, *Mao's Last Revolution* (Cambridge, MA: Harvard University Press, 2006), p. 12.

wanted to save the country rather than preserve socialism. They were patriots first and socialists second. But by this time, Mao was obsessed with the threat of revolutionary decay in the form of "revisionism," and the national interest had become less important to him than establishing China as the new revolutionary bastion with his thought as its guiding light. For this purpose, he was prepared to throw the achievements of 17 years of nation building into the melting pot of the Cultural Revolution.

So even Deng had to be sacrificed, but clearly, Mao never lost faith in his abilities and his reeducatibility. And when Lin Biao seemed to Mao to have become dangerously too powerful,[49] and Zhou was dying, Deng was brought back to run the country. But why did Mao not finally throw him out of the party when it became clear in 1976 that Deng was no more a supporter of the Cultural Revolution than he had been in 1966? There is no easy answer, but maybe even at the end of his life when he was congratulating himself on his two revolutions, Mao still retained the core of patriotism that had taken him into the CCP in the first place. Maybe he knew that of all the protagonists and antagonists of the Cultural Revolution, only Deng could run China successfully, and he hoped that he would be faithful to his memory, if not his legacy.

And so it proved: Deng blamed Mao for the idea of the Cultural Revolution but excused him from blame for its execution and insisted that "Comrade Mao Zedong was a great Marxist and a great proletarian revolutionary, strategist and theorist."[50] Most important, on June 4, 1989, he ensured that Mao's other revolution was preserved when it seemed destined to topple.

Of course, Deng decided to suppress the 1989 student movement for the sake of the CCP. And the centrality of the Chairman's reputation to the party's legitimacy dictated Deng's judgment on Mao. But what should ours be? Mao's revolution brought the great boon of peace and unity to China for the first time in over a century. Courtesy of the PLA, the Chinese people *had* stood up. But then Mao proceeded to knock them down again. He proclaimed the "Liberation," but he imposed a straitjacket. Class struggle ruled. All those campaigns of the early 1950s taught the Chinese people to fear the CCP. The terror of land reform lubricated the collectivization process. Thought reform frightened the intellectuals into banality or silence; the Anti-Rightist Movement dispersed half a million of them to menial labor or the gulag, a squandering

[49] *Ibid.*, pp. 324–336.
[50] *Decision*, p. 56.

of vital personnel. Collectivization destroyed the incentives briefly promised by land reform. The lives of millions were either cut short or gravely distorted. Yet, for many CCP leaders who survived the Cultural Revolution, that was a golden age before Mao was consumed by leftist paroxysms from the late 1950s on. Their judgment was justified only in the sense that the loss of life and the disruption of the country's polity and economy during the Great Leap Forward, and the famine that it engendered, and the Cultural Revolution were enormously greater than what had gone before. But since the Chairman's death, the policies of the whole Maoist era have been abandoned, most important, his collectivist triumph. Class struggle has formally been discarded, although the party still rules, corruptly and lawlessly in many areas.[51] Yet even minorities are now relatively liberated in thought and action, prepared to protest like Han Chinese, even violently, if the party harms them. Many Chinese are certainly getting rich before others, as Deng wanted, some egregiously so. But can this be worse than the unending egalitarian poverty of the Maoist era?

As the post–Cultural Revolution leadership debated what official analysis of the Maoist era they should hand down, one very senior leader reportedly said that if the Chairman had died in 1956, there would have been no problem; even if he had died in 1966, after the Great Leap, his reputation could have been safeguarded, but he had died in 1976! But perhaps 1950 would have been a better year for his reputation: Mao could have gone down as a great Han-type founding emperor instead of the draconian Qin Shi Huangdi to whom he liked to be compared. In short, by 1950, Mao had performed his historic role. Thereafter, overall, his rule was disastrous. But a counterfactual question arises: Absent Mao and his predilection for class struggle and utopian excesses, would Liu Shaoqi ever have led China down the road of radical reform? Probably not more likely and better still, Liu and Zhou Eulai could have persisted with New Democracy, liberating China's peasants to get rich, and simultaneously allowing Chinese entrepreneurs to start rebuilding the industrial and commercial economy. Without Mao, the Chinese miracle might have begun 30 years earlier.

[51] Minxin Pei, *China's Trapped Transition: The Limits of Developmental Autocracy* (Cambridge, MA: Harvard University Press, 2006).

Appendix   Selected Further Readings (Annotated)

This short, selected bibliography is intended to serve the nonspecialist reader who wishes to go further in his or her readings based on the introduction provided in this book.

Mao's Writings in Translation

Mao Zedong. *Selected Works of Mao Tse-tung* (Peking: Foreign Languages Press, Vol. 1–4: 1975; Vol. 5: 1977).

Selected Works and other official Mao texts/images are available at the Mao Zedong Internet Archive: http://eprints.cddc.vt.edu/marxists/reference/archive/mao/selected-works/index.htm.

Mao's Road to Power, 1912–1949, ed. by Stuart R. Schram (Armonk, NY: M. E. Sharpe, 1992--), [Standard scholarly edition in 10 volumes, up through 1941 published by 2010.]

Mao Tse-tung Unrehearsed, ed. by Stuart R. Schram (New York: Penguin Books, 1974).

The Writings of Mao Zedong, 1949–1976, ed. by Ying-mao Kao and John Leung, 2 vols. (Armonk, NY: M. E. Sharpe, 1986, 1992). [Only covers 1949–58.]

The Secret Speeches of Chairman Mao: From the Hundred Flowers to the Great Leap Forward, ed. by Roderick MacFarquhar, Timothy Cheek, and Eugene Wu (Cambridge, MA: Council on East Asian Studies, Harvard University, 1989). [Translations of unofficial Mao texts from 1957–58 and commentary by U.S. scholars.]

Cheek, Timothy. *Mao Zedong and China's Revolutions: A Brief History with Documents* (Boston: Bedford Books, 2002). [Selected texts with historical background.]

Saich, Tony. *The Rise to Power of the Chinese Communist Party: Documents and Analysis* (Armonk, NY: M. E. Sharpe, 1996). [Reliable documents and helpful commentary.]

Stephan Landsberger's Chinese Propaganda Posters: www.iisg.nl/~landsberger/. [An excellent Web site including posters and commentary on Mao, Mao's Thought, etc.]

Biographies

Spence, Jonathan. *Mao*. Penguin Lives Series (New York: Penguin, 1999). [A short, elegantly written life.]

Davin, Delia. *Mao Zedong* (London: History Press, 2009). [Brief, reliable, and readable.]

Short, Philip. *Mao: A Life* (New York: Henry Holt, 1999). [Colorful, longer, and more detailed.]

Terrill, Ross. *Mao: A Biography* (Palo Alto, CA: Stanford University Press, 2000). [Similarly longer and colorful; Chinese edition of this biography has sold well in the PRC.]

Chang, Jung, and Jon Halliday. *Mao: The Unknown Story* (London: Jonathan Cape, 2005). [Notoriously negative biography by well-known writing couple; not accepted as reliable by most scholars; see Benton and Lin below and Andrew Nathan in *LRB*: www.lrb.co.uk/v27/n22/nath01_.html.]

Meisner, Maurice. *Mao Zedong: A Political and Intellectual Portrait* (Malden, MA: Polity Press, 2007). [A reasoned and regretful Marxist analysis of Mao's thought and work.]

Studies by Topic and Period (Per the Chapters in This Book)

Historical Context: Useful Textbooks

Fairbank, John King, and Merle Goldman. *China: A New History*, 2nd ed. (Cambridge, MA: Harvard University Press, 2006).

Schoppa, Keith. *Revolution and Its Past: Identities and Change in Modern Chinese History*, 2nd ed. (Englewood Cliffs, NJ: Prentice-Hall, 2005).

Spence, Jonathan. *In Search of Modern China* (New York: W. W. Norton, 1999).

Mao, 1920s–37

Dirlik, Arif. *Anarchism in the Chinese Revolution* (Berkeley: University of California Press, 1991).

Womack, Brantly. *The Foundations of Mao's Political Thought* (Honolulu: University of Hawaii Press, 1982).

Mao, 1937–56

Teiwes, Frederick C. *Politics & Purges in China: Rectification and the Decline of Party Norms*, 2nd ed. (Armonk, NY: M.E. Sharpe, 1993). [A detailed and insightful account of the style of politics that emerged under Mao in the 1940s and has dominated China ever since.]

Apter, David, and Tony Saich. *Revolutionary Discourse in Mao's Republic* (Cambridge, MA: Harvard University Press, 1994).

Chen, Jian. *Mao's China and the Cold War* (Chapel Hill: University of North Carolina Press, 2000). [Uses newly released materials to create a fresh interpretation of Mao's role in the Korean War and cold war more broadly.]

Mao, 1957–76

MacFarquhar, Roderick. *Origins of the Cultural Revolution*, Vols. 1–3 (New York: Columbia University Press, 1974, 1983, 1997). [The authoritative history of the politics that led to China's tragic political convulsion.]

MacFarquhar, Roderick, and Michael Schoenhals. *Mao's Last Revolution* (Cambridge, MA: Harvard University Press, 2006). [High politics and individual experience in the Cultural Revolution.]

Mao and His Followers

Gao, Wenqian. *Zhou Enlai: The Last Perfect Revolutionary* (New York: Public Affairs, 2008). [An English edition of the reflections of a PRC scholar now in the West.]

Mao and Intellectuals

Liu, Binyan. *Two Kinds of Truth: Stories and Reportage from China* (Bloomington: Indiana University Press, 2006). [A welcome reprint of the 1990 collection, *People or Monsters?* featuring the writings by one China's most notable critical party intellectuals.]

Wakeman, Frederic, Jr. *History and Will: Philosophical Perspectives on Mao Tse-tung's Thought* (Berkeley: University of California Press, 1973). [One of the most wide-ranging engagements with Mao's thought, from Hegel to Stalin by way of Confucius.]

Gendered Mao

Xueping Zhong, Wang Zheng, and Bai, Di, eds., *Some of Us: Chinese Women Growing Up in the Mao Era* (New Brunswick, NJ: Rutgers University Press, 2001).

Gilmartin, Christine, Gail Hershatter, Lisa Rofel, and Tyrene White, eds. *Engendering China: Women, Culture and the State* (Cambridge, MA: Harvard Contemporary China Series, Harvard University Press, 1994). [Still a useful collection on gender issues in Mao's China and after.]

Mao the Icon

Morning Sun (Boston: Longbow Group, 2002). [An excellent 2-hour documentary focusing on the Cultural Revolution and Mao; available on DVD and supported by an intelligent Web site: www.morningsun.org/]

Schrift, Melissa. *Biography of a Chairman Mao Badge: The Creation and Mass Consumption of a Personality Cult* (New Brunswick, NJ: Rutgers University Press, 2001).

Chinese Views of Mao

Barmé, Geremie R. *Shades of Mao: The Posthumous Cult of the Great Leader* (Armonk, NY: M. E. Sharpe, 1996). [A marvelous selection of translations and commentary.]

Knight, Nick. *The Philosophical Thought of Mao Zedong: Studies from China, 1981–1989* (Armonk, NY: M. E. Sharpe, 1992). [One of the few English resources on the voluminous official scholarship on Mao in the PRC; for the serious reader.]

Third World Maoism

Dirlik, Arif, Paul Healy, and Nick Knight. *Critical Perspectives on Mao Zedong's Thought* (Atlantic Highlands, NJ: Humanities Press, 1997). [Sympathetic chapters in this unashamedly Marxist collection address Maoism in India, Vietnam, and Latin America.]

Western Images of Mao

Herzstein, Robert. *Henry R. Luce, Time, and the American Crusade in Asia* (New York: Cambridge University Press, 2005).
Perlmutter, David D. *Picturing China in the American Press: The Visual Portrayal of Sino-American Relations in Time Magazine, 1949–1973* (Lanham, MD: Lexington Books, 2007).
Snow, Edgar. *Red Star over China* (New York: Random House, 1938). [Still in print.]

Scholarly Debates and Assessments

Benton, Gregor, and Lin Chun, eds. *Was Mao Really a Monster? The Academic Response to Chang and Halliday's* Mao: The Untold Story (London: Routledge, 2009).
Madsen, Richard. *China and the American Dream: A Moral Inquiry* (Berkeley: University of California Press, 1995).
Schram, Stuart R. *The Thought of Mao Tse-tung* (Cambridge, England: Cambridge University Press, 1989).

Index

Note: *Chinese names are alphabetized by family name. For example, Mao Zedong is "Mr. Mao" and is indexed as Mao, Zedong.*

Joffe, Adolph, 51, 88
Jowitt, Kenneth, 193

Kang, Keqing, 211–12, 216
Kang, Sheng, 87, 91, 126
Kang, Youwei, 33–34, 37–38
Kauffman, Stuart, 111
Khmer Rouge, 300–04
Khrushchev, Nikita, 10–11, 107, 271, 285–86
Kissinger, Henry, 325
Knight, Nick, 27, 194
Korean War, 10, 16, 103–04

labor organization/campaigns, 73, 209
Lan, Ping. *See* Jiang, Qing
Land Investigation Movement, 81–82
land reform/redistribution, 14, 178–79, 205, 207–08
Langton, Christopher, 111
law of avoidance, 37
leader cult, 228–29, 234–35.
    See also Mao, Zedong, as icon
Lee, Ching Kwan, 23
Lei, Feng, 234
Lenin, Vladimir, 6, 314–15
Leninist politics, rise of, 47–50
Leys, Simon, 246, 254–56, 271
Li, Da, 6–7
Li, Dazhao, 43, 44, 49–50
Li, Jie, 156, 276
Li, Lisan, 179
Li, Min, 202
Li, Na, 202
Li, Pirui, 266
Li, Rui, 277–78
Li, Weihan, 98–99
Li, Xiannian, 145–46
Li, Yinqiao, 112–13
Li, Zhisui, 3, 5–6, 231–32, 329–30
Li, Zicheng, 92, 253–54
Liang, Qichao, 31, 33–34, 37–38, 39, 198
Liao, Jun, 120–21
liberal developmentalism, 326–27
liberal intellectuals, 22–23.
    See also intellectuals
liberalism, opposition to, 190–91
Liberal school perspective, 277–80.
    See also scholarship, on Mao
Life and Death in Shanghai (Cheng), 328
Lin, Biao, 113, 146, 261–62, 293–94, 297
Lin, Liguo, 146, 261

literature/arts
    popularization of, 182–85
    rising standards/elevation of, 185–87
"Little Red Book." *See Quotations from Chairman Mao Zedong*
Liu, Baiyu, 191–92
Liu, Bang, 251–53
Liu, Binyan, 137, 142, 153
Liu, Chunhua, 236
Liu, Hulan, 189
Liu, Kang, 182–83
Liu, Shaoqi
    on bourgeois intellectuals, 124
    "correct" mass line, 194
    "Four Cleanups" and, 122
    Gao Gang affair, 135–36
    Great Leap policies, 140–41
    Mao's criticism of, 144
    Mao's image and, 226–27
    in Moscow, 89
    Politburo reelection, 145–46
    portrait of, 236
    in Revolution history, 6–7
    in Secretariat, 94
    Zhou Enlai and, 145
Liu-Wang, Liming, 207, 211–12
living standards, 209
Lo, Mai. *See* Li, Weihan
Long March, 56, 83
Lu, Xun, 222
Lu Xun Arts Academy, 186, 225.
    See also literature/arts
Luce, Henry, 319–20, 321
Luo, Ruiqing, 189
Lushan conference, 138, 139–41, 257
Lynch, Michael, 17

Ma, Yinchu, 101–02
MacFarquhar, Roderick, 121, 123
Malraux, André, 324
Manchu warriors, 31–32
Mandate of Heaven, 247–48
Mao, Anying, 231, 266–67
Mao, Dun, 101–02
"Mao Studies: Retrospect and Prospect" (Schram), 27
Mao: The Unknown Story (Chang and Halliday), 245, 330–31
Mao, Yuanxin, 151, 231
    in Xiang River Review, 70–71
Maoism, formulation of, 82–85
Maoism, in the Third World. *See* Third World Maoism